# 15
# Canadian
# Poets
# X2

# 15
# Canadian
# Poets
# X2

**Edited by GARY GEDDES**

Toronto
Oxford University Press

Oxford University Press
70 Wynford Drive, Don Mills, Ontario M3C 1J9

Toronto   Oxford   New York
Delhi   Bombay   Calcutta   Madras   Karachi   Petaling Jaya
Singapore   Hong Kong   Tokyo   Nairobi   Dar es Salaam
Cape Town   Melbourne   Auckland

and associated companies in
Berlin   Ibadan

Second printing (with corrections) 1990

Canadian Cataloguing in Publication Data
Main entry under title:
15 Canadian Poets x 2.
First ed. (1970) published under title:
15 Canadian Poets.
Second ed. (1978) published under title:
15 Canadian Poets Plus 5.
Includes index.
ISBN 0-19-540655-9
1. Canadian poetry (English) - 20th century.*
1. Geddes, Gary, 1940-    . 11. Title: 15 Canadian
poets x 2
PS8291.F53 1988   C811'.54'08   C88-093631-2
PR9195.7.F53 1988
© Oxford University Press Canada 1988
OXFORD is a trade mark of Oxford University Press
3 4 5 - 3 2 1
Typeset by Greenglass Graphics
Printed in Canada by Webcom Limited

# Contents

# Preface

The long success of *15 Canadian Poets* (1971) and the revised *15 Canadian Poets Plus 5* (1978) has prompted me—ten years later—to increase the number of poets to *15 Times 2*, and to broaden the range of the anthology in several ways. First, I have reached back to include E.J. Pratt, F.R. Scott, A.M. Klein, Miriam Waddington, and Ralph Gustafson; and forward to include work by Robert Bringhurst, Anne Szumigalski, Robert Kroetsch, Robyn Sarah, Bronwen Wallace, and myself. This extended range, covering some fifty years, should make *15 Times 2* a more useful and flexible teaching anthology of twentieth-century Canadian poetry.

In making the selections for *15 Times 2*, I have tried to keep in mind such matters as region, gender, and form. Pratt's work, an important addition in its own right, speaks eloquently of aspects of the Maritime experience; Kroetsch, Waddington, and Szumigalski have strong links with the prairies; Klein, Scott, and Gustafson help round out the picture of the modernist movement in Quebec, and Robyn Sarah represents the new ferment at work there; Ontario and British Columbia—already well served in previous editions of the anthology—are newly represented, respectively, by Bronwen Wallace and Robert Bringhurst; and my own work, with one foot in the Pacific and one in the wheatfields, spans, uncomfortably, at least two regions. Canadian poetry is no longer dominated by a single region; it is also no longer dominated by men. Much of the most exciting work is now being done by women, and additions to the Second and Third Editions reflect this change: eight of the sixteen poets added are women.

I have also tried to present a variety of poetic forms. It is gratifying to break with the normal procedure of including only short lyrics in anthologies, by offering a strong selection of longer poems by Pratt, Kroetsch, and others. The long poem is not only an important proving-ground for serious poets, but also—whether poem-sequence, narrative, or sustained meditation—allows the poet new structural challenges, a more demanding and perhaps more satisfying encounter with prosody, and the chance to explore new subjects or familiar ones more comprehensively. Livesay's 'Call My People Home' and Newlove's 'The Pride' exemplify the documentary impulse; Ondaatje, Szumigalski, and Sarah make fascinating excursions into the terrain of the prose poem; and Kroetsch, a poet of infinite surprises who has played an important role as mentor and catalyst in recent Canadian poetry, offers a fine example in 'Seed Catalogue' of the post-modern sensibility at work. Poets of the real, to use James Reaney's distinction, are here alongside poets of the imagined; and what A.J.M. Smith called our 'eclectic detachment' appears in the regional, historical, fantastical, and confessional modes, as well as in the easy shifting back and forth between closed forms, with their rhymes and metrical concerns, and open forms that favour the rhythms of the speaking-voice and subtle internal music.

There has grown up, in the years since this anthology first appeared, a considerable body of poetics, which includes attempts to describe the creative process, the function of the line, the case for and against the long poem, the genesis of certain poems, and the nature of the documentary impulse. Margaret Atwood, for example, has on more than one occasion stressed that poetry is not self-expression but a *making*, and that poems not only change the way we feel—'A poem that uses language or image in a new or unexpected way causes the electrical impulses in the brain to jump their habitual paths and form new synaptical connections'—but also may profoundly alter our behaviour: 'A voice is a gift; it should be cherished and used, to utter fully human speech if possible. Powerlessness and silence go together; one of the first efforts made in any totalitarian takeover is to suppress the writers, the singers, the journalists, those who are the collective voice.... The writer, unless he is a mere word processor, retains three attributes that power-mad regimes cannot tolerate: a human imagination, in the many forms it may take; the power to communicate; and hope' ('Amnesty International: An Address').

D.G. Jones makes a not unrelated point about translation, the kind that turns feelings and ideas into living language, as well as the kind that attempts to export, or smuggle, poetry from one language to another. 'No text can be free from radical ambiguity, equivocation, indeterminacy,' he writes in 'Grounds for Translation' (*The Insecurity of Art*, 1982, edited by Ken Norris and Peter Van Toorn). 'Since a word only finds its meaning in relation to other words, as used by the writer, by his contemporaries, by his predecessors, the pursuit of its potential meanings ramifies out through the whole history of language and culture. It leads to a semantic abyss: no single meaning is ever final, no single interpretation.' And yet, however much feeling may resist being translated into text and text may resist translation, the task, be it a reading or mis-reading of the text, must take place:

> *We live by a strange dynamic: to communicate, to translate, and to produce the untranslatable, to cultivate silence. But, if it is true that Babel may be our secret delight, that mankind may indeed have been kept vital and creative by being scattered among tongues so that there is in every act of translation, as Steiner says, a touch of treason, it is equally true that we delight in sharing our most intimate secrets, that we must speak and be heard, listen and translate, or go mad.*

I have tried to introduce as much of each authors' poetics into the notes as space would allow. Any anthology restricted, for teaching purposes, to thirty Canadian poets unavoidably omits many fine writers. To the list of established poets who might have been included in the first two editions—Milton Acorn, George Johnston, James Reaney, Jay Macpherson, Anne Wilkinson, and Dennis Lee—must be added a host of lesser-known poets who have published collections of exceptional interest over the past ten years. Many of these poets appear in other anthologies; all deserve attention.

For this Third Edition I owe a debt of gratitude to my original co-editor, Phyllis Bruce, who chose to leave me to my own devices; to Bill Toye and other friends who helped me make my difficult decisions; to Laurie Ricou, who wrote the note on my work; and to my wife Jan, who knows the poems better than I do.

Gary Geddes

# Acknowledgements

MARGARET ATWOOD Reprinted by permission of Oxford University Press Canada: 'The Animals in That country', 'A Night in the Royal Ontario Museum', 'Progressive Insanities of A Pioneer' from *The Animals in That Country* © Oxford University Press (Canadian Branch) 1968; 'Game After Supper' from *Procedures for Underground* © Oxford University Press (Canadian Branch) 1971; 'You Are Happy' from *You Are Happy* © Margaret Atwood 1974; 'Five Poems for Dolls' from *Two-Headed Poems* © Margaret Atwood 1978; 'Notes Towards a Poem That Can Never Be Written', 'A Women's Issue' from *True Stories* © Margaret Atwood 1981. Reprinted by House of Anansi Press: "They Eat Out' from *Power Politics*. MARGARET AVISON 'July Man', 'The Absorbed', 'In a Season of Unemployment', 'A Nameless One', 'Pace', 'Black and White Under Green: May 18, 1965' reprinted from *The Dumbfounding, Poems by Margaret Avison*, by permission of W.W. Norton Company, Inc. © 1966 by Margaret Avison. 'Snow', 'The World Still Needs', 'New Year's Poem', 'To Professor X, Year Y', 'The Swimmer's Moment', 'Voluptuaries and Others', 'Birth Day' from *Winter Sun and other Poems* by Margaret Avison. Used by permission of The Canadian Publishers, McClelland & Stewart, Toronto. EARLE BIRNEY Used by permission of The Canadian Publishers, McClelland & Stewart, Toronto: 'From the Hazel Bough', 'Bushed', 'A Walk in Kyoto', 'The Bear on the Delhi Road', 'El Greco: Espolio', 'Cartagena de Indias' from *The Poems of Earle Birney* by Earle Birney; 'Vancouver Lights', 'Anglosaxon Street', 'November Walk Near False Creek Mouth' from *Selected Poems* by Earle Birney. GEORGE BOWERING Used by permission of The Canadian Publishers, McClelland & Stewart, Toronto: 'Grandfather' from *Points on the Grid* by George Bowering; 'Esta Muy Caliente' from *The Man in Yellow Boots* by George Bowering; 'Indian Summer', 'Albertasaurus' from *Rocky Mountain Foot* by George Bowering; 'Summer Solstice' from *The Catch* by George Bowering. All other poems reprinted by permission of the author. ROBERT BRINGHURST Used by permission of The Canadian Publishers, McClelland & Stewart, Toronto: 'For the Bones of Josef Mengele, Disinterred June 1985' from *Pieces of Map, Pieces of Music* by Robert Bringhurst; 'The Song of Ptahhotep', 'Xenophanes' from *The Beauty of the Weapons* by Robert Bringhurst. Used by permission of the author: 'The Stonecutter's Horses' from *The Stonecutter's Horses*, 1979 (Standard Edition); 'Anecdote of the Squid', 'Poem About Crystal' from *Bergschrund*, 1975 (Sono Nis Press); 'The Sun and the Moon', 'The Beauty of the Weapons' from *The Shipwright's Log* (Kanchenjunga Press). LEONARD COHEN Used by permission of The Canadian Publishers, McClelland & Stewart, Toronto: 'Elegy', 'Story', 'I Have Not Lingered in European Monasteries', 'You Have the Lovers', 'As Mist Leaves No Scar', 'Now of Sleep', 'The Genius', 'Style', 'For E.J.P.', 'The Music Crept By Us', 'Two Went to Sleep' from *Selected Poems 1956-1968* by Leonard Cohen; 'God Is Alive' from *Beautiful Losers* by Leonard Cohen; 'How To

Speak Poetry' from *Death of a Lady's Man* by Leonard Cohen; 'Number 24' from *Book of Mercy* by Leonard Cohen. GARY GEDDES Reprinted by permission of Oberon Press: 'Charioteer', 'Paymaster', 'Blacksmith' from *The Terracotta Army* by Gary Geddes; 'Sullivan', '250-Word Essay Required by the Japanese on the Battle of Hong Kong' from *Hong Kong* by Gary Geddes. Reprinted by permission of Coteau Books: 'The Strap', 'Jimmy's Place', 'Saskatchewan', 'Philip Larkin' from *Changes of State* by Gary Geddes. Reprinted by permission of the author: 'Sandra Lee Scheuer' from *The Acid Test*; 'Letter of the Master of Horse' from *Letter of the Master of Horse*. RALPH GUSTAFSON Used by permission of The Canadian Publishers, McClelland & Stewart, Toronto: 'Five Transparencies' from *Directives of Autumn* by Ralph Gustasfson; all other poems from *The Moment Is All* by Ralph Gustafson. D.G. JONES All poems are from *A Throw of Particles* by D.G. Jones. Reprinted by permission of Stoddart Publishing Co. Limited, Toronto, Ontario. A.M. KLEIN All poems are from *The Collected Poems of A.M. Klein*. Reprinted by permission of McGraw-Hill Ryerson Limited. ROBERT KROETSCH All poems are reprinted by permission of the author. PATRICK LANE All poems are reprinted by permission of the author. IRVING LAYTON All poems from *Collected Poems* by Irving Layton. Used by permission of The Canadian Publishers, McClelland & Stewart, Toronto. DOROTHY LIVESAY All poems are reprinted by permission of the author. PAT LOWTHER 'Regard to Neruda', 'Touch Home', from *Milk Stone*. Reprinted by permission of Borealis Press Ltd. All other poems reprinted by permission from *A Stone Diary* © Oxford University Press 1977. GWENDOLYN MACEWEN 'Apologies', 'Nitroglycerin Tulips', 'Deraa', 'Ghazala's Foal', 'Tall Tales', 'Notes from the Dead Land' from *The T.E. Lawrence Poems* by Gwendolyn MacEwen. Published 1982, second printing 1983 by Mosaic Press. Reprinted by permission. 'Poems in Braille', 'Manzini: Escape Artist', 'Poem Improvised Around a First Line', 'The Red Bird You Wait For', 'The Discovery', 'Dark Pines Under Water', 'The Child Dancing' from *Magic Animals* by Gwendolyn MacEwen. ELI MANDEL All poems reprinted by permission of the author. JOHN NEWLOVE Reprinted by permission of ECW Press: 'Driving', 'The Weather' from *The Night the Dog Smiled*. Used by permission of The Canadian Publishers, McClelland & Stewart, Toronto: 'The Arrival', 'Then, If I Cease Desiring', 'Verigin, Moving In Alone', from *The Fat Man* by John Newlove; 'The Pride', 'Lady, Lady', 'Ride Off Any Horizon', 'In This Reed' from *Black Night Window* by John Newlove; 'The Engine and the Sea' from *The Cave* by John Newlove. ALDEN NOWLAN Used by permission of Irwin Publishing Inc.: 'I, Icarus', 'And He Wept Aloud, So That the Egyptians Heard It', 'Britian Street', 'July 15', 'The Mysterious Naked Man', 'For Claudine Because I Love Her', 'Ypres: 1915', 'The First Stirring of the Beasts', 'The Middle-Aged Man in the Supermarket', 'The Broadcaster's Poem' from *An Exchange of Gifts: Poems New and Selected* by Alden Nowlan © 1967, 1969, 1971, 1974, 1977, 1982 Irwin Publishing Inc.; 'In Those Old Wars' from *Bread, Wine and Salt* by Alden Nowlan © 1967 by Clarke, Irwin & Company Limited; 'Another Parting' from *The Mysterious Naked Man* by Alden Nowlan © 1969 by Clarke, Irwin & Company Limited. All other poems reprinted by permission of Claudine Nowlan, Executor for the Estate of Alden Nowlan. MICHAEL ONDAATJE All poems reprinted by permission of the author. P.K. PAGE All poems reprinted by permission of the author. E.J. PRATT All poems reprinted by permission of the University of

Toronto Press. AL PURDY Used by permission of The Canadian Publishers, McClelland & Stewart, Toronto: 'The Country North of Belleville', 'The Cariboo Horses', 'Song of the Impermanent Husband', 'Wilderness Gothic' from *The Cariboo Horses* by Al Purdy; 'Eskimo Graveyard', 'Arctic Rhododendrons' from *North of Summer* by Al Purdy; 'Detail', 'Lament for the Dorsets', 'The Runners' from *Wild Grape Wine* by Al Purdy; 'The Beavers of Renfrew' from *Sex and Death* by Al Purdy. ROBYN SARAH All poems are reprinted by permission of the author. F.R. SCOTT All poems are from *Selected Poems* by F.R. Scott. Used by permission of The Canadian Publishers, McClelland & Stewart, Toronto. RAYMOND SOUSTER All poems reprinted from *Collected Poems of Raymond Souster* by the permission of Oberon Press. ANNE SZUMIGALSKI Reprinted by permission of Doubleday Canada Limited: 'Victim', 'Girl With Basket' from *Woman Reading in Bath*. Reprinted by permission of the author: 'Fishhawks', 'The Lullaby' from *A Game of Angels*; all other poems from *Dogstones* (Fifth House). MIRIAM WADDINGTON All poems are reprinted from *Collected Poems* © Miriam Waddington 1986 by permission of Oxford University Press. BRONWEN WALLACE 'Particulars' from *The Stubborn Particulars of Grace* by Bronwen Wallace. Used by permission of The Canadian Publishers, McClelland & Stewart, Toronto. All other poems reprinted from *Signs of the Former Tennant* by Bronwen Wallace by permission of Oberon Press. PHYLLIS WEBB All poems reprinted by permission of the author.

## PHOTOGRAPH CREDITS

ATWOOD Graeme Gibson. BIRNEY Sheldon Grimson. BRINGHURST Anne Taylor. COHEN Agence Sygma, France. GEDDES c.j. sweet. GUSTAFSON Betty Gustafson. JONES Monique Grandmangin. LANE Brenda Pelky. LIVESAY Lawrence Eddy, Victoria. LOWTHER *Vancouver Sun*. MACEWEN Sheldon Grimson. NEWLOVE Franke E. Brooke. ONDAATJE Marlene Brody. PRATT Ashley & Crippen. PURDY Intelligencer photo by Julia Drake. SARAH D.R. Cowles. SCOTT William Toye. SOUSTER John Ayris. WEBB Betty Fairbank.

# E. J. Pratt

## Newfoundland

Here the tides flow,
And here they ebb;
Not with that dull, unsinewed tread of waters
Held under bonds to move
Around unpeopled shores—
Moon-driven through a timeless circuit
Of invasion and retreat;
But with a lusty stroke of life
Pounding at stubborn gates,
That they might run
Within the sluices of men's hearts,
Leap under throb of pulse and nerve,
And teach the sea's strong voice
To learn the harmonies of new floods,
The peal of cataract,
And the soft wash of currents
Against resilient banks,
Or the broken rhythms from old chords
Along dark passages
That once were pathways of authentic fires.

*Red is the sea-kelp on the beach,*
*Red as the heart's blood,*
*Nor is there power in tide or sun*
*To bleach its stain.*
*It lies there piled thick*
*Above the gulch-line.*
*It is rooted in the joints of rocks,*
*It is tangled around a spar,*
*It covers a broken rudder,*

*It is red as the heart's blood,*
*And salt as tears.*

Here the winds blow,
And here they die,
Not with that wild, exotic rage
That vainly sweeps untrodden shores,
But with familiar breath
Holding a partnership with life,
Resonant with the hopes of spring,
Pungent with the airs of harvest.
They call with the silver fifes of the sea,
They breathe with the lungs of men,
They are one with the tides of the sea,
They are one with the tides of the heart,
They blow with the rising octaves of dawn,
They die with the largo of dusk,
Their hands are full to the overflow,
In their right is the bread of life,
In their left are the waters of death.

*Scattered on boom*
*And rudder and weed*
*Are tangles of shells;*
*Some with backs of crusted bronze,*
*And faces of porcelain blue,*
*Some crushed by the beach stones*
*To chips of jade;*
*And some are spiral-cleft*
*Spreading their tracery on the sand*
*In the rich veining of an agate's heart;*
*And others remain unscarred,*
*To babble of the passing of the winds.*

Here the crags
Meet with winds and tides—
Not with that blind interchange
Of blow for blow

That spills the thunder of insentient seas;
But with the mind that reads assault
In crouch and leap and the quick stealth,
Stiffening the muscles of the waves.
Here they flank the harbours,
Keeping watch
On thresholds, altars and the fires of home,
Or, like mastiffs,
Over-zealous,
Guard too well.

*Tide and wind and crag,*
*Sea-weed and sea-shell*
*And broken rudder—*
*And the story is told*
*Of human veins and pulses,*
*Of eternal pathways of fire,*
*Of dreams that survive the night,*
*Of doors held ajar in storms.*

## The Shark

He seemed to know the harbour,
So leisurely he swam;
His fin,
Like a piece of sheet-iron,
Three-cornered,
And with knife-edge,
Stirred not a bubble
As it moved
With its base-line on the water.

His body was tubular
And tapered
And smoke-blue,
And as he passed the wharf
He turned,

And snapped at a flat-fish
That was dead and floating.
And I saw the flash of a white throat,
And a double row of white teeth,
And eyes of metallic grey,
Hard and narrow and slit.

Then out of the harbour,
With that three-cornered fin
Shearing without a bubble the water
Lithely,
Leisurely,
He swam—
That strange fish,
Tubular, tapered, smoke-blue,
Part vulture, part wolf,
Part neither—for his blood was cold.

## Sea-gulls

For one carved instant as they flew,
The language had no simile—
Silver, crystal, ivory
Were tarnished.  Etched upon the horizon blue.
The frieze must go unchallenged, for the lift
And carriage of the wings would stain the drift
Of stars against a tropic indigo
Or dull the parable of snow.

Now settling one by one
Within green hollows or where curled
Crests caught the spectrum from the sun,
A thousand wings are furled.
No clay-born lilies of the world
Could blow as free
As those wild orchids of the sea.

## Erosion

It took the sea a thousand years,
A thousand years to trace
The granite features of this cliff,
In crag and scarp and base.

It took the sea an hour one night,
An hour of storm to place
The sculpture of these granite seams
Upon a woman's face.

## The Man and the Machine

By right of fires that smelted ore
Which he had tended years before,
The man whose hands were on the wheel
Could trace his kinship through her steel,
Between his body warped and bent
In every bone and ligament,
And this 'eight-cylinder' stream-lined,
The finest model yet designed.
He felt his lesioned pulses strum
Against the rhythm of her hum,
And found his nerves and sinews knot
With sharper spasm as she climbed
The steeper grades, so neatly timed
From storage tank to piston shot—
This creature with the cougar grace,
This man with slag upon his face.

## From Stone to Steel

From stone to bronze, from bronze to steel
Along the road-dust of the sun,
Two revolutions of the wheel
From Java to Geneva run.

The snarl Neanderthal is worn
Close to the smiling Aryan lips,
The civil polish of the horn
Gleams from our praying finger tips.

The evolution of desire
Has but matured a toxic wine,
Drunk long before its heady fire
Reddened Euphrates or the Rhine.

Between the temple and the cave
The boundary lies tissue-thin:
The yearlings still the altars crave
As satisfaction for a sin.

The road goes up, the road goes down—
Let Java or Geneva be—
But whether to the cross or crown,
The path lies through Gethsemane.

## Newfoundland Seamen

This is their culture, this—their master passion
Of giving shelter and of sharing bread,
Of answering rocket signals in the fashion
Of losing life to save it.  In the spread
Of time—the Gilbert-Grenfell-Bartlett span—
The headlines cannot dim their daily story,
Nor calls like London!  Gander!  Teheran!
Outplay the drama of the sled and dory.

The wonders fade.  There overhead a mile,
Planes bank like gulls:  like curlews scream the jets.
The caravans move on in radar file
Scarce noticed by the sailors at their nets,
Bracing their bodies to their tasks, as when,
Centuries before Argentia's smoking funnels,
That small ancestral band of Devon men
Red-boned their knuckles on the *Squirrel* gunwales.

As old as it is new, as new as old,
Enduring as a cape, as fresh as dulse,
This is the Terra Nova record told
Of uncontractual blood behind the pulse
On sea or land.  Was it but yesterday
That without terms and without drill commands,
A rescue squad found Banting where he lay
With the torn tissues of his healing hands?

## The Titanic

HARLAND & WOLFF WORKS, BELFAST, MAY 31, 1911

The hammers silent and the derricks still,
And high-tide in the harbour! Mind and will
In open test with time and steel had run
The first lap of a schedule and had won.
Although a shell of what was yet to be
Before another year was over, she,
Poised for the launching signal, had surpassed
The dreams of builder or of navigator.
The Primate of the Lines, she had out-classed
That rival effort to eliminate her
Beyond the North Sea where the air shots played
The laggard rhythms of their fusillade
Upon the rivets of the *Imperator*.
The wedges in, the shores removed, a girl's
Hand at a sign released a ribbon braid;
Glass crashed against the plates; a wine cascade,
Netting the sunlight in a shower of pearls,
Baptized the bow and gave the ship her name;
A slight push of the rams as a switch set free
The triggers in the slots, and her proud claim
On size—to be the first to reach the sea—
Was vindicated, for whatever fears
Stalked with her down the tallow of the slips
Were smothered under by the harbour cheers,
By flags strung to the halyards of the ships.

MARCH 31, 1912

Completed! Waiting for her trial spin—
Levers and telegraphs and valves within
Her intercostal spaces ready to start
The power pulsing through her lungs and heart.
An ocean lifeboat in herself—so ran
The architectural comment on her plan.
No wave could sweep those upper decks—unthinkable!

No storm could hurt that hull—the papers said so.
The perfect ship at last—the first unsinkable,
Proved in advance—had not the folders read so?
Such was the steel strength of her double floors
Along the whole length of the keel, and such
The fine adjustment of the bulkhead doors
Geared to the rams, responsive to a touch,
That in collision with iceberg or rock
Or passing ship she could survive the shock,
Absorb the double impact, for despite
The bows stove in, with forward holds aleak,
Her aft compartments buoyant, watertight,
Would keep her floating steady for a week.
And this belief had reached its climax when,
Through wireless waves as yet unstaled by use,
The wonder of the ether had begun
To fold the heavens up and reinduce
That ancient *hubris* in the dreams of men,
Which would have slain the cattle of the sun,
And filched the lightnings from the fist of Zeus.
What mattered that her boats were but a third
Of full provision—caution was absurd:
Then let the ocean roll and the winds blow
While the risk at Lloyds remained a record low.

THE ICEBERG

Calved from a glacier near Godhaven coast,
It left the fiord for the sea—a host
Of white flotillas gathering in its wake,
And joined by fragments from a Behring floe,
Had circumnavigated it to make
It centre of an archipelago.
Its lateral motion on the Davis Strait
Was casual and indeterminate,
And each advance to southward was as blind
As each recession to the north.  No smoke
Of steamships nor the hoist of mainsails broke

The polar wastes—no sounds except the grind
Of ice, the cry of curlews and the lore
Of winds from mesas of eternal snow;
Until caught by the western undertow,
It struck the current of the Labrador
Which swung it to its definite southern stride.
Pressure and glacial time had stratified
The berg to the consistency of flint,
And kept inviolate, through clash of tide
And gale, façade and columns with their hint
Of inward altars and of steepled bells
Ringing the passage of the parallels.
But when with months of voyaging it came
To where both streams—the Gulf and Polar—met,
The sun which left its crystal peaks aflame
In the sub-arctic noons, began to fret
The arches, flute the spires and deform
The features, till the batteries of storm,
Playing above the slow-eroding base,
Demolished the last temple touch of grace.
Another month, and nothing but the brute
And palaeolithic outline of a face
Fronted the transatlantic shipping route.
A sloping spur that tapered to a claw
And lying twenty feet below had made
It lurch and shamble like a plantigrade;
But with an impulse governed by the raw
Mechanics of its birth, it drifted where
Ambushed, fog-grey, it stumbled on its lair,
North forty-one degrees and forty-four,
Fifty and fourteen west the longitude,
Waiting a world-memorial hour, its rude
Corundum form stripped to its Greenland core.

SOUTHAMPTON, WEDNESDAY, APRIL 10, 1912

An omen struck the thousands on the shore—
A double accident! And as the ship

Swung down the river on her maiden trip,
Old sailors of the clipper decades, wise
To the sea's incantations, muttered fables
About careening vessels with their cables
Snapped in their harbours under peaceful skies.
Was it just suction or fatality
Which caused the *New York* at the dock to turn,
Her seven mooring ropes to break at the stern
And writhe like anacondas on the quay,
While tugs and fenders answered the collision
Signals with such trim margin of precision?
And was it backwash from the starboard screw
Which, tearing at the big *Teutonic*, drew
Her to the limit of her hawser strain,
And made the smaller tethered craft behave
Like frightened harbour ducks?  And no one knew
For many days the reason to explain
The rise and wash of one inordinate wave,
When a sunken barge on the Southampton bed
Was dragged through mire eight hundred yards ahead,
As the *Titanic* passed above its grave.
But many of those sailors wise and old,
Who pondered on this weird mesmeric power,
Gathered together, lit their pipes and told
Of portents hidden in the natal hour,
Told of the launching of some square-rigged ships,
When water flowed from the inverted tips
Of a waning moon, of sun-hounds, of the shrieks
Of whirling shags around the mizzen peaks.
And was there not this morning's augury
For the big one now heading for the sea?
So long after she passed from landsmen's sight,
They watched her with their Mother Carey eyes
Through Spithead smoke, through mists of Isle of Wight,
Through clouds of sea-gulls following with their cries.

WEDNESDAY EVENING

Electric elements were glowing down
In the long galley passages where scores
Of white-capped cooks stood at the oven doors
To feed the population of a town.
Cauldrons of stock, purées and consommés,
Simmered with peppercorns and marjoram.
The sea-shore smells from bisque and crab and clam
Blended with odours from the fricassées.
Refrigerators, hung with a week's toll
Of the stockyards, delivered sides of lamb
And veal, beef quarters to be roasted whole.
Hundreds of capons and halibut. A shoal
Of Blue-Points waited to be served on shell.
The boards were loaded with pimolas, pails
Of lobster coral, jars of Béchamel,
To garnish tiers of rows of chilled timbales
And aspics. On the shelves were pyramids
Of truffles, sprigs of thyme and water-cress,
Bay leaf and parsley, savouries to dress
Shad roes and sweetbreads broiling on the grids.
And then in diamond, square, crescent and star,
Hors d'oeuvres were fashioned from the toasted bread,
With paste of anchovy and caviare,
Paprika sprinkled and pimento spread,
All ready, for the hour was seven!
                                     Meanwhile,
Rivalling the engines with their steady tread,
Thousands of feet were taking overhead
The fourth lap round the deck to make the mile.
Squash racquet, shuffle board and quoits; the cool
Tang of the plunge in the gymnasium pool,
The rub, the crisp air of the April night,
The salt of the breeze made by the liner's rate,
Worked with an even keel to stimulate
Saliva for an ocean appetite;
And like storm troops before a citadel,

At the first summons of a bugle, soon
The army massed the stairs towards the saloon,
And though twelve courses on the cards might well
Measure themselves against Falstaffian juices,
But few were found presenting their excuses,
When stewards offered on the lacquered trays
The Savoy chasers and the canapés.

The dinner gave the sense that all was well:
That touch of ballast in the tanks; the feel
Of peace from ramparts unassailable,
Which, added to her seven decks of steel,
Had constituted the *Titanic* less
A ship than a Gibraltar under heel.
And night had placed a lazy lusciousness
Upon a surfeit of security.
Science responded to a button press.
The three electric lifts that ran through tiers
Of decks, the reading lamps, the brilliancy
Of mirrors from the tungsten chandeliers,
Had driven out all phantoms which the mind
Had loosed from ocean closets, and assigned
To the dry earth the custody of fears.
The crowds poured through the sumptuous rooms and halls,
And tapped the tables of the Regency;
Smirked at the caryatids on the walls;
Talked Jacobean-wise; canvassed the range
Of taste within the Louis dynasty.
Grey-templed Caesars of the world's Exchange
Swallowed liqueurs and coffee as they sat
Under the Georgian carved mahogany,
Dictating wireless hieroglyphics that
Would on the opening of the Board Rooms rock
The pillared dollars of a railroad stock.

IN THE GYMNASIUM

A group had gathered round a mat to watch
The pressure of a Russian hammerlock,

A Polish scissors and a German crotch,
Broken by the toe-hold of Frank Gotch;
Or listened while a young Y.M.C.A.
Instructor demonstrated the left-hook,
And that right upper-cut which Jeffries took
From Johnson in the polished Reno way.
By midnight in the spacious dancing hall,
Hundreds were at the Masqueraders' Ball,
The high potential of the liner's pleasures,
Where mellow lights from Chinese lanterns glowed
Upon the scene, and the *Blue Danube* flowed
In andantino rhythms through the measures.

By three the silence that proceeded from
The night-caps and the soporific hum
Of the engines was far deeper than a town's:
The starlight and the low wash of the sea
Against the hull bore the serenity
Of sleep at rural hearths with eiderdowns.

The quiet on the decks was scarcely less
Than in the berths: no symptoms of the toil
Down in the holds; no evidence of stress
From gears drenched in the lubricating oil.
She seemed to swim in oil, so smooth the sea.
And quiet on the bridge: the great machine
Called for laconic speech, close-fitting, clean,
And whittled to the ship's economy.
Even the judgment stood in little need
Of reason, for the Watch had but to read
Levels and lights, meter or card or bell
To find the pressures, temperatures, or tell
Magnetic North within a binnacle,
Or gauge the hour of docking; for the speed
Was fixed abaft where under the Ensign,
Like a flashing trolling spoon, the log rotator
Transmitted through a governor its fine
Gradations on a dial indicator.

Morning of Sunday promised cool and clear,
Flawless horizon, crystal atmosphere;
Not a cat's paw on the ocean, not a guy
Rope murmuring: the steamer's columned smoke
Climbed like extensions of her funnels high
Into the upper zones, then warped and broke
Through the resistance of her speed—blue sky,
Blue water rifted only by the wedge
Of the bow where the double foam line ran
Diverging from the beam to join the edge
Of the stern wake like a white unfolding fan.
Her maiden voyage was being sweetly run,
Adding a half-knot here, a quarter there,
Gliding from twenty into twenty-one.
She seemed so native to her thoroughfare,
One turned from contemplation of her size,
Her sixty thousand tons of sheer flotation,
To wonder at the human enterprise
That took a gamble on her navigation—
Joining the mastiff strength with whippet grace
In this head-strained, world-watched Atlantic race:
Her less than six days' passage would combine
Achievement with the architect's design.

9 A.M.

A message from *Caronia: advice*
*From ships proceeding west; sighted field ice*
*And growlers; forty-two north; forty-nine*
*To fifty-one west longitude. S.S.*
*'Mesaba' of Atlantic Transport Line*
*Reports encountering solid pack: would guess*
*The stretch five miles in width from west to east,*
*And forty-five to fifty miles at least*
*In length.*

1 P.M.

> *Amerika* obliged to slow
Down: warns all steamships in vicinity
Presence of bergs, especially of three
Upon the southern outskirts of the floe.

1.42 P.M.

The *Baltic* warns *Titanic:* so *Touraine;*
Reports of numerous icebergs on the Banks,
The floe across the southern traffic lane.

5 P.M.

The *Californian* and *Baltic* again
Present their compliments to Captain.

'TITANIC'              .

> *Thanks.*

THREE MEN TALKING ON DECK

*'That spark's been busy all the afternoon—*
*Warnings! The Hydrographic charts are strewn*
*With crosses showing bergs and pack-ice all*
*Along the routes, more south than usual*
*For this time of the year.'*
> *'She's hitting a clip*
*Instead of letting up while passing through*
*This belt. She's gone beyond the twenty-two.'*

*'Don't worry—Smith's an old dog, knows his ship,*
*No finer in the mercantile marine*
*Than Smith with thirty years of service, clean*
*Record, honoured with highest of all commands,*
*"Majestic", then "Olympic" on his hands,*
*Now the "Titanic".'*
> *'Twas a lucky streak*

That at Southampton dock he didn't lose her,
And the "Olympic" had a narrow squeak
Some months before rammed by the British Cruiser,
The "Hawke".'
                    'Straight accident.  No one to blame:
'Twas suction—Board absolved them both. The same
With the "Teutonic" and "New York". No need
To fear she's trying to out-reach her speed.
There isn't a sign of fog. Besides by now
The watch is doubled at crow's nest and bow.'
'People are talking of that apparition,
When we were leaving Queenstown—that head showing
Above the funnel rim, and the fires going!
A stoker's face—sounds like a superstition.
But he was there within the stack, all right;
Climbed up the ladder and grinned.  The explanation
Was given by an engineer last night—
A dummy funnel built for ventilation.'

'That's queer enough, but nothing so absurd
As the latest story two old ladies heard
At a rubber o' bridge.  They nearly died with fright;
Wanted to tell the captain—of all things!
The others sneered a bit but just the same
It did the trick of breaking up the game.
A mummy from The Valley of the Kings
Was brought from Thebes to London.  Excavators
Passed out from cholera, black plague or worse.
Egyptians understood—an ancient curse
Was visited on all the violators.
One fellow was run over, one was drowned,
And one went crazy.  When in time it found
Its way to the Museum, the last man
In charge—a mothy Aberdonian—
Exploding the whole legend with a laugh,
Lost all his humour when the skeleton
Appeared within the family photograph,
And leered down from a corner just like one

*Of his uncles.'*
      *'Holy Hades!'*

        *'The B.M.*
*Authorities themselves were scared and sold*
*It to New York. That's how the tale is told.'*
*'The joke is on the Yanks.'*
      *'No, not on them,*
*Nor on The Valley of the Kings. What's rummy*
*About it is—we're carrying the mummy.'*

7.30 P.M. AT A TABLE IN THE DINING SALOON

Green Turtle!
     Potage Romanoff!
         *'White Star*
*Is out this time to press Cunarders close,*
*Got them on tonnage—fifty thousand gross.*
*Preferred has never paid a dividend.*
*The common's down to five—one hundred par.*
*The double ribbon—size and speed—would send*
*Them soaring.'*

     *'Speed is not in her design,*
*But comfort and security. The Line*
*Had never advertised it—'twould be mania*
*To smash the record of the "Mauretania".'*
Sherry!
   *'The rumour's out.'*
      *'There's nothing in it.'*
*'Bet you she docks on Tuesday night.'*
       *'I'll take it.'*
*'She's hitting twenty-two this very minute.'*
*'That's four behind—She hasn't a chance to make it.'*
Brook Trout!
    Fried Dover Sole!
      *'Her rate will climb*
*From twenty-two to twenty-six in time.*

*The Company's known never to rush their ships*
*At first or try to rip the bed-bolts off.*
*They run them gently half-a-dozen trips,*
*A few work-outs around the track to let*
*Them find their breathing, take the boiler cough*
*Out of them. She's not racing for a cup.'*
Claret!

        *'Steamships like sprinters have to get*
*Their second wind before they open up.'*

*'That group of men around the captain's table,*
*Look at them, count the aggregate—the House*
*Of Astor, Guggenheim, and Harris, Straus,*
*That's Frohman, isn't it? Between them able*
*To halve the national debt with a cool billion!*
*Sir Hugh is over there, and Hays and Stead.*
*That woman third from captain's right, it's said,*
*Those diamonds round her neck—a quarter million!'*
Mignon of Beef!

        Quail!

            *'I heard Phillips say*
*He had the finest outfit on the sea;*
*The new Marconi valve; the range by day,*
*Five hundred miles, by night a thousand. Three*
*Sources of power. If some crash below*
*Should hit the engines, flood the dynamo,*
*He had the batteries: in emergency,*
*He could switch through to the auxiliary*
*On the boat deck.'*

        Woodcock *and* Burgundy!
*'Say waiter, I said* RARE*, you understand.'*
Escallope of Veal!

        Roast Duckling!

           Snipe! *More* Rhine!
*'Marconi made the sea as safe as land:*
*Remember the "Republic"—White Star Line—*
*Rammed off Nantucket by the "Florida",*
*One thousand saved—the "Baltic" heard the call.*

*Two steamers answered the "Slavonia",*
*Disabled off the Azores. They got them all,*
*And when the "Minnehaha" ran aground*
*Near Bishop's Rock, they never would have found*
*Her—not a chance without the wireless. Same*
*Thing happened to that boat—what was her name?*
*The one that foundered off the Alaska Coast—*
*Her signals brought a steamer in the nick*
*Of time. Yes, sir—Marconi turned the trick.'*

*The* Barcelona salad; *no,* Beaucaire;
*That* Russian dressing;

Avocado pear;

*'They wound her up at the Southampton dock,*
*And then the tugs gave her a push to start*
*Her off—as automatic as a clock.'*

Moselle!
*'For all the hand work there's to do*
*Aboard this liner up on deck, the crew*
*Might just as well have stopped ashore. Apart*
*From stokers and the engineers, she's run*
*By gadgets from the bridge—a thousand and one*
*Of them with a hundred miles of copper wire.*
*A filament glows at the first sign of fire,*
*A buzzer sounds, a number gives the spot,*
*A deck-hand makes a coupling of the hose.*
*That's all there's to it; not a whistle; not*
*A passenger upon the ship that knows*
*What's happened. The whole thing is done without*
*So much as calling up the fire brigade.*
*They don't need even the pumps—a gas is sprayed,*
*Carbon dioxide—and the blaze is out.'*

A Cherry Flan!
Champagne!

Chocolate parfait!

*'How about a poker crowd to-night?*
*Get Jones, an awful grouch—no good to play,*
*But has the coin. Get hold of Larry.'*

> *'Right.'*

*'You fetch Van Raalte: I'll bring in MacRae.*
*In Cabin D, one hundred seventy-nine.*
*In half-an-hour we start playing.'*

> *'Fine.'*

ON DECK

The sky was moonless but the sea flung back
With greater brilliance half the zodiac.
As clear below as clear above, the Lion
Far on the eastern quarter stalked the Bear:
Polaris off the starboard beam—and there
Upon the port the Dog-star trailed Orion.
Capella was so close, a hand might seize
The sapphire with the silver Pleiades.
And further to the south—a finger span,
Swam Betelgeuse and red Aldebaran.
Right through from east to west the ocean glassed
The billions of that snowy caravan
Ranging the highway which the Milkmaid passed.

9.05 P.M.

'CALIFORNIAN' FLASHING

*I say, old man, we're stuck fast in this place,*
*More than an hour. Field ice for miles about.*

'TITANIC'

*Say, 'Californian', shut up, keep out,*
*You're jamming all my signals with Cape Race.*

## 10 P.M.

A group of boys had gathered round a spot
Upon the rail where a dial registered
The speed, and waiting each three minutes heard
The taffrail log bell tallying off a knot.

## 11.20 P.M.

### BEHIND A DECK HOUSE

First act to fifth act in a tragic plan,
Stage time, real time—a woman and a man,
Entering a play within a play, dismiss
The pageant on the ocean with a kiss.
Eleven-twenty curtain! Whether true
Or false the pantomimic vows they make
Will not be known till at the *fifth* they take
Their mutual exit twenty after two.

## 11.25 P.M.

Position half-a-mile from edge of floe,
Hove-to for many hours, bored with delay,
The *Californian* fifteen miles away,
And fearful of the pack, has now begun
To turn her engines over under slow
Bell, and the operator, his task done,
Unclamps the 'phones and ends his dullest day.

The ocean sinuous, half-past eleven;
A silence broken only by the seven
Bells and the look-out calls, the log-book showing
Knots forty-five within two hours—not quite
The expected best as yet—but she was going
With all her bulkheads open through the night,
For not a bridge induction light was glowing.
Over the stern zenith and nadir met
In the wash of the reciprocating set.
The foam in bevelled mirrors multiplied

And shattered constellations.  In between,
The pitch from the main drive of the turbine
Emerged like tuna breaches to divide
Against the rudder, only to unite
With the converging wake from either side.
Under the counter, blending with the spill
Of stars—the white and blue—the yellow light
Of Jupiter hung like a daffodil.

D-179

*'Ace full!  A long time since I had a pot.'*

*'Good boy, Van Raalte.  That's the juiciest haul
To-night.  Calls for a round of roodles, what?
Let's whoop her up.  Double the limit.  All
In.'* (Jones, heard muttering as usual,
Demurs, but over-ruled.) *'Jones sore again.'*

VAN RAALTE (DEALER)
*'Ten dollars and all in!*
                              *The sea's like glass
To-night.  That fin-keel keeps her steady.'*

JONES:                                    *'Pass.'*
(Not looking at his hand.)

LARRY:                   *'Pass.'*

CRIPPS:                          *'Open for ten.'*
(Holding a pair of aces.) *'Say, who won
The sweep to-day?'*
                        *'A Minnesota guy
With olive-coloured spats and a mauve tie.
Five hundred and eighty miles—Beat last day's run.'*

MAC: *'My ten.'*

HARRY: (Taking a gamble on his four
Spades for a flush) *'I'll raise the bet ten more.'*

VAN R.: (Two queens) 'AND *ten.'*

JONES: (Discovering three kings)
*'Raise you to forty'* (face expressing doubt.)

LARRY: (Looking hard at a pair of nines) *'I'm out.'*

CRIPPS: (Flirts for a moment with his aces, flings
His thirty dollars to the pot.)

MAC: (The same.)

HARRY: *'My twenty. Might as well stay with the game.'*

VAN R.: *'I'm in. Draw! Jones, how bloody long you wait.'*

JONES: (Withholds an eight) *'One.'* (And then draws an eight.)

CRIPPS: *'Three.'* (Gets another pair.)
*'How many, Mac?'*

MAC: *'Guess I'll take two, no, three.'* (Gets a third Jack.)

HARRY: *'One.'* (Draws the ace of spades.)

VAN R.: *'Dealer takes three.'*

CRIPPS (THE OPENER): (Throws in a dollar chip.)

MAC: (The same.)

HARRY: *'I'll raise
You ten.'*

VAN R.: *'I'll see you.'*

JONES:                          (Hesitates, surveys
The chips.)  *'Another ten.'*

CRIPPS:                    *'I'll call you.'*

MAC:                                  *'See.'*

HARRY:  *'White livers!  Here she goes to thirty.'*

VAN R.:                              *'Just*
*The devil's luck.'*  (Throws cards down in disgust.)

JONES:
*'Might as well raise.'*  (Counts twenty sluggishly,
Tosses them to the centre.)
                          *'Staying, Cripps?'*

CRIPPS:  *'No, and be damned to it.'*

MAC:                    *'My ten.'*  (With groans.)

HARRY:
(Looks at the pyramid and swears at Jones,
Then calls, pitching ten dollars on the chips.)

JONES:
(Cards down.)  *'A full house tops the flush.'*  (He spreads
His arms around the whites and blues and reds.)

MAC:
*'As the Scotchman once said to the Sphinx,*
*I'd like just to know what he thinks,*
*I'll ask him, he cried,*
*And the Sphinx—he replied,*
*It's the hell of a time between drinks.'*

CRIPPS (WATCH IN HAND):
*'Time?  Eleven forty-four, to be precise.'*

HARRY:
*'Jones—that will fatten up your pocket-book.*
*My throat's like charcoal. Ring for soda and ice.'*

VAN R.:
*'Ice: God! Look—take it through the port-hole—look!'*

11.45 P.M.

A signal from the crow's nest. Three bells pealed:
The look-out telephoned—*Something ahead,*
*Hard to make out, sir; looks like . . . . iceberg dead*
*On starboard bow!*

MURDOCH HOLDING THE BRIDGE-WATCH

       *Starboard your helm:* ship heeled
To port. From bridge to engine-room the clang
Of the telegraph. *Danger. Stop.* A hand sprang
To the throttle; the valves closed, and with the churn
Of the reverse the sea boiled at the stern.
Smith hurried to the bridge and Murdoch closed
The bulkheads of the ship as he supposed,
But could not know that with those riven floors
The electro-magnets failed upon the doors.
No shock! No more than if something alive
Had brushed her as she passed. The bow had missed.
Under the vast momentum of her drive
She went a mile. But why that ominous five
Degrees (within five minutes) of a list?

IN A CABIN:
*'What was that, steward?'*
          *'Seems like she hit a sea, sir.'*
*'But there's no sea; calm as a landlocked bay*
*It is; lost a propeller blade?'*
            *'Maybe, sir.'*
*'She's stopped.'*

> 'Just cautious like, feeling her way,
> There's ice about. It's dark, no moon to-night,
> Nothing to fear, I'm sure, sir.'

For so slight
The answer of the helm, it did not break
The sleep of hundreds: some who were awake
Went up on deck, but soon were satisfied
That nothing in the shape of wind or tide
Or rock or ice could harm that huge bulk spread
On the Atlantic, and went back to bed.

CAPTAIN IN WIRELESS ROOM:
*'We've struck an iceberg—glancing blow: as yet*
*Don't know extent; looks serious; so get*
*Ready to send out general call for aid;*
*I'll tell you when—having inspection made.'*

REPORT OF SHIP'S CARPENTER AND FOURTH OFFICER:
A starboard cut three hundred feet or more
From foremast to amidships. Iceberg tore
Right at the bilge turn through the double skin:
Some boiler rooms and bunkers driven in;
The forward five compartments flooded—mail
Bags floating. Would the engine power avail
To stem the rush?

WIRELESS ROOM, FIRST OFFICER PHILLIPS AT KEY:
*Titanic, C.Q.D.*
*Collision: iceberg: damaged starboard side:*
*Distinct list forward.* (Had Smith magnified
The danger? Over-anxious certainly.)
The second (joking)—*'Try new call, maybe*
*Last chance you'll have to send it.'*

*S.O.S.*

Then back to older signal of distress.

On the same instant the *Carpathia* called,
The distance sixty miles—*Putting about,*
*And heading for you; Double watch installed*
*In engine-room, in stokehold and look-out.*
*Four hours the run, should not the ice retard*
*The speed; but taking chances: Coming hard!*

THE BRIDGE

As leaning on her side to ease a pain,
The tilted ship had stopped the captain's breath:
The inconceivable had stabbed his brain,
This thing unfelt—her visceral wound of death?
Another message—this time to report her
Filling, taxing the pumps beyond their strain.
Had that blow rent her from the bow to quarter?
Or would the aft compartments still intact
Give buoyancy enough to counteract
The open forward holds?
                                    The carpenter's
Second report had offered little chance,
And panic—heart of God—the passengers,
The fourteen hundred—seven hundred packed
In steerage—seven hundred immigrants!
Smith thought of panic clutching at their throats,
And feared that Balkan scramble for the boats.

No call from bridge, no whistle, no alarm
Was sounded. Have the stewards quietly
Inform the passengers: no vital harm,
Precautions merely for emergency;
Collision? Yes, but nature of the blow
Must not be told: not even the crew must know:
Yet all on deck with lifebelts, and boats ready,
The sailors at the falls, and all hands steady.

WIRELESS ROOM

The lilac spark was crackling at the gap,
Eight ships within the radius of the call
From fifteen to five hundred miles, and all
But one answering the operator's tap.
*Olympic* twenty hours away had heard;
The *Baltic* next and the *Virginian* third;
*Frankfurt* and *Burma* distant one-half day;
*Mount Temple* nearer, but the ice-field lay
Between the two ships like a wall of stone;
The *Californian* deaf to signals though
Supreme deliverer an hour ago:
The hope was on *Carpathia* alone.


ON THE DECKS

So suave the fool-proof sense of life that fear
Had like the unforeseen become a mere
Illusion—vanquished by the towering height
Of funnels pouring smoke through thirty feet
Of bore; the solid deck planks and the light
From a thousand lamps as on a city street;
The feel of numbers; the security
Of wealth; the placid surface of the sea,
Reflecting on the ship the outwardness
Of calm and leisure of the passengers;
Deck-hands obedient to their officers;
Pearl-throated women in their evening dress
And wrapped in sables and minks; the silhouettes
Of men in dinner jackets staging an act
In which delusion passed, deriding fact
Behind the cupped flare of the cigarettes.

Women and children first! Slowly the men
Stepped backward from the rails where number ten,
Its cover off, and lifted from the chocks,
Moved outward as the Welin davits swung.
The new ropes creaking through the unused blocks,

The boat was lowered to B deck and hung
There while her load of sixty stepped inside,
Convinced the order was not justified.

*Rockets, one, two,* God! Smith—what does he mean?
The sounding of the bilges could not show
This reason for alarm—the sky serene
And not a ripple on the water—no
Collision.  What report came from below?
No leak accounts for this—looks like a drill,
A bit of exhibition play—but still
Stopped in mid-ocean! and those rockets—*three!*
More urgent even than a tapping key
And more immediate as a protocol
To a disaster. *There!*  An arrow of fire,
A fourth sped towards the sky, its bursting spire
Topping the foremast like a parasol
With fringe of fuchsia,—more a parody
Upon the tragic summons of the sea
Than the real script of unacknowledged fears
Known to the bridge and to the engineers.

Midnight!  The Master of the ship presents
To the Master of the Band his compliments,
Desiring that the Band should play right through;
No intermission.

CONDUCTOR:              *'Bad?'*

OFFICER:                      *'Yes, bad enough,*
*The half not known yet even to the crew;*
*For God's sake, cut the sentimental stuff,*
*The* BLUE BELLS *and Kentucky lullabies.*
*Murdoch will have a barrel of work to do,*
*Holding the steerage back, once they get wise;*
*They're jumpy now under the rockets' glare;*
*So put the ginger in the fiddles—Zip*
*Her up.'*

CONDUCTOR:  *'Sure, number forty-seven.'*  E-Yip
I Addy-I-A, I Ay . . . I don't care . . .

NUMBER TEN GOES OVER THE SIDE

Full noon and midnight by a weird design
Both met and parted at the median line.
Beyond the starboard gunwale was outspread
The jet expanse of water islanded
By fragments of the berg which struck the blow.
And further off towards the horizon lay
The loom of the uncharted parent floe,
Merging the black with an amorphous grey.
On the port gunwale the meridian
Shone from the terraced rows of decks that ran
From gudgeon to the stem nine hundred feet;
And as the boat now tilted by the stern,
Or now resumed her levels with the turn
Of the controlling ropes at block and cleat,
How easy seemed the step and how secure
Back to the comfort and the warmth—the lure
Of sheltered promenade and sun decks starred
By hanging bulbs, amber and rose and blue,
The trellis and palms lining an avenue
With all the vista of a boulevard:
The mirror of the ceilings with festoon
Of pennants, flags and streamers—and now through
The leaded windows of the grand saloon,
Through parted curtains and the open doors
Of vestibules, glint of deserted floors
And tables, and under the sorcery
Of light excelling their facsimile,
The periods returning to relume
The panels of the lounge and smoking-room,
Holding the mind in its abandonment
During those sixty seconds of descent.
*Lower away!* The boat with its four tons
Of freight went down with jerks and stops and runs

Beyond the glare of the cabins and below
The slanting parallels of port-holes, clear
Of the exhaust from the condenser flow:
But with the uneven falls she canted near
The water line; the stern rose; the bow dipped;
The crew groped for the link-releasing gear;
The lever jammed; a stoker's jack-knife ripped
The aft ropes through, which on the instant brought her
With rocking keel though safe upon the water.

### THE 'CARPATHIA'

Fifteen, sixteen, seventeen, eighteen—three
Full knots beyond her running limit, she
Was feeling out her port and starboard points,
And testing rivets on her boiler joints.
The needle on the gauge beyond the red,
The blow-offs feathered at the funnel head.
The draught-fans roaring at their loudest, now
The quartermaster jams the helm hard-over,
As the revolving searchlight beams uncover
The columns of an iceberg on the bow,
Then compensates this loss by daring gains
Made by her passage through the open lanes.

### THE BAND

*East side, West side, all around the town,*
*The tots sang 'Ring-a-Rosie'*
*'London Bridge is falling down',*
*Boys and girls together . . . .*

The cranks turn and the sixth and seventh swing
Over and down, the 'tiller' answering
*'Aye, Aye, sir'* to the shouts of officers—
*'Row to the cargo ports for passengers.'*
The water line is reached, but the ports fail
To open, and the crews of the boats hail
The decks; receiving no response they pull

Away from the ship's side, less than half full.
The eighth caught in the tackle foul is stuck
Half-way. With sixty-five capacity,
Yet holding twenty-four, goes number three.

The sharp unnatural deflection, struck
By the sea-level with the under row
Of dipping port-holes at the forward, show
How much she's going by the head. Behind
The bulkheads, sapping out their steel control,
Is the warp of the bunker press inclined
By many thousand tons of shifting coal.

The smoothest, safest passage to the sea
Is made by number one—the next to go—
Her space is forty—twelve her company:
*'Pull like the devil from her—harder—row!*
*The minute that she founders, not a boat*
*Within a mile around that will not follow.*
*What nearly happened at Southampton? So*
*Pull, pull, I tell you—not a chip afloat,*
*God knows how far, her suction will not swallow.'*

*Alexander's rag-time band. . . .*
*It's the best band in the land. . . .*

VOICES FROM THE DECK:
*'There goes the Special with the toffs. You'll make*
*New York to-night rowing like that. You'll take*
*Your death o' cold out there with all the fish*
*And ice around.'*
                    *'Make sure your butlers dish*
*You up your toddies now, and bring hot rolls*
*For breakfast.'*
                    *'Don't forget the finger bowls.'*

The engineering staff of thirty-five
Are at their stations: those off-duty go
Of their free will to join their mates below

In the grim fight for steam, more steam, to drive
The pressure through the pumps and dynamo.
Knee-deep, waist-deep in water they remain,
Not one of them seen on the decks again.
The under braces of the rudder showing,
The wing propeller blades began to rise,
And with them, through the hawse-holes, water flowing—
The angle could not but assault the eyes.
A fifteen minutes, and the fo'c'sle head
Was under.  And five more, the sea had shut
The lower entrance to the stairs that led
From C deck to the boat deck—the short cut
For the crew.  Another five, the upward flow
Had covered the wall brackets where the glow
Diffusing from the frosted bulbs turned green
Uncannily through their translucent screen.

ON THE 'CARPATHIA'

White Star—Cunarder, forty miles apart,
Still eighteen knots!  From coal to flame to steam—
Decision of a captain to redeem
Errors of brain by hazards of the heart!
Showers of sparks danced through the funnel smoke,
The firemen's shovels, rakes and slice-bars broke
The clinkers, fed the fires, and ceaselessly
The hoppers dumped the ashes on the sea.

As yet no panic, but none might foretell
The moment when the sight of that oblique
Breath-taking lift of the taffrail and the sleek
And foamless undulation of the swell
Might break in meaning on those diverse races,
And give them common language.  As the throng
Came to the upper decks and moved along
The incline, the contagion struck the faces
With every lowering of a boat and backed
Them towards the stern.  And twice between the hush
Of fear and utterance the gamut cracked,

When with the call for women and the flare
Of an exploding rocket, a short rush
Was made for the boats—fifteen and two.
'Twas nearly done—the sudden clutch and tear
Of canvas, a flurry of fists and curses met
By swift decisive action from the crew,
Supported by a quartermaster's threat
Of three revolver shots fired on the air.

But still the fifteenth went with five inside,
Who, seeking out the shadows, climbed aboard
And, lying prone and still, managed to hide
Under the thwarts long after she was lowered.

*Jingle bells, jingle bells,*
*Jingle all the way,*
*O what fun. . . .*

'Some men in number two, sir!'

The boat swung

Back.
'Chuck the fellows out.'

Grabbed by the feet,
The lot were pulled over the gunwale and flung
Upon the deck.
'Hard at that forward cleat!
A hand there for that after fall. Lower
Away—port side, the second hatch, and wait.'

With six hands of his watch, the bosun's mate,
Sent down to open up the gangway door,
Was trapped and lost in a flooded alley way,
And like the seventh, impatient of delay,
The second left with room for twenty more.

The fiddley leading from a boiler room
Lay like a tortuous exit from a tomb.
A stoker climbed it, feeling by the twist

From vertical how steep must be the list.
He reached the main deck where the cold night airs
Enswathed his flesh with steam.  Taking the stairs,
He heard the babel by the davits, faced
The forward, noticed how the waters raced
To the break of the fo'c'sle and lapped
The foremast root.  He climbed again and saw
The resolute manner in which Murdoch's rapped
Command put a herd instinct under law;
No life-preserver on, he stealthily
Watched Phillips in his room, bent at the key,
And thinking him alone, he sprang to tear
The jacket off.  He leaped too soon.  *'Take that!'*
The second stove him with a wrench.  *'Lie there,*
*Till hell begins to singe your lids—you rat!'*

But set against those scenes where order failed,
Was the fine muster at the fourteenth where,
Like a zone of calm along a thoroughfare,
The discipline of sea-worn laws prevailed.
No women answering the repeated calls,
The men filled up the vacant seats:  the falls
Were slipping through the sailors' hands,
When a steerage group of women, having fought
Their way over five flights of stairs, were brought
Bewildered to the rails.  Without commands
Barked from the lips of officers; without
A protest registered in voice or face,
The boat was drawn up and the men stepped out
Back to the crowded stations with that free
Barter of life for life done with the grace
And air of a Castilian courtesy.

*I've just got here through Paris,*
*From the sunny Southern shore,*
*I to Monte Carlo went...*

ISIDOR AND IDA STRAUS

At the sixteenth—a woman wrapped her coat
Around her maid and placed her in the boat;
Was ordered in but seen to hesitate
At the gunwale, and more conscious of her pride
Than of her danger swiftly took her fate
With open hands, and without show of tears
Returned unmurmuring to her husband's side;
*'We've been together now for forty years,*
*Whither you go, I go.'*

     A boy of ten,
Ranking himself within the class of men,
Though given a seat, made up his mind to waive
The privilege of his youth and size, and piled
The inches on his stature as he gave
Place to a Magyar woman and her child.

And men who had in the world's run of trade,
Or in pursuit of the professions, made
Their reputation, looked upon the scene
Merely as drama in a life's routine:
Millet was studying eyes as he would draw them
Upon a canvas; Butt, as though he saw them
In the ranks; Astor, social, debonair,
Waved *'Good-bye'* to his bride—*'See you to-morrow'*,
And tapped a cigarette on a silver case;
Men came to Guggenheim as he stood there
In evening suit, coming this time to borrow
Nothing but courage from his calm, cool face.

And others unobserved, of unknown name
And race, just stood behind, pressing no claim
Upon priority but rendering proof
Of their oblation, quiet and aloof
Within the maelstrom towards the rails. And some
Wavered a moment with the panic urge,

But rallied to attention on the verge
Of flight as if the rattle of a drum
From quarters faint but unmistakable
Had put the stiffening in the blood to check
The impulse of the feet, leaving the will
No choice between the lifeboats and the deck.

The four collapsibles, their lashings ripped,
Half-dragged, half-lifted by the hooks, were slipped
Over the side. The first two luckily
Had but the forward distance to the sea.
Its canvas edges crumpled up, the third
Began to fill with water and transferred
Its cargo to the twelfth, while number four,
Abaft and higher, nose-dived and swamped its score.

The wireless cabin—Phillips in his place,
Guessing the knots of the Cunarder's race.
Water was swirling up the slanted floor
Around the chair and sucking at his feet.
*Carpathia*'s call—the last one heard complete—
*Expect to reach position half-past four.*
The operators turned—Smith at the door
With drawn incredulous face. *'Men, you have done
Your duty. I release you. Everyone
Now for himself.'* They stayed ten minutes yet,
The power growing fainter with each blue
Crackle of flame. Another stammering jet—
*Virginian* heard 'a tattering C.Q.'.
Again a try for contact but the code's
Last jest had died between the electrodes.

Even yet the spell was on the ship: although
The last lifeboat had vanished, there was no
Besieging of the heavens with a crescendo
Of fears passing through terror into riot—
But on all lips the strange narcotic quiet
Of an unruffled ocean's innuendo.

In spite of her deformity of line,
Emergent like a crag out of the sea,
She had the semblance of stability,
Moment by moment furnishing no sign,
So far as visible, of that decline
Made up of inches crawling into feet.
Then, with the electric circuit still complete,
The miracle of day displacing night
Had worked its fascination to beguile
Direction of the hours and cheat the sight.
Inside the recreation rooms the gold
From Arab lamps shone on the burnished tile.
What hindered the return to shelter while
The ship clothed in that irony of light
Offered her berths and cabins as a fold?
And, was there not the *Californian*?
Many had seen her smoke just over there,
But two hours past—it seemed a harbour span—
So big, so close, she could be hailed, they said;
She must have heard the signals, seen the flare
Of those white stars and changed at once her course.
There under the *Titanic*'s foremast head,
A lamp from the look-out cage was flashing Morse.
No ship afloat unless deaf, blind and dumb
To those three sets of signals but would come.
And when the whiz of a rocket bade men turn
Their faces to each other in concern
At shattering facts upon the deck, they found
Their hearts take reassurance with the sound
Of the violins from the gymnasium, where
The bandsmen in their blithe insouciance
Discharged the sudden tension of the air
With the fox-trot's sublime irrelevance.

The fo'c'sle had gone under the creep
Of the water.  Though without a wind, a lop
Was forming on the wells now fathoms deep.
The seventy feet—the boat deck's normal drop—

Was down to ten.  Rising, falling, and waiting,
Rising again, the swell that edged and curled
Around the second bridge, over the top
Of the air-shafts, backed, resurged and whirled
Into the stokehold through the fiddley grating.

Under the final strain the two wire guys
Of the forward funnel tugged and broke at the eyes:
With buckled plates the stack leaned, fell and smashed
The starboard wing of the flying bridge, went through
The lower, then tilting at the davits crashed
Over, driving a wave aboard that drew
Back to the sea some fifty sailors and
The captain with the last of the bridge command.

Out on the water was the same display
Of fear and self-control as on the deck—
Challenge and hesitation and delay,
The quick return, the will to save, the race
Of snapping oars to put the realm of space
Between the half-filled lifeboats and the wreck.
The swimmers whom the waters did not take
With their instant death-chill struck out for the wake
Of the nearer boats, gained on them, hailed
The steersmen and were saved:  the weaker failed
And fagged and sank.  A man clutched at the rim
Of a gunwale, and a woman's jewelled fist
Struck at his face:  two others seized his wrist,
As he released his hold, and gathering him
Over the side, they staunched the cut from the ring.
And there were many deeds envisaging
Volitions where self-preservation fought
Its red primordial struggle with the 'ought',
In those high moments when the gambler tossed
Upon the chance and uncomplaining lost.

Aboard the ship, whatever hope of dawn
Gleamed from the *Carpathia*'s riding lights was gone,

For every knot was matched by each degree
Of list. The stern was lifted bodily
When the bow had sunk three hundred feet, and set
Against the horizon stars in silhouette
Were the blade curves of the screws, hump of the rudder.
The downward pull and after buoyancy
Held her a minute poised but for a shudder
That caught her frame as with the upward stroke
Of the sea a boiler or a bulkhead broke.

Climbing the ladders, gripping shroud and stay,
Storm-rail, ringbolt or fairlead, every place
That might befriend the clutch of hand or brace
Of foot, the fourteen hundred made their way
To the heights of the aft decks, crowding the inches
Around the docking bridge and cargo winches.
And now that last salt tonic which had kept
The valour of the heart alive—the bows
Of the immortal seven that had swept
The strings to outplay, outdie their orders, ceased.
Five minutes more, the angle had increased
From eighty on to ninety when the rows
Of deck and port-hole lights went out, flashed back
A brilliant second and again went black.
Another bulkhead crashed, then following
The passage of the engines as they tore
From their foundations, taking everything
Clean through the bows from 'midships with a roar
Which drowned all cries upon the deck and shook
The watchers in the boats, the liner took
Her thousand fathoms journey to her grave.

*   *   *   *   *

And out there in the starlight, with no trace
Upon it of its deed but the last wave
From the *Titanic* fretting at its base,
Silent, composed, ringed by its icy broods,
The grey shape with the palaeolithic face
Was still the master of the longitudes.

# F. R. Scott

*Lakeshore*

The lake is sharp along the shore
Trimming the bevelled edge of land
To level curves; the fretted sands
Go slanting down through liquid air
Till stones below shift here and there
Floating upon their broken sky
All netted by the prism wave
And rippled where the currents are.

I stare through windows at this cave
Where fish, like planes, slow-motioned, fly.
Poised in a still of gravity
The narrow minnow, flicking fin,
Hangs in a paler, ochre sun,
His doorways open everywhere.

And I am a tall frond that waves
Its head below its rooted feet
Seeking the light that draws it down
To forest floors beyond its reach
Vivid with gloom and eerie dreams.

The water's deepest colonnades
Contract the blood, and to this home
That stirs the dark amphibian
With me the naked swimmers come
Drawn to their prehistoric womb.

They too are liquid as they fall
Like tumbled water loosed above

Until they lie, diagonal,
Within the cool and sheltered grove
Stroked by the fingertips of love.

Silent, our sport is drowned in fact
Too virginal for speech or sound
And each is personal and laned
Along his private aqueduct.

Too soon the tether of the lungs
Is taut and straining, and we rise
Upon our undeveloped wings
Toward the prison of our ground
A secret anguish in our thighs
And mermaids in our memories.

This is our talent, to have grown
Upright in posture, false-erect,
A landed gentry, circumspect,
Tied to a horizontal soil
The floor and ceiling of the soul;
Striving, with cold and fishy care
To make an ocean of the air.

Sometimes, upon a crowded street,
I feel the sudden rain come down
And in the old, magnetic sound
I hear the opening of a gate
That loosens all the seven seas.
Watching the whole creation drown
I muse, alone, on Ararat.


*Old Song*

far voices
and fretting leaves
this music the

hillside gives

but in the deep
Laurentian river
an elemental song
for ever

a quiet calling
of no mind
out of long aeons
when dust was blind
and ice hid sound

only a moving
with no note
granite lips
a stone throat

## Laurentian Shield

Hidden in wonder and snow, or sudden with summer,
This land stares at the sun in a huge silence
Endlessly repeating something we cannot hear.
Inarticulate, arctic,
Not written on by history, empty as paper,
It leans away from the world with songs in its lakes
Older than love, and lost in the miles.

This waiting is wanting.
It will choose its language
When it has chosen its technic,
A tongue to shape the vowels of its productivity.

*A language of flesh and of roses.*

Now there are pre-words,

Cabin syllables,
Nouns of settlement
Slowly forming, with steel syntax,
The long sentence of its exploitation.

The first cry was the hunter, hungry for fur,
And the digger for gold, nomad, no-man, a particle;
Then the bold commands of monopoly, big with machines,
Carving their kingdoms out of the public wealth;
And now the drone of the plane, scouting the ice,
Fills all the emptiness with neighbourhood
And links our future over the vanished pole.

But a deeper note is sounding, heard in the mines,
The scattered camps and the mills, a language of life,
And what will be written in the full culture of occupation
Will come, presently, tomorrow,
From millions whose hands can turn this rock into children.


## Overture

In the dark room, under a cone of light,
You precisely play the Mozart sonata.  The bright
Clear notes fly like sparks through the air
And trace a flickering pattern of music there.

Your hands dart in the light, your fingers flow.
They are ten careful operatives in a row
That pick their packets of sound from steel bars
Constructing harmonies as sharp as stars.

But how shall I hear old music?  This is an hour
Of new beginnings, concepts warring for power,
Decay of systems—the tissue of art is torn
With overtures of an era being born.

And this perfection which is less yourself

Than Mozart, seems a trinket on a shelf,
A pretty octave played before a window
Beyond whose curtain grows a world crescendo.

## Charity

A code of laws
Lies written
On this beggar's hand.

My small coin
Lengthens
The harsh sentence.

## W.L.M.K.

How shall we speak of Canada,
Mackenzie King dead?
The Mother's boy in the lonely room
With his dog, his medium and his ruins?

He blunted us.

We had no shape
Because he never took sides,
And no sides
Because he never allowed them to take shape.

He skilfully avoided what was wrong
Without saying what was right,
And never let his on the one hand
Know what his on the other hand was doing.

The height of of his ambition

Was to pile a Parliamentary Committee on a Royal Commission,
To have 'conscription if necessary
But not necessarily conscription',
To let Parliament decide—
Later.

Postpone, postpone, abstain.

Only one thread was certain:
After World War I
Business as usual,
After World War II
Orderly decontrol.
Always he led us back to where we were before.

He seemed to be in the centre
Because we had no centre,
No vision
To pierce the smoke-screen of his politics.

Truly he will be remembered
Wherever men honour ingenuity,
Ambiguity, inactivity, and political longevity.

Let us raise up a temple
To the cult of mediocrity,
Do nothing by halves
Which can be done by quarters.


## The Canadian Authors Meet

Expansive puppets percolate self-unction
Beneath a portrait of the Prince of Wales.
Miss Crotchet's muse has somehow failed to function,
Yet she's a poetess. Beaming, she sails

From group to chattering group, with such a dear
Victorian saintliness, as is her fashion,
Greeting the other unknowns with a cheer—
Virgins of sixty who still write of passion.

The air is heavy with Canadian topics,
And Carman, Lampman, Roberts, Campbell, Scott,
Are measured for their faith and philanthropics,
Their zeal for God and King, their earnest thought.

The cakes are sweet, but sweeter is the feeling
That one is mixing with the *literati;*
It warms the old, and melts the most congealing.
Really, it is a most delightful party.

Shall we go round the mulberry bush, or shall
We gather at the river, or shall we
Appoint a Poet Laureate this fall,
Or shall we have another cup of tea?

O Canada, O Canada, Oh can
A day go by without new authors springing
To paint the native maple, and to plan
More ways to set the selfsame welkin ringing?


## Saturday Sundae

The triple-decker and the double-cone
I side-swipe swiftly, suck the coke-straws dry.
Ride toadstool seat beside the slab of morgue—
Sweet corner drug-store, sweet pie in the sky.

Him of the front-flap apron, him I sing,
The counter-clockwise clerk in underalls.
Swing low, sweet chocolate, Oh swing, swing,
While cheek by juke the jitter chatter falls.

I swivel on my axle and survey
The latex tintex kotex cutex land.
Soft kingdoms sell for dimes, Life Pic Look Click
Inflate the male with conquest girly grand.

My brothers and my sisters, two by two,
Sit sipping succulence and sighing sex.
Each tiny adolescent universe
A world the vested interests annex.

Such bread and circuses these times allow,
Opium most popular, life so small and slick,
Perhaps with candy is the new world born
And cellophane shall wrap the heretic.


## Martinigram

The key person in the whole business
I said raising my Martini damn that woman
she didn't look where she was going sorry
it won't stain the key person what?  oh it's
you Georgina no I won't be there tomorrow
see you some day the key person in the whole
business is not the one oh hello James yes
we're having a wonderful time not the one you
love but it's no thank you no more just now
not the one you love but it's the one who
does the hell's bells there's a stone in my olive


## Eclipse

I looked the sun straight in the eye.
He put on dark glasses.

## A Lass in Wonderland

I went to bat for the Lady Chatte
  Dressed in my bib and gown.
The judges three glared down at me
  The priests patrolled the town.

My right hand shook as I reached for that book
And rose to play my part,
For out on the street there were the marching feet
Of the League of the Sacred Heart.

The word 'obscene' was supposed to mean
  'Undue exploitation of sex'.
This wording's fine for your needs and mine
  But it's far too free for Quebec's.

I tried my best, with unusual zest,
  To drive my argument through,
But I soon got stuck on what rhymes with 'muck'
  And that dubious word 'undue'.

So I raised their sights to the Bill of Rights
  And cried: 'Let freedom ring!',
Showed straight from the text that freedom of sex
  Was as clear as anything.

Then I plunged into love, the spell that it wove,
  And its attributes big and bold
Till the legal elect all stood erect
  As my rapturous tale was told.

The judges' sighs and rolling of eyes
  Gave hope that my case was won,
Yet Mellors and Connie still looked pretty funny
  Dancing about in the sun.

What hurt me was not that they did it a lot

And even ran out in the rain,
'Twas those curious poses with harebells and roses
  And that dangling daisy-chain.

Then too the sales made in the paper-back trade
  Served to aggravate judicial spleen,
For it seems a high price will make any book nice
  While its mass distribution's obscene.

Oh Letters and Law are found in the raw
  And found on the heights sublime,
But D.H. Lawrence would view with abhorrence
  This Jansenist pantomime.


## Bonne Entente

The advantages of living with two cultures
Strike one at every turn,
Especially when one finds a notice in an office building:
'This elevator will not run on Ascension Day';
Or reads in the *Montreal Star:*
'Tomorrow being the Feast of the Immaculate Conception,
There will be no collection of garbage in the city';
Or sees on the restaurant menu the bilingual dish:

DEEP APPLE PIE
TARTE AUX POMMES PROFONDES


## A Grain of Rice

Such majestic rhythms, such tiny disturbances.
The rain of the monsoon falls, an inescapable treasure,
Hundreds of millions live

Only because of the certainty of this season,
　　　The turn of the wind.

The frame of our human house rests on the motion
Of earth and of moon, the rise of continents,
Invasion of deserts, erosion of hills,
　　　The capping of ice.

Today, while Europe tilted, drying the Baltic,
I read of a battle between brothers in anguish,
　　　A flag moved a mile.

And today, from a curled leaf cocoon, in the course of its rhythm,
I saw the break of a shell, the creation
Of a great Asian moth, radiant, fragile,
Incapable of not being born, and trembling
　　　To live its brief moment.

Religions build walls round our love, and science
Is equal of error and truth.  Yet always we find
Such ordered purpose in cell and in galaxy,
So great a glory in life-thrust and mind-range,
Such widening frontiers to draw out our longings,
　　　We grow to one world
　　　Through enlargement of wonder.


## Creed

The world is my country
The human race is my race
The spirit of man is my God
The future of man is my heaven

## Union

Come to me
Not as a river willingly downward falls
To be lost in a wide ocean
But come to me
As flood-tide comes to shore-line
Filling empty bays
With a white stillness
Mating earth and sea.


## For Bryan Priestman

*(Drowned while attempting to save a child.)*

The child fell, turning slowly with arms outstretched like a doll,
One shrill cry dying under the arches,
And floated away, her time briefer than foam.

Nothing was changed on the summer's day. The birds sang,
The busy insects followed their fixed affairs.
Only a Professor of Chemistry, alone on the bridge,
Suddenly awoke from his reverie, into the intense moment,
Saw all the elements of his life compounded for testing,
And plunged with searching hands into his last experiment.

This was a formula he had carried from childhood,
That can work but once in the life of a man.
His were the labels of an old laboratory,
And the long glass tubes of the river.

# Earle Birney

*From the Hazel Bough*

I met a lady
  on a lazy street
hazel eyes
  and little plush feet

her legs swam by
  like lovely trout
eyes were trees
  where boys leant out

hands in the dark and
  a river side
round breasts rising
  with the fingers' tide

she was plump as a finch
  and live as a salmon
gay as silk and
  proud as a Brahmin

we winked when we met
  and laughed when we parted
never took time
  to be brokenhearted

but no man sees
  where the trout lie now
or what leans out
  from the hazel bough

## Vancouver Lights

About me the night    moonless    wimples the mountains
wraps ocean    land    air    and mounting
sucks at the stars    The city    throbbing below
webs the peninsula    Streaming    the golden
strands overleap the seajet    by bridge and buoy
vault the shears of the inlet    climb the woods
toward me    falter    and halt    Across to the firefly
haze of a ship on the gulf's erased horizon
roll the spokes of a restless lighthouse

Through the feckless years we have come to the time
when to look on this quilt of lamps is a troubling delight
Welling from Europe's bog    through Africa flowing
and Asia    drowning the lonely lumes on the oceans
tiding up over Halifax    now to this winking
outpost comes flooding the primal ink

On this mountain's brutish forehead with terror of space
I stir    of the changeless night and the stark ranges
of nothing    pulsing down from beyond and between
the fragile planets    We are a spark beleaguered
by darkness    this twinkle we make in a corner of emptiness
how shall we utter our fear that the black Experimentress
will never in the range of her microscope find it? Our Phoebus
himself is a bubble that dries on Her slide    while the Nubian
wears for an evening's whim a necklace of nebulae

Yet we must speak    we the unique glowworms
Out of the waters and rocks of our little world
we cunningly conjured these flames    hooped these sparks
by our will    From blankness and cold we fashioned stars
to our size    and signalled Aldebaran    This must we say
whoever may be to hear us    if murk devour
and none weave again in gossamer:

                              These rays were ours

we made and unmade them    Not the shudder of continents
doused us    the moon's passion    nor crash of comets
In the fathomless heat of our dwarfdom    our dream's combustion
we contrived the power    the blast that snuffed us
No one bound Prometheus    Himself he chained
and consumed his own bright liver    O stranger
Plutonian    descendant    or beast in the stretching night—
there was light

## Anglosaxon Street

Dawndrizzle ended    dampness steams from
blotching brick and    blank plasterwaste
Faded housepatterns    hoary and finicky
unfold stuttering    stick like a phonograph

Here is a ghetto    gotten for goyim
O with care denuded    of nigger and kike
No coonsmell rankles    reeks only cellarrot
ottar of carexhaust    catcorpse and cookinggrease
Imperial hearts    heave in this haven
Cracks across windows    are welded with slogans
There'll Always Be An England    enhances geraniums
and V's for a Victory    vanquish the housefly

Ho! with beaming sun    march the bleached beldames
festooned with shopping bags    farded    flatarched
bigthewed Saxonwives    stepping over buttrivers
waddling back wienerladen    to suckle smallfry

Hoy! with sunslope    shrieking over hydrants
flood from learninghall    the lean fingerlings
Nordic    nobblecheeked    not all clean of nose
leaping Commandowise    into leprous lanes

What! after whistleblow!    spewed from wheelboat

after daylight doughtiness    dire handplay
in sewertrench or sandpit    come Saxonthegns
Junebrown Jutekings    jawslack for meat

Sit after supper    on smeared doorsteps
not humbly swearing    hatedeeds on Huns
profiteers politicians    pacifists Jews

Then by twobit magic    to muse in movie
unlock picturehoard    or lope to alehall
soaking bleakly    in beer skittleless
Home again to hotbox    and humid husbandhood
in slumbertrough adding    sleepily to Anglekin

Alongside in lanenooks    carling and leman
caterwaul and clip    careless of Saxonry
with moonglow and haste    and a higher heartbeat

Slumbers now slumtrack    unstinks cooling
waiting brief for milkmaid    mornstar and worldrise


## Bushed

He invented a rainbow but lightning struck it
shattered it into the lake-lap of a mountain
so big his mind slowed when he looked at it

Yet he built a shack on the shore
learned to roast porcupine belly and
wore the quills on his hatband

At first he was out with the dawn
whether it yellowed bright as wood-columbine
or was only a fuzzed moth in a flannel of storm
But he found the mountain was clearly alive
sent messages whizzing down every hot morning
boomed proclamations at noon and spread out

a white guard of goat
before falling asleep on its feet at sundown

When he tried his eyes on the lake   ospreys
would fall like valkyries
choosing the cut-throat
He took then to waiting
till the night smoke rose from the boil of the sunset

But the moon carved unknown totems
out of the lakeshore
owls in the beardusky woods derided him
moosehorned cedars circled his swamps and tossed
their antlers up to the stars
Then he knew   though the mountain slept   the winds
were shaping its peak to an arrowhead
poised

And now he could only
bar himself in and wait
for the great flint to come singing into his heart

1951

## A Walk in Kyoto

All week   the maid tells me   bowing
her doll's body at my mat   is Boys' Day
Also please Man's Day   and gravely
bends deeper   The magnolia sprig in my alcove
is it male?   The ancient discretions of Zen were not shaped
for my phallic western eye   There is so much discretion
in this small bowed body of an empire
the wild hair of waterfalls combed straight
in the ricefields   the inn-maid retreating
with the face of a shut flower   I stand hunched
and clueless like a castaway in the shoals of my room

When I slide my parchment door to stalk awkward
through Lilliput gardens framed and untouchable
as watercolors    the streets look much the same
the Men are being pulled past on the strings of their engines
the legs of the Boys are revolved by a thousand pedals
and all the faces as taut and unfestive as Moscow's
or Chicago's    or mine

Lord Buddha help us all there is vigor enough
in these islands and in all islands reefed and resounding
with cities    But the pitch is high as the ping
of cicadas    those small strained motors concealed
in the propped pines by the dying river    and only
male as the stretched falsetto of actors mincing
the women's roles in *kabuki*    or female only
as the lost heroes womanized in the Ladies' Opera
Where in these alleys jammed with competing waves
of signs in two tongues and three scripts
can the simple song of a man be heard?

By the shoguns' palace    the Important Cultural Property
stripped for tiptoeing schoolgirls    I stare at the staring
penned carp that flail on each other's backs
to the shrunk pool's edge for the crumb this non-fish
tossed    Is this the Day's one parable?
Or under that peeling pagoda the five hundred tons
of hermaphrodite Word?

At the inn I prepare to surrender again my defeated
shoes to the bending maid    But suddenly the closed
lotus opens to a smile and she points
over my shoulder    above the sagging tiles    to where
tall in the bare sky and huge as Gulliver
a carp is rising    golden and fighting
thrusting its paper body up from the fist
of a small boy on an empty roof    higher
and higher    into the endless winds of the world

*Kyoto & Hong Kong 1958*

## The Bear on the Delhi Road

Unreal    tall as a myth
by the road the Himalayan bear
is beating the brilliant air
with his crooked arms
About him two men    bare
spindly as locusts    leap

One pulls on a ring
in the great soft nose    His mate
flicks    flicks with a stick
up at the rolling eyes

They have not led him here
down from the fabulous hills
to this bald alien plain
and the clamorous world    to kill
but simply to teach him to dance

They are peaceful both    these spare
men of Kashmir    and the bear
alive is their living    too
If    far on the Delhi way
around him galvanic they dance
it is merely to wear    wear
from his shaggy body the tranced
wish forever to stay
only an ambling bear
four-footed in berries

It is no more joyous for them
in this hot dust to prance
out of reach of the praying claws
sharpened to paw for ants
in the shadows of deodars
It is not easy to free
myth from reality

or rear this fellow up
to lurch   lurch with them
in the tranced dancing of men

*Srinagar 1958—Ile des Porquerolles 1959*

## El Greco: *Espolio*

The carpenter is intent on the pressure of his hand

on the awl   and the trick of pinpointing his strength
through the awl to the wood   which is tough
He has no effort to spare for despoilings
or to worry if he'll be cut in on the dice
His skill is vital to the scene   and the safety of the state
Anyone can perform the indignities   It's his hard arms
and craft that hold the eyes of the convict's women
There is the problem of getting the holes exact
(in the middle of this elbowing crowd)
and deep enough to hold the spikes
after they've sunk through those bared feet
and inadequate wrists he knows are waiting behind him

He doesn't sense perhaps that one of the hands
is held in a curious gesture over him—
giving   or asking   forgiveness?—
but he'd scarcely take time to be puzzled by poses
Criminals come in all sorts
as anyone knows who makes crosses
are as mad or sane as those who decide on their killings
Our one at least has been quiet so far
though they say he talked himself into this trouble
a carpenter's son who got notions of preaching

Well here's a carpenter's son who'll have carpenter sons
God willing   and build what's wanted
temples or tables   mangers or crosses

and shape them decently
working alone in that firm and profound abstraction
which blots out the bawling of rag-snatchers
To construct with hands   knee-weight   braced thigh
keeps the back turned from death

But it's too late now for the other carpenter's boy
to return to this peace before the nails are hammered

*Point Grey 1960*


## Cartagena de Indias

*'Ciudad triste, ayer reina de la mar.'*-HEREDIA

Each face its own phantom
its own formula of breed and shade
but all the eyes accuse me back and say

> There are only two races here:
> we human citizens
> who are poor but have things to sell
> and you   from outer space
> unseasonable   our one tourist
> but plainly able to buy

This arthritic street
where Drake's men and Cole's ran
swung cutlasses   where wine and sweet blood
snaked in the cobble's joints
> leaps now in a sennet of taxi horns
> to betray my invasion
All watch my first retreat
to barbizans patched from Morgan's grapeshot
and they rush me
> three desperate tarantula youths
> waving Old Golds unexcised

By an altar blackened
where the Indian silver was scratched away
in sanctuary leaning    on lush cool marble
   I am hemmed by a Congo drum man in jeans
 He bares a brace of Swiss watches
   whispers in husky Texan

Where gems and indigo were sorted
   in shouting arcades
   I am deftly shortchanged
and slink to the trees that lean
and flower tall in the Plaza
   Nine shoeboys wham their boxes
   slap at my newshined feet

Only in the Indio market
mazed on the sodden quais
I am granted uneasy truce
Around the ritual braidings of hair
the magical arrangements of fish
the piled rainbows of rotting fruit
I cast a shadow of silence
   blue-dreaded eyes
   corpse face
   hidalgo clothes
   tall one    tall as a demon
   pass O pass us quickly

Behind me the bright blaze of patois
   leaps again

I step to the beautiful slave-built bridge
and a mestiza girl
   levels Christ's hands at me
   under a dangling goitre

Past the glazed-eyed screamers of *dulces*

swing to a pink lane
where a poxed and slit-eyed savage
    pouts an obscenity
    offering a sister
    as he would spit me
    a dart from a blowpipe

Somewhere there must be another bridge
from my stupid wish
to their human acceptance
but what can I offer—
my tongue half-locked in the cell
of its language—other than pesos
    to these old crones of thirty
    whose young sink in pellagra
    as I clump unmaimed
    in the bright shoes
    that keep me from hookworm
    lockjaw and snakebite

It's written in the cut of my glasses
I've a hotelroom all to myself
with a fan    and a box of Vitamin C
It can be measured
in my unnatural stride
that my life expectation
is more than forty
especially now that I'm close to sixty

older than ever bankrupt Bolivar was
who sits now in a frozen prance
high over the coconut trays
quivering on the heads
    of three gaunt mulatto ladies
    circling in a pavane of commerce
    down upon spotlit me

Out of the heaving womb of independence

Bolivar rode    and over the bloody afterbirth
into coffee and standard oil
    from inquisitional baroque
    to armed forces corbusier
He alone has nothing more    to sell me

I come routed now    scuffling
through dust in a nameless square
treeless    burning    deserted
come lost and guiltily wakeful
in the hour of siesta
    at last to a message

    to a pair of shoes
    in a circle of baked mud
    worn    out of shape    one on its side
For a second I am shaken by panic
heat? humidity? something has got me
    the shoes are concrete
    and ten feet long

    the sight of a plaque calms
    without telling me much
                    *En homenaje de la memoria de*
                        *LUIS LOPEZ*
                    *se erigió este monumento*
                    *a los zapatos viejos*
                    *el día 10 de febrero de 1957*

Luis Lopez?    Monument to his old shoes?
What???    There was nothing else

Back through the huckster streets
the sad taxi men still awake and horn-happy

    *Si señor    Luis Lopez el poeta*
    Here is his book
    Unamuno praised it    *si si*

You have seen *los zapatos*?    Ah?
But they are us, *señor*
It was about us he wrote
about Cartagena where he was born
and died    See here this sonnet
always he made hard words
Said we were lazy except to make noise
we only shout to get money
ugly too, backward . . . why not?
It is for a poet to write these things
Also *plena*—how say it?—
*plena de rancio desaliño*
Full of rancid disarray!
  *Si si* but look, at the end, when old
  he come to say one nice thing
   only one ever about us
   He say we inspire that love a man has
   for his old shoes—*Entonces*
   we give him a monument to the shoes

I bought the book    walked back
sat on the curb happier than Wordsworth
gazing away at his daffodils
Discarded queen    I thought    I love you too
Full of rancid disarray
city like any city
full of the stench of human indignity
and disarray of the human proportion
full of the noisy always poor
and the precocious dying
stinking with fear    the stale of ignorance
I love you first for giving birth
to Luis Lopez    suffering him
honouring him at last
in the grand laconic manner
he taught you

—and him I envy

I who am seldom read by my townsmen

Descendants of pirates    grandees
galleyslaves and cannibals
I love the whole starved cheating
poetry-reading lot of you    most of all
for throwing me the shoes of deadman Luis
to walk me back into your brotherhood

*Colombia 1962—Greece 1963*


## November Walk Near False Creek Mouth

*The time is the last of warmth*
*and the fading of brightness*
  *before the final flash and the night*

I walk as the earth turns
from its burning father
here on this lowest edge of mortal city
where windows flare on faded flats
and the barren end of the ancient English
    who tippled mead in Alfred's hall
    and took tiffin in lost Lahore
drink now their fouroclock chainstore tea
sighing like old pines as the wind turns

*The beat is the small    slap    slapping*
*of the tide sloping    slipping*
*its long soft fingers into the tense*
*joints of the trapped seawall*

More ones than twos on the beaches today
strolling    or stranded as nations
woolly mermaids    dazed on beachlogs
a kept dog    sniffing    leading his woman

Seldom the lovers    seldom as reason
They will twine indoors from now to May
or ever to never    except the lovers
of what is not city    the refugees
   from the slow volcano
   the cratered rumbling    sirening vents
   the ashen air    the barren spilling
   compulsive rearing of glassy cliff
   from city
they come to the last innocent warmth
and the fading
before the unimaginable brightness

*The theme lies in the layers*
*made and unmade by the nudging    lurching*
*spiralling down from nothing*

down through the common explosion of time
through the chaos of suns
to the high seas of the spinning air
where the shelves form    and re-form down
through cirrus to clouds on cracking peaks
to the terraced woods and the shapeless town
and its dying shapers

The act is the sliding out
to the shifting rotting
folds of the sands that lip
slipping to reefs and sinking cliffs
that ladder down to the ocean's abyss
and farther down through a thousand seas
of the mantling rock
to the dense unbeating black unapproachable
heart of this world

Lanknosed lady sits on a seawall
not alone    she sits with an older book
Who is it? Shakespeare    Sophocles    Simenon?

They are tranced as sinners unafraid
in the common gaze to pursue
under hard covers their private quaint barren
affair   though today there is no unbusy body
but me to throw them a public look

    not this wrinkled triad of tourists
    strayed off the trail from the rank zoo
    peering away from irrelevant sea
    seeking a starred sign for the bus-stop
    They dangle plastic totems   a kewpie
    a Hong Kong puzzle for somebody's child
    who waits to be worshipped
    back on the prairie farm

    No nor the two manlings
    all muscles and snorkels and need to shout
    with Canadian voices   Nipponese bodies
    racing each other into the chilling waters
    last maybe of whatever summer's swimmers

    Nor for certain the gamey old gaffer
    asleep on the bench like a local Buddha
    above them   buttonedup mackinaw
    Sally Ann trousers   writing in stillness
    his own last book   under the squashed
    cock of his hat   with a bawdy plot
    she never will follow

A tremor only of all his dream
runs like fear from under the hat
through the burned face to twitch
one broken boot   at the other end
of the bench as I pass

dreaming my own unraveled plots
between eating water and eaten shore
    in this hour of the tired and homing

retired    dissolving
in the days of the separate wait
for the mass dying

and I    having clambered down to the last
shelf of the gasping world of lungs
do not know why I too wait    and stare
before descending the final step
into the clouds of the sea

*The beat beating    is the soft cheek*
*nudging of the sly    shoving    almost*
*immortal ocean at work*
*on the earth's liquidation*

Outward the sun    explodes light
like a mild rehearsal of light to come
over the vitreous waters
At this edge of the blast
a young girl sits on a granite bench
so still as if already only
silhouette burned in the stone

Two women pass in a cloud of words
    . . . so I said    You're *not*!?
    and she said    I *am*!
    I'm one of the Lockeys!
    *Not* the Lockeys of *Out*garden surely
    I said    *Yes*    she said    but I live
    in Winnipeg now    Why for heaven's *sake*
    I said    then you *must* know Carl *Thor*son?
    *Carl?*    she said    he's my cousin by marriage
    He is    I said    why he's *mine* too! So . . .

Born from the glare come the freakish forms
of tugs    all bows and swollen funnels
straining to harbor in False Creek
and blindly followed by mute scows

with islets of gravel to thicken the city
and square bowls of saffron sawdust
the ground meal of the manstruck forest
or towing shining grids of the trees stricken

At the edge of knowledge the *Prince Apollo*
(or is it the *Princess Helen?*)
floats in a paperblue fusion of air
gulf    Mykenean islands
and crawls with its freight of flesh
toward the glare and the night waiting
behind the hidden Gate of the Lions

*The beat is the slap slip    nudging*
*as the ledges are made    unmade*
*by the lurching swaying of all the world*
*that lies under the spinning air*

from the dead centre and the fiery circles
up through the ooze to black liquidities
up to the vast moats
where the doomed whales are swimming
by the weedy walls of sunless Carcassonnes
rising    rising    to the great eels waiting
in salt embrasures    and swirling up
to the twilit roofs that floor the Gulf
up to the crab-scratched sands
of the dappled Banks
into the sunblazed living mud
and the radiant mussels
that armor the rocks

and I on the path at the high-tide edge
wandering under the leafless maples
between the lost salt home
and the asphalt ledge where carhorns call
call in the clotting air by a shore
where shamans never again will sound

with moon-snail conch the ritual plea
to brother salmon or vanished seal
and none ever heard
the horn of Triton or merman

*The beat is the bob    dip    dipping*
*in the small waves    of the ducks shoring*
*and the shored rocks that seem to move*
*from turning earth or breathing ocean*
*in the dazzling slant of the cooling sun*

Through piled backyards of the sculptor sea
I climb    over discarded hemlock saurians
   Medusae cedar-stumps    muscled horsemen
   Tartars or Crees    sandsunk forever
and past the raw sawed butt
   telltale with brands
of a buccaneered boom-log
   whisked away to a no-question mill

all the swashing topmost reach of the sea
   that is also the deepest
   reach of wrens    the vanishing squirrel
   and the spilling city
the stinking ledge disputed by barnacles
waiting for tiderise to kick in their food
contested by jittery sandfleas
and hovering gulls that are half-sounds only
traced overhead    lone as my half-thoughts
   wheeling too with persistence of hunger
   or floating on scraps of flotsam

*Slowly    scarcely sensed    the beat*
*has been quickening now as the air*
*from the whitened peaks is falling*
*faraway sliding    pouring down*
*through the higher canyons and over*
*knolls and roofs to a oneway urgent*

*procession of rhythms*

blowing the haze from False Creek's girders
where now I walk as the waves stream
from my feet to the bay to the far shore
Where they lap like dreams that never reach
The tree-barbed tip of Point Grey's lance
has failed again to impale the gone sun
Clouds and islands float together
out from the darkening bandsaw of suburbs
and burn like sodium over the sunset waters

Something   is it only the wind?
above a jungle of harbor masts
is playing paperchase with the persons
of starlings   They sift and fall
stall and soar   turning
   as I too turn   with the need to feel
   once more the yielding of moist sand
   and thread the rocks back to the seawall

shadowed and empty now
of booklost ladies or flickering wrens

   and beyond to the Boats for Hire
   where a thin old Swede clings in his chair
   like hope to the last light
   eyeing bluely the girls with rackets
   padding back from belated tennis
   while herring gulls make civic statues
   of three posts on the pier
   and all his child-bright boats
   heave unwanted to winter sleep

Further the shore dips   and the sea   sullen
with sludge from floors of barges   spits
arrogantly over the Harbour Board's wall
and only the brutish prow of something

a troller perhaps    lies longdrowned
on an Ararat of broken clamshells
and the flakings of dead crabs

The shore snouts up again
spilling beachlogs glossy and dry
as sloughed snakeskins
but with sodden immovable hearts
heigh ho the logs that no one wants
and the men that sit on the logs
that no one wants
while the sea repeats what it said
to the first unthinking frogs
and the green wounds of the granite stones

By cold depths and by cliffs
whose shine will pass any moment now
the shore puts an end to my ledge
and I climb past the dried shell
of the children's pool    waiting like faith
for summer   to where the last leaves
of the shore's alders    glistening with salt
have turned the ragged lawns
to a battlefield bright with their bodies

*For the time is after the scarring of maples*
*torn by the fall's first fury of air*
*on the nearest shelf above brine and sand*
*where the world of the dry troubling begins*

the first days of the vitreous fusing
of deserts   the proud irradiations of air
in the time when men rise
and fall   from the moon's ledge

while the moon sends    as before
the waters swirling up and back
from the bay's world

to this darkening bitten shore

I turn to the terraced road
the cold steps to the bland new block
the human-encrusted reefs
that rise here higher than firs or singing
up to aseptic penthouse hillforts
to antennae above the crosses
pylons marching over the peaks
of mountains without Olympus

Higher than clouds and strata of jetstreams
the air-roads wait the two-way traffic
And beyond?    The desert planets
What else?    a galaxy-full perhaps
of suns and penthouses waiting

But still on the highest shelf of ever
washed by the curve of timeless returnings
lies the unreached unreachable nothing
whose winds wash down to the human shores
and slip   shoving

into each thought nudging my footsteps now
as I turn to my brief night's ledge

*in the last of warmth*
*and the fading of brightness*
*on the sliding edge of the beating sea*

*Vancouver 1961—Ametlla, Spain 1963*

# Ralph Gustafson

## 'S.S.R., Lost at Sea.'  The Times

What heave of grapnels will resurrect the fabric
Of him, oceans drag, whereof he died,
Drowning sheer fathoms down, liquid to grab on—
Sucked by the liner, violence in her side?
Of no more sorrow than a mottled Grief
In marble.  There fantastic in the murk,
Where saltwhite solitary forests leaf,
He swings:  the dark anonymously works.
For who shall count the countless hands and limbs
In ditch and wall and wave, dead, dead
In Europe:  touch with anguished name and claim
And actual tear, what must be generally said?
O let the heart's tough riggings salvage him,
Only whose lengths can grapple with these dead.

S.S. *Athenia*
September 3, 1939


## Now at the Ocean's Verge

After great expectations, what
It is the time of life declares, that
Was there, is as the ebbtide shows:
These miles of sand packt and under a slant
Moon, the piling granite throw of surf,
Nothing but the beauty of itself.
Conch and shell and tugged weed cling
To the wave and are thrown.

I turn to the seamark,
Climb descensions of pebbles and under the moon
Sit arms on knees, the night of stars,
Each in apportioned stance, intolerable before
The initialling mind.  Indigence is all.
Concrete heaven only must suffice,
What expectation thought was possible:
Packt sand; a grasp, whorled and beautiful
Tossed by the tide, this accessible,
Reached for, empty shell.

## The Newspaper

That photo of the little Jew in the cap,
Back to the gun held by the Nazi
With splay feet aware of the camera,
The little boy his hands in the air,
I turn over, I don't want to see it.
As a member of the human race. I am
Civilized. I am happy. I flap the
Newspaper with the picture over
So that when it is picked up to be taken
Down cellar to be put with the trash
I won't see it. I am sensitive.
The little boy is dead. He went
Through death. The cap is his best one.
He has brown eyes. He does not
Understand. Putting your hands
Up in front of a carbine prevents
The bullet. He is with the others.
Some of them he knows, so
It is all right. I turn
The paper over, the picture face
Down.

## Wednesday at North Hatley

It snows on this place
And a gentleness obtains.
The garden fills with white,
Last summer's hedgerow
Bears a burden and birds
Are scarce. The grosbeak
Fights for seeds, the squirrel
Walks his slender wire.
There is a victory;
The heart endures, the house
Achieves its warmth and where
He needs to, man in woollen
Mitts, in muffler, without
A deathwish, northern, walks.
Except he stop at drifts
He cannot hear this snow,
The wind has fallen, and where
The lake awaits, the road
Is his. Softly the snow
Falls. Chance is against him.
But softly the snow falls.

## In the Yukon

In Europe, you can't move without going down into history.
Here, all is a beginning. I saw a salmon jump,
Again and again, against the current,
The timbered hills a background, wooded green
Unpushed through; the salmon jumped, silver.
This was news, was commerce, at the end of the summer
The leap for dying. Moose came down to the water edge
To drink and the salmon turned silver arcs.
At night, the northern lights played, great over country

Without tapestry and coronations, kings crowned
With weights of gold.  They were green,
Green hangings and great grandeur, over the north
Going to what no man can hold hard in mind,
The dredge of that gravity, being without experience.


## I Think of All Soft Limbs

Many victims are around.
There are Greeks beaten
Over the kidneys with rifle
Butts.  There are the four
Hundred of Phu Cam,
'The eyeholes,' it is reported, 'deep
And black, the water broken
Over the ribs.'  A somewhat
Agitated description,
But one can get what's going
On—apparently they were bludgeoned
To death and the creek was shallow.
Others were found elsewhere.
A farmer stumbled on
A wire; when he tugged,
A hand rose from the dirt.
In other places the grass
Grew abnormally green
And long.  This was at Hué—
They showed the corpses on
The TV.  I looked
For genitals but they had fixed
Up the film or else
It was luck.

   Then there are the children
Who must die so the others may eat.
The worst were obviously expendable.

You could tell: though they moved their heads
They were no longer eager.
The ones who got the food
Jumped in the stream laughing,
To show the cameras. . . . That
Is clear? Or should it be
Gone over? I mean, the others
Might just as well die. . . .

Anyway, 2000 a day
Did in Biafra. Of course,
That is not all children—
Just mostly children.
Major General Yakubu
Gowon of Nigeria explains
It all. 'We must live together,'
He rightly says. Meanwhile,
He expresses regrets. This,
Like the crucifixion of Christ,
Is past history, of course.

Still, within memory, are Sinyavsky
And Daniel, writers mixed
Up in Marxist realism
And Siberia: Solzhenitsyn—
Unassailable really:
He has stomach cancer.
Natalya Gorbanevskaya
Though, can be mentioned, a poet
Arrested on Red Square
Not far from Lobnoye Mesto,
'The place of the forehead' where intellects
Were beheaded under the Czars.
She was against Soviet
Tanks liberating
Czechoslovakia. She
Is not in Siberia, however,
But in a mental home:

She has a three-months-old
Son.  As they said:
'These are all Jews!'

Then there are those who sit
In student unions hearing
Ceremony is bullshit;
Students dragged along
Stone stairways face
Down; and those in Vaclav
Square who place fresh flowers
Daily on the Wenceslas monument.

Many are around.  One
Could bring up Bill Terry,
First Class, black,
The corpse, kept out of the white
Cemetery in Alabama,
Buried finally by law
Six months to the day.

I think of all soft limbs:
The VC stripped, wrists
Wired behind, kicked
In the cheeks and groin, going
Back to foetal position
Each time, the GI
Standing by, reasonably
Not offering much advice,
His buddy on being picked
Up the day before,
Leaving his leg behind.

The trouble is there is too
Much death for compassion.

## Ramble on What in the World Why

Making a meaning out of everything that has happened,
The there-it-is, plainsong, pitch and pinnacle:
All is blanket-plucking otherwise.  My father
Lighted a pipe out in a rowboat on the lake
When he fished and brought up Leviathan on a wormy
Hook, Ahab's pegleg in the belly,
So the watching boy said.  Brahms
Percolated coffee, something to fiddle with,
The cup, the pot, the burner, to duck having
To write down music.  Meaning is wearying, hammers,
Level, hacking out hunks of marble to raise
Cathedrals.  I travel to get out of it to walk in them—
And run slambang into gospels of course,
Pegasus loose and the barndoor slammed.
Berryman took poems and jumped off a bridge.
It all comes down to making oneself one
With sea-slime.  Knowing what is OK,
It's the why we've got to, the prehensile toes
And all the rest of it, slops, jade and Jesus,
Venice, murder, virgins and music, that counts.


## The Sun in the Garden

Wallace Stevens is wrong: he says,
'A poem need not have a meaning
And like most things in nature
Often does not have.'  He is slipshod.
He was in the insurance business,
He ought to have known better.

I examine this slug that has crawled up
Into the saucer of my cup of tea.
It has two protrusions out of its head

And apparently absorbs food
Through its foot's peristalsis:
Repugnance after my sugar.

Also after the roses. The garden
Looks like it. The protuberances
Move out almost imperceptibly
But it doesn't fool what it senses
Or me. Beauty is taken in,
Blind repugnance or not. It squashes.

I snip it with my fingers off
The saucer, enough of it had. I walk
The rest of the day in the garden knowing
Something is futile. I have meaning.
I have to counteract it. I look up
*Evolution, religion, love.*

## The Arrival of Wisdom

Of course the truth is there's no design,
Just process: which settles all-seeing God for good
And Him as a chemist mixing combinations
To get what He could declare without it,
Wanting to be worshipped, pitching beginnings
With a Bang into teleological void.

Truth goes on solving nothing, gluons
And quarks combine, come apart, not caring, stars
Go out, suns come on, the clutter ever
Expanding; sheep on the meadow chew, chew,
Man makes mince, until his neck-thongs shrivel
And breath departs lugging its baggage
Of unaccomplished dreams. What a celestial
Tautology to get there! fun in the dreaming,
Irony in choice, tragedy in the waste,

Getting nowhere with injustice.

Faith is an ignorance.  Love without hurt
The only choice.

## At the Café at Night

All this uproar under the stars
Only art makes sense of.  The houses
Pay no heed to the passing night,
The moon is an object—it takes art
To get to the bottom of it.  Men
Hate one another.  The uproar
Of consent tingles the pulse.  This
Disbelieved, ask the next
Person.  The noise assails the stars.

Let us refer to those two at the café
Sitting outside in the night, the electric
Bulb bare, the street past the chairs
Empty, they tolerate one another
Only because of Van Gogh's paint.

## State of Affairs

This is a world of small boys with legs off.
*Hip.  Hip.*  They walk the world grown up.
Bitterness is not unknown.

Of course always there have been legs off
In a manner of speaking, taking legs off
To stand for eyes out,

But that is expected—the previous century is barbaric,

Few university degrees were granted,
TV was unknown.

It is too bad since we have so many computers,
So many carbines and combines that we have
So many legs off

But it can't be helped, boys must hop as best
They can, bitterness or not, there must be legs off
So there can be progress,

That is to say democratic election,
Culture for the collectivity and less
In the future legs off.


## Hunter's Moon

The moon was gold and the leaves were gold.
The red leaves had fallen and the pallor
Of the soft aspen was lighted, as gold,
By the hunter's moon, the first full
Moon of October.  She stood on the verandah,
Facing that upper gold moon
(My arms lightly, closely around her
As if the time would come now).
Foliage was fallen thickly, the lawn
Almost uncertain, the dry brown leaves
Fallen.  Across the pathway
The last flowers, a further frost
Was promised.

        She did not like the deer
To be in the forested hills.  It is a hunter's
Moon, she said.  But it was beautiful,
The dense covered hills, the moon above,
The moment, the way it was,
The moment.

## Aspect of a Cut Peach

Succulent as morning were the pieces of that peach.
Cut on the china plate of mint foliage
Around the rim, a cool gathering circle
Of indentation holds the fragments of quench
And question. What has this to do with hunger
And Ethiopia; rotten weather in Ontario
Raised the rarity of that peach; the skin peeled
Back like a sexual nonpresbyterian pleasure,
What of the cry of children that runs off
The guilty blade of silver? Heaven is doomed
Here. Only in paradise are peaches
Prized purely and is pith succulent.

## Five Transparencies:

TAO IN NORTH HATLEY

Picking red currants by the western hedge
I catch a glimpse of the silver lake
Every once in a while as I raise my body
To ease the muscles of my thighs and back.

The unknown bird sings and then stops.
I listen to the sudden silence,
Then begin picking red berries again,
Dropping them in the deep pan with the handle

Brought from the kitchen. Fingers of both hands
Are stained with the red juice, some
Of the berries are very ripe. I like
The stain. I am one with the bird again

And the quiet reminds me of that scholar, Tao Qian,
In his garden tending his fourth-century

Chrysanthemums, eighty-eight days
Out of the court and its weary obeisances.

Among these hedges and the red currant bush
In the corner, apart, listening to the bird
And picking berries, I too have a fundamental
Truth to tell if only the words could be found.

OF LU HONG THE SCHOLAR

For his learning and integrity Lu Hong
Received from Xuan Zong his emperor
One hundred pecks of rice
And fifty bolts of silk.

His thatched hut on Mount Song
Had a brook, a bridge to cross it,
And a glass house, not large,
To care for delicate seeds.

Ten views of Lu's hut
Are still to be seen with poems to go
With each view well apart
From the purlieus of the court.

THE STORY OF WANG WEI

More elaborate was Wang Wei's eighth-century villa.
Rambling houses, pavilions and galleries
Connected by bridges and paths (famed
Among architects)

Imposed neither isolation nor abnegation.
Wang was no happier but he had
Many perspectives to describe with ink and colour
On rice paper.

He commanded visual inspiration walking
His courts and gardens.  He was wise
However.  Dynasties of vast wealth
And pleasure foundered

On unrestrained expenditure.  (By the third century
Gardens were already synonyms for extravagance.)
Wang walked his garden paths laughing
At the intricacies.

## THE OPINION OF JI CHENG

A better view even
Than you would have
Sitting in trees,
Says Ji Cheng the author
Of a treatise on gardens,
Is through the moon gate,
The far willow in it,
And across the lotus pond
Where the blossom
Unfolds, from the mud,
Unstained petals.
All this even in the midst
Of a marketplace!
Noise is shut out
When the gates are closed,
Notes Ji in his book *Yuan Ye*.

## AT THE ORCHID PAVILION

Amid the harshness of pebbles
My reluctant feet wander,
At sundown I sit by the willow
Listening to the plucked lute.

# A.M. Klein

*Heirloom*

My father bequeathed me no wide estates;
No keys and ledgers were my heritage;
Only some holy books with *yahrzeit* dates
Writ mournfully upon a blank front page—

Books of the Baal Shem Tov, and of his wonders;
Pamphlets upon the devil and his crew;
Prayers against road demons, witches, thunders;
And sundry other tomes for a good Jew.

Beautiful: though no pictures on them, save
The scorpion crawling on a printed track;
The Virgin floating on a scriptural wave,
Square letters twinkling in the Zodiac.

The snuff left on this page, now brown and old,
The tallow stains of midnight liturgy—
These are my coat of arms, and these unfold
My noble lineage, my proud ancestry!

And my tears, too, have stained this heirloomed ground,
When reading in these treatises some weird
Miracle, I turned a leaf and found
A white hair fallen from my father's beard.

## Autobiographical

Out of the ghetto streets where a Jewboy
Dreamed pavement into pleasant Bible-land,
Out of the Yiddish slums where childhood met
The friendly beard, the loutish Sabbath-goy,
Or followed, proud, the Torah-escorting band,
Out of the jargoning city I regret,
Rise memories, like sparrows rising from
The gutter-scattered oats,
Like sadness sweet of synagogal hum,
Like Hebrew violins
Sobbing delight upon their Eastern notes.

Again they ring their little bells, those doors
Deemed by the tender-year'd, magnificent:
Old Ashkenazi's cellar, sharp with spice;
The widows' double-parloured candy-stores
And nuggets sweet bought for one sweaty cent;
The warm fresh-smelling bakery, its pies,
Its cakes, its navel'd bellies of black bread;
The lintels candy-poled
Of barber-shop, bright-bottled, green, blue, red;
And fruit-stall piled, exotic,
And the big synagogue door, with letters of gold.

Again my kindergarten home is full—
Saturday night—with kin and compatriot:
My brothers playing Russian card-games; my
Mirroring sisters looking beautiful,
Humming the evening's imminent fox-trot;
My uncle Mayer, of blessed memory,
Still murmuring maariv, counting holy words;
And the two strangers, come
Fiery from Volhynia's murderous hordes—
The cards and humming stop.
And I too swear revenge for that pogrom.

Occasions dear: the four-legged aleph named
And angel pennies dropping on my book;
The rabbi patting a coming scholar-head;
My mother, blessing candles, Sabbath-flamed,
Queenly in her Warsovian perruque;
My father pickabacking me to bed
To tell tall tales about the Baal Shem Tov—
Letting me curl his beard.
Oh memory of unsurpassing love,
Love leading a brave child
Through childhood's ogred corridors, unfear'd!

The week in the country at my brother's—(May
He own fat cattle in the fields of heaven!)
Its picking of strawberries from grassy ditch,
Its odour of dogrose and of yellowing hay—
Dusty, adventurous, sunny days, all seven!—
Still follow me, still warm me, still are rich
With the cow-tinkling peace of pastureland.
The meadow'd memory
Is sodded with its clover, and is spanned
By that same pillow'd sky
A boy on his back one day watched enviously.

And paved again the street: the shouting boys,
Oblivious of mothers on the stoops,
Playing the robust robbers and police,
The corncob battle—all high-spirited noise
Competitive among the lot-drawn groups.
Another day, of shaken apple trees
In the rich suburbs, and a furious dog,
And guilty boys in flight;
Hazelnut games, and games in the synagogue—
The burrs, the Haman rattle,
The Torah dance on Simchas Torah night.

Immortal days of the picture calendar
Dear to me always with the virgin joy

Of the first flowering of senses five,
Discovering birds, or textures, or a star,
Or tastes sweet, sour, acid, those that cloy;
And perfumes. Never was I more alive.
All days thereafter are a dying off,
A wandering away
From home and the familiar. The years doff
Their innocence.
No other day is ever like that day.

I am no old man fatuously intent
On memories, but in memory I seek
The strength and vividness of nonage days,
Not tranquil recollection of event.
It is a fabled city that I seek;
It stands in Space's vapours and Time's haze;
Thence comes my sadness in remembered joy
Constrictive of the throat;
Thence do I hear, as heard by a Jewboy,
The Hebrew violins,
Delighting in the sobbed Oriental note.


## For the Sisters of the Hotel Dieu

In pairs,
as if to illustrate their sisterhood,
the sisters pace the hospital garden walks.
In their robes black and white immaculate hoods
they are like birds,
the safe domestic fowl of the House of God.

O biblic birds,
who fluttered to me in my childhood illnesses
—me little, afraid, ill, not of your race,—
the cool wing for my fever, the hovering solace,
the sense of angels—
be thanked, O plumage of paradise, be praised.

## Grain Elevator

Up from the low-roofed dockyard warehouses
it rises blind and babylonian
like something out of legend. Something seen
in a children's coloured book. Leviathan
swamped on our shore? The cliffs of some other river?
The blind ark lost and petrified? A cave
built to look innocent, by pirates? Or
some eastern tomb a travelled patron here makes local?

But even when known, it's more than what it is:
for here, as in a Josephdream, bow down
the sheaves, the grains, the scruples of the sun
garnered for darkness; and Saskatchewan
is rolled like a rug of a thick and golden thread.
O prison of prairies, ship in whose galleys roll
sunshines like so many shaven heads,
waiting the bushel-burst out of the beachhead bastille!

Sometimes, it makes me think Arabian,
the grain picked up, like tic-tacs out of time:
first one; an other; singly; one by one;—
to save life. Sometimes, some other races claim
the twinship of my thought,—as the river stirs
restless in a white Caucasian sleep,
or, as in the steerage of the elevators,
the grains, Mongolian and crowded, dream.

A box: cement, hugeness, and rightangles—
merely the sight of it leaning in my eyes
mixes up continents and makes a montage
of inconsequent time and uncontiguous space.
It's because it's bread. It's because
bread is its theme, an absolute. Because
always this great box flowers over us
wth all the coloured faces of mankind. . . .

## Indian Reservation: Caughnawaga

Where are the braves, the faces like autumn fruit,
who stared at the child from the coloured frontispiece?
And the monosyllabic chief who spoke with his throat?
Where are the tribes, the feathered bestiaries?—
Rank Aesop's animals erect and red,
with fur on their names to make all live things kin—
Chief Running Deer, Black Bear, Old Buffalo Head?

Childhood, that wished me Indian, hoped that
one afterschool I'd leave the classroom chalk,
the varnish smell, the watered dust of the street,
to join the clean outdoors and the Iroquois track.
Childhood; but always,—as on a calendar,—
there stood that chief, with arms akimbo, waiting
the runaway mascot paddling to his shore.

With what strange moccasin stealth that scene is changed!
With French names, without paint, in overalls,
their bronze, like their nobility expunged,—
the men. Beneath their alimentary shawls
sit like black tents their squaws; while for the tourist's
brown pennies scattered at the old church door,
the ragged papooses jump, and bite the dust.

Their past is sold in a shop: the beaded shoes,
the sweetgrass basket, the curio Indian,
burnt wood and gaudy cloth and inch-canoes—
trophies and scalpings for a traveller's den.
Sometimes, it's true, they dance, but for a bribe;
after a deal don the bedraggled feather
and welcome a white mayor to the tribe.

This is a grassy ghetto, and no home.
And these are fauna in a museum kept.
The better hunters have prevailed. The game,

losing its blood, now makes these grounds its crypt.
The animals pale, the shine of the fur is lost,
bleached are their living bones.  About them watch
as through a mist, the pious prosperous ghosts.


## Political Meeting

For Camillien Houde

On the school platform, draping the folding seats,
they wait the chairman's praise and glass of water.
Upon the wall the agonized Y initials their faith.

Here all are laic; the skirted brothers have gone.
Still, their equivocal absence is felt, like a breeze
that gives curtains the sounds of surplices.

The hall is yellow with light, and jocular;
suddenly some one lets loose upon the air
the ritual bird which the crowd in snares of singing

catches and plucks, throat, wings, and little limbs.
Fall the feathers of sound, like *alouette's*.
The chairman, now, is charming, full of asides and wit,

building his orators, and chipping off
the heckling gargoyles popping in the hall.
(Outside, in the dark, the street is body-tall,

flowered with faces intent on the scarecrow thing
that shouts to thousands the echoing
of their own wishes.)  The Orator has risen!

Worshipped and loved, their favourite visitor,
a country uncle with sunflower seeds in his pockets,
full of wonderful moods, tricks, imitative talk,

he is their idol: like themselves, not handsome,
not snobbish, not of the *Grande Allée! Un homme!*
Intimate, informal, he makes bear's compliments

to the ladies; is gallant; and grins;
goes for the balloon, his opposition, with pins;
jokes also on himself, speaks of himself

in the third person, slings slang, and winks with folklore;
and knows now that he has them, kith and kin.
Calmly, therefore, he begins to speak of war,

praises the virtue of being *Canadien,*
of being at peace, of faith, of family,
and suddenly his other voice: *Where are your sons?*

He is tearful, choking tears; but not he
would blame the clever English; in their place
he'd do the same; maybe.

Where *are* your sons?
                    The whole street wears one face,
shadowed and grim; and in the darkness rises
the body-odour of race.


## Montreal

O city metropole, isle riverain!
Your ancient pavages and sainted routs
Traverse my spirit's conjured avenues!
Splendour erablic of your promenades
Foliates there, and there your maisonry
Of pendant balcon and escalier'd march,
Unique midst English habitat,
Is vivid Normandy!

You populate the pupils of my eyes:
Thus, does the Indian, plumed, furtivate
Still through your painted autumns, Ville-Marie!
Though palisades have passed, though calumet
With tabac of your peace enfumes the air,
Still do I spy the phantom, aquiline,
Genuflect, moccasin'd, behind
His statue in the square!

Thus, costumed images before me pass,
Haunting your archives architectural:
*Coureur de bois*, in posts where pelts were portaged;
Seigneur within his candled manoir; Scot
Ambulant through his bank, pillar'd and vast.
Within your chapels, voyaged mariners
Still pray, and personage departed,
All present from your past!

Grand port of navigations, multiple
The lexicons uncargo'd at your quays,
Sonnant though strange to me; but chiefest, I,
Auditor of your music, cherish the
Joined double-melodied vocabulaire
Where English vocable and roll Ecossic,
Mollified by the parle of French
Bilinguefact your air!

Such your suaver voice, hushed Hochelaga!
But for me also sound your potencies,
Fortissimos of sirens fluvial,
Bruit of manufactory, and thunder
From foundry issuant, all puissant tone
Implenishing your hebdomad; and then
Sanct silence, and your argent belfries
Clamant in orison!

You are a part of me, O all your quartiers—
And of dire pauvrete and of richesse—

To finished time my homage loyal claim;
You are locale of infancy, milieu
Vital of institutes that formed my fate;
And you above the city, scintillant,
Mount Royal, are my spirit's mother,
Almative, poitrinate!

Never do I sojourn in alien place
But I do languish for your scenes and sounds,
City of reverie, nostalgic isle,
Pendant most brilliant on Laurentian cord!
The coigns of your boulevards—my signiory—
Your suburbs are my exile's verdure fresh,
Your parks, your fountain'd parks—
Pasture of memory!

City, O city, you are vision'd as
A parchemin roll of saecular exploit
Inked with the script of eterne souvenir!
You are in sound, chanson and instrument!
Mental, you rest forever edified
With tower and dome; and in these beating valves,
Here in these beating valves, you will
For all my mortal time reside!


## Lone Bather


Upon the ecstatic diving board the diver,
poised for parabolas, lets go
lets go his manshape to become a bird.
Is bird, and topsy-turvy
the pool floats overhead, and the white tiles snow
their crazy hexagons. Is dolphin. Then
is plant with lilies bursting from his heels.

Himself, suddenly mysterious and marine,
bobs up a merman leaning on his hills.

Plashes and plays alone the deserted pool;
as those, is free, who think themselves unseen.
He rolls in his heap of fruit,
he slides his belly over
the melonrinds of water, curved and smooth and green.
Feels good: and trains, like little acrobats
his echoes dropping from the galleries;
circles himself over a rung of water;
swims fancy and gay; taking a notion, hides
under the satins of his great big bed,—
and then comes up to float until he thinks
the ceiling at his brow, and nowhere any sides.
His thighs are a shoal of fishes: scattered: he
turns with many gloves of greeting
towards the sunnier water and the tiles.

Upon the tiles he dangles from his toes
lazily the eight reins of his ponies.
An afternoon, far from the world
a street sound throws like a stone, with paper, through the glass.
Up, he is chipped enamel, grained with hair.
The gloss of his footsteps follows him to the showers,
the showers, and the male room, and the towel
which rubs the bird, the plant, the dolphin back again
personable plain.


## Portrait of the Poet as Landscape

I

Not an editorial-writer, bereaved with bartlett,
mourns him, the shelved Lycidas.
No actress squeezes a glycerine tear for him.
The radio broadcast lets his passing pass.

And with the police, no record.  Nobody, it appears,
either under his real name or his alias,
missed him enough to report.

It is possible that he is dead, and not discovered.
It is possible that he can be found some place
in a narrow closet, like the corpse in a detective story,
standing, his eyes staring, and ready to fall on his face.
It is also possible that he is alive
and amnesiac, or mad, or in retired disgrace,
or beyond recognition lost in love.

We are sure only that from our real society
he has disappeared; he simply does not count,
except in the pullulation of vital statistics—
somebody's vote, perhaps, an anonymous taunt
of the Gallup poll, a dot in a government table—
but not felt, and certainly far from eminent—
in a shouting mob, somebody's sigh.

O, he who unrolled our culture from his scroll—
the prince's quote, the rostrum-rounding roar—
who under one name made articulate
heaven, and under another the seven-circled air,
is, if he is at all, a number, an x,
a Mr  Smith in a hotel register,—
incognito, lost, lacunal.

II

The truth is he's not dead, but only ignored—
like the mirroring lenses forgotten on a brow
that shine with the guilt of their unnoticed world.
The truth is he lives among neighbours, who, though they will allow
him a passable fellow, think him eccentric, not solid,
a type that one can forgive, and for that matter, forgo.

Himself he has his moods, just like a poet.
Sometimes, depressed to nadir, he will think all lost,

will see himself as throwback, relict, freak,
his mother's miscarriage, his great-grandfather's ghost,
and he will curse his quintuplet senses, and their tutors
in whom he put, as he should not have put, his trust.

Then he will remember his travels over that body—
the torso verb, the beautiful face of the noun,
and all those shaped and warm auxiliaries!
A first love it was, the recognition of his own.
Dear limbs adverbial, complexion of adjective,
dimple and dip of conjugation!

And then remember how this made a change in him
affecting for always the glow and growth of his being;
how suddenly was aware of the air, like shaken tinfoil,
of the patents of nature, the shock of belated seeing,
the loneliness peering from the eyes of crowds;
the integers of thought; the cube-roots of feeling.

Thus, zoomed to zenith, sometimes he hopes again,
and sees himself as a character, with a rehearsed role:
the Count of Monte Cristo, come for his revenges;
the unsuspecting heir, with papers; the risen soul;
or the chloroformèd prince awakening from his flowers;
or—deflated again—the convict on parole.

III

He is alone; yet not completely alone.
Pins on a map of a colour similar to his,
each city has one, sometimes more than one;
here, caretakers of art, in colleges;
in offices, there, with arm-bands, and green-shaded;
and there, pounding their catalogued beats in libraries,—

everywhere menial, a shadow's shadow.
And always for their egos—their outmoded art.
Thus, having lost the bevel in the ear,
they know neither up nor down, mistake the part

for the whole, curl themselves in a comma,
talk technics, make a colon their eyes.  They distort—

such is the pain of their frustration—truth
to something convolute and cerebral.
How they do fear the slap of the flat of the platitude!
Now Pavlov's victims, their mouths water at bell,
the platter empty.
           See they set twenty-one jewels
into their watches; the time they do not tell!

Some, patagonian in their own esteem,
and longing for the multiplying word,
join party and wear pins, now have a message,
an ear, and the convention-hall's regard.
Upon the knees of ventriloquists, they own,
of their dandled brightness, only the paint and board.

And some go mystical, and some go mad.
One stares at a mirror all day long, as if
to recognize himself; another courts
angels,—for here he does not fear rebuff;
and a third, alone, and sick with sex, and rapt,
doodles him symbols convex and concave.

O schizoid solitudes!  O purities
curdling upon themselves!  Who live for themselves,
or for each other, but for nobody else;
desire affection, private and public loves;
are friendly, and then quarrel and surmise
the secret perversions of each other's lives.

IV

He suspects that something has happened, a law
been passed, a nightmare ordered.  Set apart,
he finds himself, with special haircut and dress,
as on a reservation.  Introvert.
He does not understand this; sad conjecture

muscles and palls thrombotic on his heart.

He thinks an impostor, having studied his personal biography,
his gestures, his moods, now has come forward to pose
in the shivering vacuums his absence leaves.
Wigged with his laurel, that other, and faked with his face,
he pats the heads of his children, pecks his wife,
and is at home, and slippered, in his house.

So he guesses at the impertinent silhouette
that talks to his phone-piece and slits open his mail.
Is it the local tycoon who for a hobby
plays poet, he so epical in steel?
The orator, making a pause? Or is that man
he who blows his flash of brass in the jittering hall?

Or is he cuckolded by the troubadour
rich and successful out of celluloid?
Or by the don who unrhymes atoms? Or
the chemist death built up? Pride, lost impostor'd pride,
it is another, another, whoever he is,
who rides where he should ride.

V

*Fame*, the adrenalin: to be talked about;
to be a verb; to be introduced as *The:*
to smile with endorsement from slick paper; make
caprices anecdotal; to nod to the world; to see
one's name like a song upon the marquees played;
to be forgotten with embarrassment; to be—
to be.

It has its attractions, but is not the thing;
nor is it the ape mimesis who speaks from the tree
ancestral; nor the merkin joy. . .
Rather it is stark infelicity
which stirs him from his sleep, undressed, asleep
to walk upon roofs and window-sills and defy
the gape of gravity.

VI

Therefore he seeds illusions. Look, he is
the nth Adam taking a green inventory
in world but scarcely uttered, naming, praising,
the flowering fiats in the meadow, the
syllabled fur, stars aspirate, the pollen
whose sweet collusion sounds eternally.
For to praise

the world—he, solitary man—is breath
to him. Until it has been praised, that part
has not been. Item by exciting item—
air to his lungs, and pressured blood to his heart—
they are pulsated, and breathed, until they map,
not the world's, but his own body's chart!

And now in imagination he has climbed
another planet, the better to look
with single camera view upon this earth—
its total scope, and each afflated tick,
its talk, its trick, its tracklessness—and this,
this, he would like to write down in a book!

To find a new function for the *déclassé* craft
archaic like the fletcher's; to make a new thing;
to say the word that will become sixth sense;
perhaps by necessity and indirection bring
new forms to life, anonymously, new creeds—
O, somehow pay back the daily larcenies of the lung!

These are not mean ambitions. It is already something
merely to entertain them. Meanwhile, he
makes of his status as zero a rich garland,
a halo of his anonymity,
and lives alone, and in his secret shines
like phosphorus. At the bottom of the sea.

# Dorothy Livesay

## Fire and Reason

I cannot shut out the night—
Nor its sharp clarity.

The many blinds we draw,
You and I,
The many fires we light
Can never quite obliterate
The irony of stars,
The deliberate moon,
The last, unsolved finality of night.

## Going to Sleep

I shall lie like this when I am dead—
But with one more secret in my head.

## Green Rain

I remember long veils of green rain
Feathered like the shawl of my grandmother—
Green from the half-green of the spring trees
Waving in the valley.

I remember the road
Like the one which leads to my grandmother's house,
A warm house, with green carpets,
Geraniums, a trilling canary

And shining horse-hair chairs;
And the silence, full of the rain's falling
Was like my grandmother's parlour
Alive with herself and her voice, rising and falling—
Rain and wind intermingled.

I remember on that day
I was thinking only of my love
And of my love's house.
But now I remember the day
As I remember my grandmother.
I remember the rain as the feathery fringe of her shawl.

## Spain

When the bare branch responds to leaf and light
Remember them: it is for this they fight.
It is for haze-swept hills and the green thrust
Of pine, that they lie choked with battle dust.
You who hold beauty at your finger-tips
Hold it because the splintering gunshot rips
Between your comrades' eyes; hold it across
Their bodies' barricade of blood and loss.

You who live quietly in sunlit space
Reading The Herald after morning grace
Can count peace dear, when it has driven
Your sons to struggle for this grim, new heaven.

# Call My People Home

*A Documentary Poem for Radio or Choral Presentation*

ANNOUNCER:

Now after thirty years come from a far island
Of snow and cherry blossoms, holy mountains,
To make a home near water, near
The blue Pacific; newcomers and strangers
Circled again and shaped by snow-white mountains,
These put down their roots, the Isseis:*
The older generation. This is their story.

CHORUS OF ISSEIS:

Home, they say, is where the heart is:
Transplanted walls, and copper-coloured gardens
Or where the cherry bough can blow
Against your pain, and blow it cool again—
This they call home.

But for ourselves we learned
How home was not
Even the small plot, raspberry laden
Nor shack on stilts, stooping over the water,
Nor the brown Fraser's whirl,
Sucking the salmon upward.

Home was the uprooting:
The shiver of separation,
Despair for our children
Fear for our future.

Home was the finding of a dry land
Bereft of water or rainfall
Where water is cherished
Where our tears made channels

*Isseis—generation born in Japan.*

And became irrigation.

Home was in watching:
The fruit growing and pushing
So painfully watered;
The timber hewn down
The mill run completed.

Home was in waiting:
For new roots holding
For young ones branching
For our yearning fading . . .

ANNOUNCER:

His ancestors had lived near water
Been fishermen under Fujiyama's shadow.

Each season in the new land found him struggling
Against the uncertain harvest of the sea,
The uncertain temper of white fishermen
Who hungered also, who had mouths to feed.
So these men cut his share
From half to one-eighth of the fishing fleet:
But still he fished, finding the sea his friend.

FIRST FISHERMAN:

Home was my boat: T.K. 2930—
Wintering on the Skeena with my nets
Cast up and down the river, to lure and haul
The dogfish. (His oil, they said, was needed overseas
For children torn from home, from a blitzed town.)
We made good money, and the sockeye run
That summer had outdone all the remembered seasons.
Now I could own my boat, *Tee Kay*, the Gillnetter
The snug and round one, warm as a woman
With her stove stocked at night and her lanterns lit
And anchor cast, brooding upon the water

Settled to sleep in the lap of the Skeena.

Now after thirty years, come from an island
To make a home near water: first on a sailing vessel
Towed, each season, to the fishing grounds:
Then the small gasboat, the gillnetter, that belonged
Not to the man who fished, but to the cannery.
Now after thirty years a free man, naturalized,
A man who owned his boat! I smelt the wind
Wetting my face, waves dashing against the *Tee Kay*'s sides
The grey dawn opening like a book
At the horizon's rim. I was my own master—
Must prove it now, today! Stooping over the engine
Priming the starter, opening the gas valve,
I felt her throbbing in answer; I laughed
And grasped the fly wheel, swung her over.
She churned off up the river—my own boat, my home.
That was before Pearl Harbor: before a December day
Spent on a restless sea; then anchor in the dusk
And down to bunk to have a bowl of rice.
By lantern light I turned the battery set
To hear brief messages from fishermen
From boat to shore, to learn the weather forecast.
Must have been dozing when I woke up sharp—
What was he saying? Some kind of government order?
'All fishing craft on the high seas must head at once
To the nearest port, report to authorities.'
Did they not want our fish, the precious oil?
'No,' said the voice, 'Our boats were to be examined, searched
For hidden guns, for maps, for treachery. . .'
I heard, but could not understand. Obeyed,
But as a blind man. The numb fear about my boat,
*Tee Kay*, found no release in port, off shore,
Rubbing against a fleet of trollers, frail gillnetters
All heading down the Inverness and Tusk
All in the dark, with rumor flying fast.
No one knew more than his fear whispered,
No one explained.

We thought:  perhaps it's all a mistake
Perhaps they'll line us up and do a search
Then leave us free for Skeena, Ucluelet—
The time is ripe, the season's fish are running.

SECOND FISHERMAN:

There was no mistake. It wasn't a joke:
At every fishing port more boats fell in.
Some had no wood, no gasoline; and some
Barely a day's store of food aboard.
So we waited at the Inlet's mouth, till the 16th.

FIRST FISHERMAN:

How speak about the long trip south, the last
We ever made, in the last of our boats?
The time my life turned over, love went under
Into the cold unruly sea. Those waves
Washing the cabin's walls
Lashed hate in me.

SECOND FISHERMAN:

We left Rupert in two long lines of sixty boats
Strung to the seiners, met and tugged
By *Starpoint* and the naval escort, the corvette.
All day we watched the gloomy sea roughed up
By westerlies, but had to tough it out
Glued to the wheel, weary for sleep, till 2 a.m.

Then, at Lowe Inlet, had brief anchorage.
At Milbanke Sound we ran into heavier seas
The buffeted boats like so many bobbing corks
Strung on a thin rope line that over and over
Would break, be mended by the corvette's men
And then again be snapped by snarling sea.

Day emerged into night and day again
Found us with six boats broken loose; some torn

And others gashed with bumping in the dark—
If some drugged fisherman fell off to sleep
And left craft pilotless,
Smashing like blind birds through a log-strewn sea.
Some boats that had no gasoline to keep
Heart thumping in their engines, these
Were plucked aloft in fistfuls by the waves
Then brought down with a thud—
Propellers spinning helpless in mid-air.
So we proceeded into colder, rougher seas,
Seasick and sore, nodding at the wheel,
Then stamping up and down to keep the winter out.

FIRST FISHERMAN:

Christmas at sea. The bitterest for me
That any year had given. Even so
Some had a celebration, pooled their funds
And bought the only chicken left in Alert Bay.
Others boiled cabbages in salt sea water,
Pulled out the playing cards and shrugged, and laughed.
As we set sail at midnight, now a thousand boats
Chained to the naval escort, steadily south
Into familiar waters where the forests cooled their feet
At rocks'-end, mountains swam in mist—
As we set sail for home, the young ones, born here, swore
Not softly, into the hissing night. The old men wept.

The rest takes little telling. On the fifteenth night
We passed Point Grey's low hulk, our long line wavered shoreward.
Dirty and hungry, sleep lying like a stone
Stuck in our heads, we nosed our broken craft
Into the wharf at Steveston, 'Little Tokyo.'
The crowd on the dock was silent. Women finding their men
Clung to them searchingly, saying never a word,
Leading them home to the *ofuro** and supper.
Others of us, like me, who knew no one,
Who had no place near the city's centre

*Ofuro—the bath.

Stood lonely on the wharf, holding the *Tee Kay*'s line
For the last time, watching the naval men
Make a note of her number, take my name.
That was the end of my thirty years at the fishing
And the end of my boat, my home.

ANNOUNCER:

These their children, the Niseis,† were born
Into the new world, called British Columbia home,
Spoke of her as mother, and beheld
Their future in her pungent evergreen.

GIRL'S VOICE:

*We lived into ourselves*
*Thinking so to be free.*
*Locked in the harbour*
*Of father and mother*
*The children incoming*
*The tide inflowing.*

BOY'S VOICE:

Sometimes at remote midnight
With a burnt-out moon
An orange eye on the river
Or rising before dawn
From a house heavy with sleepers
The man touching my arm
Guiding my hand through the dark
To the boat softly bumping and sucking
Against the wharf;
We go out toward misty islands
Of fog over the river
Jockeying for position;
Till morning steals over, sleepy,
And over our boat's side, leaning
The word comes, Set the nets!

*\*Niseis—generation born in Canada.*

Hiding the unannounced prayer
Resounding in the heart's corners:
May we have a high boat
And the silver salmon leaping!

GIRL'S VOICE:

*We lived unto ourselves*
*Locked in the harbour*

BOY'S VOICE:

I remember the schoolhouse, its battered doorway
The helter-skelter of screaming children
Where the old ones went, my sisters
Soberly with books strapped over their shoulders:
Deliberately bent on learning—
(And learned, soon enough, of
The colour of their skin, and why
Their hair would never turn golden.)

GIRL'S VOICE:

But before the bell rang
For me
My turn at becoming
Before the bell rang
I was out on the hillside
Reaching high over my head for the black ones
The first plump berries of summer;
A scratch on the arm, maybe, a tumble
But filling my pail and singing my song
With the bees humming
And the sun burning.

Then no bell rang for me;
Only the siren.
Only the women crying and the men running.
Only the Mounties writing our names

In the big book; the stifled feeling
Of being caught, corralled.
Only the trucks and a scramble to find
A jacket, a ball, for the bundle.

My blackberries spilled
Smeared purple
Over the doorway.
Never again did I go
Blackberry picking on the hillside.
Never again did I know
That iron schoolbell ringing.

BOY'S AND GIRL'S VOICES:

*The children incoming*
*The tide inflowing.*

ANNOUNCER:

From the upper islands of the coast
With only one day's notice to depart
Came these, and hundreds like them:  Mariko and her mother.
In the re-allocation centre, Hastings Park
Mariko writes a letter.

THE LETTER:

I wonder where in the inner country
On what train shooting between two mountains
You fly tonight, Susumu?
When I explain to you how it is here
You will understand, perhaps,
Why I have not been able to tell my mother
About you and me.

It is this:  she is continually frightened—
Never having lived so. in a horse stall before.
My bunk is above hers, and all night I lie rigid

For fear to disturb her; but she is disturbed.
She has hung her pink petticoat from my bunk rail
Down over her head, to be private; but nothing is private.
Hundreds of strangers lie breathing around us
Wakeful, or coughing; or in sleep tossing;
Hundreds of strangers pressing upon us
Like horses tethered, tied to a manger.

My mother lies wakeful with her eyes staring.
I cannot see her, but I know. She is thinking:
*This is a nightmare.* She is back in her home
Embroidering blossoms on a silk kimono
Talking to me Yosh (the boy I mentioned,
The one I grew up with). She is making plans
To visit the go-between, to bake for a wedding.

My mother cannot believe her dream is over,
That she lies in a manger with her hands tethered.
So you will understand now, Susumu:
I have not been able to tell my mother.
It is hard for me to believe, myself,
How you said the words, how you spoke of a garden
Where my name, MARIKO, would be written in flowers. . . .
I wonder where in the inner country
On what train far from this animal silence
This thick night stifling my heart, my nostrils—
Where like a rocket shooting between two planets
Have you flown, Susumu? Have you gone?

ANNOUNCER:

Between the fury and the fear
The window-breaking rabble and the politican's blackout,
(Wartime panic fed
On peacetime provocations)
Between the curfew rung
On Powell Street
And the rows of bunks in a public stable
Between the line-ups and the labels and the presentation

of a one-way ticket
Between these, and the human heart—
There was in every centre one man, a white man—
A minister, a layman—a mayor.

THE MAYOR:

That year the snow came early, lay lightly on our hills
Cooling their colours, pointing up the evergreen
Scribbled over the ledges; at valley's end
Snow muffled with its mantle the gaunt shape,
The smokeless chimney of the copper smelter.

I stood on the station platform reading the message
Telegraphed from Vancouver:   'The first contingent,
Sixty-eight persons, arriving on the night train.'
Then I looked down our narrow, funnelled valley
My ghost-town village, with hotels closed up
Since gold-rush days; post office perched
Upon a down-hill lurch, leaning towards empty stores.
At seven-fifteen the evening train pulled in.
I stood alone on the platform, waiting.
Slowly the aliens descended, in huddled groups,
Mothers and crying children; boys and girls
Holding a bundle of blankets, cardboard boxes,
A basket of pots and pans, a child's go-cart—
Looking bewildered up and down the platform,
The valley closing in, the hostile village. . . .

I stepped forward, urged into sudden action.
The women cowered, fell back, cried words
In panic to the old men standing surly, helpless.
I collared a young kid, bright, with his eyes snapping:
'You there, you speak English?' 'Why, yah! You bet.'
We eyed each other, and I smiled. 'You see,'
I said, 'I'm mayor here . . . your mayor.
This is your home. Can you tell the people that?
Tell them I'm here to meet them, get acquainted,

Find a place for them to sleep.' The boy
Nodded. 'Okay, I'll tell my mother, sure.
The rest will believe whatever she says to do.'

Their conference began. I waited, tense;
Then plunged into the job of lifting crates
And scanty furnishings, getting local lads
To pile it up on trucks; until I felt
A timid touch upon my arm; I turned
And saw the Issei mother.
                                        Putting out my hand
I felt hers move, rest for a moment in mine—
Then we were free. We began to work together. . . .

Then I went out to find some carpenters
To build a village in a single day. . . .
It was cold. Light snow covered the hills.

By spring, I vowed, those people would be mine!
This village would be home.

ANNOUNCER:

These were the fathers, mothers, those
Who had to choose another home, another way.
What would they choose? The questioner
Paused with his pencil lifted; gave them a day
To talk together, choose.

THE WIFE:

Either to be a ghost in mountain towns
Abandoned by the seekers after gold,
There to sit with idle hands,
Embroidering the past upon a window-pane
Fed on foreign food
And crowded together in government huts
The men torn from our arms, the family parted,
Or to face the longer, stranger journey
Over the mountain ranges, barred from the sea—
To labour in uncertain soil, inclement weather

Yet labour as one—all the family together?

THE HUSBAND:

We looked at each other, you and I, after
So many doubtful years binding our struggles:
Our small plot grown to wider green
Pastured within the Fraser's folds, the shack
Upbuilded to a cottage, now a house—
The cherry trees abloom and strawberry fields
White with the snow of blossom, of promise.

THE WIFE:

Had it all to be done again, worked at again
By our gnarled hands, in a harsh new land
Where summer passes like a quick hot breath
And winter holds you chained for half the year?
You took my hands, and said: 'It's the children's country.
Let them choose.' They chafed for independence
Scenting the air of freedom in far fields.
Therefore we had no choice, but one straight way:
The eastward journey into emptiness,
A prairie place called home.

THE HUSBAND:

It was harder than hate. Home was a blueprint only.
We lived in a hen coop perched on a farmer's field
Soaked by the sudden storms, the early rains of April.
Yet there was time for ploughing, time to sow
Beet seed upon the strange black soil in rows
Of half an acre; we saw in neighbouring fields'
Bleak tableland, the stabbing green
Of the young wheat; and heard the sweet
Heart-snaring song of meadow-larks; in grass
Withered and brown saw maps move, empty patches
Purple with crocus underneath our feet.

In summer the sun's beak
Tore at our backs bending over the rows
Endless for thinning; the lumpy soil left callouses
Upon our naked knees; mosquitoes swarmed
In frenzied choruses above our heads
Sapping the neck; until a hot wind seared
The field, drove them away in clouds.

THE WIFE:

I think we had nearly given up, and wept
And gone for government help, another home—
Until, one evening lull, work done
You leaned upon the poplar gate to watch
A lime green sky rim the mauve twilight
While in the pasture fireflies danced
Like lanterns of Japan on prairie air.

Leaning the other way spoke our new friend
The neighbour from the Ukraine;
Touching your arm, using words more broken
Than yours, like scraps of bread left over.
'See how tomorrow is fine. You work
Hard, same as me. We make good harvest time.'
He came from a loved land, too, the mild
Plains of the Dneiper where, in early spring
(He said) the violets hid their sweetness. 'This land
Is strange and new. But clean and big
And gentle with the wheat. For children too,
Good growing.'
He lifted up his hands, his praise; we heard
Over the quickening fields a fresh wind blowing.

ANNOUNCER:

This one was young, a renegade. He wanted the world
In his two hands. He would not make the choice,
But cast it back in their teeth.

NISEI VOICE:

They can't do this to me, Shig said
(Once a Jap, always a Jap)
Why, I went to school with those kids
Vancouver's my home town.

They can't do this to me, Shig said
(Once a Jap, always a Jap)
I'll spend my life in a road camp
In a freight car bunk in the bush.

They'll get tired of me, Shig said
(Once a Jap, always a Jap)
And some dark night I'll buckle my belt
And hitch-hike to the sea.

The Mounties won't get me, Shig said
(Once a Jap, always a Jap)
I'll say I'm a Chinese, see?
It's the underworld for me.

They picked Shig up on a robbery charge
(Once in jail, always in jail)
There were only a few of us such as he
But he blackened our name
Shut the gates to the sea.

ANNOUNCER:

This one was young; but he wanted the world
For others. A philosopher,
He accepted the blow, Pearl Harbor.
He learned the way of waiting.

THE PHILOSOPHER:

To be alone is grace; to see it clear
Without rancour; to let the past be
And the future become. Rarely to remember

The painful needles turning in the flesh.

(I had looked out of the schoolroom window
And could not see the design, held dear
Of the shaken maples; nor the rain, searing and stinging
The burning rain in the eye.

I could not see, nor hear my name called:
Tatsuo, the Pythagoras theorem!
I could not think till the ruler rapped
On the desk, and my mind snapped.

The schoolroom faded, I could not hold
A book again in my hand.
It was the not knowing; the must be gone
Yet the continual fear of going.

Yes, to remember is to go back; to take
The path along the dyke, the lands of my uncle
Stretching away from the river—
The dykeside where we played

Under his fruit trees, canopied with apples,
Falling asleep under a hedgerow of roses
To the gull's shrill chatter and the tide's recurrent
Whisper in the marshland that was home. . . .)

So must I remember. It cannot be hid
Nor hurried from. As long as there abides
No bitterness; only the lesson learned
And the habit of grace chosen, accepted.

CHORUS OF NISEIS:

Home, we discover, is where life is:
Not Manitoba's wheat
Ontario's walled cities
Nor a B.C. fishing fleet.

Home is something more than harbour—
Than father, mother, sons;
Home is the white face leaning over your shoulder
As well as the darker ones.

Home is labour, with the hand and heart,
The hard doing, and the rest when done;
A wider sea than we knew, a deeper earth,
A more enduring sun.

## The Three Emily's*

These women crying in my head
Walk alone, uncomforted:
The Emily's, these three
Cry to be set free—
And others whom I will not name
Each different, each the same.

Yet they had liberty!
Their kingdom was the sky:
They batted clouds with easy hand,
Found a mountain for their stand;
From wandering lonely they could catch
The inner magic of a heath—
A lake their palette, any tree
Their brush could be.

And still they cry to me
As in reproach—
I, born to hear their inner storm
Of separate man in woman's form,
I yet possess another kingdom, barred
To them, these three, this Emily.

*Emily Bronte, Emily Dickinson and Emily Carr.

I move as mother in a frame,
My arteries
Flow the immemorial way
Towards the child, the man;
And only for brief span
Am I an Emily on mountain snows
And one of these.

And so the whole that I possess
Is still much less—
They move triumphant through my head:
I am the one
Uncomforted.

## Bartok and the Geranium

She lifts her green umbrellas
Towards the pane
Seeking her fill of sunlight
Or of rain;
Whatever falls
She has no commentary
Accepts, extends,
Blows out her furbelows,
Her bustling boughs;
And all the while he whirls
Explodes in space,
Never content with this small room:
Not even can he be
Confined to sky
But must speed high and higher still
From galaxy to galaxy,
Wrench from the stars their momentary notes
Steal music from the moon.

She's daylight

He is dark
She's heaven-held breath
He storms and crackles
Spits with hell's own spark.

Yet in this room, this moment now
These together breathe and be:
She, essence of serenity,
He in a mad intensity
Soars beyond sight
Then hurls, lost Lucifer,
From heaven's height.

And when he's done, he's out:
She leans a lip against the glass
And preens herself in light.

## Without Benefit of Tape

The real poems are being written in outports
on backwoods farms
in passageways where pantries still exist
or where geraniums
nail light to the window
while out of the window boy in the flying field
is pulled to heaven on the keel of a kite.

Stories breed in the north:
men with snow in their mouths
trample and shake at the bit
kneading the woman down under blankets of snow
icing her breath, her eyes.

The living speech is shouted out
by men and women leaving railways lines
to trundle home, pack-sacked
just company for deer or bear—

　　Hallooed
across the counter, in a corner store
it booms upon the river's shore:
on midnight roads where hikers flag you down
speech echoes from the canyon's wall
　　resonant
　　indubitable.


## Bellhouse Bay

Last night a full silver
moon
shone in the waters of the bay
so serene
one could believe in
an ongoing universe

And today it's summer
noon heat soaking into
arbutus trees　blackberry bushes
Today in the cities
rallies and peace demonstrations exhort

SAVE OUR WORLD　SAVE OUR CHILDREN

But save also　I say
the towhees under the blackberry bushes
eagles playing a mad caper
in the sky above Bellhouse Bay

This is not paradise
dear adam　dear eve
but it is a rung on the ladder
upwards
towards a possible
breathtaking landscape

# Irving Layton

*The Swimmer*

The afternoon foreclosing, see
The swimmer plunges from his raft,
Opening the spray corollas by his act of war—
The snake heads strike
Quickly and are silent.

Emerging see how for a moment
A brown weed with marvellous bulbs,
He lies imminent upon the water
While light and sound come with a sharp passion
From the gonad sea around the Poles
And break in bright cockle-shells about his ears.

He dives, floats, goes under like a thief
Where his blood sings to the tiger shadows
In the scentless greenery that leads him home,
A male salmon down fretted stairways
Through underwater slums . . .

Stunned by the memory of lost gills
He frames gestures of self-absorption
Upon the skull-like beach;
Observes with instigated eyes
The sun that empties itself upon the water,
And the last wave romping in
To throw its boyhood on the marble sand.

## Look, the Lambs
## Are All Around Us!

Your figure, love,
curves itself
into a man's memory;
or to put it the way
a junior prof
at Mount Allison might,
Helen with her thick
absconding limbs
about the waist
of Paris
did no better.

Hell, my back's sunburnt
from so much love-making
in the open air.
The Primate (somebody
made a monkey of him)
and the Sanhedrin
(long on the beard, short
on the brain)
send envoys to say
they don't approve.
You never see them, love.
You toss me in the air
with such abandon,
they take to their heels and run.
I tell you
each kiss of yours
is like a blow on the head!

What luck, what luck to be loved
by the one girl
in this Presbyterian
country
who knows how to give
a man pleasure.

## The Cold Green Element

At the end of the garden walk
the wind and its satellite wait for me;
their meaning I will not know
          until I go there,
but the black-hatted undertaker

who, passing, saw my heart beating in the grass,
is also going there. Hi, I tell him,
a great squall in the Pacific blew a dead poet
          out of the water,
who now hangs from the city's gates.

Crowds depart daily to see it, and return
with grimaces and incomprehension;
if its limbs twitched in the air
          they would sit at its feet
peeling their oranges.

And turning over I embrace like a lover
the trunk of a tree, one of those
for whom the lightning was too much
          and grew a brilliant
hunchback with a crown of leaves.

The ailments escaped from the labels
of medicine bottles are all fled to the wind;
I've seen myself lately in the eyes
          of old women,
spent streams mourning my manhood,

in whose old pupils the sun became
a bloodsmear on broad catalpa leaves
and hanging from ancient twigs,
          my murdered selves
sparked the air like the muted collisions

of fruit. A black dog howls down my blood,
a black dog with yellow eyes;
he too by someone's inadvertence
⠀⠀⠀⠀⠀saw the bloodsmear
on the broad catalpa leaves.

But the furies clear a path for me to the worm
who sang for an hour in the throat of a robin,
and misled by the cries of young boys
⠀⠀⠀⠀⠀I am again
a breathless swimmer in that cold green element.

## The Fertile Muck

There are brightest apples on those trees
⠀⠀but until I, fabulist, have spoken
they do not know their significance
or what other legends are hung like garlands
⠀⠀on their black boughs twisting
like a rumour. The wind's noise is empty.

Nor are the winged insects better off
⠀⠀though they wear my crafty eyes
wherever they alight. Stay here, my love;
you will see how delicately they deposit
⠀⠀me on the leaves of elms
or fold me in the orient dust of summer.

And if in August joiners and bricklayers
⠀⠀are thick as flies around us
building expensive bungalows for those
who do not need them, unless they release
⠀⠀me roaring from their moth-proofed cupboards
their buyers will have no joy, no ease.

I could extend their rooms for them without cost

and give them crazy sundials
to tell the time with, but I have noticed
how my irregular footprint horrifies them
    evenings and Sunday afternoons:
they spray for hours to erase its shadow.

How to dominate reality? Love is one way;
    imagination another. Sit here
beside me, sweet; take my hard hand in yours.
We'll mark the butterflies disappearing over the hedge
    with tiny wristwatches on their wings:
our fingers touching the earth, like two Buddhas.


## On Seeing the Statuettes
## of Ezekiel and Jeremiah in the
## Church of Notre Dame

They have given you French names
    and made you captive, my rugged
troublesome compatriots;
    your splendid beards, here, are epicene,
plaster white
        and your angers
unclothed with Palestinian hills quite lost
in this immense and ugly edifice.

You are bored—I see it—sultry prophets
    with priests and nuns
(What coarse jokes must pass between you!)
    and with those morbidly religious
i.e. my prize brother-in-law
             ex-Lawrencian
pawing his rosary, and his wife
sick with many guilts.

Believe me I would gladly take you
    from this spidery church
its bad melodrama, its musty smell of candle
    and set you both free again
in no make-believe world
              of sin and penitence
but the sunlit square opposite
alive at noon with arrogant men.

Yet cheer up Ezekiel and you Jeremiah
    who were once cast into a pit;
I shall not leave you here incensed, uneasy
    among alien Catholic saints
but shall bring you from time to time
             my hot Hebrew heart
as passionate as your own, and stand
with you here awhile in aching confraternity.


## Sacrament by the Water

How shall I sing the accomplished waters
Whose teeming cells make green my hopes
How shall the Sun at daybreak marry us
Twirling these waters like a hoop.

Gift of the waters that sing
Their eternal passion for the sky,
Your cunning beauty in a wave of tumult
Drops an Eden about your thighs.

Green is the singing singing water
And green is every joyous leaf
White myrtle's in your hand and in the other
The hairy apple bringing life.

## Whatever Else Poetry Is Freedom

Whatever else poetry is freedom.
Forget the rhetoric, the trick of lying
All poets pick up sooner or later. From the river,
Rising like the thin voice of grey castratos—the mist;
Poplars and pines grow straight but oaks are gnarled;
Old codgers must speak of death, boys break windows;
Women lie honestly by their men at last.

And I who gave my Kate a blackened eye
Did to its vivid changing colours
Make up an incredible musical scale;
And now I balance on wooden stilts and dance
And thereby sing to the loftiest casements.
See how with polish I bow from the waist.
Space for these stilts! More space or I fail!

And a crown I say for my buffoon's head.
Yet no more fool am I than King Canute,
Lord of our tribe, who scanned and scorned;
Who half-deceived, believed; and, poet, missed
The first white waves come nuzzling at his feet;
Then damned the courtiers and the foolish trial
With a most bewildering and unkingly jest.

It was the mist. It lies inside one like a destiny.
A real Jonah it lies rotting like a lung.
And I know myself undone who am a clown
And wear a wreath of mist for a crown;
Mist with the scent of dead apples,
Mist swirling from black oily waters at evening,
Mist from the fraternal graves of cemeteries.

It shall drive me to beg my food and at last
Hurl me broken I know and prostrate on the road;
Like a huge toad I saw, entire but dead,
That Time mordantly had blacked; O pressed

To the moist earth it pled for entry.
I shall be I say that stiff toad for sick with mist
And crazed I smell the odour of mortality.

And Time flames like a paraffin stove
And what it burns are the minutes I live.
At certain middays I have watched the cars
Bring me from afar their windshield suns;
What lay to my hand were blue fenders,
The suns extinguished, the drivers wearing sunglasses.
And it made me think I had touched a hearse.

So whatever else poetry is freedom. Let
Far off the impatient cadences reveal
A padding for my breathless stilts. Swivel,
 O hero, in the fleshy groves, skin and glycerine,
And sing of lust, the sun's accompanying shadow
Like a vampire's wing, the stillness in dead feet—
Your stave brings resurrection, O aggrievèd king.


## Berry Picking

Silently my wife walks on the still wet furze
Now darkgreen the leaves are full of metaphors
Now lit up is each tiny lamp of blueberry.
The white nails of rain have dropped and the sun is free.

And whether she bends or straightens to each bush
To find the children's laughter among the leaves
Her quiet hands seem to make the quiet summer hush—
Berries or children, patient she is with these.

I only vex and perplex her; madness, rage
Are endearing perhaps put down upon the page;
Even silence daylong and sullen can then
Enamour as restraint or classic discipline.

So I envy the berries she puts in her mouth,
The red and succulent juice that stains her lips;
I shall never taste that good to her, nor will they
Displease her with a thousand barbarous jests.

How they lie easily for her hand to take,
Part of the unoffending world that is hers;
Here beyond complexity she stands and stares
And leans her marvellous head as if for answers.

No more the easy soul my childish craft deceives
Nor the simpler one for whom yes is always yes;
No, now her voice comes to me from a far way off
Though her lips are redder than the raspberries.


## Cain

Taking the air rifle from my son's hand,
I measured back five paces, the Hebrew
In me, narcissist, father of children,
Laid to rest. From there I took aim and fired.

The silent ball hit the frog's back an inch
Below the head. He jumped at the surprise
Of it, suddenly tickled or startled

(He must have thought) and leaped from the wet sand
Into the surrounding brown water. But
The ball had done its mischief. His next spring
Was a miserable flop, the thrust all gone
Out of his legs. He tried—like Bruce—again,
Throwing out his sensitive pianist's
Hands as a dwarf might or a helpless child.
His splash disturbed the quiet pondwater
And one old frog behind his weedy moat
Blinking, looking self-complacently on.

The lin's surface at once became closing
Eyelids and bubbles like notes of music
Liquid, luminous, dropping from the page
White, white-bearded, a rapid crescendo
Of inaudible sounds and a crones' whispering
Backstage among the reeds and bulrushes
As for an expiring Lear or Oedipus.

But Death makes us all look ridiculous.
Consider this frog (dog, hog, what you will)
Sprawling, his absurd corpse rocked by the tides
That his last vain spring had set in movement.
Like a retired oldster, I couldn't help sneer,
Living off the last of his insurance:
Billows—now crumbling—the premiums paid.
Absurd, how absurd. I wanted to kill
At the mockery of it, kill and kill
Again—the self-infatuate frog, dog, hog,
Anything with the stir of life in it,
Seeing the dead leaper, Chaplin-footed,
Rocked and cradled in this afternoon
Of tranquil water, reeds, and blazing sun,
The hole in his back clearly visible
And the torn skin a blob of shadow
Moving when the quiet poolwater moved.

O Egypt, marbled Greece, resplendent Rome,
Did you also finally perish from a small bore
In your back you could not scratch? And would
Your mouths open ghostily, gasping out
Among the murky reeds, the hidden frogs,
We climb with crushed spines toward the heavens?

When the next morning I came the same way
The frog was on his back, one delicate
Hand on his belly, and his white shirt front
Spotless. He looked as if he might have been
A comic; tapdancer apologizing

For a fall, or an Emcee, his wide grin
Coaxing a laugh from us for an aside
Or perhaps a joke we didn't quite hear.

## Keine Lazarovitch 1870-1959

When I saw my mother's head on the cold pillow,
Her white waterfalling hair in the cheeks' hollows,
I thought, quietly circling my grief, of how
She had loved God but cursed extravagantly his creatures.

For her final mouth was not water but a curse,
A small black hole, a black rent in the universe,
Which damned the green earth, stars and trees in its stillness
And the inescapable lousiness of growing old.

And I record she was comfortless, vituperative,
Ignorant, glad, and much else besides; I believe
She endlessly praised her black eyebrows, their thick weave,
Till plagiarizing Death leaned down and took them for his mould.

And spoiled a dignity I shall not again find,
And the fury of her stubborn limited mind;
Now none will shake her amber beads and call God blind,
Or wear them upon a breast so radiantly.

O fierce she was, mean and unaccommodating;
But I think now of the toss of her gold earrings,
Their proud carnal assertion, and her youngest sings
While all the rivers of her red veins move into the sea.

## A Tall Man Executes a Jig

I

So the man spread his blanket on the field
And watched the shafts of light between the tufts
And felt the sun push the grass towards him;
The noise he heard was that of whizzing flies,
The whistlings of some small imprudent birds,
And the ambiguous rumbles of cars
That made him look up at the sky, aware
Of the gnats that tilted against the wind
And in the sunlight turned to jigging motes.
Fruitflies he'd call them except there was no fruit
About, spoiling to hatch these glitterings,
These nervous dots for which the mind supplied
The closing sentences from Thucydides,
Or from Euclid having a savage nightmare.

II

Jig jig, jig jig. Like minuscule black links
Of a chain played with by some playful
Unapparent hand or the palpitant
Summer haze bored with the hour's stillness.
He felt the sting and tingle afterwards
Of those leaving their orthodox unrest,
Leaving their undulant excitation
To drop upon his sleeveless arm. The grass,
Even the wildflowers became black hairs
And himself a maddened speck among them.
Still the assaults of the small flies made him
Glad at last, until he saw purest joy
In their frantic jiggings under a hair,
So changed from those in the unrestraining air.

III

He stood up and felt himself enormous.
Felt as might Donatello over stone,
Or Plato, or as a man who has held
A loved and lovely woman in his arms
And feels his forehead touch the emptied sky
Where all antinomies flood into light.
Yet jig jig jig, the haloing black jots
Meshed with the wheeling fire of the sun:
Motion without meaning, disquietude
Without sense or purpose, ephemerides
That mottled the resting summer air till
Gusts swept them from his sight like wisps of smoke.
Yet they returned, bringing a bee who, seeing
But a tall man, left him for a marigold.

IV

He doffed his aureole of gnats and moved
Out of the field as the sun sank down,
A dying god upon the blood-red hills.
Ambition, pride, the ecstasy of sex,
And all circumstance of delight and grief,
That blood upon the mountain's side, that flood
Washed into a clear incredible pool
Below the ruddied peaks that pierced the sun.
He stood still and waited. If ever
The hour of revelation was come
It was now, here on the transfigured steep.
The sky darkened. Some birds chirped. Nothing else.
He thought the dying god had gone to sleep:
An Indian fakir on his mat of nails.

V

And on the summit of the asphalt road
Which stretched towards the fiery town, the man
Saw one hill raised like a hairy arm, dark

With pines and cedars against the stricken sun
—The arm of Moses or of Joshua.
He dropped his head and let fall the halo
Of mountains, purpling and silent as time,
To see temptation coiled before his feet:
A violated grass snake that lugged
Its intestine like a small red valise.
A cold-eyed skinflint it now was, and not
The manifest of that joyful wisdom,
The mirth and arrogant green flame of life;
Or earth's vivid tongue that flicked in praise of earth.

VI

And the man wept because pity was useless.
'Your jig's up; the flies come like kites,' he said
And watched the grass snake crawl towards the hedge,
Convulsing and dragging into the dark
The satchel filled with curses for the earth,
For the odours of warm sedge, and the sun,
A blood-red organ in the dying sky.
Backwards it fell into a grassy ditch
Exposing its underside, white as milk,
And mocked by wisps of hay between its jaws;
And then it stiffened to its final length.
But though it opened its thin mouth to scream
A last silent scream that shook the black sky,
Adamant and fierce, the tall man did not curse.

VII

Beside the rigid snake the man stretched out
In fellowship of death; he lay silent
And stiff in the heavy grass with eyes shut,
Inhaling the moist odours of the night
Through which his mind tunnelled with flicking tongue
Backwards to caves, mounds, and sunken ledges
And desolate cliffs where come only kites,
And where of perished badgers and racoons

The claws alone remain, gripping the earth.
Meanwhile the green snake crept upon the sky,
Huge, his mailed coat glittering with stars that made
The night bright, and blowing thin wreaths of cloud
Athwart the moon; and as the weary man
Stood up, coiled above his head, transforming all.


*For Mao Tse-Tung:*
*A Meditation on Flies and Kings*

So, circling about my head, a fly.
Haloes of frantic monotone.
Then a smudge of blood smoking
On my fingers, let Jesus and Buddha cry.

Is theirs the way? Forgiveness of hurt?
Leprosariums? Perhaps. But I
Am burning flesh and bone,
An indifferent creature between
Cloud and a stone;
Smash insects with my boot,
Feast on torn flowers, deride
The nonillion bushes by the road
(Their patience is very great.)
Jivatma, they endure,
Endure and proliferate.

And the meek-browed and poor
In their solid tenements
(Etiolated, they do not dance.)
Worry of priest and of commissar:
None may re-create them who are
Lowly and universal as the moss
Or like vegetation the winds toss
Sweeping to the open lake and sky.
I put down these words in blood

And would not be misunderstood:
They have their Christs and their legends
And out of their pocks and ailments
Weave dear enchantments—
Poet and dictator, you are as alien as I.

On this remote and classic lake
Only the lapsing of the water can I hear
And the cold wind through the sumac.
The moneyed and their sunburnt children
Swarm other shores.  Here is ecstasy,
The sun's outline made lucid
By each lacustral cloud
And man naked with mystery.
They dance best who dance with desire,
Who lifting feet of fire from fire
Weave before they lie down
A red carpet for the sun.

I pity the meek in their religious cages
And flee them; and flee
The universal sodality
Of joy-haters, joy-destroyers
(O Schiller, wine-drunk and silly!)
The sufferers and their thick rages;
Enter this tragic forest where the trees
Uprear as if for the graves of men,
All function and desire to offend
With themselves finally done;
And mark the dark pines farther on,
The sun's fires touching them at will,
Motionless like silent khans
Mourning serene and terrible
Their Lord entombed in the blazing hill.

*1958*

## Rhine Boat Trip

The castles on the Rhine
are all haunted
by the ghosts of Jewish mothers
looking for their ghostly children

And the clusters of grapes
in the sloping vineyards
are myriads of blinded eyes
staring at the blind sun

The tireless Lorelei
can never comb from their hair
the crimson beards
of murdered rabbis

However sweetly they sing
one hears only
the low wailing of cattle-cars
moving invisibly across the land


## Israelis

It is themselves they trust and no one else;
Their fighter planes that screech across the sky,
Real, visible as the glorious sun;
Riflesmoke, gunshine, and rumble of tanks.

Man is a fanged wolf, without compassion
Or ruth: Assyrians, Medes, Greeks, Romans,
And devout pagans in Spain and Russia
—Allah's children, most merciful of all.

Where is the Almighty if murder thrives?

He's dead as mutton and they buried him
Decades ago, covered him with their own
Limp bodies in Belsen and Babi Yar.

Let the strong compose hymns and canticles,
Live with the Lord's radiance in their hard skulls
Or make known his great benevolences;
Stare at the heavens and feel glorified

Or humbled and awestruck buckle their knees:
They are done with him now and forever.
Without a whimper from him they returned,
A sign like an open hand in the sky.

The pillar of fire: Their flesh made it;
It burned briefly and died—you all know where.
Now in their own blood they temper the steel,
God being dead and their enemies not.

# P.K. Page

*The Stenographers*

After the brief bivouac of Sunday,
their eyes, in the forced march of Monday to Saturday,
hoist the white flag, flutter in the snow-storm of paper,
haul it down and crack in the mid-sun of temper.

In the pause between the first draft and the carbon
they glimpse the smooth hours when they were children—
the ride in the ice-cart, the ice-man's name,
the end of the route and the long walk home;

remember the sea where floats at high tide
were sea marrows growing on the scatter-green vine
or spools of grey toffee, or wasps' nests on water;
remember the sand and the leaves of the country.

Bell rings and they go and the voice draws their pencil
like a sled across snow; when its runners are frozen
rope snaps and the voice then is pulling no burden
but runs like a dog on the winter of paper.

Their climates are winter and summer—no wind
for the kites of their hearts—no wind for a flight;
a breeze at the most, to tumble them over
and leave them like rubbish—the boy-friends of blood.

In the inch of the noon as they move they are stagnant.
The terrible calm of the noon is their anguish;
the lip of the counter, the shapes of the straws
like icicles breaking their tongues, are invaders.

Their beds are their oceans—salt water of weeping
the waves that they know—the tide before sleep;
and fighting to drown they assemble their sheep
in columns and watch them leap desks for their fences

and stare at them with their own mirror-worn faces.
In the felt of the morning the calico-minded,
sufficiently starched, insert papers, hit keys,
efficient and sure as their adding machines;

yet they weep in the vault, they are taut as net curtains
stretched upon frames. In their eyes I have seen
the pin men of madness in marathon trim
race round the track of the stadium pupil.

## The Landlady

Through sepia air the boarders come and go,
impersonal as trains. Pass silently
the craving silence swallowing her speech;
click doors like shutters on her camera eye.

Because of her their lives become exact:
their entrances and exits are designed;
phone calls are cryptic. Oh, her ticklish ears
advance and fall back stunned.

Nothing is unprepared. They hold the walls
about them as they weep or laugh. Each face
is dialled to zero publicly. She peers
stippled with curious flesh;

pads on the patient landing like a pulse,
unlocks their keyholes with the wire of sight,
searches their rooms for clues when they are out,
pricks when they come home late.

Wonders when they are quiet, jumps when they move,
dreams that they dope or drink, trembles to know
the traffic of their brains, jaywalks their street
in clumsy shoes.

Yet knows them better than their closest friends:
their cupboards and the secrets of their drawers,
their books, their private mail, their photographs
are theirs and hers.

Knows when they wash, how frequently their clothes
go to the cleaners, what they like to eat,
their curvature of health, but even so
is not content.

And like a lover must know all, all, all.
Prays she may catch them unprepared at last
and palm the dreadful riddle of their skulls—
hoping the worst.


## Stories of Snow

Those in the vegetable rain retain
an area behind their sprouting eyes
held soft and rounded with the dream of snow
precious and reminiscent as those globes—
souvenir of some never-nether land—
which hold their snow-storms circular, complete,
high in a tall and teakwood cabinet.

In countries where the leaves are large as hands
where flowers protrude their fleshy chins
and call their colours,
an imaginary snow-storm sometimes falls
among the lilies.
And in the early morning one will waken

to think the glowing linen of his pillow
a northern drift, will find himself mistaken
and lie back weeping.
And there the story shifts from head to head,
of how in Holland, from their feather beds
hunters arise and part the flakes and go
forth to the frozen lakes in search of swans—
the snow-light falling white along their guns,
their breath in plumes.
While tethered in the wind like sleeping gulls
ice-boats wait the raising of their wings
to skim the electric ice at such a speed
they leap jet strips of naked water,
and how these flying, sailing hunters feel
air in the mouths as terrible as ether.
And on the story runs that even drinks
in that white landscape dare to be no colour;
how flasked and water clear, the liquor slips
silver against the hunters' moving hips.
And of the swan in death these dreamers tell
of its last flight and how it falls, a plummet,
pierced by the freezing bullet
and how three feathers, loosened by the shot,
descend like snow upon it.
While hunters plunge their fingers in its down
deep as a drift, and dive their hands
up to the neck of the wrist
in that warm metamorphosis of snow
as gentle as the sort that woodsmen know
who, lost in the white circle, fall at last
and dream their way to death.

And stories of this kind are often told
in countries where great flowers bar the roads
with reds and blues which seal the route to snow—
as if, in telling, raconteurs unlock
the colour with its complement and go
through to the area behind the eyes
where silent, unrefractive whiteness lies.

## Photos of a Salt Mine

How innocent their lives look,
how like a child's
dream of caves and winter, both combined;
the steep descent to whiteness
and the stope
with its striated walls
their folds all leaning as if pointing to
the greater whiteness still,
that great white bank
with its decisive front,
that seam upon a slope,
salt's lovely ice.

And wonderful underfoot the snow of salt
the fine
particles a broom could sweep,
one thinks
muckers might make angels in its drifts
as children do in snow,
lovers in sheets,
lie down and leave imprinted where they lay
a feathered creature holier than they.

And in the outworked stopes
with lamps and ropes
up miniature matterhorns
the miners climb
probe with their lights
the ancient folds of rock—
syncline and anticline—
and scoop from darkness an Aladdin's cave:
rubies and opals glitter from its walls.

But hoses douse the brilliance of these jewels,
melt fire to brine.
Salt's bitter water trickles thin and forms,

slow fathoms down,
a lake within a cave,
lacquered with jet—
white's opposite.
There grey on black the boating miners float
to mend the stays and struts of that old stope
and deeply underground
their words resound,
are multiplied by echo, swell and grow
and make a climate of a miner's voice.

So all the photographs like children's wishes
are filled with caves or winter,
innocence
has acted as a filter,
selected only beauty from the mine.
Except in the last picture,
it is shot
from an acute high angle. In a pit
figures the size of pins are strangely lit
and might be dancing but you know they're not.
Like Dante's vision of the nether hell
men struggle with the bright cold fires of salt,
locked in the black inferno of the rock:
the filter here, not innocence but guilt.


## The Permanent Tourists

Somnolent through landscapes and by trees
nondescript, almost anonymous,
they alter as they enter foreign cities—
the terrible tourists with their empty eyes
longing to be filled with monuments.

Verge upon statues in the public squares
remembering the promise of memorials

yet never enter the entire event
as dogs, abroad in any kind of weather,
move perfectly within their rainy climate.

Lock themselves into snapshots on the steps
of monolithic bronze as if suspecting
the subtle mourning of the photograph
might later conjure in the memory
all they are now incapable of feeling.

And search all heroes out: the boy who gave
his life to save a town; the stolid queen;
forgotten politicians minus names
and the plunging war dead, permanently brave,
forever and ever going down to death.

Look, you can see them nude in any café
reading their histories from the bill of fare,
creating futures from a foreign teacup.
Philosophies like ferns bloom from the fable
that travel is broadening at the café table.

Yet somehow beautiful, they stamp the plaza.
Classic in their anxiety they call
all sculptured immemorial stone
into their passive eyes, as rivers
draw ruined columns to their placid glass.


## Cook's Mountains

By naming them he made them.
They were there
before he came
but they were not the same.
It was his gaze
that glazed each one.

He saw
the Glass House Mountains in his glass.
They shone.

And still they shine.
We saw them as we drove—
sudden, surrealist, conical
they rose
out of the rain forest.
The driver said,
'Those are the Glass House Mountains up ahead.'

And instantly they altered to become
the sum of shape and name.
Two strangenesses united into one
more strange than either.
Neither of us now
remembers how they looked before they broke
the light to fragments as the driver spoke.

Like mounds of mica,
hive-shaped hothouses,
mountains of mirror glimmering
they form
in diamond panes behind the tree ferns of
the dark imagination,
burn and shake
the lovely light of Queensland like a bell
reflecting Cook upon a deck
his tongue
silvered with paradox and metaphor.

## Arras

Consider a new habit—classical,
and trees espaliered on the wall like candelabra.
How still upon that lawn our sandalled feet.

But a peacock rattling his rattan tail and screaming
has found a point of entry. Through whose eye
did it insinuate in furled disguise
to shake its jewels and silk upon that grass?

The peaches hang like lanterns. No one joins
those figures on the arras.
                          Who am I
or who am I become that walking here
I am observer, other, Gemini,
starred for a green garden of cinema?

I ask, what did they deal me in this pack?
The cards, all suits, are royal when I look.
My fingers slipping on a monarch's face
twitch and grow slack.
I want a hand to clutch, a heart to crack.

No one is moving now, the stillness is
infinite. If I should make a break. . . .
take to my springy heels. . . . ?  But nothing moves.
The spinning world is stuck upon its poles,
the stillness points a bone at me. I fear
the future on this arras.
                          I confess:

It was my eye.

Voluptuous it came.
Its head the ferrule and its lovely tail
folded so sweetly; it was strangely slim
to fit the retina. And then it shook

and was a peacock—living patina,
eye-bright, maculate!
Does no one care?

I thought their hands might hold me if I spoke.
I dreamed the bite of fingers in my flesh,
their poke smashed by an image, but they stand
as if within a treacle, motionless,
folding slow eyes on nothing. While they stare
another line has trolled the encircling air,
another bird assumes its furled disguise.


## After Rain

The snails have made a garden of green lace:
broderie anglaise from the cabbages,
chantilly from the choux-fleurs, tiny veils—
I see already that I lift the blind
upon a woman's wardrobe of the mind.

Such female whimsy floats about me like
a kind of tulle, a flimsy mesh,
while feet in gum boots pace the rectangles—
garden abstracted, geometry awash—
an unknown theorem argued in green ink,
dropped in the bath.
Euclid in glorious chlorophyl, half drunk.

I none too sober slipping in the mud
where rigged with guys of rain
the clothes-reel gauche
as the rangey skeleton of some
gaunt delicate spidery mute
is pitched as if
listening;
while hung from one thin rib

a silver web—
its infant, skeletal, diminutive,
now sagged with sequins, pulled ellipsoid,
glistening.

I suffer shame in all these images.
The garden is primeval, Giovanni
in soggy denim squelches by my hub
over his ruin,
shakes a doleful head.
But he so beautiful and diademmed,
his long Italian hands so wrung with rain
I find his ache exists beyond my rim
and almost weep to see a broken man
made subject to my whim.

O choir him, birds, and let him come to rest
within this beauty as one rests in love,
till pears upon the bough
encrusted with
small snails as pale as pearls
hang golden in
a heart that knows tears are a part of love.

And choir me too to keep my heart a size
larger than seeing, unseduced by each
bright glimpse of beauty striking like a bell,
so that the whole may toll,
its meaning shine
clear of the myriad images that still—
do what I will—encumber its pure line.

## Brazilian Fazenda

That day all the slaves were freed
their manacles, anklets
left on the window ledge to rust in the moist air

and all the coffee ripened
like beads on a bush or balls of fire
as merry as Christmas

and the cows all calved and the calves all lived
such a moo.
On the wide verandah where birds in cages
sang among the bell flowers
I in a bridal hammock
white and tasselled
whistled

and bits fell out of the sky near Nossa Senhora
who had walked all the way in bare feet from Bahia

and the chapel was lit by a child's
fistful of marigolds on the red velvet altar
thrown like a golden ball.

Oh let me come back on a day
when nothing extraordinary happens
so I can stare
at the sugar white pillars
and black lace grills
of this pink house.

# Cry Ararat!

### I

In the dream the mountain near
but without sound.
A dream through binoculars
seen sharp and clear:
the leaves moving, turning
in a far wind
no ear can hear.

First soft in the distance,
blue in blue air
then sharpening, quickening
taking on green.
Swiftly the fingers
seek accurate focus
(the bird
has vanished so often
before the sharp lens
could deliver it)
then as if from the sea
the mountain appears
emerging new-washed
growing maples and firs.
The faraway, here.

Do not reach to touch it
nor labour to hear.
Return to your hand
the sense of the hand;
return to your ear
the sense of the ear.
Remember the statue,
that space in the air
which with nothing to hold
what the minute is giving

*is* through each point
where its marble touches air.

Then will each leaf and flower
each bird and animal
become as perfect as
the thing its name evoked
when busy as a child
the world stopped at the Word
and Flowers more real than flowers
grew vivid and immense;
and Birds more beautiful
and Leaves more intricate
flew, blew and quilted all
the quick landscape.

So flies and blows the dream
embracing like a sea
all that in it swims
when dreaming, you desire
and ask for nothing more
than stillness to receive
the I-am animal,
the We-are leaf and flower,
the distant mountain near.


II

So flies and blows the dream that haunts us when we wake
to the unreality of bright day:
the far thing almost sensed by the still skin
and then the focus lost, the mountain gone.
This is the loss that haunts our daylight hours
leaving us parched at nightfall
blowing like last year's leaves
sibilant on blossoming trees
and thirsty for the dream of the mountain

more real than any event:
more real than strangers passing on the street
in a city's architecture white as bone
or the immediate companion.

But sometimes there is one
raw with the dream of flying:
'I, a bird,
landed that very instant
and complete—
as if I had drawn a circle in my flight
and filled its shape—
find air a perfect fit.
But this my grief,
that with the next tentative lift
of my indescribable wings
the ceiling looms
heavy as a tomb.

'Must my most exquisite and private dream
remain unleavened?
Must this flipped and spinning coin that sun
could gild and make miraculous become
so swiftly pitiful?
The vision of the flight it imitates
burns brightly in my head as if a star
rushed down to touch me where I stub against
what must forever be my underground.'


III

These are the dreams that haunt us,
these the fears.
Will the grey weather wake us,
toss us twice in the terrible night to tell us
the flight is cancelled
and the mountain lost?

O, then cry Ararat!

The dove believed
in her sweet wings and in the rising peak
with such a washed and easy innocence
that she found rest on land for the sole of her foot
and, silver, circled back,
a green twig in her beak.

The leaves that make the tree by day,
the green twig the dove saw fit
to lift across a world of water
break in a wave about our feet.
The bird in the thicket with his whistle
the crystal lizard in the grass
the star and shell
tassel and bell
of wild flowers blowing where we pass,
this flora-fauna flotsam, pick and touch,
requires the focus of the total I.

A single leaf can block a mountainside;
all Ararat be conjured by a leaf.


## Sestina for Pat Lane after Reading 'Albino Pheasants'

*Pale beak . . . pale eye . . .* the dark imagination
flares like magnesium. Add but *pale flesh*
and I am lifted to a weightless world:
watered cerulean, chrome-yellow (light)
and green, veronese—if I remember—a soft wash
recalls a summer evening sky.

At Barro de Navidad we watched the sky
fade softly like a bruise.   Was it imagination

that showed us Venus phosphorescent in a wash
of air and ozone?—a phosphorescence flesh
wears like a mantle in bright moonlight,
a natural skin-tone in that other world.

Why do I wish to escape this world?
Why do three phrases alter the color of the sky
the clarity, texture even, of the light?
What is there about the irrepressible imagination
that the adjective *pale* modifying *beak, eye* and *flesh*
can set my sensibilities awash?

If with my thickest brush I were to lay a wash
of thinnest water-color I could make a world
as unlike my own dense flesh
as the high-noon midsummer sky;
but it would not catch at my imagination
or change the waves or particles of light

yet *pale* can tip the scales, make light
this heavy planet.   If I were to wash
everything I own in mercury, would imagination
run rampant in that suddenly silver world—
free me from gravity, set me floating skyward—thistledown—permanently disburdened of my flesh?

Like cygnets hatched by ducks, our minds and flesh
are imprinted early—what to me is light
may be dark to one born under a sunny sky.
And however cool the water my truth won't wash
without shrinking except in my own world
which is one part matter, nine parts imagination.

I fear flesh which blocks imagination,
the light of reason which constricts the world.
*Pale beak . . . pale eye . . . pale flesh . . .* My sky's awash.

# Miriam Waddington

*Girls*

In summer the light flushed faces of my girls
Rush to me with hullos along the green street of their growing,
And from their freckled smiles all their hopes bloom out
And in their curving laughter all their past is carolled
While the strands of hair damp against their foreheads
Are tendrils reaching from the roots of their joy.

Oh my girls, as you rush to me with your swift hullos
I see over your shoulders the years like a fascist army
Advancing against your love, burning your maiden villages,
I see your still minorities destroyed in lethal chambers
Your defenceless dreams shot backward into the pit,
And I see
The levelling down of all your innocent worlds.

I offer myself a splint against your sorrows
And I kiss the broken wings of your future.


*At Midnight*

Wife goes to husband now
And husband to his wife
The bells ring midnight on the winter street.

Outside the wandering cats
Are still and the rooster
In his silky wing is soft asleep.

Inside the dark now

Husband turns to wife,
Precious and single as the guarded seal

Of ancient kings
Merge they and mingle,
Folded limbs and lips.

Softly now falls the rhythm
Of their breathing through the house,
And the frost against the window flickers low.

## My Lessons in the Jail

Walk into the prison, that domed citadel,
That yellow skull of stone and sutured steel,
Walk under their mottoes, show your pass,
Salute their Christ to whom you cannot kneel.

In the white-tiled room arrange the interview
With the man who took his daughter, and learn
That every man is usual but none are equal
In the dark rivers that in them burn.

And take this man's longest, bleakest year,
Between done act and again-done act, and take
His misery and need, stand against his tears
And transform them to such a truth as slakes

The very core of thirst, and be you sure
The thirst is his and not your own deep need
To spurt fine fountains; accept, accept
His halting words—since you must learn to read

Between the lines his suffering and doubt.
Be faithful to your pity, be careworn,
Though all this buffet you, and beat, and cruelly

Test you—you chose this crown of thorns.

Wear it with grace and when you rise to go
Thank him, and don't let yourself forget
How hard it is to thank, and to beholden be
One to another, and spin your role out yet

For moments in the hallway, compose your face
To false good humor, conceal your sex:
Smile at the brute who runs the place
And memorize the banner, *Christus Rex.*


## On My Birthday

There was nothing   not a white bone
or the hard dry skeleton of half a leaf,
only the wind in the transmitter singing
when I fronted the winter so sick and halfhearted,
denying my body's wholeness from my head to my feet
as I turned with the world to the high wind's song.

There was nothing   and turning I cried
for a white bone found or the half-moon's token,
there was only the heel of the beer bottle lying
on the humped-up earth in the net of snow,
and the wild parsley like a green wound showing
as the world turned and the high wind lay low.

And I guessed at the beggar's steep celebration
and the pitch of his wailing in four-legged joy
at his being a man inside of a woman
at her being a woman with a man inside,
both tossed on the bed of the mounting darkness
when the world turned to the high wind's song.

And I turned blind to the dead mating season

with my nerve-ends crying at lovers broken.
I heard the rain on the vowelled whisper
of the man and the woman in leafy autumn;
their bodies sank in their love's last labour
as he lay a Hans Andersen prince in her arms,
and she, muted mermaid that he wished her.

And I listened to my own my blind bone groaning
and to all the children that lay in my womb,
to the landlocked sailors and men in prison
and the pimply youths in the pin-ball cafés
as I choked on the cry of my white bone wailing
the wilding boy the self I never was.

In my darkest year at the deadness of mating,
in my dismalest year and the years still passing,
how could I guess that all waters flow downward,
that the womb-held child must swim out downward
and the man through the woman moves deep downward,
but the woman from downward is never retrieved?

And I listened to the world loud with my wailing
for the selves not dead who were never born,
and all the tongue-tied rage of my losing
shook me and roared through my solemn aging,
and I was a child in the wind's high singing
turning the world to be born again.

For how could I guess and to whom confide
my dreadness of losing and the gone bone wailing
the man's hard absence from winter's white side?
With my blind rooted body defenceless and falling
I guessed at the cry of my birth that first morning
when the world turned to the high wind's song.

## The Mile Runner

You are my buzz my hive   you are my honey steeple,
you are my me my how my pray and also prithee,
my mile runner and spinning helicopter,
my rescue from the wilderness of river.

And are you not my this my that of prairie,
my weathered granary   my nuisance crow?
My miles of sameness and my endless railway,
my gone-astray   my slow unlabelled freight?

So add the fishes' double-quick of colour,
the while-away of summer's brazen boys,
the golden eye of lakes   the fresh of beaches,
and I'm the eyelid and the tongue   and I'm the ear.


## Ukrainian Church

Little father your
rhythmic black robe
against white snow
improvises you
a black note
on a white keyboard;

let me follow
into your churchbarn
through the gate
to the onion domes
where your carrot
harvest burns
a fire of candles,

let me follow
in the cool light

as you move through
God's storehouse
as you put the bins
in order as you set
each grain in place;

let me follow
as your voice
moves in the
familiar liturgy
through the low caves
of Gregorian chant
and let me hear
little father

how you pray
for all your geese
for the cow fertile
at Easter and the
foundations of new
houses to be strong
and firmly set;

let me hear
how you beseech
for all your people
a clear road, an
open gate and
a new snowfall
fresh, dazzling,
white as birchbark.

## Gossip

Professor Waddington will not be
joining the academic procession
she wrote a note to the Dean she

said that her gown was moth-eaten
and she had to stay home to tie up
the chrysanthemums or else they
would flop all over and kill the grass
and she would have to resod around
the flowerbeds a nuisance so she regrets
she will not be able to join the academic
procession if you ask me that woman has
a nerve she's not friendly and furthermore I hear that she keeps late hours
looks at men what kind of example is that
for young girls all I can say is some
people are never satisfied

## The Survivors

In your quiet hand I touch
the touch of your gentle mother's hand
and hold her death in mine;

and in your opened eyes I see
the bareness of your younger brother's eyes
and miss your missed farewell.

The troubled journeys that you since have made
from war to war, record the faulty pulse
of time so timeless lost between the wars,

and wake the terrible child in us all
to rage against fixed bedtime and to cry
himself to lonesome sleep inside a world

of you-can't-go-home-again or painted cities
flat as lakes and bland as German summers:
the innocent seasons of the never never

are unmarked graveyards of the spoiled time

where even your hand must mourn against mine
to mark the graveyard of that other time

with angers that your Jewish father's face
buried against your will in every act
to make your hearing deaf   your speaking dumb;

and what I touch with my uninjured hand
is your survival:  immune to love we move
to ancient Jewish law   and strict command.


## A Morning Like
## the Morning
## When Amos Awoke

Let me sing
of reality
let me forget
the contingencies
houses mortgages
cars children
music lessons
loneliness;
let me sing
of the terrible
cities the dry
furnaces when
autumn was
spread over
Manhattan and
brandy burned
in the (polluted)
air and Hart
Crane's Indian
maiden danced
on the autumn

water of the
icy Hudson:

Whitman's lilacs
were folded deep
in his leaves of
grass loose manu-
scripts planted
with people (and
this was almost
the last week to
be wearing sandals)
and all the time
the crabapples were
ripening behind
my back in a
Toronto garden
just like on the
morning when Amos
awoke from his
figsticking job
on his father's
estate and filled
the world with
his stern *take
away from me the
noise of your songs
to the melody of
your harps I will
not listen but
let justice roll
down like waters*
let me sing of
reality forget
the contingencies
to the melody of
harps I will not
listen   take away
from me the noise
of my songs

## How I Spent the Year
## Listening to the
## Ten O'clock News

Last year
there were executions
in Chile
bribes in
America no
transit for Jews
in Austria
and lies
lies everywhere.

The children
of Ireland are
also in the news,
they have become
hardened street
fighters some of
them murderers,
I ask myself
where will it
all end?

Of course
the interests of
Canadian citizens
(read corporations)
must be protected
at any cost no
matter how many
good men are
shot like dogs
in the streets
of Chile or
how many poets
die of a broken
heart.

They claim
the world is
changing getting
better they have
the moon walk
and moon walkers
to prove it,
but my brain
is bursting my
guts are twisted
I have too much
to say thank
God I am too old
to bear children.

## Ten Years and More

When my husband
lay dying a mountain
a lake three
cities ten years
and more
lay between us:

There were our
sons my wounds
and theirs,
despair loneliness,
handfuls of un-
hammered nails
pictures never
hung all

The uneaten
meals and unslept

sleep; there was
retirement, and
worst of all
a green umbrella
he can never
take back.

I wrote him a
letter but all
I could think of
to say was: do you
remember Severn
River, the red canoe
with the sail
and lee-boards?

I was really saying
for the sake of our
youth and our love
I forgave him for
everything
and I was asking him
to forgive me too.

## Downtown Streets

There are still people
who write each other
intimate letters who
sing their personal arias
to an audience of white
paper; is it pain they
score, bursts of light they
note after a dark illness,
a childish jump, or some

mongrel dance-step in the
icicled rooms of snow?

Sometimes I still stand
outside a lighted window
on downtown streets (just
as I used to thirty years
ago) a woman sits at a
table writing intimate
letters, she is asking, *do
you really like the smell
of my perfume*, she is saying
*next time you come it will
be winter the season of
mandarin oranges.*

Standing there under
the window
I think I can hear
the sound
of her ghostly pen
moving across the page,
I think I can hear it
singing
in the downtown streets.

## *Elegies for a Composer*

1

Now there is only
the whisper of grass,
gentle under the flight
of your song's swallow.

Now there is only
the motion of earth that
sleeps under the mountain
beyond your song's sorrow.

2

You have crossed
into the world
below the frost line,
you have gone to join
the effigies of
our immigrant parents
who lie frozen
into statues under
fields of snow.

They lie there
and wait for us
under the wild sage
of their summer,
they look out at us
from the hundred white
eyes of the stinkweed
that grows so modestly
on the prairie.

Muffled by mouthfuls
of earth their voices
sing to us in the lost
tongues of our childhood,
they sing to us
the buried truth
of ourselves.

3

Why did it take us
a lifetime to hear
through the strange

accents of our parents
our own songs?

4

Now you are dead
and your song is
digging its way up
through the garden;
it emerges slow and
glistening with the
earthworms who labour
so earnestly for every
new planting.

## Lately I've Been
## Feeling Very Jewish

Jews are soft
touches:  I'm a soft
touch too I
melt like snow
in February I
step down disappear
leave patches of
bare earth in
the backyard for
other soft touches
and touchers; it
makes the world
less lonesome when
you can feel/see
the soft/yellow not-
especially-Jewish-touch
of a daffodil.

# Margaret Avison

## Snow

Nobody stuffs the world in at your eyes.
The optic heart must venture: a jail-break
And re-creation. Sedges and wild rice
Chase rivery pewter. The astonished cinders quake
With rhizomes. All ways through the electric air
Trundle candy-bright disks; they are desolate
Toys if the soul's gates seal, and cannot bear,
Must shudder under, creation's unseen freight.
But soft, there is snow's legend: colour of mourning
Along the yellow Yangtze where the wheel
Spins an indifferent stasis that's death's warning.
Asters of tumbled quietness reveal
Their petals. Suffering this starry blur
The rest may ring your change, sad listener.

## The World Still Needs

Frivolity is out of season.
Yet, in this poetry, let it be admitted
The world still needs piano-tuners
And has fewer, and more of these
Gray fellows prone to liquor
On an unlikely Tuesday, gritty with wind,
When somewhere, behind windows,
A housewife stays for him until the
    Hour of the uneasy bridge-club cocktails
    And the office rush at the groceteria
    And the vesper-bell and lit-up buses passing
    And the supper trays along the hospital corridor,

Suffering from
Sore throat and dusty curtains.

Not all alone on the deserted boathouse
Or even on the prairie freight
(The engineer leaned out, watchful and blank
And had no Christmas worries
Mainly because it was the eve of April),
Is like the moment
When the piano in the concert-hall
Finds texture absolute, a single solitude
For those hundreds in rows, half out of overcoats,
Their eyes swimming with sleep.

From this communal cramp of understanding
Springs up suburbia, where every man would build
A clapboard in a well of Russian forest
With yard enough for a high clothesline strung
To a small balcony . . .
A woman whose eyes shine like evening's star
Takes in the freshblown linen
While sky a lonely wash of pink is still
Reflected in brown mud
Where lettuces will grow, another spring.


## New Year's Poem

The Christmas twigs crispen and needles rattle
Along the windowledge.
   A solitary pearl
Shed from the necklace spilled at last week's party
Lies in the suety, snow-luminous plainness
Of morning, on the windowledge beside them.
And all the furniture that circled stately
And hospitable when these rooms were brimmed
With perfumes, furs, and black-and-silver

Crisscross of seasonal conversation, lapses
Into its previous largeness.
            I remember
Anne's rose-sweet gravity, and the stiff grave
Where cold so little can contain;
I mark the queer delightful skull and crossbones
Starlings and sparrows left, taking the crust,
And the long loop of winter wind
Smoothing its arc from dark Arcturus down
To the bricked corner of the drifted courtyard,
And the still windowledge.
            Gentle and just pleasure
It is, being human, to have won from space
This unchill, habitable interior
Which mirrors quietly the light
Of the snow, and the new year.


## To Professor X, Year Y

The square for civic receptions
Is jammed, static, black with people in topcoats
Although November
Is mean, and day grows late.

The newspapermen, who couldn't
Force their way home, after the council meeting
&c., move between windows and pressroom
In ugly humour. They do not know
What everybody is waiting for
At this hour
To stand massed and unmoving
When there should be—well—nothing to expect
Except the usual hubbub
Of city five o'clock.

Winter pigeons walk the cement ledges

Urbane, discriminating.

Down in the silent crowd few can see anything.
It is disgusting, this uniformity
Of stature.
If only someone climbed in pyramid
As circus families can . . .
Strictly, each knows
Downtown buildings block all view anyway
Except, to tease them,
Four narrow passages, and ah
One clear towards open water
(If 'clear'
Suits with the prune and mottled plumes of
Madam night).

Nobody gapes skyward
Although the notion of
Commerce by air is utterly
familiar.

Many citizens at this hour
Are of course miles away, under
Rumpus-room lamps, dining-room chandeliers,
Or bound elsewhere.
One girl who waits in a lit drugstore doorway
North 48 blocks for the next bus
Carries a history, an ethics, a Russian grammar,
And a pair of gym shoes.

But the few thousand inexplicably here
Generate funny currents, zigzag
Across the leaden miles, and all suburbia
Suffers, uneasily.

You, historian, looking back at us,
Do you think I'm not trying to be helpful?
If I fabricated cause-and-effect

You'd listen? I've been dead too long for fancies.
Ignore us, hunched in these dark streets
If in a minute now the explosive
Meaning fails to disperse us and provide resonance
Appropriate to your chronicle.

But if you do, I have a hunch
You've missed a portent.
('Twenty of six.' 'Snow?—I wouldn't wonder.')


## The Swimmer's Moment

For everyone
The swimmer's moment at the whirlpool comes,
But many at that moment will not say
'This is the whirlpool, then.'
By their refusal they are saved
From the black pit, and also from contesting
The deadly rapids, and emerging in
The mysterious, and more ample, further waters.
And so their bland-blank faces turn and turn
Pale and forever on the rim of suction
They will not recognize.
Of those who dare the knowledge
Many are whirled into the ominous centre
That, gaping vertical, seals up
For them an eternal boon of privacy,
So that we turn away from their defeat
With a despair, not for their deaths, but for
Ourselves, who cannot penetrate their secret
Nor even guess at the anonymous breadth
Where one or two have won:
(The silver reaches of the estuary).

## Voluptuaries and Others

That Eureka of Archimedes out of his bath
Is the kind of story that kills what it conveys;
Yet the banality is right for that story, since it is not a
    communicable one
But just a particular instance of
The kind of lighting up of the terrain
That leaves aside the whole terrain, really,
But signalizes, and compels, an advance in it.
Such an advance through a be-it-what-it-may but take-it-not
    quite-as-given locale:
Probably that is the core of being alive.
The speculation is not a concession
To limited imaginations. Neither is it
A constrained voiding of the quality of immanent death.
Such near values cannot be measured in values
Just because the measuring
Consists in that other kind of lighting up
That shows the terrain comprehended, as also its containing
    space,
And wipes out adjectives, and all shadows
    (or, perhaps, all but shadows).

The Russians made a movie of a dog's head
Kept alive by blood controlled by physics, chemistry, equip-
    ment, and
Russian women scientists in cotton gowns with writing tablets.
The heart lay on a slab midway in the apparatus
And went phluff, phluff.
Like the first kind of illumination, that successful experiment
Can not be assessed either as conquest or as defeat.
But it is living, creating the chasm of creation,
Contriving to cast only man to brood in it, further.

History makes the spontaneous jubilation at such moments
    less and less likely though,
And that story about Archimedes does get into public school
    textbooks.

## Birth Day

Saturday I ran to Mitilene.

Bushes and grass along the glass-still way
Were all dabbled with rain
And the road reeled with shattered skies.

Towards noon an inky, petulant wind
Ravelled the pools, and rinsed the black grass round them.

Gulls were up in the late afternoon
And the air gleamed and billowed
And broadcast flung astringent spray
                              All swordy-silver.
I saw the hills lie brown and vast and passive.

The men of Mitilene waited restive
Until the yellow melt of sun.
I shouted out my news as I sped towards them
That all, rejoicing, could go down to dark.

All nests, with all moist downy young
Blinking and gulping daylight; and all lambs
Four-braced in straw, shivering and mild;
And the first blood-root up from the ravaged beaches
Of the old equinox; and frangible robins' blue
Teethed right around to sun:
These first we loudly hymned;
And then
The hour of genesis
When first the moody firmament
Swam out of Arctic chaos,
Orbed solidly as the huge frame for this
Cramped little swaddled creature's coming forth
To slowly, foolishly, marvellously
Discover a unique estate, held wrapt

Away from all men else, which to embrace
Our world would have to stretch and swell with strangeness.

This made us smile, and laugh at last. There was
Rejoicing all night long in Mitilene.


## Pace

Plump raindrops in these
faintly clicking groves,
the pedestrians' place, July's
violet and albumen
close?'

'No. No. It is perhaps the conversational side-effect
among the pigeons; behold
the path-dust is nutmeg powdered and
bird-foot embroidered.'

> The silk-fringed hideaway
> permits the beechnut-cracking
> squirrels to plumply
> pick and click and
>   not listen.

Pedestrians linger
striped stippled sunfloating
    at the rim of the
        thin-wearing groves

letting the ear experience this
discrete, delicate
clicking.

## Black-White Under Green:
## May 18, 1965

This day of the leafing-out
speaks with blue power—
among the buttery grassblades
white, tiny-spraying spokes on the end of a weed-stem
and in the formal beds, tulips
and invisible birds inaudibly hallooing,
enormous, their beaks out wide, throats bulging, aflutter,
eyes weeping with speed
where the ultraviolets play and the scythe of the jets
flashes, carrying
the mind-wounded heartpale person, still a boy, a pianist, dying
        not
of the mind's wounds (as they read the x-rays) but
dying, fibres separated, parents ruddy and
American, strong, sheathed in the cold of
years of his differentness, clustered by two at
the nether arc of his flight.

This day of the leafing-out is one to remember
        how the ice crackled among
            stiff twigs. Glittering strongly
                the old trees sagged. Boughs
        abruptly unsocketed. Dry, orange gashes
the dawn's fine snowing discovered and powdered over.
. . . to remember the leaves ripped loose
the thudding of the dark sky-beams
and the pillared plunging sea
shelterless. Down the centuries
a flinching speck
        in the white fury found of itself—and another—
the rich blood spilling, mother to child, threading
the perilous combers, marbling
the surges, flung
out, and ten-fingered, feeling for
the lollop, the fine-wired

music, dying skyhigh
still between carpets and the
cabin-pressuring windows
on the day of the leafing.

Faces fanned by
rubberized, cool air
are opened; eyes wisely
smile.
The tulips, weeds, new leaves
neither smile nor are scorning to smile nor uncertain,
dwelling in light.
A flick of ice, fire, flood,
far off from
the day of the leafing-out I knew
when knee-wagon small, or from my
father's once at a horse-tail silk-shiny
fence-corner or this
day when the runways wait
white in the sun, and a new leaf is
metal, torn out of that blue
afloat in the dayshine.

## July Man

Old, rain-wrinkled, time-soiled, city-wise, morning man
whose weeping is for the dust of the elm-flowers
and the hurting motes of time,
rotted with rotting grape,
sweet with the fumes,
puzzled for good by fermented potato-
peel out of the vat of the times,
turned out and left
in this grass-patch, this city-gardener's place
under the buzzing populace's
square shadows, and the green shadows

of elm and ginkgo and lime
(planted for Sunday strollers and summer evening
families, and for those
bird-cranks with bread-crumbs
and crumpled umbrellas who come
while the dew is wet on the park, and beauty
is fan-tailed, gray and dove gray, aslant, folding in
from the white fury of day).

In the sound of the fountain
you rest, at the cinder-rim, on your bench.

The rushing river of cars
makes you a stillness, a pivot, a heart-stopping
blurt, in the sorrow
of the last rubbydub swig, the searing, and
stone-jar solitude lost, and yet,
and still—wonder (for good now) and
trembling:

    The too much none of us knows
    is weight, sudden sunlight, falling
    on your hands and arms, in your lap,
    all, all, in time.


## The Absorbed

The sun has not absorbed
this icy day, and this day's industry—in
behind glass—hasn't the blue and gold, cold
outside. Though not absorbing, this
sought that:

    sheeted, steely, vaulted,
    all gleam, this morning;
    bright blue with one stained wing in the

.northeast, at lunch hour;
in early afternoon
abruptly a dust-flurry,
     all but this private coign of place
     deafened, all winding in one cloth of moth.
Then space breathed, hollowing twilight
     on ice and the pale-gray, pale-blue,
     and far fur-colored wooden trees
     and ornamental trees.

Towards sundown
a boy came with an aluminum toboggan.
He worked his way, absorbed,
past footmark pocks, on crust,
up ice-ridge, sometimes bumping
down to the Japanese yews, sometimes
scooter-shoving athwart the hill,
then, with a stake,
kneeling,
he paddles, thrusting, speed-wise, then
stabbing, uphill; then
dangling the rope and poring on
slope-sheen, standing, he stashes
the aluminum, upright, in a frost-lumpy shoal
and beside coasting motorcars and parked cars
listens . . . and off again, toque to the eyebrows,
alone still in the engulfing dark.

The inside breathing here
closes down all the window but a visor-slit
on the night glare.
               New cold is
in dry-thorn nostrils.

Alone,  he plays, still there. We
struggle, our animal fires
pitted against those
several grape-white stars,
their silence.

## In a Season of Unemployment

These green painted park benches are
all new. The Park Commissioner had them
planted.
Sparrows go on
having dust baths at the edge of
the park maple's shadow, just where
the bench is cemented down, planted
and then cemented.

   Not a breath moves
   this newspaper.
   I'd rather read it by the Lapland sun at midnight. Here we're
   bricked in early by a
   stifling dark.

On that bench a man in a
pencil-striped white shirt
keeps his head up and steady.

   The newspaper-astronaut says
   'I feel excellent under the condition of weightlessness.'
And from his bench a
scatter of black bands in the hollow-air
ray out—too quick for the eye—
and cease.

   'Ground observers watching him on a TV circuit said
   At the time of this report he
   was smiling,' Moscow radio reported.
I  glance across at him, and mark that
he is feeling
excellent too, I guess, and
weightless and
'smiling'.

## A Nameless One

Hot in June a narrow winged
long-elbowed-thread-legged
living insect lived
and died within
the lodgers' second-floor bathroom here.

At six a.m.
wafting ceilingward,
no breeze but what it living made there;

at noon standing
still as a constellation of spruce needles
before the moment of
making it, whirling;

at four a
wilted flotsam, cornsilk, on the linoleum:
now that it is
over, I
look with new eyes
upon this room
adequate for one to
be, in.

Its insect-day
has threaded a needle
for me for my eyes dimming
over rips and tears and
thin places.

# Al Purdy

*The Country North of Belleville*

Bush land scrub land—
      Cashel Township and Wollaston
Elzevir McClure and Dungannon
green lands of Weslemkoon Lake
where a man might have some
      opinion of what beauty
is and none deny him
          for miles—

Yet this is the country of defeat
where Sisyphus rolls a big stone
year after year up the ancient hills
picnicking glaciers have left strewn
with centuries' rubble
          backbreaking days
          in the sun and rain
when realization seeps slow in the mind
without grandeur or self-deception in
          noble struggle
of being a fool—

A country of quiescence and still distance
a lean land
      not like the fat south
with inches of black soil on
      earth's round belly—
And where the farms are
      it's as if a man stuck
both thumbs in the stony earth and pulled

it apart
to make room
enough between the trees
for a wife
and maybe some cows and
room for some
of the more easily kept illusions—
And where the farms have gone back
to forest
are only soft outlines
shadowy differences—

Old fences drift vaguely among the trees
a pile of moss-covered stones
gathered for some ghost purpose
has lost meaning under the meaningless sky
—they are like cities under water
and the undulating green waves of time
are laid on them—

This is the country of our defeat
and yet
during the fall plowing a man
might stop and stand in a brown valley of the furrows
and shade his eyes to watch for the same
red patch mixed with gold
that appears on the same
spot in the hills
year after year
and grow old
plowing and plowing a ten-acre field until
the convolutions run parallel with his own brain—

And this is a country where the young
leave quickly
unwilling to know what their fathers know
or think the words their mothers do not say—

Herschel Monteagle and Faraday
lakeland rockland and hill country
a little adjacent to where the world is
a little north of where the cities are and
sometime
we may go back there
                              to the country of our defeat
Wollaston Elzevir and Dungannon
and Weslemkoon lake land
where the high townships of Cashel
                              McClure and Marmora once were—
But it's been a long time since
and we must enquire the way
            of strangers—


## The Cariboo Horses

 At 100 Mile House the cowboys ride in rolling
stagey cigarettes with one hand reining
half-tame bronco rebels on a morning grey as stone
—so much like riding dangerous women
            with whiskey coloured eyes—
such women as once fell dead with their lovers
with fire in their heads and slippery froth on thighs
—Beaver and Carrier women maybe or
            Blackfoot squaws far past the edge of this valley
on the other side of those two toy mountain ranges
            from the sunfierce plains beyond—

But only horses
                        waiting in stables
hitched at taverns
                        standing at dawn
pastured outside the town with
jeeps and fords and chevvys and

busy muttering stake trucks rushing
importantly over roads of man's devising
over the safe known roads of the ranchers
families and merchants of the town—
          On the high prairie
are only horse and rider
             wind in dry grass
clopping in silence under the toy mountains
dropping sometimes and
          lost in the dry grass
          golden oranges of dung—

Only horses
      no stopwatch memories or palace ancestors
not Kiangs hauling undressed stone in the Nile Valley
and having stubborn Egyptian tantrums or
Onagers racing thru Hither Asia and
the last Quagga screaming in African highlands
      lost relatives of these
      whose hooves were thunder
the ghosts of horses battering thru the wind
whose names were the wind's common usage
whose life was the sun's
      arriving here at chilly noon
      in the gasoline smell of the
      dust and waiting 15 minutes
      at the grocer's—


## Song of the Impermanent Husband

Oh I would
        I would in a minute
if the cusswords and bitter anger couldn't—
if the either/or quarrel didn't—
and the fat around my middle wasn't—

if I was young if
                I wasn't so damn sure
I couldn't find another maddening bitch
like you holding on for dear life to
all the different parts of me for
twenty or twenty
                        thousand years
I'd leave in the night like
a disgraced caviar salesman
                        descend the moonlight
stairs to Halifax
        (uh—no—not Halifax)
well then Toronto
                uh
I guess not Toronto either/or
nouveau riche Vancouver down
                                down
                                        down
the dark stairs to
the South Seas' sunlit milky reefs and
        the jungle's green
                unending bank account with
all the brown girls being brown
                as they can be and all
the one piece behinds stretched tight tonight
in small sarongs not to be touched tho Oh
beautiful as an angel's ass without the genitals
and me
        in Paris like a smudged Canadian postcard and
(dear me)
        all the importuning white and lily girls
of Rue Pigalle
                and stroll
the sodden London streets and
                find a sullen foggy woman who
enjoyed my odd colonial ways and send
a postcard back to you about my faithfulness and
talk about the lovely beastly English weather

I'd be the slimiest most uxorious wife deserter
           my shrunk amoeba self absurd inside
a saffron girl's geography and
hating me between magnetic nipples
but
     fooling no one in all the sad
     and much emancipated world
Why then I'll stay at least for tea for
all the brownness is too brown and
all the whiteness too damned white
and I'm afraid
           afraid of being
any other woman's man who
might be me
        afraid
the unctuous and uneasy self I glimpse
sometimes might lose my faint and yapping cry for
being anything was never quite what I intended
And you you
           bitch no irritating
questions re love and permanence only
           an unrolling lifetime here
between your rocking thighs and
           the semblance of motion


## Wilderness Gothic

Across Roblin Lake, two shores away,
they are sheathing the church spire
with new metal.  Someone hangs in the sky
over there from a piece of rope,
hammering and fitting God's belly-scratcher,
working his way up along the spire
until there's nothing left to nail on—

Perhaps the workman's faith reaches beyond:

touches intangibles, wrestles with Jacob,
replacing rotten timber with pine thews,
pounds hard in the blue cave of the sky,
contends heroically with difficult problems of
gravity, sky navigation and mythopoeia,
his volunteer time and labour donated to God,
minus sick benefits of course on a non-union job—

Fields around are yellowing into harvest,
nestling and fingerling are sky and water borne,
death is yodelling quiet in green woodlots,
and bodies of three young birds have disappeared
in the sub-surface of the new county highway—

That picture is incomplete, part left out
that might alter the whole Dürer landscape:
gothic ancestors peer from medieval sky,
dour faces trapped in photographic albums escaping
to clop down iron roads with matched greys:
work-sodden wives groping inside their flesh
for what keeps moving and changing and flashing
beyond and past the long frozen Victorian day.
A sign of fire and brimstone?  A two-headed calf
born in the barn last night?  A sharp female agony?
An age and a faith moving into transition,
the dinner cold and new-baked bread a failure,
deep woods shiver and water drops hang pendant,
double-yolked eggs and the house creaks a little—
Something is about to happen.  Leaves are still.
Two shores away, a man hammering in the sky.
Perhaps he will fall.

## Eskimo Graveyard

Walking in glacial litter
frost boils and boulder pavements

of an old river delta
where angry living water
changes its mind every half century
and takes a new direction
to the blue fiord
The Public Works guy I'm with
says you always find good gravel
for concrete near a graveyard
where digging is easy maybe
a footnote on human character
But wrapped in blankets
above ground a dead old woman
(for the last few weeks I'm told)
without a grave marker
And a hundred yards away
the Anglican missionary's grave
with whitewashed cross
that means equally nothing
The river's soft roar
drifts to my ears and changes
tone when the wind changes
ice debris melts at low tide
& the Public Works guy is mildly pleased
with the good gravel we found
for work on the schoolhouse
which won't have to be shipped in
from Montreal
and mosquitoes join happily
in our conversation      Then
he stops to consult
with the construction foreman
I walk on
toward the tents of The People
half a mile away
at one corner of the picture
Mothers with children on their backs
in the clean white parkas
they take such pride in

buying groceries at H.B.C.
boys lounging under the store
in space where timber stilts
hold it above the permafrost
with two of them arm in arm
in the manner of Eskimo friends
After dinner
I walk down among the tents
and happen to think of the old woman
neither wholly among the dead
nor quite gone from the living
and wonder how often
a thought of her enters the minds
of people she knew before
and what kind of flicker it is
as lights begin to come on
in nightlong twilight
and thoughts of me
occur to the mosquitoes
I keep walking
as if something ought to happen
(I don't know what)
with the sun stretching
a yellow band across the water
from headland to black headland
at high tide in the fiord
sealing in the settlement
as if there was no way out
and indeed there isn't
until the looping Cansos come
dropping thru the mountain doorway
That old woman?
it occurs to me
I might have been thinking
about human bookkeeping
debits and credits that is
or profit and loss
(and laugh at myself)

among the sealed white tents
like glowing swans
hoping
for a most improbable
birth

*Pangnirtung*


## Arctic Rhododendrons

They are small purple surprises
in the river's white racket
and after you've seen them
a number of times
in water-places
where their silence seems
related to river-thunder
you think of them as 'noisy flowers'
Years ago
it may have been
that lovers came this way
stopped in the outdoor hotel
to watch the water floorshow
and lying prone together
where the purged green
boils to a white heart
and the shore trembles
like a stone song
with bodies touching
flowers were their conversation
and love the sound of a colour
that lasts two weeks in August
and then dies
except for the three or four
I pressed in a letter
and sent whispering to you

*Pangnirtung*

## Detail

The ruined stone house
has an old apple tree
left there by the farmer
whatever else he took with him
It bears fruit every year
gone wild and wormy
with small bitter apples
nobody eats
even children know better
I passed that way on the road
to Trenton twice a month
all winter long
noticing how the apples clung
in spite of hurricane winds
sometimes with caps of snow
little golden bells
And perhaps none of the other
travellers looked that way
but I make no parable of them
they were there and that's all
For some reason I must remember
and think of the leafless tree
and its fermented fruit
one week in late January
when wind blew down the sun
and earth shook like a cold room
no one could live in
with zero weather
soundless golden bells
alone in the storm

## Lament for the Dorsets

*(Eskimos extinct in the 14th century A.D.)*

Animal bones and some mossy tent rings
scrapers and spearheads   carved ivory swans
all that remains of the Dorset giants
who drove the Vikings back to their long ships
talked to spirits of earth and water
—a picture of terrifying old men
so large they broke the backs of bears
so small they lurk behind bone rafters
in the brain of modern hunters
among good thoughts and warm things
and come out at night
to spit on the stars

The big men with clever fingers
who had no dogs and hauled their sleds
over the frozen northern oceans
awkward giants
                    killers of seal
they couldn't compete with little men
who came from the west with dogs
Or else in a warm climatic cycle
the seals went back to cold waters
and the puzzled Dorsets scratched their heads
with hairy thumbs around 1350 A.D.
—couldn't figure it out
went around saying to each other
plaintively
              'What's wrong? What happened?
              Where are the seals gone?'
And died

Twentieth century people
apartment dwellers
executives of neon death

warmakers with things that explode
—they have never imagined us in their future
how could we imagine them in the past
squatting among the moving glaciers
six hundred years ago
with glowing lamps?
As remote or nearly
as the trilobites and swamps
when coal became
or the last great reptile hissed
at a mammal the size of a mouse
that squeaked and fled

Did they ever realize at all
what was happening to them?
Some old hunter with one lame leg
a bear had chewed
sitting in a caribou skin tent
—the last Dorset?
Let's say his name was Kudluk
carving 2-inch ivory swans
for a dead grand-daughter
taking them out of his mind
the places in his mind
where pictures are
He selects a sharp stone tool
to gouge a parallel pattern of lines
on both sides of the swan
holding it with his left hand
bearing down and transmitting
his body's weight
from brain to arm and right hand
and one of his thoughts
turns to ivory
The carving is laid aside
in beginning darkness
at the end of hunger
after a while wind

blows down the tent and snow
begins to cover him
After 600 years
the ivory thought
is still warm


## The Runners

"It was when Leif was with King Olaf Tryggvason, and he bade him proclaim Christianity
to Greenland, that the king gave him two Gaels; the man's name was Haki, and the woman's
Haekia. The king advised Leif to have recourse to these people, if he should stand in need of
fleetness, for they were swifter than deer. Erick and Leif had tendered Karlsefni the services
of this couple. Now when they had sailed past Marvel-Strands (to the New World) they put
the Gaels ashore, and directed them to run to the southward, and investigate the nature of
the country, and return again before the end of the third half-day.'
                                               —From ERICK THE REDY'S SAGA

Brother, the wind of this place is cold,
and hills under our feet tremble,
the forests are making magic against us—
I think the land knows we are here,
I think the land knows we are strangers.
Let us stay close to our friend the sea,
or cunning dwarves at the roots of darkness
shall seize and drag us down—

Sister, we must share our strength between us,
until the heat of our bodies makes a single flame,
and one that we are is more than two that we were:
while the moon sees only one shadow,
and the sun knows only our double heartbeat,
and the rain does not come between—

Brother, I am afraid of this dark place,
I am hungry for the home islands,
and wind blowing the waves to coloured spray,
I am sick for the sun—

Sister, we must not think those thoughts again,
for three half-days have gone by,
and we must return to the ship.
If we are away longer,
the Northmen will beat us with thongs,
until we cry for death—
Why do you stare at nothing?

Brother, a cold wind touched me,
tho I stand in your arms' circle:
perhaps the Northmen's runes have found us,
the runes they carve on wood and stone.
I am afraid of this dark land,
ground mist that makes us half ghosts,
and another silence inside silence . . .
But there are berries and fish here,
and small animals by the sea's edge
that crouch and tremble and listen . . .
If we join our words to the silence,
if our trails cross the trails we made,
and the sun remembers what the moon forgets . . .
Brother, it comes to me now,
the long ship must sail without us,
we stay here—

Sister, we should die slowly,
the beasts would gnaw at our bodies,
the rains whiten our bones.
The Northmen's runes are strong magic,
the runes would track us down,
tho we keep on running
past the Land of Flat Stones
over the Marvel-Strands
beyond the land of great trees . . .
Tho we ran to the edge of the world,
our masters would track us down—

Brother, take my hand in your hand,
this part of ourselves between us

while we run together,
over the stones of the sea-coast,
this much of ourselves is our own:
while rain cries out against us,
and darkness swallows the evening,
and morning moves into stillness,
and mist climbs to our throats,
while we are running,
while we are running—

Sister—


## The Beavers of Renfrew

By day
chain saws stencil the silence in my head,
black quotes appear on the red brain—
Across glacial birth marks old Jake
Loney is cutting his winter wood,
tongue drowned in a chaw of tobacco—
The belly button pond at one
end of the farm brims
full its cockleshell three acres:
—tonight the beaver are back,
and work their swing shift
under the moon.
Sometimes at low earthen dams
where the pouring spillway empties,
they stand upright in a pride of being,
holding rainbow trout like silver thoughts,
or pale gold Indian girls
arriving here intact from bone cameras
ten thousand ancestors ago,
before letting them spin down the moonlight
rapids as mortal lures
for drowned fishermen—

Among the beaver lodges
I stand unable to sleep,
but cannot stay awake
while poplar and birch fall around me.
I am not mistaken for a tree,
but almost totally ignored,
pissed on by mistake occasionally—
Standing here long enough,
seeing the gentle bodies moving
close to what they truly are,
I wonder what screwed-up philosophy,
what claim to a god's indulgence,
made men decide their own importance?
And what is great music and art
but an alibi for murderers?
Perhaps in the far-off beginnings
of things they made a pact with men,
dammed the oceans for us,
chewed a hole in the big log bridge
wedged between Kamchatka and Alaska,
tore open the Mediterranean,
parted the Red Sea for Moses,
drowned Atlantis and the Eden-myth,
original sin and all that,
in the great salt womb of the sea—
And why?
Because they pitied men.
To the wet animal shivering in a tree
they said,
              'Come on down—
                        It's all right.'
And he shinnied down with hairless
purple behind pointed east for heat,
tail between hind legs,
humbly standing on all fours,
touching his forelock muttering,
'Yessir yessir thank'ee kindly,'
but not knowing how to speak yet of course—
Beaver looked at this dripping creature,

a miserable biological dead end:
but every failure has flashes of genius
exploding out of death:
and the man listened
to an agreement of the water beings
and land beings together
which men have forgotten since:
the secret of staying completely still,
allowing ourselves to catch up
with the shadow just ahead of us
we have lost,
when the young world was a cloudy room
drifting thru morning stillness—
But the rest of it
I have forgotten,
and the gentle beaver will not remind us:
standing upright at their earthen dams
holding the moonlit reins of water,
at peace with themselves—

'Why not make a left turn
and just stay here,'
I said next day to old Jake Loney,
'instead of going forward to the planets?'
The chain saw bucked in his hands,
chewing out chunks of pine that toppled
and scarred the air with green absence.
Far off a beaver tail slapped water,
a bird looked for the tree that was gone—
Old Jake's cheek bulged its chaw of tobacco—
'Well, why not?' I said argumentatively,
before he could spit,
                    'Why not?'
And the log bridge across the Bering
burst with a roar around
me again nothing but water,
brown water—
                    'Why not?'

# Raymond Souster

## The Nest

It will have to be near some water
so there can be moonlight like a pool
to bathe our tired, sleep-returning eyes.

There must be a high, strong roof
so the rain children will not break
the step of their marching above us.

White sheets to lull our flesh asleep
after we've squeezed all the love from our bodies,
with God's hand on the door
so none can touch the slightest scattered hair
of your head on its pillow, that none
will hand me a gun again and say,
leave her, there's new blood to be spilled
in the name of our latest lie.

## Young Girls

With the night full of spring and stars we stand
here in this dark doorway and watch the young
girls pass, two, three together, hand in hand.
Like flowers they are whose fragrance has not sprung
or awakened, whose bodies dimly feel
the flooding upward welling of the trees;
whose senses, caressed by the wind's soft fingers, reel
with a delirium that makes them ill at ease.

They lie awake at night unable to sleep
and walk the streets kindled by strange desires;
they steal glances at us, unable to keep
control upon those subterranean fires.
We whistle after them, then laugh, for they
stiffen, not knowing what to do or say.

## Lagoons, Hanlan's Point

Mornings
 before the sun's liquid
spilled gradually, flooding
the island's cool cellar,
there was the boat
and the still lagoons,
with the sound of my oars
the only intrusion
over cries of birds
in the marshy shallows,
or the loud thrashing
of the startled crane
rushing the air.

And in one strange
dark, tree-hung entrance,
I followed the sound
of my heart all the way
to the reed-blocked ending,
with the pads of the lily
thick as green-shining film
covering the water.

And in another
where the sun came
to probe the depths
through a shaft of branches,

I saw the skeletons
of brown ships rotting
far below in their burial-ground,
and wondered what strange fish
with what strange colours
swam through these palaces
under the water. . . .

A small boy
with a flat-bottomed punt
and an old pair of oars
moving with wonder
through the antechamber
of a waking world.


## The Lilac Poem

Before the lilacs are over and they are only
shrunken stalks at the ends of drooping branches,
I want to write a poem about them and their beauty
brief and star-shining as a young girl's promise.

Because there is so much made of strength and wealth and power,
because the little things are lost in this world,
I write this poem about lilacs knowing that both
are this day's only: tomorrow they will lie forgotten.


## Downtown Corner News Stand

It will need all of death to take you from this corner.
It has become your world, and you its unshaved
bleary-eyed, foot-stamping king. In winter
you curse the cold, huddled in your coat from the wind,
you fry in summer like an egg hopping on a griddle;

and always the whining voice, the nervous-flinging arms,
the red face, shifting eyes watching, waiting
under the grimy cap for God knows what
to happen. (But nothing ever does, downtown Toronto
goes to sleep and wakes the next morning
always the same, except a little dirtier.)
And you stand with your armful of *Stars* and *Telys*,
the peak of your cap well down against the sun,
and all the city's restless seething river
surges beside you, but not once do you plunge
into its flood, are carried or tossed away:
but reappear always, beard longer than ever, nose running,
to catch the noon editions at King and Bay.


## Study: The Bath

In the almost dim light
of the bathroom a woman
steps from white tub
towel around her shoulders.

Drops of water glisten
on her body, slight buttocks,
neck, tight belly,
fall at intervals
from the slightly plumed
oval of crotch.

Neck bent forward
eyes collected
her attention gathered
at the ends of fingers

as she removes
dead skin from her nipples.

## Flight of the Roller-Coaster

Once more around should do it, the man confided . . .

and sure enough, when the roller-coaster reached the peak
of the giant curve above me, screech of its wheels
almost drowned out by the shriller cries of the riders,

instead of the dip and plunge with its landslide of screams,
it rose in the air like a movieland magic carpet,
     some wonderful bird,

and without fuss or fanfare swooped slowly across
     the amusement-park,
over Spook's Castle, ice-cream booths, shooting-gallery.
     And losing no height

made the last yards above the beach, where the cucumber-cool
brakeman in the last seat saluted
a lady about to change from her bathing-suit.

Then, as many witnesses reported, headed leisurely
     out over the water,
disappearing all too soon behind a low-flying flight of clouds.


## All This Slow Afternoon

All this slow afternoon
the May winds blowing
honey of the lilacs,
sounds of waves washing
through the highest branches
of my poplar tree.

Enough in such hours

to be simply alive;
I will take death tomorrow
without bitterness.

Today all I ask
is to be left alone
in the wind
in the sunshine,
with the honey of lilacs
down the garden;

to fall asleep tired
of small birds' gossip,
of so much greenness
pushed behind my eyes.

## The Six-Quart Basket

The six-quart basket
one side gone
half the handle torn off

sits in the centre of the lawn
and slowly fills up
with the white fruits of the snow.

## The Death of the Grenadiers

It was over the ice
of this bottomless pond
(so the story goes)
that the Grenadiers
chased those Indians,

and the ice that gave way
to the marching step
of the English held up
for the braves' single file. . . .
And girls have told me
they've felt that someone
was looking up their legs
as they skated the pond,
and looking down they've seen
(noses close to the ice
on the underneath side),
the white-bearded faces
of lonely soldiers
looking up at them
with lascivious winks
in their socketless eyes.

## A Morning in Brussels

—Granted the most subtle torture that in which the victim
knows each step of his pain but is powerless to change
it in any way—

Then become this moment the young French-Canadian airman
of twenty, who, having watched in the cellar of the Rue
Royale the most expert monsters of the Gestapo stalk
round on cat-silent shoes behind the line of prisoners
(faces held six inches back from dripping walls), lashing
out with rubber truncheons now at this head and now this,
quite at random, never the same pattern repeated—

Knowing this then stand in line yourself, lips held
tightly together until the first searing terror of your
face smashed against the stone, pain in your nose like
a knife-slit, lips moving tremblingly in prayer, Holy

Mary, Mother of God, as you wait for the warning of
footsteps which never comes, as you wait for an end,
any end. . . .

## Memory of Bathurst Street

'Where are you, boy?'
my Aunt Maggie's calling,
but I can't hear her
in my attic eyrie,
where I watch the heat
swirl up from the tar roofs,
and wait for the cry
of the bearded rag-picker
down the lane from Ulster Street.

'Where are you, boy?'
my Uncle Jim's calling,
but I can't hear him
for the cooing of birds
inside this pigeon-house
at the back of the garden,
where I scrape up the droppings
to learn my allowance.

'Where are you, boy?'
my Aunt Lizzie's calling,
but I can't hear her
from the upstairs sitting-room,
as I turn the pages
of my favourite book
where the Highlanders lie
in the blood of their death
on green Spion Kop.

## St Catherine Street East

For Louis Dudek

Beer on a hot afternoon?—what else
in this Bon Marché of the World,
earth's narrowest, most crowded rabbit-run,
sweating under loud sunshine that glints off
baby carriages, tin cups of beggars,
silver balls of pawnshops, making
the rouge-layered, powder-dipped girls
squint hard but not taking anything off
their free-swinging walk on the stilt-heels.

Beer you said? Right back here
behind giant cheeses, wienerwurst truncheons,
hungry smells of bread, perfumes of coffee.
Look, the cold-sweated bottles count out
to a dozen, and we fight our way
past the check-out counter to the street
where sun, traffic, noise, faces, heat-breath
hit, stun us.
                    Every face in every window
of each building watching as we go
down the steaming pavement, on, out of this jungle
where the dead are never buried by the living,
but crowd onto buses, sit late at bar stools, or wait
in the darkness of always airless rooms.

## On the Rouge

I can almost see
my father's canoe
pointing in from the lake,
him paddling,
mother hidden

in a hat of fifty years ago.

Turning now up a stream
clear-flowing through marsh
(not mud-brown like today):

gliding under the same
railway bridge we cross under,
slipping by the same giant
stepping-stones of rock
standing up so like ramparts:

moving on to those quieter
summer-singing reaches,
the calling of birds
making speech difficult.

Lost finally, perhaps forever,
behind ferns swallowing banks,
bent trees overarching sky,

drifting the summer
labyrinths of love.


## Night Raider

Something getting its Christmas dinner early
in the narrow alley that flanks
our apartment house.
                          Gorging so frantically
it can't hear the noise it makes
rattling trash-can lids, ripping skins
of newspaper-wrapping off the choicest refuse.
This to the sleepy steadiness of rain falling,
so that I get a picture of my animal,
head down in garbage, busy, steam ascending
like a grace from its breathing coat.

## Among the Willows

When summer returns, these same willows will
        come alive,
burst bud and throw
a green band along
the mud banks of the river.

When I was a kid, nine or ten years old,
we played our games of cowboys and Indians
among them. More than once surprised
young couples in those thickets,
who, thinking themselves well-hidden,
had abandoned themselves to their loving.

I think we were more
surprised and embarrassed than they were,
for they said nothing to us, made no move
to leave off their pleasure,
while we retreated, confused,
not old or bold enough to know
our easy advantage.

Was it later we collected
soiled sheaths of their mating, spearing them
on the points of sticks?

It may have been.
We had that fresh innocence once,
in the summer, by the river, among the willows.

## Get the Poem Outdoors

Get the poem outdoors under any pretext,
reach through the open window if you have to,

kidnap it right off the poet's desk,
then walk the poem in the garden, hold it up
  among the soft yellow garlands of the
  willow,
command of it no further blackness, no silent
  cursing at midnight, no puny whimpering
  in the endless small hours, no more
  shivering in the cold-storage room of the
  winter heart,
tell it to sing again, loud and then louder so it
  brings the whole neighbourhood out, but
  who cares,
ask of it a more human face, a new tenderness,
  even the sentimental allowed between the
  hours of nine to five,
then let it go, stranger in a fresh green world, to
  wander down the flower beds, let it go to
  welcome each bird that lights on the still
  barren mulberry tree.


## A Letter to Archibald Lampman

Dear Archie:
if I remember correctly
it was in 1888
that you published your first book of verse
*Among the Millet*
with a legacy left to your wife.

I believe the book was published
or at any rate printed
by J. Durie & Son
of Ottawa, the city you worked in
and died in,
the city that has done exactly nothing

for you its most distinguished citizen
(for my money anyway);

and eighty-six years later
or 1974 to be precise,
you are still too big a risk
to be published in that city.

'A volume this size
concentrated on one poet
would be a risky venture.'

Now, I don't blame my publisher
who happens to locate in Ottawa,
and I can't fault your verse—
let's face it, it's the best we have,
you are not in any sense 'minor'—

I can only blame it, Archie,
on your misfortune to be born
a poet in a country

so rich and so big
yet so minor as Canada.


## Pictures of a Long-Lost World

*Passchendaele, October 1917*

Half-drowning in the miserable lean-to
that was really just a roof over mud,
my father heard a strange *plop plop plop*
almost on top of him, panicked, yelled at Fred
who was drowsing beside him, and with both hands shaking,
somehow pulled his gas-mask on.
                    But old Fred

wasn't buying it this time, he was sick of false alarms,
so didn't move until the first yellow cloud
seeped in a minute later (my father watching
through his half-fogged goggles, heard Fred cough,
then struggle with his gas-mask, cough, clutch his throat again,
then jump up, scramble out, a madman screaming
as he ran for the battery gas-curtain. . . .)

Six months later he was back
his lungs almost good as new.

# Eli Mandel

## Pillar of Fire

A man came to my tent door
in the heat of the day, the tent
stretched and slapped in the wind.
All the guy ropes went taut
And I felt my temples stretch
and throb in the noise and heat.

He talked about blowflies,
plague among the swollen cattle.
He asked about the children.
'You are a great nation.
Will you stay here long?'

That night the fire in the tent
vomited a great smoke.
The tent glowed like a furnace.
I dreamt about Egypt and its flies,
a priest dying of cancer.
I am told to breed more children,
try not to think about politics,
remember the Sabbath and my enemies.

## Thief Hanging in Baptist Halls

*After a Sculpture by George Wallace*

Amid the congratulations of summer,
polite vegetation, deans, a presbyterian sun,
brick minds quaintly shaped in gothic and glass,

here where the poise and thrust of speech
gleams like polished teak
I did not expect to see myself.

But there he hangs
shrugging on his hung lines,
soft as a pulped fruit or bird
in his welded soft suit of steel.

I wish he would not shrug
and smile weakly at me
as if ashamed that he is hanging there,
his dean's suit fallen off, his leg cocked
as if to run
or (too weak, too tired, too undone)
to do what can be done
about his nakedness.

Why should he hang there,
my insulting self, my deanship, all undone?

He dangles while the city bursts in green and steel,
black flower in the mouth of my speech:
the proud halls reel,
gothic and steel melt in the spinning sun.


## The Meaning of the I CHING

I

unopened
        book of old men
        orange-blossom book
                                before me
you were
        how could you contain me?

do you not see I am the mouths
of telegraphs and cemeteries?
my mother groaned like the whole
of Western Union to deliver
my message
    and yelling birthdays
that unrolled from my lungs
like ticker-tape for presidents
about to be murdered
     I sped
on a line that flew
to the vanishing point of the west

before I was
    you were
unopened book
     do not craze me
with the odour of orange-blossom

do not sit there
like smiling old men

   how could you contain me?

II

under my fingers words form themselves
it's crazy to talk of temples in this day
but light brightens on my page
like today moving against the wooden house
all shapes change and yet stay
as if they were marble in autumn
as if in the marbled yellow autumn
each western house becomes a shrine
stiff against the age of days
under my fingers stiffly formed

one cannot be another, I cry,
let me not be crazed by poetry

I will walk in streets that vanish
noting peculiar elms like old women
who will crash under the storm of sun
that breaks elm, woman, man
into a crumble of stump and bark
until the air is once more clear
in the sane emptiness of fall

III

my body speaks to me
as my arms say:   two are one
as my feet say:   earth upon earth
as my knees say:   bow down, unhinge yourself
as my cells say:   we repeat the unrepeatable

the book speaks:   arrange yourself in the form
                   that will arrange you

before I was:   colours that hurt me
                arranged themselves in me

before I was:   horizons that blind me
                arranged themselves in me

before I was:   the dead who speak to me
                arranged themselves in me

IV

I am the mouths
of smiling old men

there rises from me
the scent of orange-blossoms

I speak in the words
of the ancient dead

arranged
in the raging sun

in the stiffening age of days

and in the temple of my house

one becomes another
I am crazed by poetry


## Houdini

I suspect he knew that trunks are metaphors,
could distinguish between the finest rhythms
unrolled on rope or singing in a chain
and knew the metrics of the deepest pools

I think of him listening to the words
spoken by manacles, cells, handcuffs,
chests, hampers, roll-top desks, vaults,
especially the deep words spoken by coffins

escape, escape: quaint Harry in his suit
his chains, his desk, attached to all attachments
how he'd sweat in that precise struggle
with those binding words, wrapped around him
like that mannered style, his formal suit

and spoken when? by whom? What thing first said
'there's no way out'?; so that he'd free himself,
leap, squirm, no matter how, to chain himself again,
once more jump out of the deep alive
with all his chains singing around his feet
like the bound crowds who sigh, who sigh.

## Pictures in an Institution

I

Notice:  all mirrors will be covered
the mailman is forbidden to speak
professors are confined to their offices
faculties no longer exist.

II

I speak of what I know,
how uncle Asher, spittle on his lips,
first typed with harvest hands the fox
across a fence and showing all good men
come to their country's aid rushed off to Israel
there to brutalize his wife and son

how step-grandfather Barak wiped
sour curds out of his curly beard
before he roared the Sabbath in my ears
what Sara, long his widow, dreamed
the night she cried: God, let him die at last,
thinking perhaps of Josef who had lost
jewels in Russia where the Cossack rode
but coughed his stomach out in Winnipeg

Your boredom does not matter.  I take,
brutal to my thoughts, these lives, defy
your taste in metaphor; the wind-break
on the farm that Barak plowed to dust
makes images would ruin public poetry.

The rites of love I knew:
how father cheated brother, uncle, son,
and bankrupt-grocer, that we might eat
wrote doggerel verse, later took his wife,
my mother, in the English way beside my bed.
Why would he put his Jewishness aside?

Because there was no bread?
                              Or out of spite
that doctors sliced his double rupture,
fingered spleen, and healed his bowel's ache?

Lovers lie down in glades, are glad.
These, now in graves, their headstones sunk,
knew nothing of such marvels, only God, his ways,
owning no texts of Greek or anthropology.

III

Notice:  the library is closed to all who read
             any student carrying a gun
             registers first, exempt from fines,
             is given thirteen books per month,
             one course in science, one in math,
             two options
                       campus police
             will see to co-eds' underwear

IV

These names I rehearse:
                           Eva, Isaac,
Charley, Yetta, Max
                       now dead
or dying or beyond my lies

till I reeling with messages
and sick to hold again their bitter lives
put them, with shame, into my poetry.

V

Notice:  there will be no further communication
             lectures are cancelled
             all students are expelled
             the reading of poetry is declared a public
                                            crime

## Woodbine

When a crooked man meets beauty
You think there'd be shouting in the streets

I wish there were no allegories
I wish the doctors could do something about my forked tongue

Believe me, I have gone about with pails on my head
so that my friends would recognize me.

Lord, Lord, pollution everywhere
But I breathe still
                and breathless, sweet
woodbine, colour of honey, touches my skin
as if my unbelieving eyes made no difference at all


## The Speaking Earth

grandfathers fall into it
their mighty beards muffled in grass

and admirals, the sea-sounding men

lovers fall into the earth
like rain on wet dark bodies

listen, our lady earth flowers
into the sea-green language
of grass and drowned admirals

listen: in bearded branches
clasped like broken hands
admiring birds
lovers singing of their kiss
before and after all the words

## From the North Saskatchewan

when on the high bluff discovering
the river cuts below
                              send messages
we have spoken to those on the boats

I am obsessed by the berries they eat
all night odour of Saskatoon
and an unidentifiable odour
something baking
                              the sun
never reaches the lower bank

I cannot read the tree markings

today the sky is torn by wind:
a field after a long battle
strewn with corpses of cloud

give blessings to my children
speak for us to those who sent us here
say we did all that could be done
we have not learned
what lies north of the river
or past those hills that look like beasts


## Marina

Because she spoke often of the sea we thought she had known
        another country, her people distant, not forgotten

We did not know then who was calling her or what songs she
        listened to or why the sea-birds came to rest
        upon her long fingers

Or why she would shudder like a sea-bird about to take flight,
    her eyes changing with the changing light

As the sea-changing opal changes, as a shell takes its
    colours from the sea as if it were the sea

As if the great sea itself were held in the palm of a hand

They say the daughters of the sea know the language of birds,
    that in their restless eyes the most fortunate learn
    how the moon rises and sets

We do not know who is calling her or why her eyes change
    or what shore she will set her foot upon


*On the 25th Anniversary of the*
*Liberation of Auschwitz:*
*Memorial Services, Toronto, YMHA,*
*Bloor & Spadina, January 25, 1970*

the name is hard
a German sound made out of
the gut guttural throat
y scream yell   ing  open
voice mouth growl
                 and sweat

the only way out of Auschwitz
is through the chimneys'
                 of course
that's second hand   that's told
again Sigmund Sherwood (Sobolewski)
twisting himself into that sentence
before us on the platform

                          the poem
shaping itself late in the after
noon later than it would be:

Pendericki's 'Wrath of God'
moaning electronic Polish theatric
the screen silent
                    framed by the name
looking away from/pretending not there
no   name   no not   name   no

        Auschwitz
        in   GOTHIC   lettering
                        the hall
a parody a reminiscence a nasty memory
the Orpheum in Estevan before Buck Jones
the Capital in Regina before Tom Mix
waiting for the guns
waiting for the cowboy killers
one two three
                    Legionnaires
Polish ex-prisoners Association
Legions
        their medals their flags

so the procession, the poem gradually
insistent beginning to shape itself
with the others
                    walked with them
into the YMHA Bloor & Spadina
thinking apocalypse shame degradation
thinking bones and bodies melting
thickening thinning melting bones and bodies
thinking not mine/speak clearly
the poet's words/Yevtyshenko at Baba-Yar

there   this January   snow
heavy wet   the wind   heavy wet

the street grey white slush melted concrete
bones and bodies melting slush
                              saw
with the others
                    the prisoner
in the YMHA hall Bloor & Spadina
arms wax stiff body stiff unnatural
coloured face blank eyes
                              walked
with the others toward the screen
toward the pictures
                         SLIDES
          this is mother
          this is father
          this is
                    the one who is
waving her arms like that
is the one who
                    like
I mean running with her breasts bound
ing
     running
               with her hands here and there
with her here and
                         there
hands
          that          that is

the poem becoming the body
becoming the faint hunger
ing body
          prowling
                    through
words the words words the words
opening  mouths  ovens
the generals smiling saluting
in their mythic uniforms god-like
generals uniforms with the black leather
with the straps and intricate leather

the phylacteries the prayer shawl
corsets and the boots and the leather straps
and the shining faces of the generals in their boots
and their stiff wax bodies their unnatural faces
and their blank eyes and their hands their stiff hands
and the generals in their straps and wax and stiff
staying standing
           melting bodies and thickening
           quick flesh on flesh handling
           hands


    the poem flickers, fades
the four Yarzeit candles guttering   one
    each four million lights dim
my words drift
          smoke from chimneys and ovens
    a bad picture, the power failing
   pianist clattering on and over and through
the long Saturday afternoon in the Orpheum
     while the whitehatted star spangled cowboys
       shot the dark men and shot the dark men
       and we threw popcorn balls and grabbed
   each other and cheered:
             me jewboy yelling
for the shot town and the falling men
     and the lights come on
           and
    with the others
standing in silence


    the gothic word hangs
    over us on a shroud-white screen
and we drift away
       to ourselves
        to the late Sunday *Times*


       the wet snow
       the city


       a body melting

## Two Dream Songs for John Berryman

I

Henry, it says to me here
you took yourself to a bridge.
And you, weary and wavery,
walked, bone and brain, all
to the rail
        there perched
waved farewell from rail

Is that how it was done?

Is it only possible to live
how we have done backwards
dreaming our way from death to
bony life?
        Well, it was gaily
done
      but, here on the coast of Spain,
heartsick like you
          and hurt too
by burning poems that will not write
themselves I
      say
now fare-you-well
with Sylvia, Ted, Randall,

and all your hurt friends,

God notwithstanding

II

It is done but not done well
Henry   to betake yourself to ice
and death in a Minnesota morning

or a bruise
throwing yourself from bridge
to ice
     why would you want so
to say to me or to God once more
that nothing is fair
among fair women and hardy men

to God
       who never once cared
now name him as you will

it's both night and day
not done well to you or anyone
less or better
           not well


## Agatha Christie

being civil she saw poison
as a flaw in character
and the use of a knife
a case history in Freud

difficult to explain
her dislike of jews
or why night upon night
she plotted solutions
to deaths she must have dreamed

her 200,000,000 readers
how much longing for murder
the neatness of England
is and still remains

though in Belfast, say,
bombs have other reasons
and no one explains


## On the Death of Ho Chi Minh

toward the end
he became frail as rice paper
his beard whispering thin ideograms

how unlike the great carved storm
that was Marx's face
                        how unlike
the darkness and fury
in Beethoven's head
                        scarcely
anything to be consumed

bombs destroy   destroy
you cannot touch his body now
or burn his poems

# Anne Szumigalski

*Victim*

Ah the cliff edge—where so many murders are done
Can't you see the body among the boulders
Far down on the beach?
While seagulls scream they are filming
A frail girl in a thin nightgown
Prone on the distant rocks

Mr. B and I are walking hand in hand
Up the cliff path knowing
That under our feet
Disaster and drama are making a second-rate movie
Take no notice my darling Mr. B
Tell me a simple answer to the urgent question
Who am I?  Who are we?

Mr. B is a known madman   a suspected murderer
I think the cops are after him for being himself
For not sobbing
For not beating his breast
When he finds a victim on the beach
Bloody and wet in the tide
Was that my body we saw down there Mr. B
Twisted in seaweed   Who am I?  Who was I?

He picked me up on the beach
I am the tiny girl in the thin nightgown
That Mr. B carries in a seashell
In his trousers pocket among
The sticks of Dentyne gum and the spent flashbulbs
Oh I am glad I am dead and can't see

The dirty darkness in here

I was murdered last Thursday but even so
The heat of his groin
And all the fumbling that goes on there
Is disturbing my final rest


## Girl with a Basket

Now comes dusty Beatrice drab girl
With her arms full of bales wound with fresh linen
She lets fall white coils down between long gray fingers
Nor smudges nor smears clear light   cold linen

Beatrice why are you crying as you smooth the sheet
With your dark hand?
She makes a short drain snort in her nose
Being fearful and glad to watch the head cut open
Or green shell belly slit with small sharp knife
Looks down and sees eight rows of seeds
Neatly knitted into a web of pith   her one comfort
The sweet drops that drip from the flesh
Not like tears they run
Like whey from squeezed cheeses


## Fishhawks

my son stands in waist-high water
the salt reddens his skin
out of his face spring wiry hairs
thickening to a beard
his arms have become wide and heavy

he splices rope

smells of the tar that blackens his fingers
he has learned to make his living from the sea

(the huge shadow of a bird
darkens the sand around us
I speak, say to you *look*
*at that rare creature*
*an osprey)*

further out from the shore
your daughter is a rock
jutting from the waves
she is rounded and hollow
within her is a sea-cave
her face is a pearly shell
a shining operculum
stoppers up her mouth
her singing is muffled, a murmur

the boy smiles
his semen darts out of him
a shoal of swift fishes
entering her secret place
he stretches out his finger
flicks away the shell plug from her mouth
so that she may cry out

you look at me, say
*this has all happened far too quickly*
we wade out        I say:
*there is just time for us to bless them*
but in that glance they have crossed the horizon
are washed away out of our sight

we two return to the beach
the salt water drips from us
making the dull shingles glisten
our wet clothes cling to our legs

behind us the sun is clouded
the sea is cold not splendid
*I am a widow* I tell you
*but we are just strangers* you reply

out there where the great bird hovers
mantling preparing to spiral
there is a faint wailing

## The Lullaby

a woman offers a man an orange
it is heavy and cold in her hand

the man is afraid of the woman's gift
is afraid to accept anything
especially an orange
for who knows it may contain
the woman's liver and heart
her thighs and her low breasts hanging
it may contain her children
with their night cries
and their noses running

the woman turns to her child
who has dirtied himself again
she strips him as usual
and washes him off in the creek
and the creek runs on
taking the child's dirt to the river
and the river carries it to the sea

the man settles himself in a treefork
with his back against a branch
for he's afraid to follow
the woman into the house

dark comes and the woman lights a lamp
he watches her shadow cross the window
he hears her laughing her child to sleep

## The Disc

over and over a woman is told that she's not what she seems to be
at first she fights this *I am* she says *what I seem to be*:  sand, twigs,
stones, and waves of disturbed air through which a bird has just
flown, also light refracted from the lid of a syrup tin  the disc of light
wobbles on the floor and ceiling

she begins to have second thoughts  perhaps after all she is not what
she seems:  a laurel hedge, a butterfly flagging on the beach, a scale
from the wing of that butterfly, a rhubarb bush, the oiled wheel of
a train

she could indeed be something not yet mentioned not yet named *for
always* she tells herself *before you have finished naming a thing the
meaning has changed*  no one can speak as fast as a thought darts
across the mind no one can speak faster than the sound of words

*I'm not what I seem to be* she confesses at last then a warm subservi-
ence floods through her and she becomes the fluent shadow of any
names we may choose to throw at her

## The Flight

at the beginning of winter an old woman lies dying in her poor
cottage at the end of a village in her extremity she is enlightened and
can clearly see not only all the details of the life she is now leaving
but every moment of every day of all the lives she has led since god
created her

the thing that impresses her most is the deathbed of the life immediately before this one   that time she was a man, one who had a great name for himself in this world

the famous man lies in a large polished brass bed surrounded by his sorrowing family and admirers   his fine soft hands pick at the coverlet which is fashioned of many squares of rich velvet embroidered in featherstitching and edged with a heavy fringe of yellow silk   his handsome grizzled beard fans out on the quilt and the sidewhiskers which frame his large florid face are spread carefully over the lace-edged pillow   his favourite niece, the one who is expecting to inherit his considerable fortune, has just finished brushing them with his ebony-backed silver-initialled hairbrushes

as the old woman watches her former self she sees him lift his hand and bless his family and friends with a noble gesture   a bell tinkles and the servant who has been kneeling modestly beside the great mahogany commode gets quietly to his feet and opens the door

in sweeps the cardinal attended by three young acolytes: one to carry the holy oils: one to swing the smoking censer: one to ring the little bell and carry in his other hand the tall lighted candle that will be extinguished when the famous man is declared dead by the family doctor   the cardinal in his most splendid vestments bears the holy viaticum which the dying man is to receive in preparation for his entry into the next world

the old woman lies on her hard pallet feasting her inner eye on this glorious scene   how different it is from her present death   this time just two old cronies have come to bid her goodbye she can hear them now in the kitchen enjoying a sad cup of tea and rifling the biscuitbox   in the plain little bedroom the fire has gone out for lack of coal and the poor woman cannot tell whether the cold she feels creeping up from her feet is the chill of death or simply the november frost penetrating the thin walls of the house

the village doctor is at the door *to do what I can for the poor creature* she hears him whisper to one of the old biddies on the other side of the partition     when the older of the two gossips ushers him into the bedroom the dying woman waves him away *I haven't so much as a penny in the house to pay you with doctor so be off and take your nasty potions with you* after a few laboured breaths she adds more gently *but please be good enough if you are passing the rectory to ask the priest to call*

this long speech so exhausts her that she falls back senseless on the hard grey pillow and the two cronies begin to mutter the prayers for the dead they are just about to pull the threadbare blanket over her face when the doctor who has been listening with his ear to her chest pronounces her still alive

perhaps the young priest can be forgiven for dawdling a little on receiving the old woman's message     he has ministered to this village for three years already and has officiated at seven christenings and two weddings but has never yet been called upon to administer the last rites of the church indeed he has never known death to visit this place where rosy children grow up into rudely healthy men and women where old pensioners sit outside their cottages on sunny days knitting and chatting until their century is past

excitement is in the air as the priest walks solemnly through the village clothed in a clumsy countrymade surplice and carrying the blessed sacrament veiled with a scrap of homespun     men doff their caps women fall to their knees on the chilly stones murmuring almost forgotten prayers the young man is enjoying the drama of the occasion and does not hurry it is only afterwards that he realizes that not one of his parishioners has asked who the dying person might be

at last he comes to the end of the village and enters the old woman's cottage     he is barely in time has hardly dipped his finger into the holy oil when the soul leaves the body and flies up into the rafters where it roosts on a crossbeam above the narrow bed     it gazes down upon the dead old woman whose white hair sticks out all around her head like a crown of thorns as soon as the priest has left the two friends wash the withered old body and clothe it in a worn linen shift which is the only suitable garment they can find in the house then they rummage in all the cupboards and drawers looking for *a few little things to remember her by* the elder hides the teacaddy and a framed holy picture under her ample skirts while the younger finds two spoons and a tin locket in the shape of a heart these she tucks away in her reticule and carries home

now it is time for the soul too to leave the house it flutters desperately in the eaves and around the door lintel for in all the excitement no one has remembered to open the window for it to escape and fly back to its creator    it is forced to remain in the house for several days strutting about on the cold floor and roosting in the rafters

at last the carpenter and his son come bringing the rough pine coffin which is to be the old woman's last bed and the imprisoned soul is able to escape through the open door

but it does not fly away immediately it rests for a little while on the topmost twigs of the tall elm which grows behind the cottage from there it can see the whole village with its neat rows of whitewashed houses every one with a well kept backyard from which the winter's supply of carrots and potatoes have recently been dug   at the bottom of each garden is a small bonfire for the villagers are a tidy lot and do not care to see fallen leaves scuttering about the street and the village pump all winter

today there is no wind    from each little fire a thin twist of smoke rises straight upward towards the frosty sky

## The Arrangement

she's arranging irises in a polished brass vase as elegant and narrow-shouldered as herself *made from a bombcase* she explains to the tall blue flags stiff as april that will not obey her arthritic fingers *1916* she adds softening the effect with a spray of ferny leaves

bombs falling on london all around the town whistling down from silvery zeppelins which nose about in the sky huge docile fish swimming in the upper air

she stalks naked through the dark rooms watching her reflection flicker in grey mirrors soft thin body, pale legs, wiry red hair resting uneasily on white shoulders and freckled arms    she peers closer examines the small uneven face the emphatic mouth the smallpox scar between the foxy brows

this is the first time she has ever been alone in the forest-hill house where she was born

if ever she was born for there's no record of any such birth of any such person as herself, none    she found that out at her wedding five months ago *you are marrying nobody* and she rests her fingers lightly on the two stars on william's epaulette then leans forward and kisses him on the mouth she can feel that her warm lips shock him for he's younger and much shyer than she is    *bill my will* she whispers again to the dark house this lonely night *can you survive all this? can I?*

for she carries in her velvet belly a weight lighter than a burr a kernel from which a red-haired child may grow

now she's in the cool garden hugging her thin arms round her fine nakedness chalkwhite roses bloom in their beds their stems and thorns black as blood one open flower stares up at her with the pinched face of an infant about to cry

the earth shrieks    cracks apart    rumbles    shakes    shakes    and trembles to a stop

fish has laid his tumble of eggs among the pavements and the houses    the school crumples    the churchtower falls into the park the walls of the prison break open and men rush out thanking the fishgod for their deliverance almost at once they turn into muddy soldiers grumbling and joking about the war, the mud, wet feet, rats and the rotten bitter war

she lies flat in the roses covered with plaster dust from next door thorns clawing at her chin and her breasts the cocklebur little nut moves within her parts from its seedcase and drops from her to the earth followed by a narrow warm trickle

she scratches among the roses as a cat might then buries the tiny thing without a tear stands up dizzy lighter by the weight of a handful of leaves

in the house she draws the heavy curtain so close that not a chink parts them then lights a candle and flings herself onto the wide bed a small empty space aches within her, aches coldly through her sleep which lasts long into the next day

downstairs in the back kitchen where the window is broken and the door swings loose on its hinges the small debris of the city has been sifting into the house all night a layer of fine particles covers the sink and the green glass flower-holders    by morning the shelf and the vases that stand there—blue raku, enamelled chinoiserie, silver beaten thin as steam—are greyed with a layer of fine detritus which might be the dust of a century


## Summer 1928

almost asleep charles hears his mother say to her friend I don't care what you're wearing I don't care what you've been eating just come over here and sit down beside me at the piano   in bed the child is telling himself the story of everything that has happened   the man sitting beside his mother playing and singing *to althea from prison* which the boy interprets as the tale of the heart's refusal he falls into a dream of wisteria a bower outside a tavern in italy where anything grows claims his mother but here in this beastly climate it's hard to find a flowering creeper though there are climbing shrubs enough to cover any balcony with a thicket of tender leaves where linnets nest and sing

the boy sees himself in the attic fondling the trailing teagown his aunt is said to have put away forever when word came that her lover had been picked off by a sniper charles lifts it out of its squashed cardboard box and slips it over his head the chiffon is a turbid green like ditchwater for a moment the gown hangs silkily on his naked shoulders then with a whisper falls apart and floats to the floor each piece no bigger than an envelope he gathers them all up and folds them back into the blue tissue assuring himself that after a year the garment will heal and become whole and beautiful again he has only to be patient and wait the twelvemonth through

from downstairs the sound of the two voices the four hands trails away to silence the child makes himself think of those twenty fingers resting on the piano keys he would like to be another person a boy his own age but with different coloured eyes and hair lying on the bottom of the sea looking up through grey water at the metal hull of a ship passing overhead   in the first class ballroom two golden-haired women have just finished playing a duet on the piano the last trickle of sound dribbles out into the ocean   the strange boy puts out a languid hand and catches the music in the guise of undulating seaweed

*charles darling* his mother has said it more than once your uncle norman is the owner of an excellent baritone when she says *charles darling* he's always startled because that's how she speaks to his father the first charles who perhaps has returned and is standing behind him in his majesty's uniform the tropical one because he's just arrived from a redhot place where mangos grow on a tall tree a man in a turban shakes the tree and when the fruit falls he makes it into chutney which the officers eat from dishes like pink porcelain blossoms while the brown soldiers sit on blankets spread over the dead grass and are served nothing but hard round cakes of river-mud arranged in neat rows on old tin trays rusting a little at the rims it's afternoon and nurse is pinning a terry square on one of the twins who are the result she says candidly of his father's last leave or maybe that mr norman but no she laughs darkly he'd rather be godfather to many than father to one   he's not such a bad sort for doesn't he take the twins off our hands most afternoons and give us all a rest from their squalling

the man whom the boy hates picks up the babies one under each arm and dumps them into the perambulator   as he starts off it begins to rain pittering on the pramhoods but that doesn't bother uncle who strides away up the village singing his loudest nurse and charles watch him go until they can't hear the singing and crying any more then she goes upstairs to tidy and he picks up the book he's decided to read about fighter aircraft not that he cares much for it but it makes him feel more like some of the boys he goes to school with

norman is back the babies are asleep in their soft white shawls smelling of their mother's sandlewood soap she's in a silly mood and comes giggling out of the drawing room inviting the man to stay as though he was a stranger she was meeting for the first time it's tea and cake in the summerhouse charles is not included he has his in the kitchen with nurse

when he turns his head and looks through the kitchen window he can see the creepers growing up the side of the summerhouse where rain is still dripping from the eaves a large drop is hanging from the lip of one of the greenish cobea blossoms he can't make up his mind whether it will trickle down the striped purple throat of the flower or whether is will fall outwards onto the leaves which are withering and turning pink with autumn

a storm comes at night and charles gets up trembling wanting to creep into bed with nurse who is not afraid of anything he knows her back turned towards him in sleep will smell reassuringly of buttered bread on the turn of the stair he sees his mother with uncle norman their hands are clasped tightly but she is holding the man away from her by the length of her white freckled arms   thunder breaks the air then hush a very faint word comes from between her lips what's she saying what's she saying?

the next streak of lightning lifts her hair which stands up all around her head like a brilliant fox-fur halo   little white tongues of flame flash from the curled ends of her red hair

uncle norman whimpers and lets go and she sinks down onto the stairs moaning or crying or laughing it's difficult to tell which charles decides she is laughing and goes back to bed to dream of italy where the three of them stayed in a room above a courtyard *so long* father says buckling on his sam browne looking into his son's eyes for a long time

then he picks up his cap and swaggerstick from the chair by the brass bed where his wife is lying with the quilt pulled up over her face refusing to look refusing to say goodbye

## Shrapnel

shrapnel has torn the man's ribs apart
there is a shabby wound in his breast
his mouth opens innocently upon a cry

he wants to curse his enemies but cannot
for he sees them as striplings lying in the grass
each with a girl beneath him
the long grass full of clover and fieldherbs
waves gently in the heat
the men get up from the women
and buckle on their belts
the women just lie there looking up at the thundery sky
*we are wounded with joy* they tell each other
*we are happy happy happy*

the soldier sees this he hears all this

as he lies there asking the earth
*is this my final place my own place*
he glances upwards to where
the tops of the trees almost meet
there is just a small patch of empty sky showing
it must be spring for a bird with a straw in its beak
swoops down to a low bough   he tries to think
of the name of the bird
he tries to think of his own name
the name of his son who has learned to speak already
so his wife writes   he has seen the child only once
and that was more than a year ago

he tries to remember the colour of his wife's eyes
he sees only her frailty those little narrow birdbones
beneath the soft flesh
he wishes she was another woman
one easier to abandon   one calm and robust
with a wide smooth brow

but who could forget that pitiful teat
in the child's mouth
the curious maze of the blue milkveins whose pattern
he traces in the dirt   his hand touches a broken brick
here was a house   now he remembers the collapse
of its walls

he licks his lips tasting for brickdust
he counts his strong teeth with his tongue
they are all there unchipped   he hears the bland
voice of the dentist telling him he has perfect bite

he shuts his eyes against the light but it shines on
through rosy lids which are the same colour exactly
as his wife's secret he wants to part her legs
and touch her glistening vermillion lining
now at last he understands
why he loves the bodies of women

more than the bodies of men   for pale skin covers
a man all over and only a wound can show his lining

carefully he passes his hands over his body
buttoned into its tunic of stiff drab wool
until he finds the hole in his chest
he thrusts in his fist to staunch the blood
a pulse beats close to his folded fingers
it is insistent and strong
it is pushing him away from himself

## Desire

desire is not like a wedding which rushes relentlessly towards us
from the other end of time   it comes unexpected as a cloud inviting
questions and implying answers   *can three lovers meet as two* we ask
can they walk out of a summer's morning and roll as all true lovers
must in the dewy wayside grass without one of them feeling
neglected, worse still pitied, by the other two   can four lovers meet
as three or must they remain always two pairs as isolated from each
other as we all are from the begetter of our uncertainties   and does
all this apply not only to lovers but to brothers and sisters both
secular and holy

*darling* we shall say to our child *you were born of our surprising ability
to couple and couple again without weariness without a thought for the
garden half-planted for the book half-read* certainly we shall never tell
her of our present condition what an effort it is to keep up an interest
for the sake of our tinpot relationship for the sake of our parenthood
for the sake of the future which while we lie here locked in each
other is rapidly crumbling into the past

# Robert Kroetsch

*Poem of Albert Johnson**

It is his silence    they cannot allow
offended into a blood reason    the hunters
surround his cabin    with their loud law

he will give no name    to hate or love
neither forgive nor blame    the righteous
fusillade    no word of hurt or mercy

no word    only his rivalling guns
confide his awareness    of their assault
confuse the hunters    into the bomb-blast

unhousing the harried trapper    bare
to the Arctic night    the brave running
by which he will become    poet of survival

to our suburban pain    the silent man
circling back    to watch them coming
giving new tracks    to the blizzard-white trail

leaving the faint sleigh dogs    scent
of their lost game    (police and Indians
together at last    punished by dark

and wind    neglect the weather
of their intent)    he will give no name
only the cold camp    where he almost slept

*The so-called 'Mad Trapper of Rat River' was hunted to death by a small army
of men in the Northwest Territories and the Yukon in the winter of 1932.

letting gunshot   into his best pursuer
his self's shadow   dressed in red authority
and after the quick exchanging   unspeakably dead

and gone beyond all living   the silent man
made the impossible crossing   the snowshoe pattern
over the closed pass   into the caribou herd

that gave him a gap   out of the closing frame
the trap   forged by the roaring bush plane
out of six weeks' hunting   the silent man

having leapt their ring   walked back
and baited their pride   with his spent body
bought them the cry they sought   and only kept

his silence   (we stand at his grave in Aklavik
mosquitoes swarming at our heads   like the posse
that slammed him   out of his last loading)

the poet of our survival   his hands and feet
frozen   no name on his dead mouth
no words betraying   either love or hate


## Elegy for Wong Toy

Charlie   you are dead now
but I dare to speak because
in China the living speak
to their kindred   dead.
And you are one of my fathers:

Your iron bachelorhood perplexed
our horny youth:   we were born
to the snow of a prairie town
to the empty streets of our

longing.     You built a railway
                              to get there.

You were your own enduring     winter.
You were your abacus, your Chinaman's
eyes.  You were the long reach up
to the top of that bright showcase
where    for a few pennies
we bought a whole childhood.

Only a Christmas calendar
told us your name:
Wong Toy, prop., Canada Cafe:
above the thin pad of months,
under the almost naked girl
in the white leather boots
who was never allowed to undress
in the rows of God-filled houses

which you were never
invited to enter.

Charlie, I knew my first touch
of Ellen Kiefer's young breasts
in the second booth from the back
                              in your cafe.
It was the night of a hockey game.
You were out in the kitchen
making sandwiches and coffee.

You were your own enduring
winter.    You were our spring
and we    like meadowlarks
hearing the sun    boom
under the flat horizon
cracked the still dawn alive
with one ferocious    song.

So Charlie    this is a thank you

poem.  You are twenty years
dead.  I hope they buried you
sitting upright in your grave
the way you sat    pot-bellied
behind your jawbreakers
and your licorice plugs,
behind your tins of Ogden's fine cut,
your treasury of cigars,

and the heart-shaped box of chocolates
that no one ever took home.


## Meditation on Tom Thomson

Tom Thomson I love you    therefore I apologize
for what I must say    but I must say
damn your jack pines    they are beautiful

I love your bent trees    and I love your ice
in spring    candled into its green rot
and I love the way you drowned    all alone

with your canoe    and our not even knowing
the time of day    and the grave mystery
of your genius    interrupted    is *our* story

and art, man, art    is the essential
luxury    the imperative QUESTION(?)
the re-sounding say    of the night's loon

and holy shit mother    the muskeg snatch
of the old north    the bait that caught
the fishing father    into his own feast

the swimming art-man    who did not drown
in the lake    in his pictures

who drowned    for murder or grief or

the weave of the water    would not hold
the shoulders of the sky    were deep
the maelstrom would not spin    to spit him

free, daddy, FREE FREE FREE    (but I must say
DAMN your jack pines)    for the whorl
of the whirlpool breaks us    one by one

we stretch and tear    the joints
opening like curtains    on a cool
Algonquin morning    onto a red sun

or down onto the black bottom    or far
(the grammar of our days    is ill defined)
or rapt in the root and fire    of that wind

bent forest    (about your pine trees
this evening    one of them moved
across my wall)    daring the light

daring the bright and lover's leap    across
the impassible gap    the uncertain
principle of time and space    straight down

he dove    and he would seize unearthly
shades    and he would seize the drowned land
the picture from the pool    the pool's picture

and the gods cried    Tom, Tom, you asshole
let go    and you had found their secret
and would not ever    let go    they cry

## Seed Catalogue

1

No. 176—*Copenhagen Market Cabbage:* ' This *new introduction,
strictly speaking,* is in every respect a *thoroughbred,* a *cabbage* of
*highest pedigree,* and is *creating considerable flurry* among *profes-
sional gardeners* all *over the world.'*

We took the storm windows/off
the south side of the house
and put them on the hotbed.
Then it was spring. Or, no:
then winter was ending.

> 'I wish to say we had lovely success
> this summer with the seed purchased
> of you. We had the finest Sweet
> Corn in the country, and Cabbage
> were dandy.'
> —W.W. Lyon, South Junction, Man.

> My mother said:
> Did you wash your ears?
> You could grow cabbages
> in those ears.

Winter was ending.
This is what happened:
we were harrowing the garden.
You've got to understand this:
I was sitting on the horse.
The horse was standing still.
I fell off.

> The hired man laughed: how
> in hell did you manage to
> fall off a horse that was
> *standing still?*

Bring me the radish seeds,
my mother whispered.

Into the dark of January
the seed catalogue bloomed

a winter proposition, if
spring should come, then,

with illustrations:

No. 25—*McKenzie's Improved Golden Wax Bean:* 'THE MOST
PRIZED OF ALL BEANS. *Virtue* is its own reward. We have had
*many expressions* from *keen discriminating gardeners extol-
ling our seed* and *this variety.'*

> Beans, beans,
> the musical fruit;
> the more you eat,
> the more you virtue.

My mother was marking the first row
with a piece of binder twine, stretched
between two pegs.

The hired man laughed: just
about planted the little bugger.
Cover him up and see what grows.
My father didn't laugh. He was puzzled
by any garden that was smaller than a
quarter-section of wheat and summerfallow.

the home place: N.E. 17-42-16-W4th Meridian.

the home place: one and a half miles west of Heisler, Alberta,

on the correction line road
and three miles south

No trees
around the house.
Only the wind.
Only the January snow.
Only the summer sun.
The home place:
a terrible symmetry.

*How do you grow a gardener?*

> Telephone Peas
> Garden Gem Carrots
> Early Snowcap Cauliflower
> Perfection Globe Onions
> Hubbard Squash
> Early Ohio Potatoes

This is what happened—at my mother's wake. This
is a fact—the World Series was in progress. The
Cincinnati Reds were playing the Detroit Tigers.
It was raining. The road to the graveyard was barely
passable. The horse was standing still. Bring me
the radish seeds, my mother whispered.


2

My father was mad at the badger: the badger was digging holes
in the potato patch, threatening man and beast with broken limbs
(I quote). My father took the double-barrelled shotgun out into
the potato patch and waited.

Every time the badger stood up, it looked like a little man, come
out of the ground. Why, my father asked himself—Why would
so fine a fellow live under the ground? Just for the cool of roots?
The solace of dark tunnels? The blood of gophers?

My father couldn't shoot the badger. He uncocked the shotgun, came back to the house in time for breakfast. The badger dug another hole. My father got mad again. They carried on like that all summer.

> *Love is an amplification*
> *by doing/over and over.*
>
> *Love is a standing up*
> *to the loaded gun.*
>
> *Love is a burrowing.*

One morning my father actually shot at the badger. He killed a magpie that was pecking away at a horse turd about fifty feet beyond and to the right of the spot where the badger had been standing.

A week later my father told the story again. In that version he intended to hit the magpie. Magpies, he explained, are a nuisance. They eat robins' eggs. They're harder to kill than snakes, jumping around the way they do, nothing but feathers.

Just call me sure-shot,
my father added.

3

No. 1248—*Hubbard Squash:* 'As *mankind* seems to have a *particular fondness* for squash, *Nature* appears to have *especially* provided this *matchless* variety of *superlative flavor.'*

> *Love is a leaping up*
> *and down.*
>
> *Love*
> *is a beak in the warm flesh.*

'As a cooker, it heads the list for warted squash. The

vines are of strong running growth; the fruits are large,
olive shaped, of a deep rich green color, the rind is
smooth ...'

*But how do you grow a lover?*

This is the God's own truth:
playing dirty is a mortal sin
the priest told us, you'll go to hell
and burn forever (with illustrations)—

it was our second day of catechism
—Germaine and I went home that
afternoon    if it's that bad, we
said to each other    we realized
we better quit    we realized

let's do it just one last time
and quit.

This is the God's own truth:
catechism, they called it,
the boys had to sit in the pews
on the right, the girls on the left.
Souls were like underwear that you
wore inside.  If boys and girls sat
together—

*Adam and Eve got caught
playing dirty.*

This is the truth.
We climbed up into a granary
full of wheat    to the gunny sacks
the binder twine was shipped in—

we spread the paper from the sacks
smooth sheets    on the soft wheat

Germaine and I    we were like/one

we had discovered, don't ask me
how, where—but when the priest said
*playing dirty* we knew—well—

he had named it    he had named
our world    out of existence
(the horse    was standing still)

— This is my first confession.  Bless me father I played
    dirty so long, just the other day, up in the granary
    there by the car shed—up there on the Brantford Binder
    Twine gunny sacks and the sheets of paper—Germaine
    with her dress up and her bloomers down—

— Son.  For penance, keep your peter in your pants
    for the next thirteen years.

*But how—*

        Adam and Eve and Pinch-Me
        went down to the river to swim—
        Adam and Eve got drownded.

*But how do you grow a lover?*

        We decided we could do it
        just one last time.

4

It arrived in winter, the seed catalogue, on a January
day.  It came into town on the afternoon train.

Mary Hauck, when she came west from Bruce County, Ontario,
arrived in town on a January day.  She brought along
her hope chest.

She was cooking in the Heisler Hotel. The Heisler Hotel
burned down on the night of June 21, 1919. Everything
in between: lost. Everything: an absence

of satin sheets
of embroidered pillow cases
of tea towels and English china
of silver serving spoons.

*How do you grow a prairie town?*

>The gopher was the model.
>Stand up straight:
>telephone poles
>grain elevators
>church steeples.
>Vanish, suddenly: the
>gopher was the model.

*How do you grow a past/*
to live in

the absence of silkworms
the absence of clay and wattles (whatever the hell
                    they are)
the absence of Lord Nelson
the absence of kings and queens
the absence of a bottle opener, and me with a vicious
                    attack of the 26-ounce flu
the absence of both Sartre and Heidegger
the absence of pyramids
the absence of lions
the absence of lutes, violas and xylophones
the absence of a condom dispenser in the Lethbridge Hotel and
                    me about to screw an old Blood whore. I was
                    in love.
the absence of the Parthenon, not to mention the Cathédrale de
                    Chartres

the absence of psychiatrists
the absence of sailing ships
the absence of books, journals, daily newspapers and everything
          else but the *Free Press Prairie Farmer* and *The*
          *Western Producer*
the absence of gallows (with apologies to Louis Riel)
the absence of goldsmiths
the absence of the girl who said that if the Edmonton Eskimos
          won the Grey Cup she'd let me kiss her
          nipples in the foyer of the Palliser Hotel. I
          don't know where she got to.
the absence of Heraclitus
the absence of the Seine, the Rhine, the Danube, the Tiber and
          the Thames. Shit, the Battle River ran dry
          one fall. The Strauss boy could piss across it.
          He could piss higher on a barn wall than any
          of us. He could piss right clean across the
          principal's new car.
the absence of ballet and opera
the absence of Aeneas

*How do you grow a prairie town?*

Rebuild the hotel when it burns down. Bigger. Fill it
full of a lot of A-1 Hard Northern Bullshitters.

— You ever hear the one about the woman who buried
  her husband with his ass sticking out of the ground
  so that every time she happened to walk by she could
  give it a swift kick?

— Yeh, I heard it.

5

I planted some melons, just to see what would
happen. Gophers ate everything.

                  I applied to the Government.

I wanted to become a postman,
to deliver real words
to real people.

There was no one to receive
my application.

I don't give a damn if I do die do die do die do die do die
do die do die do die do die do die do die do die do die do
die do die do die do die do die do die do die do die do die
do

6

No. 339—*McKenzie's Pedigreed Early Snowcap Cauliflower:* 'Of
the many *varieties* of *vegetables* in *existence, Cauliflower* is
*unquestionably* one of the *greatest inheritances* of the *present generation, particularly* Western Canadians. There is *no place* in the
*world* where *better cauliflowers* can be *grown* than right here in the
West. The *finest specimens* we have *ever seen,* larger and of *better
quality,* are *annually grown* here on our *prairies. Being particularly*
a *high altitude plant* it *thrives* to a *point* of *perfection* here, *seldom
seen* in *warmer climes.'*

*But how do you grow a poet?*

Start: with an invocation
invoke—

His muse is
his muse/if
memory is

and you have
no memory then
no meditation
no song (shit
we're up against it)

how about that girl
you felt up in the
school barn or that
girl you necked with
out by Hastings' slough
and ran out of gas with
and nearly froze to
death with/ or that
girl in the skating
rink shack who had on
so much underwear you
didn't have enough
prick to get past her/
CCM skates

Once upon a time in the village of Heisler—

— Hey, wait a minute.
That's a story.

*How do you grow a poet?*

For appetite: cod-liver
oil.
For bronchitis: mustard
plasters.
For pallor and failure to fill
the woodbox: sulphur
& molasses.
For self-abuse: ten Our
Fathers & ten Hail Marys.
For regular bowels: Sunny Boy
Cereal.

*How do you grow a poet?*

'It's a pleasure to advise that I
won the First Prize at the Calgary

Horticultural Show... This is my
first attempt.  I used your seeds.'

Son, this is a crowbar.
This is a willow fencepost.
This is a sledge.
This is a roll of barbed wire.
This is a bag of staples.
This is a claw hammer.

We give form to this land by running
a series of posts and three strands
of barbed wire around a quarter-section.

First off I want you to take that
crowbar and drive 1,156 holes
in that gumbo.
And the next time you want to
write a poem
we'll start the haying.

*How do you grow a poet?*

This is a prairie road.
This road is the shortest distance
between nowhere and nowhere.
This road is a poem.

Just two miles up the road
you'll find a porcupine
dead in the ditch.  It was
trying to cross the road.

As for the poet himself
we can find no record
of his having traversed
the land/in either direction

no trace of his coming
or going/only a scarred
page, a spoor of wording
a reduction to mere black

and white/a pile of rabbit
turds that tells us
all spring long
where the track was

poet ... say uncle.

*How?*

Rudy Wiebe: 'You must lay great black steel lines of
fiction, break up that space with huge design and, like
the fiction of the Russian steppes, build a giant
artifact.  No song can do that ...'

February 14, 1976.  Rudy, you
took us there:  to the Oldman River
Lorna & Byrna, Ralph & Steve and me
you showed us where
the Bloods surprised the Crees
in the next coulee/surprised
them to death.  And after
you showed us Rilke's word
*Lebensgliedes.*

Rudy:  Nature thou art.

7

*Brome Grass (Bromus Inermis):* 'No amount of cold will kill it.  It
*withstands* the summer suns.  Water may stand on it for several
weeks without apparent injury.  The roots push through the soil,
throwing up new plants continually.  It *starts quicker* than other
grasses in the spring.  *Remains green* longer in the fall.  *Flourishes*
*under absolute neglect.'*

The end of winter:
seeding/time.

*How do you grow*
*a poet?*

(a)

I was drinking with Al Purdy. We went round and round
in the restaurant on top of the Chateau Lacombe. We
were the turning center in the still world, the winter
of Edmonton was hardly enough to cool our out-sights.

The waitress asked us to leave. She was rather insistent;
we were bad for business, shouting poems at the paying
customers. Twice, Purdy galloped a Cariboo horse
right straight through the dining area.

Now that's what I call
a piss-up.

                              'No song can do that.'

(b)

No. 2362—*Imperialis Morn-*
*ing Glory:* 'This is the wonderful *Japanese Morning*
*Glory,* celebrated the world
over for its *wondrous beauty*
of both flowers and foliage.'

Sunday, January 12, 1975. This evening after
rereading *The Double Hook:* looking at Japanese prints.
Not at actors. Not at courtesans. Rather: Hiroshige's
series, *Fifty-Three Stations on the Tokaido.*

From the *Tokaido* series: 'Shono-Haku-u.' The
bare-assed travellers, caught in a sudden shower.
Men and trees, bending. How it is in a rain shower/
that you didn't see coming. And couldn't have avoided/
even if you had.

> The double hook:
> the home place.

> The stations of the way:
> the other garden

> *Flourishes.*
> *Under absolute neglect.*

(c)

Jim Bacque said (I was waiting for a plane,
after a reading; Terminal 2, Toronto)—he said,
You've got to deliver the pain to some woman,
don't you.

— Hey, Lady.
    You at the end of the bar.
    I wanna tell you something.

— Yuh?

— Peter Knight—of Crossfield,
    Alberta. Bronc-Busting Champion
    of the World. You ever hear of
    Pete Knight, the King of All
    Cowboys, Bronc-Busting Champion
    of the World?

— Huh-uh.

— You know what I mean? King

of *All* Cowboys . . . Got
killed—by a horse.
He fell off.

—You some kind of a nut
or something?

8

> We silence words
> by writing them down.

THIS IS THE LAST WILL AND TESTAMENT
OF ME, HENRY L. KROETSCH:

(a) [yes, his first bequest]

*To my son Frederick my carpenter tools.*

It was his first bequest.  First,
a man must build.

Those horse-barns around Heisler—
those perfectly designed barns
with the rounded roofs—only Freddie
knew how to build them.  He mapped
the parklands with perfect horse-barns.

> I remember my Uncle Freddie.
> (The farmers no longer
> use horses.)
>
> Back in the 30s, I remember
> he didn't have enough money
> to buy a pound of coffee.
>
> Every morning at breakfast
> he drank a cup of hot water

with cream and sugar in it.

Why, I asked him one morning—
I wasn't all that old—why
do you do that? I asked him.

Jesus Christ, he said. He was
a gentle man, really. Don't you
understand *anything?*

9

*The danger of merely living.*

a shell/exploding
in the black sky: a
strange planting

a bomb/exploding
in the earth: a
strange

man/falling
on the city.
Killed him dead.

It was a strange
planting.

the absence of my cousin who was shot down while bombing
the city that was his maternal great-grandmother's
birthplace. He was the navigator. He guided himself
to that fatal occasion:

> — a city he had
>   forgotten
> — a woman he had
>   forgotten

He intended merely to release a cargo of bombs on a
target and depart.  The exploding shell was:

a) an intrusion on a design that was not his, or

b) an occurrence which he had in fact, unintentionally,
   himself designed, or

c) it is essential that we understand this matter
   because:

He was the first descendant of that family to return
to the Old Country.  He took with him: a cargo of bombs.

> Anna Weller:  *Geboren* Cologne, 1849.
> Kenneth MacDonald:  Died Cologne, 1943.

> A terrible symmetry.

A strange muse: forgetfulness.  Feeding her far children
to ancestral guns, blasting them out of the sky, smack/
into the earth.  Oh, she was the mothering sort.  Blood/
on her green thumb.

### 10

After the bomb/blossoms  
After the city/falls  
After the rider/falls  
(the horse  
standing still)

*Poet, teach us*  
*to love our dying.*

*West is a winter place.*  
*The palimpsest of prairie*

*under the quick erasure*  
*of snow, invites a flight.*

*How/do you grow a garden?*

(a)

> No. 3060—*Spencer Sweet Pea:*
> Pkt. $.10; oz. $.25;
> $\frac{1}{4}$ lb. $.75; $\frac{1}{2}$ lb. $1.25

Your sweet peas
climbing the staked
chicken wire,
climbing the stretched
binder twine by
the front porch

taught me the smell
of morning, the grace
of your tired
hands, the strength
of a noon sun, the
colour of prairie grass

taught me the smell
of my sweating armpits.

(b)

*How do you a garden grow?*
*How do you grow a garden?*

'Dear Sir,
        The longest brome grass I remember seeing was
one night in Brooks. We were on our way up to the Calgary
Stampede, and reached Brooks about 11 pm, perhaps earlier
because there was still a movie on the drive-in screen.
We unloaded Cindy, and I remember tying her up to the truck
box and the brome grass was up to her hips. We laid down
in the back of the truck—on some grass I pulled by hand—
and slept for about three hours, then drove into Calgary.

Amie'

(c)

No trees
around the house,
only the wind.
Only the January snow.
Only the summer sun.

*Adam and Eve got drownded—*
*Who was left?*

# Phyllis Webb

## Marvell's Garden

Marvell's garden, that place of solitude,
is not where I'd choose to live
yet is the fixed sundial
that turns me round
unwillingly
in a hot glade
as closer, closer I come to contradiction,
to the shade green within the green shade.

The garden where Marvell scorned love's solicitude—
that dream—and played instead an arcane solitaire,
shuffling his thoughts like shadowy chance
across the shrubs of ecstasy,
and cast the myths away to flowering hours
as yes, his mind, that sea, caught at green
thoughts shadowing a green infinity.

And yet Marvell's garden was not Plato's
garden—and yet—he *did* care more for the form
of things than for the thing itself—
ideas and visions,
resemblances and echoes,
things seeming and being
not quite what they were.

That was his garden, a kind of attitude
struck out of an earth too carefully attended,
wanting to be left alone.
And I don't blame him for that.
God knows, too many fences fence us out

and his garden closed in on Paradise.

On Paradise! When I think of his hymning
Puritans in the Bermudas, the bright oranges
lighting up that night! When I recall
his rustling tinsel hopes
beneath the cold decree of steel,
Oh, I have wept for some new convulsion
to tear together this world and his.

But then I saw his luminous plumèd Wings
prepared for flight,
and then I heard him singing glory
in a green tree,
and then I caught the vest he'd laid aside
all blest with fire.

And I have gone walking slowly in
his garden of necessity
leaving brothers, lovers, Christ
outside my walls
where they have wept without
and I within.


## Breaking

Give us wholeness, for we are broken.
But who are we asking, and why do we ask?
Destructive element heaves close to home,
our years of work broken against a breakwater.

Shattered gods, self-iconoclasts,
it is with Lazarus unattended we belong
(the fall of the sparrow is unbroken song).
The crucifix has clattered to the ground,
the living Christ has spent a year in Paris,

travelled on the Métro, fallen in the Seine.
We would not raise our silly gods again.
Stigmata sting, they suddenly appear
on every blessed person everywhere.
If there is agitation there is cause.

Ophelia, Hamlet, Othello, Lear,
Kit Smart, William Blake, John Clare,
Van Gogh, Henry IV of Pirandello,
Gerard de Nerval, Antonin Artaud
bear a crown of darkness.
It is better so.

Responsible now each to his own attack,
we are bequeathed their ethos and our death.
Greek marble white and whiter grows
breaking into history of a west.
If we could stand so virtuously white
crumbling in the terrible Grecian light.

There is a justice in destruction.
It isn't 'isn't fair'.
A madhouse is designed for the insane,
a hospital for wounds that will re-open;
a war is architecture for aggression,
and Christ's stigmata body-minted token.
What are we whole or beautiful or good for
but to be absolutely broken?

## Making

Quilted
patches, unlike the smooth slick loveliness
of the bought,
this made-ness out of self-madness

thrown across their bones to keep them warm.
It does.

Making
under the patches a smooth silk loveliness
of parts;
two bodies are better than one for this quilting,
throwing into the dark a this-ness that was not.
It does.

Fragments
of the splintered irrelevance of doubt, sharp
hopes, spear and splice into a nice consistency as once
under the pen, the brush, the sculptor's hand
music was made, arises now, blossom on fruit-tree bough.
It does.

Exercise
exegesis of the will captures and lays
haloes around bright ankles of a saint.
Exemplary under the tree,
Buddha glows out now
making the intolerable, accidental sky
patch up its fugitive ecstasies.
It does.

It does,
and, all doing done, a child on the street runs
dirty from sun
to the warm infant born to soiled sheets
and stares at the patched external face.
It does.

From the making made and, made, now making
certain order—thus excellent despair
is laid, and in the room the patches of the quilt
seize light and throw it back upon the air.
A grace is made, a loveliness is caught

quilting a quiet blossom as a work.
It does.

And do you,
doubting, fractured, and untaught, St. John of the Cross,
come down and patch the particles and throw
across the mild unblessedness of day
lectures to the untranscended soul.
Then lotus-like, you'll move upon the pond,
the one-in-many, the many-in-the-one,
making a numbered floral-essenced sun
resting upon the greening padded frond,
a patched, matched protection for Because.
And for our dubious value it will do.
It always does.


## Love Story

It was easy to see what he was up to,
the grey, bundled ape,
as he sidled half-playfully
up to the baby
and with a sly look behind
put his hands onto the crib
and leapt in.

The child's pink, beginning face
stared up as the hair-handed monkey
explored the flesh, so soft, of our infant race.
The belly spread like plush to the monkey's haunch,
he settled, heavy and gay, his nuzzling
mouth at the baby's neck.

But, no answer accurate to a smile,
he bit, tasted time, maddened,
and his nails rooted sudden fire in the ribs of Adam,

towered, carnivorous, for aim
and baby face, ears, arms
were torn and taken in his ravaging.

And so the killing, too-late parents came,
hysteric, after their child's
futile pulse had stopped its beating.
Only the half-pathetic, half-triumphant
monkey peered out from the crib,
bobbed nervously on the dead infant's belly,
then stopped, suddenly paralyzed on that soft tomb.

Was it the donkey Death brayed out at him
from the human mother's eyes,
or did his love for her in that pause
consume him?

The jealous ape's death was swift
and of natural cause. 'Died of shame,'
some said, others, 'of shock.'
But his death was Othello's death,
as great, as picayune,
he died of envy, lacking the knack of wisdom.


## Sitting

The degree of nothingness
is important:
to sit emptily
in the sun
receiving fire
that is the way
to mend
an extraordinary world,
sitting perfectly
still

and only
remotely human.


## A Tall Tale

The whale, improbable as lust,
carved out a cave
for the seagirl's rest;
with rest the seagirl, sweet as dust, devised
a manner for the whale
to lie between her thighs.
Like this they lay
within the shadowed cave
under the waters, under the waters wise,
and nested there, and nested there and stayed,
this coldest whale aslant the seagirl's thighs.

Two hundred years perhaps swam by them there
before the cunning waters so distilled the pair
they turned to brutal artifacts of stone
polished, O petrified prisoners of their lair.
And thus, with quiet, submerged in deathly calm,
the two disclosed a future geologic long,
lying cold, whale to thigh revealed
the secret of their comfort
to the marine weeds,
to fish, to shell, sand, sediment and wave,
to the broken, dying sun
which probed their ocean grave.
These, whale and seagirl, stone gods,
stone lust, stone grief,
interred on the sedimented sand
amongst the orange starfish,
these cold and stony mariners
invoked the moral snail
and in sepulchral voice intoned a moral tale:

'Under the waters, under the waters wise,
all loving flesh will quickly meet demise,
the cave, the shadow cave is nowhere wholly safe
and even the oddest couple can scarcely find relief:
appear then to submit to this tide and timing sea,
but secrete a skilful shell and stone and perfect be.'

## To Friends
## Who Have Also
## Considered Suicide

It's still a good idea.
Its exercise is discipline:
to remember to cross the street without looking,
to remember not to jump when the cars side-swipe,
to remember not to bother to have clothes cleaned,
to remember not to eat or want to eat,
to consider the numerous methods of killing oneself,
that is surely the finest exercise of the imagination:
death by drowning, sleeping pills, slashed wrists,
kitchen fumes, bullets through the brain or through
the stomach, hanging by the neck in attic or basement,
a clean frozen death—the ways are endless.
And consider the drama! It's better than a whole season
at Stratford when you think of the emotion of your
family on hearing the news and when you imagine
how embarrassed some will be when the body is found.
One could furnish a whole chorus in a Greek play
with expletives and feel sneaky and omniscient
at the same time. But there's no shame
in this concept of suicide.
It has concerned our best philosophers
and inspired some of the most popular
of our politicians and financiers.
Some people swim lakes, others climb flagpoles,

some join monasteries, but we, my friends,
who have considered suicide take our daily walk
with death and are not lonely.
In the end it brings more honesty and care
than all the democratic parliaments of tricks.
It is the 'sickness unto death'; it is death;
it is not death; it is the sand from the beaches
of a hundred civilizations, the sand in the teeth
of death and barnacles our singing tongue:
and this is 'life' and we owe at least this much
contemplation to our western fact: to Rise,
Decline, Fall, to futility and larks,
to the bright crustaceans of the oversky.

## Occasions of Desire

Occasions of desire with their attendant envies,
the white heat of the cold swan dying,
create their gestures, obscene or most beautiful.
Oh, the clear shell of a swan's fluted wings!

And as the old swan calls clarity from dark waters,
sailing triumphant into the forgotten,
desire in its moving is that rapacious cry,
gorgeous as the torrent Lethe, and as wise.

And if the curl of cygnets on the Avon,
so freshly broken from their perfect shells,
take from a dying bird not moral or enticement,
but float with their own white mother, that is just.
Oh, imperious innocence to envy
only the water bearing such beauty!

## Poetics Against
## the Angel
## of Death

I am sorry to speak of death again
(some say I'll have a long life)
but last night Wordsworth's 'Prelude'
suddenly made sense—I mean the measure,
the elevated tone, the attitude
of private Man speaking to public men.
Last night I thought I would not wake again
but now with this June morning I run ragged to elude
The Great Iambic Pentameter
who is the Hound of Heaven in our stress
because I want to die
writing Haiku
or, better,
long lines, clean and syllabic as knotted bamboo. Yes!


## Rilke

Rilke, I speak your name I throw it away
with your angels, your angels, your statues
and virgins, and a horse in a field held
at the hoof by wood. I cannot take so much
tenderness, tenderness, snow falling like lace
over your eyes year after year as the poems
receded, roses, the roses, sinking in snow
in the distant mountains.

Go away with your women to Russia or take them
to France, and take them or don't the poet is
in you, the spirit, they love that.
(I met one in Paris, her death leaning outward,
death in all forms. The letters you'd sent her,

she said, stolen from a taxi.)

Rilke.
Clowns and angels held your compassion.
You could sit in a room saying nothing,
nothing. Your admirers thought you were there,
a presence, a wisdom. But you had to leave
everyone once, once at least. That was your
hardness.

This page is a shadowed hall in Duino Castle.
Echoes. The echoes.
I don't know why I'm here.


*For Fyodor*

I am a beetle in the cabbage soup they serve up for geniuses
in the House of the Dead.

I am a black beetle and loll seductively at the bottom of the
warm slop.

Someday, Fyodor, by mistake you'll swallow me down and I'll
become a part of your valuable gutworks.

In the next incarnation I hope to imitate that idiot and saint
Prince Myshkin, drop off my wings for his moronic glory.

Or, if I miss out on the Prince, Sonya or Dunya might do.

I'm not joking. I am not the result of bad sanitation in the
kitchen, as you think.

Up here in Omsk in Siberia beetles are not accidents but desti-
nies.

I'm drowning fast but even in this condition I realize your bad tempered haughtiness is part of your strategy.

You are about to turn this freezing hell into an ecstatic emblem.
A ferocious shrine.

Ah, what delicious revenge. But take care! A fit is coming!
Now, now, I'll leap into your foaming mouth and jump
your tongue.
Now I stamp on this not quite famous tongue

shouting: Remember Fyodor, you may hate men but it's here in
Omsk you came to love mankind.

But you don't hear, do you: there you are writhing in epileptic
visions.

Hold your tongue! You can't speak yet. You are mine, Dos-
toevsky.

I aim to slip down your gullet and improve myself.
I can almost hear what you'll say:

> Crime and Punishment
> Suffering and Grace

and of the dying

> Pass by and forgive
> us our happiness

## Eschatology of Spring

Death, Judgement, Heaven, Hell,
and Spring. The Five Last Things,
the least of which I am, being in
the azaleas and dog-toothed violets

of the South of Canada.  Do not tell me
this is a cold country.  I am also in
the camelias and camas of early, of
abrupt birth.
We are shooting up for the bloody
judgement of the six o'clock news.
Quick, cut us out from the deadlines
of rotting newspapers, quick, for the
tiny skeletons and bulbs will tell you
how death grows and grows in Chile and
Chad.  Quick, for the small bones pinch
me and insects divulge occult excrement
in the service of my hyacinth, my trailing
begonia.  And if you catch me resting
beside the stream, sighing against
the headlines of this pastoral, take
up your gun, the flowers blossoming
from its barrel, and join this grief, this
grief:  that there are lambs, elegant black-
footed lambs in this island's eschatology,
Beloved.

## Prison Report

The eye of Jacobo Timerman looks through the hole and sees
another eye looking through a hole.

These holes are cut into steel doors in prison cells in Argentina.

Both eyes are wary.
They disappear.

Timerman rests his cheek on the icy door,
amazed at the sense of space he feels—the joy.

He looks again:  the other's eye is there,

then vanishes like a spider.

Comes back, goes, comes back.

This is a game of hide-and-seek.
This is intelligence with a sense of humour.
Timerman joins the game.

Sometimes two eyes meet at exactly the same moment.

This is music. This is love
playing in the middle of a dark night
in a prison in Argentina.

My name is Jacobo one eye says.
Other eye says something, but Jacobo can't quite catch it.

Now a nose appears in the vision-field
of Timerman. It rubs cold edges of the hole,
a love-rub for Jacobo.

This is a kiss, he decides, a caress,
an emanation of solitude's tenderness.

In this prison everything is powered electrically
for efficiency and pain. But tenderness is also
a light and a shock.

An eye, a nose, a cheek resting against a steel door
in the middle of the dark night.
These are parts of bodies, parts of speech,
saying,
I am with you.

## Treblinka Gas Chamber

*'Klostermayer ordered another count of the children.*
*Then their stars were snipped off and thrown into*
*the center of the courtyard. It looked like a field of*
*buttercups.'*
—A Field of Buttercups *by Joseph Hymans*

fallingstars
        'a field of
                buttercups'

          yellow stars
              of David
                  falling

the prisoners
        the children
           falling

       in heaps
          on one another
              they go down

Thanatos
      showers
         his dirty breath
            they must breathe
                him in

       they see stars
          behind their
              eyes

David's
     'a field of
        buttercups'

> a metaphor
>> where all that's
>>> left lies down

## Leaning

I am half-way up the stairs
of the Leaning Tower of Pisa.

Don't go down.  You are in this
with me too.

I am leaning out of the Leaning
Tower heading into the middle distance

where a fur-blue star contracts, becomes
the ice-pond Brueghel's figures are skating on.

North Magnetic pulls me like a flower
out of the perpendicular

angles me into outer space
an inch at a time, the slouch

of the ground, do you hear that?
the hiccup of the sludge about the stone.

(Rodin in Paris, his amanuensis, a torso . . .)
I must change my life or crunch

over in vertigo, hands
bloodying the inside tower walls

lichen and dirt under the fingernails
Parsifal vocalizing in the crazy night

my sick head on the table where I write
slumped one degree from the horizontal

the whole culture leaning . . .

the phalloi of Miës, Columbus returning
stars all shot out—

And now this. Smelly tourists
shuffling around my ears

climbing into the curvature.
They have paid good lira to get in here.

So have I. So did Einstein and Bohr.
Why should we ever come down, ever?

And you, are you still here

tilting in this stranded ark
blind and seeing in the dark.

# D.G. Jones

*Portrait of Anne Hébert*

The sunlight, here and there,
Touches a table

And a draught at the window
Announces your presence,

You take your place in the room
Without fuss,

Your delicate bones,
Your frock,
Have the grace of disinterested passion.

Words are arrayed
Like surgical instruments
Neatly in trays.

Deftly, you make an incision
Probing
The obscure disease.

Your sensibility
Has the sure fingers of the blind:

Each decision
Cuts like a scalpel
Through tangled emotion.

You define
The morbid tissue, laying it bare

Like a tatter of lace
Dark
On the paper.


## Beautiful Creatures Brief as These

For Jay Macpherson

Like butterflies but lately come
From long cocoons of summer
These little girls start back to school
To swarm the sidewalks, playing-fields,
And litter air with colour.

So slight they look within their clothes,
Their dresses looser than the Sulphur's wings,
It seems that even if the wind alone
Were not to break them in the lofty trees,
They could not bear the weight of *things*.

And yet they cry into the morning air
And hang from railings upside down
And laugh, as though the world were theirs
And all its buildings, trees, and stones
Were toys, were gifts of a benignant sun.


## For Françoise Adnet

It is that time of day, time
To chop the beans, to peel
Potatoes for the evening meal.

The fullness of time
Grows, at this hour,

Like the shadows on the crockery.

Mademoiselle's mauve gloves,
Alone, tell of the afternoon, the dried
Flowers, the delicate hands among the stalks.

For once things are what they are,
Until my little girl
Comes in from outdoors, the melting snow

Cool in her nostrils,
Sky, blue without clouds,
Behind her eyes.

But even these dissolve.
Fingering an orange
She lets her bare legs dangle.

Time is space, it glows
Like the white tablecloth,
The breadboard where I slice the onions.

The kitchen floats in my tears—
And the sun
In its brazier of urban trees.


## These Trees Are No Forest of Mourners

They had dragged for hours.
The weather was like his body,
Cold, though May. It rained.

It had rained for three days—
In the grass, in the new leaves,
In the black boughs against the sky.

The earth oozed,
Like the bottom of the lake—
Like a swamp. They stared

At the drowned grass, at the leaves
That dripped in the water—aware
Of their own death, heavy

As the black boughs of the spruce
Moving in a current under the grey
Surface of the sky—aware

Of a supreme ugliness, which seemed
In its very indifference,
Somehow, to defy them:

The sodden body of the world
And of their only son.

Let them be. Oh hear me,

Though it cannot help you. They exist
Beyond your grief; they have their own
Quiet reality.


## Summer Is a Poem by Ovid

For Michael Ondaatje

The fire falls, the night
Grows more profound.
The music is composed
Of clear chords
And silence. We become
Clear and simple as the forms
Of music; we are dumb

As water
Mirroring the stars.

Then summer is
Ovidian, and every sun
Is but a moth evolving
In the large gloom,
An excerpt from
*Ars Amoris*: flame
Is no more fleeting than the limbs
Of boy and girl: the conflagration
Is the same.

While the fire falls, and night
Grows more profound, the flesh,
The music and the flame
All undergo
Metamorphosis. The sounds
Of music make a close,
So with our several selves,
Together, until silence shall compose
All but the ashes in the pale dawn
And even those.

## *I Thought There Were Limits*

I thought there were limits, Newtonian
Laws of emotion—

I thought there were limits to this falling away,
This emptiness. I was wrong.

The apples, falling, never hit the ground.

So much for grass, and animals—
Nothing remains,

No sure foundation on the rock. The cat

Drifts, or simply dissolves.

*L'homme moyen sensuel*
Had better look out: complete
Deprivation brings

Dreams, hallucinations which reveal
The sound and fury of machines
Working on nothing—which explains

God's creation: *ex nihilo fecit.*

Wrong again. I now suspect
The limit is the sea itself,
The limitless.

So, neither swim nor float. Relax.
The void is not so bleak.

Conclude: desire is but an ache,
An absence. It creates
A dream of limits

And it grows in gravity as that takes shape.


## The Stream Exposed With All Its Stones

The stream exposed with all its stones
Flung on a raw field
Is covered, once again,

With snow.

It is not hidden. It

Still flows.

The houses in the valley, standing
Motionless below,
Seem wrapped in sunlight like a snow

And are deceptive. Even stones
Deceive us.

The creator goes
Rampaging through our lives: winter
Is a masquerade.

I tell you
Nakedness is a disguise: the white
Is dark below.

This silence is the water's cry.

I tell you in those silent houses girls
Are dancing like the stones.


## Words From the Aviary

For Monique

I would clothe you in feathers

You are too bare
in your long bones when the wind
sighs in the snow

You are a movement of birds

I would clothe you in voices
appellations, words

spare as the mirror of a young girl

or raw, and deliquescent as the crow's
cawing over chill fields

It is not a clothing but a call

of voices, nameless
gone into the still air

of the small birds that drift
above a river running among stones
in the Haute-Savoie

above the grasses of the steppe, and in the small
trees of the taiga

in the summer forest
north
along the Ottawa

I would surround you with a guard
of heron like a tall
smoke, I would surround you with a choir
of unrecorded waterbirds, exiguous
emerging from a wall

beyond the Nile

I would have you smile, and see the sun
arrested, rest among your bones

as glistening

you move within the garden of your names, diaphanous
innumerable

You walk as you have always walked
through desert yards, the cold

spaces where the night

sighs among the stars

the sunken orchard where the wind
sighs in the snow

You are an overture. You come

like a migration
like the first waters of the world
with their entelechy of flowers

And then your naked summer
silences my words


## Kate, These Flowers . . .
## (The Lampman Poems)

I

You picked the dead bloom
expertly, leaving one star
lifting, long-stemmed, above cascading
leaves
      my day's star

Oh, Archie, you're a fool, she said

What colours are the vireo?
Deep garden lights, the reflected lights of
apple leaves
      my dear
your shadowed flesh

like grave eyes in the afternoon
it is, under all pain, silent

laughter
      bird, flower
you, Kate, briefly on a day in June

II

Kisses are knowledge, Kate
aphasia confounds us with a new
tongue
        too Pentecostal, too
Eleusinian, perhaps, for us
moderate Anglicans

You blush and the immoderate blood
riots like a rose
            we are both
exposed
      I who hate Sundays

dream how I will boldly
rush out and overnight paint
Ottawa crimson
         I come
secretly to the fold, would find
election in your mouth

III

Wild carrot, daisy, buttercup
I scatter words in the air
like your bouquet
            petal, sepal, leaf
delicate explosions

prestidigitations, Kate
rabbits from hats, from atoms
instant nebulae

        thus fields
mimic your grace, thus words

rearticulate the trace
of outcast energy

             All day the wind
sun took tresses, ribbons, dress
Etna's vale remembered less
stripped of its flowering text

IV

Wet places, where flowers
anchor the sky,  where rain
troubles no one
           I
escape there in heavy weather
roving your veins, Kate
haptic, the hero as bare
youth adrift in the reeds

a bird sways in the swaying
cat-tails
          muted, the sun
is a wet flame
               in the hyaline
night I recognize
Thale's world
             anchored among
hyacinth, and moist curls

V

Puritan or paradox? this land
arctic, temperate
              white
like your small breasts, yet
explosive to the sun

slim margins underwrite the flowers
nudging through snow
ours too

           our kind of spare
wordless joy

                  this country where
desire becomes restraint
refractory, silence
our orator
           and thus apparent

paradox
           until the petalled flesh
speak as to the deaf and blind

VI

Guard yourself, Kate, like the wild
orchid, with neglect, with worse
loneliness
           what can escape
destructiveness, man's damage
emu, dodo, wild pigeon
numerous herds and flocks

secret places of themselves invite
lovers, and new violence
                       flowers
in deep woods, beside
pools, moist rocky soil
petals twisted like brown hair

even I could not resist
ransacking the rare, delicate purse

VII

Masts in the misty fields
udders moving among grassheads
lagging wind

        we cared
little for Arcadia, its
elementary joys, its excrement
its vulgar weeds
              we wished
noetic clouds, a marble frieze

stomach, Kate, we lacked
the stomach to be real
animals
          a carnal music among
lambs, oxen lowing or
kids prancing, the hairy
stalks glaucous among kine

VIII

This is the place, thornbush
humped grass, granite
empty except for the wind
inane except for the incessant
movement of birds, clouds, yellowing
moss, the leaves
              a random
outcrop, overcast
                  ?who
reads this landscape, windswept
thistle, aster, ghostly
everlasting
          this is the true
locus of your grey eyes
leaving us lonely, stone, flesh
each more nakedly alive

IX

Truth, Kate, all your virtues
harrow my flesh, are flesh
etching my mind
              as lately

wind was a hawk moving
aslant the land, was the sloped
transient sky, was pine
elegiac by the stream
                        the water
revealing our thirst
                        as lately
crouched among stones, curls and stray
ribbons of your shift
eddying round you, you seemed
simplicity itself
                        while the clear
spring rippled with cress


X

Gone, love's body, like a field
reclaimed by winter
all its flowers, exhausted
sick of passion, flesh itself
surrendered to the uniform
Euclidian space: blank wall
shut door, blind discreetly drawn

illusory propriety: beneath the surface
nothing is dissolved

stones in the wet weather
nudge through snow, and the black
orphaned boughs, and grass
whispering of the humpy world

XI

Loneliness becomes us, we
advance through separations, learning
to love cold skies, empty
even to the last high
hail and farewell of birds

arrowing south
                wilderness
waste flelds become us

thistles matted with their own seed
haggard thorn trees
originals
              ourselves, or mere
reticulations of the wind
nameless
              bright precipitates of our desire
scattered in grass

XII

Perverse, this trellis, this peignoir
of flowers
              Kate, this is your
invention, your insouciance
slipping naked into the cold
dismantled garden, leaving
evidence of spring
                  green sheath
stems and tendrils, butterflies
exhaling scent, the violet, the rose
nuances of remembered flesh

treacherous images, this is the real
excrement of summer
                  let the wind
undress us, frost
restore our pristine nakedness

XIII

Milkweed unpacks itself
riddling the wind with packaged
roots, parachutes, poems
ordnance for a spring offensive

Winter, then, and wars

                      and memory
lays cut flowers in
empty carpels
             absurd
yet from absurdity our love
fits out an underground
resistance

        Who foresaw?
increasing violence accompanies
technique, the empty self

heaven is a mortalflower

# Alden Nowlan

## Beginning

From that they found most lovely, most abhorred,
my parents made me: I was born like sound
stroked from the fiddle to become the ward
of tunes played on the bear-trap and the hound.

Not one, but seven entrances they gave
each to the other, and he laid her down
the way the sun comes out. Oh, they were brave,
and then like looters in a burning town.

Their mouths left bruises, starting with the kiss
and ending with the proverb, where they stayed;
never in making was there brighter bliss,
followed by darker shame. Thus I was made.


## Warren Pryor

When every pencil meant a sacrifice
his parents boarded him at school in town,
slaving to free him from the stony fields,
the meagre acreage that bore them down.

They blushed with pride when, at his graduation,
they watched him picking up the slender scroll,
his passport from the years of brutal toil
and lonely patience in a barren hole.

When he went in the Bank their cups ran over.

They marvelled how he wore a milk-white shirt
work days and jeans on Sundays. He was saved
from their thistle-strewn farm and its red dirt.

And he said nothing. Hard and serious
like a young bear inside his teller's cage,
his axe-hewn hands upon the paper bills
aching with empty strength and throttled rage.

## God Sour the Milk of the Knacking Wench

God sour the milk of the knacking wench
with razor and twine she comes
to stanchion our blond and bucking bull,
pluck out his lovely plumbs.

God shiver the prunes on her bark of chest,
who capons the prancing young.
Let maggots befoul her alive in bed,
and dibble thorns in her tongue.

## For Nicholas of All the Russias

Wind in a rocky country and the harvest
meagre, the sparrows eaten, all the cattle
gone with the ragged troopers, winter coming,
mother will starve for love of you and wrapping
newest and least accustomed leave him squalling
out in the hills beside the skulls of foxes,
it cold and snow in the air. Stranger, knocking,
(now in this latter time even the poor
have bread and sleep on straw) what silly rumour
tells me your eyes are yellow and your lips

once rose trout-quick to suck a she-wolf's teats?

Our Lord, his peaked heir and hawk-faced daughters
are gone, although they say one severed finger
was found after the soldiers cleaned the cellar.

## I, Icarus

There was a time when I could fly. I swear it.
Perhaps, if I think hard for a moment, I can even tell you
    the year.
My room was on the ground floor at the rear of the house.
My bed faced a window.
Night after night I lay on my bed and willed myself to fly.
It was hard work, I can tell you.
Sometimes I lay perfectly still for an hour before I felt
    my body rising from the bed.
I rose slowly, slowly until I floated three or four feet
    above the floor.
Then, with a kind of swimming motion, I propelled myself
    toward the window.
Outside, I rose higher and higher, above the pasture fence,
    above the clothesline, above the dark, haunted trees
    beyond the pasture.
And, all the time, I heard the music of flutes.
It seemed the wind made this music.
And sometimes there were voices singing.

## And He Wept Aloud,
## So That the Egyptians Heard It

In my grandfather's house
for the first time in years,

houseflies big as bumblebees
playing crazy football
in the skim-milk-coloured windows,

leap-frogging from
the cracked butter saucer
to our tin plates of
rainbow trout and potatoes, catching the bread
on its way to our mouths,
    mounting one another
    on the rough deal table.

It was not so much their filth
as their numbers and persistence and—
oh, admit this, man, there's no point in poetry
if you withhold the truth
once you've come by it—
    their symbolism:
    Baal-Zebub,
god of the poor and outcast,

that enraged me, made me snatch the old man's
*Family Herald*, attack them like a maniac,
lay to left and right until the window sills
over-flowed with their smashed corpses,
until bits of their wings
stuck to my fingers,
until the room buzzed with their terror . . .

And my grandfather, bewildered and afraid,
came to help me:
    'never seen a year
    when the flies were so thick'
as though he'd seen them at all before I came!

His voice so old and baffled and pitiful
that I threw my club into the wood box and sat down
    and wanted to beg his forgiveness

as we ate on in silence broken only
by the almost inaudible humming
of the flies rebuilding their world.

## Britain Street

*Saint John, New Brunswick*

This is a street at war.
The smallest children
battle with clubs
till the blood comes,
shout 'fuck you!'
like a rallying cry—

while mothers shriek
from doorsteps and windows
as though the very names
of their young were curses:

'Brian! Marlene!
Damn you! God damn you!'

or waddle into the street
to beat their own with switches:
'I'll teach you, Brian!
I'll teach you, God damn you!'

On this street,
even the dogs
would rather fight
than eat.

I have lived here nine months
and in all that time
have never once heard
a gentle word spoken.

I like to tell myself
that is only because
gentle words are whispered
and harsh words shouted.


## In Those Old Wars

In those old wars
where generals wore yellow ringlets
and sucked lemons at their prayers,
other things being equal
the lost causes were the best.

Lee rode out of history
on his gray horse, Traveller,
so perfect a hero
had he not existed
it would have been necessary to invent him—
war stinks without gallantry.

An aide, one of the few who survived,
told him,
Country be damned, general,
for six months these men
have had no country but you.
They fought barefoot
and drank blueberryleaf tea.

The politicians
strung up Grant
like a carrot,
made him a Merovingian.
They stole everything,
even the coppers from Lincoln's dead eyes.

In those days, the vanquished
surrendered their swords like gentlemen,
the victors alone
surrendered their illusions.
The easiest thing to do for a Cause
is to die for it.

## July 15

The wind is cool. Nothing is happening.
I do not strive for meaning. When I lie on my back
the wind passes over me, I do not feel it.
The sun has hands
like a woman, calling the heat
out of my body.
The trees sing. Nothing is happening.

When I close my eyes,
I hear the soft footsteps
of the grass. Nothing is happening.

How long have I lain here?
Well, it is still summer. But is it the same
summer I came?
I must remember
not to ask myself questions.
I am naked. Trees sing. The grass walks.
Nothing is happening.

## The Mysterious Naked Man

A mysterious naked man has been reported
on Cranston Avenue. The police are performing
the usual ceremonies with coloured lights and sirens.

Almost everyone is outdoors and strangers are conversing
     excitedly
as they do during disasters when their involvement is
     peripheral.
'What did he look like?' the lieutenant is asking.
'I don't know,' says the witness. 'He was naked.'
There is talk of dogs—this is no ordinary case
of indecent exposure, the man has been seen
a dozen times since the milkman spotted him and now
the sky is turning purple and voices
carry a long way and the children
have gone a little crazy as they often do at dusk
and cars are arriving
from other sections of the city.
And the mysterious naked man
is kneeling behind a garbage can or lying on his belly
in somebody's garden
or maybe even hiding in the branches of a tree,
where the wind from the harbour
whips at his naked body,
and by now he's probably done
whatever it was he wanted to do
and he wishes he could go to sleep
or die
or take to the air like Superman.


## Another Parting

Is this what it's like to be old?
To have endured so many partings
that this time I scarcely feel
the throat's tensing for the blow,
the sick pendulum in the belly,

feel only my pain
flowing into

an all-encompassing sadness

like the sound of that high plane,
full of people I don't know,
people I can hardly imagine,

breaking the silence
of this dark room
where I lie sleepless.


## For Claudine Because I Love Her

Love is also
my finding this house
emptier than a stranger
ever could.

Is it the sound of your movements
enlivening the chairs
although I hear nothing, is it the weight
of your small body moving the house
so little no machine
could ever assess it,
though my mind knows,
is it some old
wholly animal instinct
that fills every room with you,
gently, so I am aware of it only

when I come home
and there is nothing here.

## Ypres: 1915

The age of trumpets is passed, the banners hang
like dead crows, tattered and black,
rotting into nothingness on cathedral walls.
In the crypt of St Paul's I had all the wrong thoughts,
wondered if there was anything left of Nelson
or Wellington, and even wished
I could pry open their tombs and look,
then was ashamed
of such morbid childishness, and almost afraid.

I know the picture is as much a forgery
as the Protocols of Zion, yet it outdistances
more plausible fictions: newsreels, regimental histories,
biographies of Earl Haig.
                            It is always morning
and the sky somehow manages to be red
though the picture is in black and white.
There is a long road over flat country,
shell holes, the debris of houses,
a gun carriage overturned in a field,
the bodies of men and horses,
but only a few of them and those
always neat and distant.
                            The Moors are running
down the right side of the road.
The Moors are running
in their baggy pants and Santa Claus caps.
The Moors are running.
                            And their officers,
Frenchmen who remember
Alsace and Lorraine,
are running backwards in front of them,
waving their swords, trying to drive them back,
weeping
        at the dishonour of it all.
The Moors are running.

And on the left side of the same road,
the Canadians are marching
in the opposite direction.

The Canadians are marching
in English uniforms behind
a piper playing 'Scotland the Brave'.

The Canadians are marching
in impeccable formation,
every man in step.

The Canadians are marching.

And I know this belongs
with Lord Kitchener's mustache
and old movies in which the Kaiser and his general staff
seem to run like the Keystone Cops.

That old man on television last night,
a farmer or fisherman by the sound of him,
revisiting Vimy Ridge, and they asked him
what it was like, and he said,
There was water up to our middles, yes
and there was rats, and yes
there was water up to our middles
and rats, all right enough,
and to tell you the truth
after the first three or four days
I started to get a little disgusted.
Oh, I know they were mercenaries
in a war that hardly concerned us.
I know all that.

Sometimes I'm not even sure that I have a country.

But I know they stood there at Ypres

the first time the Germans used gas,
that they were almost the only troops
in that section of the front
who did not break and run,
who held the line.

Perhaps they were too scared to run.
Perhaps they didn't know any better
—that is possible, they were so innocent,
those farmboys and mechanics, you have only to look
at old pictures and see how they smiled.
Perhaps they were too shy
to walk out on anybody, even Death.
Perhaps their only motivation
was a stubborn disinclination.

Private MacNally thinking:
You squareheaded sons of bitches,
you want this God damn trench
you're going to have to take it away
from Billy MacNally
of the South End of Saint John, New Brunswick.

And that's ridiculous, too, and nothing
on which to found a country.
                              Still
It makes me feel good, knowing
that in some obscure, conclusive way
they were connected with me
and me with them.

## The First Stirring of the Beasts

The first stirring of the beasts
is heard at two or three or four
in the morning, depending on the season.

You lie, warm and drowsy, listening,
wondering how there is so much difference
between the sounds
cattle and horses make,
moving in their stanchions or halters,
so much difference that you can't explain,
so that if someone asked you
*which of them is moving now?*
you couldn't answer
but lying there, not quite awake,
you know, although it doesn't matter,
and then a rooster crows
and it sounds, or maybe you imagine this,
unsure and a little afraid,

                            and after a little
there are only the sounds of night
that we call silence.

The second stirring of the beasts
is the one everybody understands.
You hear it at dawn
and if you belong here
you get up.
Anyway, there is no mystery
in it, it is the other stirring,
the first brief restlessness
which seems to come for no reason
that makes you ask yourself
*what are they awake for?*

## The Middle-Aged Man in the Supermarket

I'm pretending to test the avocadoes for ripeness
while gaping obliquely at the bare brown legs
of the girl in the orange skirt selecting mushrooms

when she says, 'Hi, there, let's make love.'
At first I think that she must have caught me
and is being sarcastic and then I decide
she's joking with someone she knows, perhaps the boy
       weighing green beans
or the young man with the watercress, so I try to act
as if I hadn't heard her, walk away at what I hope
is the right speed, without looking back,
and don't stop until I come to
the frozen-food bins, where I'm still standing,
gazing down at things I almost never buy, when
       I become aware
she's near me again, although I see only
a few square inches of brown thigh, a bit of
       orange cloth
and two symmetrical bare feet. I wish I could know
her body so well I could ever afterwards identify her
by taste alone. I rattle a carton
of frozen peas, read both French and English
       directions
on a package of frozen bread dough. She still
       stands there.
I wait for her to say to me:
'I fell in love the moment I saw you.
I want us to spend our first week together
in bed. We'll have our meals sent up. I'm even
       prettier
when I'm bare and I promise I'll keep my eyes shut
while you're naked, so that you'll never worry
that I might be comparing your body with that
of a previous lover, none of whom was older
than twenty, although the truth is I like
fat hips and big bellies—it's a kink
       that I have:
my nipples harden when I envision
those mountainous moons of flesh above me.'

## The Broadcaster's Poem

I used to broadcast at night
alone in a radio station
but I was never good at it,
partly because my voice wasn't right
but mostly because my peculiar
metaphysical stupidity
made it impossible
for me to keep believing
there was somebody listening
when it seemed I was talking
only to myself in a room no bigger
than an ordinary bathroom.
I could believe it for a while
and then I'd get somewhat
the same feeling as when you
start to suspect you're the victim
of a practical joke.
          So one part of me
was afraid another part
might blurt out something
about myself so terrible
that even I had never until
that moment suspected it.
          This was like the fear
of bridges and other
high places: Will I take off my glasses
and throw them
into the water, although I'm
half-blind without them?
Will I sneak up behind
myself and push?
          Another thing:
as a reporter
I covered an accident in which a train
ran into a car, killing

three young men, one of whom
was beheaded. The bodies looked
boneless, as such bodies do.
More like mounds of rags.
And inside the wreckage
where nobody could get at it
the car radio
was still playing.
                 I thought about places
the disc jockey's voice goes
and the things that happen there
and of how impossible it would be for him
to continue if he really knew.

# Leonard Cohen

## Elegy

Do not look for him
In brittle mountain streams:
They are too cold for any god;
And do not examine the angry rivers
For shreds of his soft body
Or turn the shore stones for his blood;
But in the warm salt ocean
He is descending through cliffs
Of slow green water
And the hovering coloured fish
Kiss his snow-bruised body
And build their secret nests
In his fluttering winding-sheet.

## Story

She tells me a child built her house
one Spring afternoon,
but that the child was killed
crossing the street.

She says she read it in the newspaper,
that at the corner of this and this avenue
a child was run down by an automobile.

Of course I do not believe her.
She has built the house herself,
hung the oranges and coloured beads in the doorways,

crayoned flowers on the walls.
She has made the paper things for the wind,
collected crooked stones for their shadows in the sun,
fastened yellow and dark balloons to the ceiling.

Each time I visit her
she repeats the story of the child to me,
I never question her. It is important
to understand one's part in a legend.

I take my place
among the paper fish and make-believe clocks,
naming the flowers she has drawn,
smiling while she paints my head on large clay coins,
and making a sort of courtly love to her
when she contemplates her own traffic death.

## I Have Not Lingered in European Monasteries

I have not lingered in European monasteries
and discovered among the tall grasses tombs of knights
who fell as beautifully as their ballads tell;

I have not parted the grasses
or purposefully left them thatched.

I have not released my mind to wander and wait
in those great distances
between the snowy mountains and the fishermen,
like a moon,
or a shell beneath the moving water.

I have not held my breath
so that I might hear the breathing of God,
or tamed my heartbeat with an exercise,
or starved for visions.

Although I have watched him often
I have not become the heron,
leaving my body on the shore,
and I have not become the luminous trout,
leaving my body in the air.

I have not worshipped wounds and relics,
or combs of iron,
or bodies wrapped and burnt in scrolls.

I have not been unhappy for ten thousand years.
During the day I laugh and during the night I sleep.
My favourite cooks prepare my meals,
my body cleans and repairs itself,
and all my work goes well.


## You Have the Lovers

You have the lovers,
 they are nameless, their histories only for each other,
and you have the room, the bed and the windows.
Pretend it is a ritual.
Unfurl the bed, bury the lovers, blacken the windows,
let them live in that house for a generation or two.
No one dares disturb them.
Visitors in the corridor tip-toe past the long closed door,
they listen for sounds, for a moan, for a song:
nothing is heard, not even breathing.
You know they are not dead,
 you can feel the presence of their intense love.
Your children grow up, they leave you,
they have become soldiers and riders.
Your mate dies after a life of service.
Who knows you? Who remembers you?
But in your house a ritual is in progress:
it is not finished: it needs more people.

One day the door is opened to the lovers' chamber.
The room has become a dense garden,
full of colours, smells, sounds you have never known.
The bed is smooth as a wafer of sunlight,
in the midst of the garden it stands alone.
In the bed the lovers, slowly and deliberately and silently,
perform the act of love.
Their eyes are closed,
as tightly as if heavy coins of flesh lay on them.
Their lips are bruised with new and old bruises.
Her hair and his beard are hopelessly tangled.
When he puts his mouth against her shoulder
she is uncertain whether her shoulder
has given or received the kiss.
All her flesh is like a mouth.
He carries his fingers along her waist
and feels his own waist caressed.
She holds him closer and his own arms tighten around her.
She kisses the hand beside her mouth.
It is his hand or her hand, it hardly matters,
there are so many more kisses.
You stand beside the bed, weeping with happiness,
you carefully peel away the sheets
from the slow-moving bodies.
Your eyes are filled with tears, you barely make out the lovers.
As you undress you sing out, and your voice is magnificent
because now you believe it is the first human voice
heard in that room.
The garments you let fall grow into vines.
You climb into bed and recover the flesh.
You close your eyes and allow them to be sewn shut.
You create an embrace and fall into it.
There is only one moment of pain or doubt
as you wonder how many multitudes are lying beside your body,
but a mouth kisses and a hand soothes the moment away.

## As the Mist Leaves No Scar

As the mist leaves no scar
On the dark green hill,
So my body leaves no scar
On you, nor ever will.

When wind and hawk encounter,
What remains to keep?
So you and I encounter,
Then turn, then fall to sleep.

As many nights endure
Without a moon or star,
So will we endure
When one is gone and far.

## Now of Sleeping

Under her grandmother's patchwork quilt
a calico bird's-eye view
of crops and boundaries
naming dimly the districts of her body
sleeps my Annie like a perfect lady

Like ages of weightless snow
on tiny oceans filled with light
her eyelids enclose deeply
a shade tree of birthday candles
one for every morning
until the now of sleeping

The small banner of blood
kept and flown by Brother Wind
long after the pierced bird fell down
is like her red mouth

among the squalls of pillow

Bearers of evil fancy
of dark intention and corrupting fashion
who come to rend the quilt
plough the eye and ground the mouth
will contend with mighty Mother Goose
and Farmer Brown and all good stories
of invincible belief
which surround her sleep
like the golden weather of a halo

Well-wishers and her true lover
may stay to watch my Annie
sleeping like a perfect lady
under her grandmother's patchwork quilt
but they must promise to whisper
and to vanish by morning—
all but her one true lover.

## The Genius

For you
I will be a ghetto jew
and dance
and put white stockings
on my twisted limbs
and poison wells
across the town

For you
I will be an apostate jew
and tell the Spanish priest
of the blood vow
in the Talmud
and where the bones

of the child are hid

For you
I will be a banker jew
and bring to ruin
a proud old hunting king
and end his line

For you
I will be a Broadway jew
and cry in theatres
for my mother
and sell bargain goods
beneath the counter

For you
I will be a doctor jew
and search
in all the garbage cans
for foreskins
to sew back again

For you
I will be a Dachau jew
and lie down in lime
with twisted limbs
and bloated pain
no mind can understand


## Style

I don't believe the radio stations
of Russia and America
but I like the music and I like
the solemn European voices announcing jazz
I don't believe opium or money

though they're hard to get
and punished with long sentences
I don't believe love
in the midst of my slavery I
do not believe
I am a man sitting in a house
on a treeless Argolic island
I will forget the grass of my mother's lawn
I know I will
I will forget the old telephone number
Fitzroy seven eight two oh
I will forget my style
I will have no style
I hear a thousand miles of hungry static
and the old clear water eating rocks
I hear the bells of mules eating
I hear the flowers eating the night
under their folds
Now a rooster with a razor
plants the haemophilia gash across
the soft black sky
and now I know for certain

I will forget my style
Perhaps a mind will open in this world
perhaps a heart will catch rain
Nothing will heal and nothing will freeze
but perhaps a heart will catch rain
America will have no style
Russia will have no style
It is happening in the twenty-eighth year
of my attention
I don't know what will become
of the mules with their lady eyes
or the old clear water
or the giant rooster
The early morning greedy radio eats
the governments one by one the languages

the poppy fields one by one
Beyond the numbered band
a silence develops for every style
for the style I laboured on
an external silence like the space
between insects in a swarm
electric unremembering
and it is aimed at us
(I am sleepy and frightened)
it makes toward me brothers


*For E. J. P.*

I once believed a single line
        in a Chinese poem could change
                forever how blossoms fell
and that the moon itself climbed on
        the grief of concise weeping men
                to journey over cups of wine
I thought invasions were begun for crows
        to pick at a skeleton
                dynasties sown and spent
to serve the language of a fine lament
        I thought governors ended their lives
                as sweetly drunken monks
telling time by rain and candles
        instructed by an insect's pilgrimage
                across the page—all this
so one might send an exile's perfect letter
to an ancient home-town friend

I chose a lonely country
        broke from love
                scorned the fraternity of war
I polished my tongue against the pumice moon
        floated my soul in cherry wine

      a perfumed barge for Lords of Memory
to languish on to drink to whisper out
    their store of strength
        as if beyond the mist along the shore
their girls their power still obeyed
    like clocks wound for a thousand years
I waited until my tongue was sore

Brown petals wind like fire around my poems
    I aimed them at the stars but
        like rainbows they were bent
before they sawed the world in half
    Who can trace the canyoned paths
        cattle have carved out of time
wandering from meadowlands to feasts
    Layer after layer of autumn leaves
        are swept away
Something forgets us perfectly


## The Music Crept by Us

I would like to remind
the management
that the drinks are watered
and the hat-check girl
has syphilis
and the band is composed
of former SS monsters
However since it is
New Year's Eve
and I have lip cancer
I will place my
paper hat on my
concussion and dance

## *Two Went to Sleep*

Two went to sleep
almost every night
one dreamed of mud
one dreamed of Asia
visiting a zeppelin
visiting Nijinsky
Two went to sleep
one dreamed of ribs
one dreamed of senators
Two went to sleep
two travellers
The long marriage
in the dark
The sleep was old
the travellers were old
one dreamed of oranges
one dreamed of Carthage
Two friends asleep
years locked in travel
Good night my darling
as the dreams waved goodbye
one travelled lightly
one walked through water
visiting a chess game
visiting a booth
always returning
to wait out the day
One carried matches
one climbed a beehive
one sold an earphone
one shot a German
Two went to sleep
every sleep went together
wandering away
from an operating table
one dreamed of grass

one dreamed of spokes
one bargained nicely
one was a snowman
one counted medicine
one tasted pencils
one was a child
one was a traitor
visiting heavy industry
visiting the family
Two went to sleep
none could foretell
one went with baskets
one took a ledger
one night happy
one night in terror
Love could not bind them
Fear could not either
they went unconnected
they never knew where
always returning
to wait out the day
parting with kissing
parting with yawns
visiting Death till
they wore out their welcome
visiting Death till
the right disguise worked

*1964*

## God Is Alive

From *Beautiful Losers*

God is alive. Magic is afoot. God is alive. Magic is afoot. God is afoot. Magic is alive. Alive is afoot. Magic never died. God never sickened. Many poor men lied. Many sick men lied. Magic never weakened. Magic never hid. Magic always ruled. God is afoot. God never died. God was ruler though his funeral lengthened. Though his mourners thickened Magic never fled. Though his shrouds were hoisted the naked God did live. Though his words were twisted the naked Magic thrived. Though his death was published round and round the world the heart did not believe. Many hurt men wondered. Many struck men bled. Magic never faltered. Magic always led. Many stones were rolled but God Would not lie down. Many wild men lied. Many fat men listened. Though they offered stones Magic still was fed. Though they locked their coffers God was always served. Magic is afoot. God rules. Alive is afoot. Alive is in command. Many weak men hungered. Many strong men thrived. Though they boasted solitude God was at their side. Nor the dreamer in his cell, nor the captain on the hill. Magic is alive. Though his death was pardoned round and round the world the heart would not believe. Though laws were carved in marble they could not shelter men. Though altars built in parliaments they could not order men. Police arrested Magic and Magic went with them for Magic loves the hungry. But Magic would not tarry. It moves from arm to arm. It would not stay with them. Magic is afoot. It cannot come to harm. It rests in an empty palm. It spawns in an empty mind. But Magic is no instrument. Magic is the end. Many men drove Magic but Magic stayed behind. Many strong men lied. They only passed through Magic and out the other side. Many weak men lied. They came to God in secret and though they left him nourished they would not tell who healed. Though mountains danced before them they said that God was dead. Though his shrouds were hoisted the naked God did live. This I mean to whisper to my mind. This I mean to laugh with in my mind. This I mean my mind to serve till service is but Magic moving through the world, and mind itself is Magic coursing through the flesh, and flesh itself is Magic dancing on a clock, and time itself the Magic Length of God.

## How to Speak Poetry

Take the word butterfly. To use this word it is not necessary to make the voice weigh less than an ounce or equip it with small dusty wings. It is not necessary to invent a sunny day or a field of daffodils. It is not necessary to be in love, or to be in love with butterflies. The word butterfly is not a real butterfly. There is the word and there is the butterfly. If you confuse these two items people have the right to laugh at you. Do not make so much of the word. Are you trying to suggest that you love butterflies more perfectly than anyone else, or really understand their nature? The word butterfly is merely data. It is not an opportunity for you to hover, soar, befriend flowers, symbolize beauty and frailty, or in any way impersonate a butterfly. Do not act out words. Never act out words. Never try to leave the floor when you talk about flying. Never close your eyes and jerk your head to one side when you talk about death. Do not fix your burning eyes on me when you speak about love. If you want to impress me when you speak about love put your hand in your pocket or under your dress and play with yourself. If ambition and the hunger for applause have driven you to speak about love you should learn how to do it without disgracing yourself or the material.

What is the expression which the age demands? The age demands no expression whatever. We have seen photographs of bereaved Asian mothers. We are not interested in the agony of your fumbled organs. There is nothing you can show on your face that can match the horror of this time. Do not even try. You will only hold yourself up to the scorn of those who have felt things deeply. We have seen newsreels of humans in the extremities of pain and dislocation. Everyone knows you are eating well and are even being paid to stand up there. You are playing to people who have experienced a catastrophe. This should make you very quiet. Speak the words, convey the data, step aside. Everyone knows you are in pain. You cannot tell the audience everything you know about love in every line of love you speak. Step aside and they will know what you know because they know it already. You have nothing to teach them. You are not more beautiful than they are. You are not wiser. Do not shout at them. Do not force a dry entry. That is bad sex. If you show the lines of your genitals, then deliver what you promise. And remember that people do not really want an acrobat in bed. What is our need? To be close to the natural man, to be close to the natural woman. Do not pretend that you are a beloved singer with a vast loyal audience which has followed the ups and downs of your life to this very moment. The bombs, flame-throwers, and all the shit have destroyed more than just the trees and villages. They have also destroyed the stage. Did you think that your profession would escape the general destruction? There is no more stage. There are no more footlights. You are among the people. Then be modest. Speak the words, convey the data, step aside. Be by yourself. Be in your own room. Do not put yourself on.

This is an interior landscape. It is inside. It is private. Respect the privacy of the material. These pieces were written in silence. The courage of the play is to speak them. The discipline of the play is not to violate them. Let the audience feel your love of privacy even though there is no privacy. Be good whores. The poem is not a slogan. It cannot advertise you. It cannot promote your reputation for sensitivity. You are not a stud. You are not a killer lady. All this junk about the gangsters of love. You are students of discipline. Do not act out the words. The words die when you act them out, they wither, and we are left with nothing but your ambition.

Speak the words with the exact precision with which you would check out a laundry list. Do not become emotional about the lace blouse. Do not get a hard-on when you say panties. Do not get all shivery just because of the towel. The sheets should not provoke a dreamy expression about the eyes. There is no need to weep into the handkerchief. The socks are not there to remind you of strange and distant voyages. It is just your laundry. It is just your clothes. Don't peep through them. Just wear them.

The poem is nothing but information. It is the Constitution of the inner country. If you declaim it and blow it up with noble intentions then you are no better than the politicians whom you despise. You are just someone waving a flag and making the cheapest appeal to a kind of emotional patriotism. Think of the words as science, not as art. They are a report. You are speaking before a meeting of the Explorers' Club or the National Geographic Society. These people know all the risks of mountain climbing. They honour you by taking this for granted. If you rub their faces in it that is an insult to their hospitality. Tell them about the height of the mountain, the equipment you used, be specific about the surfaces and the time it took to scale it. Do not work the audience for gasps and sighs. If you are worthy of gasps and sighs it will not be from your appreciation of the event, but from theirs. It will be in the statistics and not the trembling of the voice or the cutting of the air with your hands. It will be in the data and the quiet organization of your presence.

Avoid the flourish. Do not be afraid to be weak. Do not be ashamed to be tired. You look good when you're tired. You look like you could go on forever. Now come into my arms. You are the image of my beauty.

## From *Book of Mercy*

### NUMBER 24

In the thin light of hunted pleasure, I become afraid that I will never know my sorrow. I call on you with a cry that concentrates the heart. When will I cry out in gratitude? When will I sing to your mercy? Tomorrow is yours, the past is in debt, and death runs toward me with the soiled white flag of surrender. O draw me out of an easy skill into the art of the holy. I am afraid of what I have done to my soul, and the judgement is established like a sudden noise. O help me bow down to your anger. I lie beside the corpse of my idol, in the spell of fire and ashes, my word for the day of atonement forgotten. Lift me up with a new heart, with an old memory, for my father's sake, for the sake of your name which rings in heaven and hell, through worlds destroyed and worlds to come, tangible music shining between the hidden and the perceived, garbled in my ear and clearly the place I stand on, O precious name of truth uncontradicting. The scornful man will bend his knee, and holy souls will be drawn down into his house. Hedges will be planted in the rotting world, the young shoots protected. Time will be measured from mother to child, from father to son, and learning will speak to learning. Even the evil are weary, the bomb falls on the pilot's son, the riot shouts out to be calmed. The wound widens every heart, the general exile thickens, the whole world becomes the memory of your absence. How long will you hunt us with sorrow? How long will they rage, the fires of refinement? Blood drinking blood, wound swallowing wound, sorrow torturing sorrow, cruelty rehearsing itself under the measureless night of your patience. When will the work of truth begin, to verify your promise? Now that all men hear each other, let your name be established in hell, and count us back to the safety of your law, father of mercy, bride of the captured earth. Speak to your child of his healing, in this place where we are for a moment.

# George Bowering

*Grandfather*

Grandfather
           Jabez Harry Bowering
strode across the Canadian prairie
hacking down trees
                and building churches
delivering personal baptist sermons in them
leading Holy holy holy lord god almighty songs in them
red haired man squared off in the pulpit
reading Saul on the road to Damascus at them
Left home
           big walled Bristol town
at age eight
             to make a living
buried his stubby fingers in root snarled earth
for a suit of clothes and seven hundred gruelly meals a year
taking an anabaptist cane across the back every day
for four years till he was whipped out of England

Twelve years old
              and across the ocean alone
to apocalyptic Canada
                Ontario of bone bending child labor
six years on the road to Damascus till his eyes were blinded
with the blast of Christ and he wandered west
to Brandon among wheat kings and heathen Saturday nights
young red haired Bristol boy shoveling coal
in the basement of Brandon college five in the morning

Then built his first wooden church and married
a sick girl who bore two live children and died

leaving several pitiful letters and the Manitoba night

He moved west with another wife and built children and churches
Saskatchewan Alberta British Columbia Holy holy holy
lord god almighty
                        struck his labored bones with pain
and left him a postmaster prodding grandchildren with crutches
another dead wife and a glass bowl of photographs
and holy books unopened save the bible by the bed

Till he died the day before his eighty fifth birthday
in a Catholic hospital of sheets white as his hair


## Esta Muy Caliente

On the highway
near San Juan del Río
we had to stop the car
for a funeral.

The whole town it was
a hundred people or
two hundred
walking slowly along the highway

toward the yellow domed church
on the top of the hill
and we pulled into the shade
of a shaggy tree.

I turned off the engine
and we heard their music
a screeching saxophone
and high broken noted trumpet

alone and sad in the hot afternoon
as they walked slow like sheep

the women with black shawls
the men in flappy trousers.

Every five minutes the men
threw cherry bombs into the air
behind them: loud gun shots
blasting the afternoon

then the saxophone: tin music
odd tortured jazz
in that mysterious Indian Christian march
up the hill: bearing a coffin to the priest.

It was a small coffin
on the shoulder of one man in front
        the father we thought
the cherry bombs were like violence

against us: but we were stopped.
An old rattling truck
nosed thru them: and they closed
together again behind it
                        ignoring us.

I walked away from the road
in among the bushes and prickly pear
looking for scorpions on the hot sand
and took a leak beside a thin horse.

An hour later the road was clear
and as I got in the car
a man on a donkey came by
a San Juan lonely in the mountains man.

Good afternoon, I said.
Good afternoon, he said, it is very hot.
Yes it is, I said, especially for us.
It is very hot for us too, he said.

## News

Every day I add an inch
to the pile of old newspapers
in the closet.

In that three foot pile now
a dozen airliner crashes,
one earthquake in Alaska,
seventeen American soldiers
face down in Asian mud

I could go on enumerating
like newsprint—we record
violent death & hockey scores
& keep the front room neat.

In front of me, on the table
my empty coffee cup, somewhat melted
butter, carbon copy of an old poem,
familiar things, nothing unexpected.

A plane could crash into the kitchen—
a fissure could jag the floor open—
some olive faced paratrooper bash
his rifle butt thru the window—

It would be news, somewhere.


## Circus Maximus

They come
            each one
of them
            a rise
like those

       who came
before them.

New heroes flexing
to fill the shape
made out for them
by the now dead

but each new man
a refutation of his predecessor.

Camus refining Dostoyevsky
yet feeling the swell
of body the Russian felt

the old man
grizzling in his beard
anticipating the African
who would fit his fingers
over the old pen
playing with down
         on his cheek.

Who knows ten of your molecules
are not in me?

but Nature helps me define
my own shape

looks on as
I stumble over the centuries'

exposed root
lost in my own
           particularity

(patterns I deny
and that
is part of a pattern).

Styles do not multiply themselves
but are all
pervasive

the suit of clothes
is nothing
without its own disfigurations.

New heroes flex into it
and bend it to their bodies.


## Indian Summer

The yellow trees
along the river

are dying I said
they are in
their moment of life
you said.

The Indians I think
are dead, you cant
immortalize them, a
leaf prest between

pages becomes a
page.


In a month
the river will move

beneath ice, moving
as it always does
south. We will

believe it as we

will no longer see
those yellow borders
of the river.

## *Albertasaurus*

The great valley of Drumheller
a silent gorge, filled
with dinosaur bones,

unexpected trees on the plains,
old ghost towns of coal
mines & dinosaurs,

the wood, petrified, the earth
streakt white & brown,
the Badlands, sea shells

caught a thousand miles
from the sea. In the town

small town cafés, restaurants
they say, with Pepsi-Cola neon
signs, old-fashioned menus,

the home of the dinosaur,
caught in a corner of the
prairie, small-town people
in a dying town, conscious
they must cling to the
dinosaur for their living.

cling to his neck, forgetting
where the dinosaur came
to rest.

## The House

I

If I describe my house
I may at last describe my self

but I will surely lie
about the house.

For there is the first lie.
It is not a house at all

but a fragment, a share
of a house, instinct drives me

to one door.  As certain as
one hair lies beside another.

As certain as these rows of books
carry me from house to house,

arrange me to their will. I
squat for an hour, eye level

to those books, saying I will
read this, or I will read this,

& this way never succeed
in reading my self, no time

left in the hour between
the news & the pants on the floor.

II

In the morning the window
is bamboo & behind that

snow. (But here I am trying
to go outside the house, remember

what I said.) My bare feet
find no wood, the water

runs warm from the tap,
the coffee in the white cup

on which is painted a green
tree. There is a newspaper

on the floor inside the door,
& a woman in the chiffon

of the bed. A salt shaker
of glass & an aluminum

pepper shaker, & in the
farthest room, papers, orderly.

Those are the reason for the house
& its enemy. I am the fisher

who lays his fish side by side
in the pan. The noise of the pen

on paper is the drift of
cigarette smoke in the window's light.

III

The house has a refrigerator
& a stove, a painting & a

husband, & the husband
has fingers from which words

fall as the wine glass falls
unbroken on the rug.

The key fits into the door
as my feet step in snow, cutting

precise patterns & the silence
of wind, & from outside

the windows are glass, &
behind that the house is not empty.


## Dobbin

For Mike Ondaatje

We found dead animals in our sagebrush hills,
every day it seems now, deer, heads of
unimaginable elk. Or rattlesnake killed
by some kids we likely knew, upside down,
wrong coloured in the burnt couchgrass.

But my first dead horse. It was something
like mother, something gone wrong at home—
his opened & scattered body was tethered,
the old shit surrounded his tufted hair
& his skin, the oil gone, just twisted
leather without eyeballs. A horse, as if
someone had lost him, obeying the rope
thru his open-air starving.

I was then, then, no longer another one
of the animals come to look, this
was no humus like the others, this
was death, not merely dead; that rope
may now hang from some rotted fence.

## Summer Solstice

I

The cool Pacific spring has gone without
my notice, now summer lies around us
once again.  How long life is, how many
more of these seasons must I see, hydrangea
& the fat rhododendron sullen on the
neighbour's lawn. & I must rise, stick
fluid in mouth, stick beaten vegetables
into my living daughter's mouth, shit, it comes
& goes, it goes, thru us pretending we are
not some more, shit, the wearisome sun
& the sad motes in its visitations envelop
my mind even when it is thinking action
& when it thinks offers impatience with this
boring reappearance of the grass.

II

.                          Must I
live longer year by year, watching from this
small mountain the heavier pall of sludge
residing over this city & the yet discernible
waterways of bygone sea manoeuvres, my baby
breathing under that?  Every midnight, every
winter, removing familiar clothes & taking
others more familiar to my bed of habit?

III

What nature gave me at my birth no more
than this, a prospectus of recurring faces, old
leaves appear above ground, old words grow
to surround them, old fingers join to pull
them & cast them to their home.

IV

The grass needs cutting, part of it
is yellow, it is dying of starvation, hell
it will be back next year, somewhere
else, & so will we, will we? Will
we endure that? The Pacific winter remembered more fondly than it is, some
unconvincing refuge of the life-giving
horror felt in the knives of Quebec December.
We congratulate each other for the snowy
re-emergence of the mountains, our mountains
we say with fancy dinners at the top
& hydroelectric sticks poking up the
slopes, our mountains re-emerging from our
papermaking smoke, our mountains showing up
each year with their peaks capt, silent
& gentle, the air restful over them, the sea
content to lie beneath them, not looking
for any entrance to that stilled heart.

V

It is slowly dying, but so slowly, the
earthquake belt is forty miles west, the sea
deterred by that long island. Every summer's
pollen mixt with more haze. We come
back here to partake of slow death, the dying
ocean so lifelike, harder to beat down than some
great lake. The mountains once promist me
a rapid death, fall is a fall, to the
rocks below—but the mountains are somebody's back yard, hydrangea bushes all round.

VI

I havent heard a timely utterance for a
long time, there we are, hung on those
hands, watching & watching, & will they
never move? We seek out ways of death,

but slowly, or given minimal expectation, why
do I climb those stairs every morning?
To visit her, lift her eighteen pounds, &
clean her, more of it she'll pass & never
recall, to bring her downstairs for more,
of the same. Some will say that is reason
enough. Few will say enough of reason. It's
not reason I seek upstairs, we ought to be
past that, it's legs take us up there, legs
more tired every season. She makes utterances
we measure her time by.

VII

Sunday, I & Thea were there when Angela
woke up. So I'm back, she said, &
reacht to touch her baby's fuzzy head. Why,
where you been, I ask her.

I went on a car ride with a Fairie,
name of Mab.

What did she tell you?

She said things are going to get better.

VIII

I am slowly dying, water evaporating
from a saucer. I saw my daughter this
morning, trying to walk, & it fell like a vial
of melted lead into my heart, my heart so
deep in my chest. She will have to do it now,
we have presented her with a world,
whose spectres take shapes before her eyes
have fully focust, poor voyager! For joy
she brings us every morning we exchange
an accelerating series of shocks. We are together
cannibals of her spirit, we feast to nurture

our tired bodies, turning music to shit, a shock
felt numbly here & radiating to collisions
at the rim of space. You dont believe me?
See her eyes when first she wakes. A visible
tyrant of light yanks their traces, demanding
they stride apace.

IX

       Then cannibal I will be—
her father. & I cant even teach her love,
but loose the horses, let a ghost ride &
call him loving, turn her away finally &
soothe her with a merry-go-round. That music
will disgust her in time, it rings & rings,
& I will instruct her of gold & gold
bedevillings, I will toil to win her trust,
& we will fall where we will rust
& watch the golden horses prancing by.

X

So fall will come
& winter too,
& she will wear
her first tight shoe

& she will wear
the seasons round
& watch the summers
wear me down.

XI

Thea, never read my lines, love your mother,
love your father, distrust circles, reach
this way & that. Remember how you can
the afternoon a bird came to sit at your shoulder
& let me remember how I dropt my game
to fly to your side, protecting your eyes.

Accept no promise from the mountains,
I have never seen your face before, & when
I leave you I will leave you time.
Forgive me the light that fades not fast away,
forgive me the continuous feast
we make from your remembered day.


## Sequestered Pop & a Stripe

fr Stephen Morrissey

Separate from let us say the trees & all that may be living
hardly significant lives in them, I stood at the back door,
drinking over-cookt coffee & trying to imagine why anyone
would dedicate a life to understanding the secret course of
nature.  I know it gets tedious, you can leave, this rant, & I am
no lover of brusht aluminum, well maybe I do have a bit of a
crush on it.

A few days earlier I'd seen from the taxi a poor raccoon in a
rich neighbourhood, trying to get back across busy Marine
Drive.  The sun was up & he was late.  I dont know whether he
made it home but I doubt it.  I did.  I sat in aluminum & fabric
35,000 feet as they still say in the sky, & I made it home.  We
burned a billion ancient sea creatures getting here, rings
around our eyes in the time differential.

Separate from the earth no more, the blue heron I saw a few
minutes later assumed an alternate shape of beauty, a kind of
folded sky; who knew what he was looking for?  Not eye in the
cab, a voice in my head multiplying by one and a half &
dividing by ten.

Separate from the boy I am reading & the boy I am writing, I
would be nothing but a hairless pronoun cat drinking coffee, I
decided, empty of intelligence like a cup stained by old brown
acid.

## Bones Along Her Body

Bones along her body show
art is never far below,
reason offers equal space
bones that glimmer in her face;
art is never far from where
reason offers up its chair—
art is never far away.

Phones ring out in open air,
ears deduce a message there,
noises all fall into place,
tones that need no special grace;
letting half her reason go,
art is never far from so,
never far when she will play
dancing bones on reason's day.

# Pat Lowther

*Coast Range*

Just north of town
the mountains start to talk
back-of-the-head buzz
of high stubbled meadows
minute flowers
moss gravel and clouds

They're not snobs, these mountains,
they don't speak Rosicrucian,
they sputter with
billygoat-bearded creeks
bumsliding down
to splat into the sea

they talk with the casual
tongues of water
rising in trees

They're so humble they'll let you
blast highways through them
baring their iron and granite
sunset-coloured bones
broken for miles

And nights when
clouds foam on a beach
of clear night sky,
those high slopes creak
in companionable sleep

Move through gray green
aurora of rain
to the bare fact:
The land is bare.

Even the curly opaque Pacific
forest, chilling you full awake
with wet branch-slaps,
is somehow bare
stainless as sunlight:

The land is what's left
after the failure
of every kind of metaphor.

*

The plainness of first things
trees
gravel
rocks
naive root atom
of philosophy's first molecule

The mountains reject nothing
but can crack
open your mind
just by being intractably there

Atom: that which can not
be reduced

You can gut them
blast them
to slag
the shapes they've made in the sky
cannot be reduced

## Octopus

The octopus is beautifully
functional as an umbrella;
at rest a bag of rucked skin
sags like an empty scrotum
his jelled eyes sad and bored

but taking flight:  look
how lovely purposeful
in every part:
the jet vent smooth
as modern plumbing
the webbed pinwheel of tentacles
moving in perfect accord
like a machine dreamed
by Leonardo


## Touch Home

My daughter, a statistic
in a population explosion
exploded
          popped
out of my body like a cork.

The doctors called for oxygen,
the birth too sudden, violent,
the child seemed pale

But my daughter lay
in perfect tranquillity
touching          the new air
          with her
  elegant          hands.

## Hotline to the Gulf

### 1

A hot wire
into the immense
turquoise
chasm of silence

this slenderest serpent
electrode fanged
excruciatingly
delicately
into my jugular
snaking under my ear
down to the heart's
chambers

it brings me new
perceptions:  the world
is not a sphere,
it's a doughnut,
there's a huge
hole at the centre

away down there
are clouds,
a static of voices
remote as angels

### 2

Write to me, darling
from the other world.
send me olives.

3

There was this woman
on the radio:
all you had to do
was phone CJOR
and she'd give you
the inside dope
on your loved ones
Passed Beyond.

Turning the dial,
what I heard was
*my sister's voice:*
*What can you tell me*
*about my little boy?*

And I ripped the cord
from the wall,
beat my fists
on the kitchen
counter, crying
against that reaching
more terrible
even than death.

4

A list of things done
with hot wires:
　　cauterizing small wounds
　　burning off warts
　　removing the eyes
　　of caged songbirds
　　shoving it up the penis
　　of prisoners

5

Speak to me
for Gods sake.
There are worse things
than death
though you and I
are not likely
to experience
any of them

6

I could almost climb
that wire down
hand over hand
like a fine chain
dangling
into the cool
abyss

a faint odour
of absence,
windless air,
buzzing
of distant voices
I dan't recognize

7

Or that imaginary
ribcage
which sheltered me like
a white picket fence
built with love
expanded,
rushed outward
out of sight:

I'm a red
thing beating
at the centre
of emptiness

only a hot vein
wires me
to the perimeter
straining
to hear syllables
in the hiss of blood


## Regard to Neruda

When I heard that
the world's greatest poet
was running for president:
being north american
I would have laughed, until
I thought of the campaign trek
over country that was
his blood and bed,
the persistent human song
for which he became
rivers, harps of forests,
metallic skies of cities.
and I thought also
of the tenderness implied
in his handshake.

Could I see with his high vision
(man with thick hands and belly
full of good things)
the naked feet of beginnings,
the sons of rare minerals
transforming the earth,

could I wash my country
with songs that settle
like haloes on the constituents,
I'd campaign
to be prime minister
without kisses.

Often now I forget
how to make love
but I think I am ready
to learn politics.


## Chacabuco, The Pit

(Information filtered out of Chile: political
prisoners formerly held in the stadium at Santiago
have been transported to a Nazi-type concentration
camp set up in a disused nitrates mine somewhere
on the Atacama desert.)

       EVERYTHING SHOULD BE DONE
QUIETLY AND EFFECTIVELY TO INSURE
THAT ALLENDE DOES NOT LAST THE NEXT
CRUCIAL SIX MONTHS.
—from 18-point plan submitted by International
Telegraph and Telephone Co. to the White House, USA.

            CONTACT TRUSTWORTHY
SOURCES
WITHIN THE CHILEAN ARMED FORCES.
—from Point 7, above.

        *I shall speak to the Lord of Heaven*
*where he sits asleep.*
—from an ancient Mayan prayer.

Atacama desert:
by day the sun lets down
his weight    everyone wears
a halo   everything quivers
sharp-sided dust refracts
blurred glitter between
creased squinting eyelids;
by night the land is naked
to the farthest reaches
between galaxies
that vacuum sucks
heat:    the land is
cold to the utter bone.

Carefully now (place
records on a turntable)
remember those 1940s movies
where virgins were sacrifices
to volcanoes:    here is
that same
                ceremonial
                        suspenseful
                                approach:
we are approaching
                        Chacabuco
                            the pit.

Notice first the magnificent sunset,
the stars, the clouds of Magellan.
Note that here as in all human places
prayer has been uttered.

Watch until morning
burns the sky white.
Wooden shacks persevere
in the dry air,
their corners banked with dust;
a grid of streets prints

an ominous white shadow
on your eyelids;
it leads
to the pit.

A huge, gouged cavity
flickering like a bad film,
the whole scene twitching
on and off
in and out of existence:
is God blinking? are you
shuttering your eyes, tourista?

I shall speak to the lord of heaven
where he sits asleep

there are men in that pit
imagine that they are chained
(they may be)
starving (they are)
watched over by jailers
with faces blank
as a leached brain

Working, that sallow bitter rock
ground to glass
powder enters their lungs
nostrils eyes pores
Sleeping, they dream of eating
rock, sucking juice from it
pissing nitrate dust

Moments of darkness film
their eyes, they stumble
in negative light
and the blows of whips

*

Do they remember
who they are? patriots
    believers
          builders

collective dreamers who woke
to find all their good wishes
happening faster
than they could move,
the people outreaching the planners
factory workers running
the factories
children wearing moustaches
of milk

Forgetting to keep guns beside their pillows
forgetting to bribe generals
breathing long breaths of peace
organizing anti-Fascist song festivals
instead of militia
seeing the people stand at last
upright in mellow light like a sound harvest
they forgot lifetimes of exile
years of held breath and stealth
seeing so many strong
they forgot the strength of I.T.& T.
United Fruit Co.
         Anaconda

who do not easily give up
what they have taken.

\*

Some one decides
who shall eat
who shall not eat
who shall be beaten

and on which
parts of his body

Some one decides
who shall be starved
who shall be fed
enough to sustain
another day's torture

A man decides.
That man does not breathe dust:
he is dust.

\*

Choirs of young boys
exquisitely trained
sing hymns in cathedrals;
jellyfish swim in the ocean
like bubbles of
purity made tangible;
whole cities lie open
to the stars;
women bake bread;
fruit trees unfold their blossoms
petal by petal;
we are continually born

but these, captive, stumble
in gross heat
in stupor of pain:
they are the fingers sliced off
when the wood was cut,
the abortions born living;
they are the mangled
parts of our bodies
screaming to be
reunited.

\*

*'If I forget thee, O Zion'*

Let statesmen's tongues lock
between their jaws,
let businessmen's cheque hands
be paralyzed,
let musicians stop building
towers of sound,
let commerce fall
in convulsions:
we have deserved this.

\*

Staircases ascending
through caverns
clefts in the root sockets
of mountains, opening
onto ocean's foot:
we have all been there,
that journey, its
hardships its surprises
stay in our cells
our footprints in clay
splayed: we were burdened.

Remember breathing on fire
a cautious husbandry
then suddenly sparks
bursting upward
like dolphins leaping
in the sunlight path
of the first boat
we had song
    mathematics
      magic

Even for torturers we have done this

journey, broken
ourselves like crumbs,
pumped children into wombs,
heaved them out,
laid stone on stone;

we forgive each other
our absurdities,
casually accept splendour;
we forgive even death

but these places
of death slowly inflicted
we can't forgive, but writhe
coiling in on ourselves
to try to forget, to deny:
*we have travelled so far*
*and these are still with us?*

Even now in our cities
churches universities
pleasant lawns we are
scrabbling with broken nails
against rock, we are
dying of flies and disease.
Until that pus is drained
we are not healed.

*

*'And the dead shall be raised incorruptible'*

When their names are called
will you answer,
will I?
for bread on the table
for salt in the bread
for bees in the cups

of flowers
will you answer to their names?

For I tell you the earth
itself is a mystery
which we penetrate constantly
and our people a holy mystery
beyond refusal

And the horrors of the mind
are the horrors of
what we allow to be done
and the grace of the soul
is what we determine shall be
made truly among us. Amen.


## The Dig

Even where traffic passes
the ancient world has exposed
a root, large and impervious,
humped like a dragon
among the city's conduits.
*Look, they say,*
*who would have thought*
*the thing so tough,*
*so secretive?*

THE DIGGERS

The bone gloved in clay
shallow perhaps where arches
of feet go over;
they see it as finished
round like a jar;
a shard they see as whole.

*Will our bones tell*
*what we died of?*

The diggers
with very gentle fingers
lift up the bones of a woman;
tenderly they take off
her stockings of earth;
they have not such love
for the living
who are not finished
or predicted.

THE BONES

The men we see always swift
moving, edged with a running light
like fire; their hands infinitely
potent, working in blood,
commanding the death of animals,
the life of the tribe.

The women we see finished
completed like fat jars,
like oil floating on water:
breasts  bellies  faces
all round and calm.

*Their bones should thrash*
*in the diggers' baskets,*
*should scream against the light.*

Their work bent them
and sex, that soft explosion
miraculous as rain
broke in them over and over,
their bodies thickened like tubers

broke and were remade
again and again crying out
in the heave of breaking
the terrible pleasure
again and again till
they fell away, at last
they became bone.

Even their hands
curved around implements,
pounding-stones, were worshipping
the cock that made them
round and hollow.

But before their falling away
was an anger,
a stone in the mouth.
They would say there is
a great fall like water,
a mask taking shape on air,
a sound coming nearer
like a heavy animal
breaking twigs.

And the flesh stamen
bursting inside them
splayed their bones
apart like spread legs.

*Will our bones tell*
*sisters, what we died of?*
*how love broke us*
*in that helplessly desired*
*breaking, and men*
*and children ransacked our flesh,*
*cracked our innermost bones*
*to eat the morrow.*

# John Newlove

*The Arrival*

Having come slowly, hesitantly
at first, as a poem comes,
and then steadily down to the marshy sea-board—

that day I ran along a stone sea-break,
plunging into the Pacific, the sun
just setting, clothed, exuberant, hot,
so happy—
           o sing!
plunging into the ocean, rolled on my back, eyes
full of salt water, hair in eyes,
shoes lost forever at the bottom, noting
as if they were trivia
the wheeling birds of the air
and gulls gorging themselves
on the sea-going garbage
of civilization, the lower mainland,
hauled away by tugs—
              the gulls,
being too heavy to fly,
and foolish-looking there,
can be knocked off with sticks
from barge into ocean—

and noting the trees whitely flowering,
took off my clothes and calmly bathed.

## Then, If I Cease Desiring

Then, if I cease desiring,
you may sing a song
of how young I was.

You may praise famous moments,
all have them, of the churches
I broke into for wine,

not praise, the highways
I travelled drunkenly
in winter, the cars I stole.

You may allow me moments,
not monuments, I being
content. It is little,
but it is little enough.


## Verigin, Moving in Alone,

(fatherless, 250 people,
counting dogs and gophers
we would say, Jmaeff's grocerystore,
me in grade 4, mother
principal of the 2-building,
3-room, 12-grade school,)

a boy sitting on the grass
of a small hill, the hot fall,
speaking no russian, an airgun
my sister gave me making me envied.

I tried all fall, all spring
the next ominous year, to kill

a crow  with it, secretly glad
I could not, the men
in winter shooting the town's
wild dogs, casually tossing
the quick-frozen barely-bleeding
head-shot corpses onto
the street-side snowbanks,

the highway crews cutting their way
through to open the road with what
I was sure was simply
some alternate of a golden summer's
wheat-threshing machine, children
running through the hard-tossed spray,
pretending war from the monster's snout,

leaping into snowbanks from
Peter The Lordly Verigin's
palace on the edge of town
in a wild 3-dimensional
cubistic game of cops and robbers,

cold spring swimming
in Dead Horse Creek and farmers'
dugouts and doomed fishing
in beastless ponds, strapped
in school for watching a fight,

coldly holding back tears
and digging for drunken father's
rum-bottle, he had finally
arrived, how I loved him,
loved him, love him, dead, still.

My mad old brother chased me
alone in the house with him
around and around
the small living room, airgun,

rifle in hand, silently,
our breaths coming together—

all sights and temperatures
and remembrances,
as a lost gull screams now
outside my window,
a 9-year-old's year-long
night and day in tiny
magnificent prairie Verigin:

the long grey cat we got,
the bruised knees, cut fingers,
nails in feet, far walks
to watch a horse's corpse
turn slowly and sweetly to bone,
white bone, and in the late spring,
too, I remember the bright
young bodies of the boys,

my friends and peers and enemies,
till everything breaks down.

## The Pride

1
The image/   the pawnees
in their earth-lodge villages,
the clear image
of teton sioux, wild
fickle people the chronicler says,

the crazy dogs, men
tethered with leather dog-thongs
to a stake, fighting until dead,

image:  arikaras
with traded spanish sabre blades
mounted on the long
heavy buffalo lances,
riding the sioux
down, the centaurs, the horsemen
scouring the level plains
in war or hunt
until smallpox got them,
the warriors,

image—of a desolate country,
a long way between fires,
unfound lakes, mirages, cold rocks,
and lone men going through it,
cree with good guns
causing terror in athabaska
among the inhabitants, frightened
stone-age people, 'so that
they fled at the mere sight
of a strange smoke miles away.'


2
This western country crammed
with the ghosts of indians,
haunting the coastal stones and shores,
the forested pacific islands,
mountains, hills and plains:

beside the ocean ethlinga,
man in the moon, empties
his bucket, on
a sign from spirit
of the wind ethlinga
empties his bucket, refreshing
the earth, and it rains
on the white cities;

that black  joker, broken-
jawed raven, most prominent
among haida and tsimshian tribes
is in the kwakiutl
dance masks too—
it was he who brought fire,
food and water to man,
the trickster;

and thunderbird hilunga,
little thought of
by haida for lack of thunderstorms
in their district, goes
by many names, exquisite disguises
carved in the painted wood,

he is nootka tootooch, the wings
causing thunder and the tongue
or flashing eyes engendering
rabid white lightning,
whose food was whales,

called kwunusela by the kwakiutl,
it was he who laid down the house-logs
for the people at the place
where kwunusela alighted;

in full force and virtue
and terror of the law, eagle—
he is authority, the sun
assumed his form once,
the sun which used to be
a flicker's egg, success-
fully tranformed;

and malevolence comes to the land,
the wild woman of the woods—
grinning, she wears

a hummingbird in her hair,
d'sonoqua, the furious one—

they are all ready
to be found, the legends
and the people, or
all their ghosts and memories,
whatever is strong enough
to be remembered.


3
But what image, bewildered
son of all men
under the hot sun,
do you worship,
what completeness
do you hope to have
from these tales,
a half-understood massiveness, mirage,
in men's minds—what
is your purpose;

with what force
will you proceed
along a line
neither straight nor short,
whose future
you cannot know
or result foretell,
whose meaning is still
obscured as the incidents
occur and accumulate?


4
The country moves on;
there are orchards in the interior,

the mountain passes
are broken, the foothills
covered with cattle and fences,
and the fading hills covered;

but the plains are bare,
not barren, easy
for me to love their people,
for me to love their people
without selection.


5

In 1787, the old cree saukamappee, aged 75 or thereabout,
speaking then of things that had happened when he was 16, just
a man, told david thompson about the raids the shoshonis, the
snakes, had made on the westward-reaching peigan, of their
war-parties sometimes sent 10 days' journey to enemy camps,
the men all afoot in battle array for the encounter, crouching
behind their giant shields. The peigan armed with guns drove
these snakes out of the plains, the plains where their strength had
been, where they had been settled since living memory (though
nothing is remembered beyond a grandfather's time), to the west
of the rockies:

these people moved without rest,
backward and forward with the wind,
the seasons, the game, great herds,
in hunger and abundance—

in summer and in the bloody fall
they gathered on the killing grounds,
fat and shining with fat, amused
with the luxuries of war and death,

relieved from the steam of knowledge,
consoled by the stream of blood
and steam rising from the fresh hides

and tired horses, wheeling in their pride
on the sweating horses, their pride.


6
Those are all stories;
the pride, the grand poem
of our land, of the earth itself,
will come, welcome, and
sought for, and found,
in a line of running verse,
sweating, our pride;

we seize on
what has happened before,
one line only
will be enough,
a single line
and then the sunlit brilliant image suddenly floods us
with understanding, shocks our
attentions, and all desire
stops, stands alone;

we stand alone,
we are no longer lonely
but have roots,
and the rooted words
recur in the mind, mirror, so that
we dwell on nothing else, in nothing else,
touched, repeating them,
at home freely
at last, in amazement;

'the unyielding phrase
in tune with the epoch,'
the thing made up
of our desires,
not of its words, not only

of them, but of something else
as well, that which we desire
so ardently, that which
will not come when
it is summoned alone,
but grows in us
and idles about and hides
until the moment is due—

the knowledge of
our origins, and where
we are in truth,
whose land this is
and is to be.

7
The unyielding phrase:
when the moment is due, then
it springs upon us
out of our own mouths,
unconsidered, overwhelming
in its knowledge, complete—

not this handful
of fragments, as the indians
are not composed of
the romantic stories
about them, or of the stories
they tell only, but
still ride the soil
in us, dry bones a part
of the dust in our eyes,
needed and troubling
in the glare, in
our breath, in our
ears, in our mouths,
in our bodies entire, in our minds, until

at last
we become them

in our desires, our desires,
mirages, mirrors, that are theirs, hard-
riding desires, and they
become our true forbears, moulded
by the same wind or rain,
and in this land we
are their people, come
back to life again.

1968


## Lady, Lady

Lady, lady, I cannot lie,
I didn't cut down your cherry tree.

It was another man, in another season,
for the same reason.

I eat the stone and not the flesh,
it is the bare bone of desire I want,

something you would throw a dog,
or me, though I insult by saying so.

God knows it is not said
of your body, that it is like

a bone thrown to a dog,
or that I would throw it away, which

moment to moment I cannot remember
under those baggy clothes you wear—

which, if I love and tell,
I love well.


## Ride Off any Horizon

Ride off any horizon
and let the measure fall
where it may—

on the hot wheat,
on the dark yellow fields
of wild mustard, the fields

of bad farmers, on the river,
on the dirty river full
of boys and on the throbbing

powerhouse and the low dam
of cheap cement and rocks
boiling with white water,

and on the cows and their powerful
bulls, the heavy tracks
filling with liquid at the edge

of the narrow prairie
river running steadily away.

\*

Ride off any horizon
and let the measure fall
where it may—

among the piles of bones
that dot the prairie

in vision and history
(the buffalo and deer,

dead indians, dead settlers
the frames of lost houses

left behind in the dust
of the depression,

dry and profound, that
will come again in the land

and in the spirit, the land
shifting and the minds

blown dry and empty—
I have not seen it! except

in pictures and talk—
but there is the fence

covered with dust, laden,
the wrecked house stupidly empty)—

here is a picture for your wallet,
of the beaten farmer and his wife
leaning toward each other—

sadly smiling, and emptied of desire.

*

Ride off any horizon
and let the measure fall
where it may—

off the edge
of the black prairie

as you thought you could fall,
a boy at sunset

not watching the sun
set but watching the black earth,

never-ending they said in school,
round: but you saw it ending,

finished, definite, precise—
visible only miles away.

\*

Ride off any horizon
and let the measure fall
where it may—

on a hot night the town
is in the streets—

the boys and girls
are practising against

each other, the men
talk and eye the girls—

the women talk and
eye each other, the indians
play pool: eye on the ball.

\*

Ride off any horizon
and let the measure fall
where it may—

and damn the troops, the horsemen

are wheeling in the sunshine,
the cree, practising

for their deaths: mr poundmaker,
gentle sweet mr bigbear,
it is not unfortunately

quite enough to be innocent,
it is not enough merely
not to offend—

at times to be born
is enough, to be
in the way is too much—

some colonel otter, some
major-general middleton will
get you, you—

indian. It is no good to say,
I would rather die
at once than be in that place—

though you love that land more,
you will go where they take you.

*

Ride off any horizon
and let the measure fall—

where it may;
it doesn't have to be

the prairie. It could be
the cold soul of the cities
blown empty by commerce

and desiring commerce
to fill up emptiness.

The streets are full of people.

It is night, the lights
are on; the wind

blows as far as it may. The streets
are dark and full of people.

Their eyes are fixed as far as
they can see beyond each other—

to the concrete horizon, definite,
tall against the mountains,
stopping vision visibly.


## In This Reed

In this reed, in this semblance
of a human body I wear
so awkwardly, unjointed,
though I hesitate to admit,

there there is life, though
once I would have denied it, thinking
my somnolence clever evidence
of a wearied intellectuality;

but in this hunger I feed on,
in the lungs heaving and the eyes,
to speak only of the eyes
that see so little
of what they ought to see (no more
than they should!), there the life is—

it is imperfection
the eyes see, it is
impreciseness they deserve,

but they desire so much more,
what they desire, what they hope,
what they invent,

is perfection, organizing
all things as they may not be,
it is what they strive for

unwillingly, against themselves,
to see a perfect order, ordained
reason—

and what they strive against
while they wish it, what they want
to see, closed, is what
they want, and will not be.


## The Engine and the Sea

The locomotive in the city's distance, obscure, misplaced,
sounds a child's horn on the flat land leading to the
cliff of dark buildings,

the foghorns on the water's edge cry back.

Between the sounds men sit in their houses watching
machines inform them in Edison's light. In the marshes,
the music of ominous living. . . .

a leggy insect runs on that surface, frogs wait, fish,
angling birds.

In the cities men wait to be told. They sit between the
locomotive and the fish. The flat sea and the prairie
that was a sea contain them. Images float before their
eyes,

men and women acting,

entertaining, rigorously dancing with fractured minds
contorted to a joyless pleasure, time sold from life.

The locomotive hums, the prairies hum. Frogs touch
insects with their long tongues, the cannibal fish and
the stabbing birds

wait.

Night actions flash before uncountable animal eyes. Mice
run. Light rain falls in the night.

The frogs are stilled. Between the engine and the sea, the
lights go out. People sleep with mechanical dreams, the sea
hums with rain, the locomotive shines black, fish wait under
the surface of a pinked pool.

Frogs shiver in the cold. The land waits, black, dreaming. Men
lie dry in their beds.

History, history!

Under the closed lids their eyes flick back and forth as they try
to follow the frightening shapes of their desires.

## Driving

You never say anything in your letters. You say,
I drove all night long through the snow
in someone else's car
and the heater wouldn't work and I nearly froze.
But I know that. I live in this country too.
I know how beautiful it is at night
with the white snow banked in the moonlight.

Around black trees and tangled bushes,
how lonely and lovely that driving is,
how deadly. You become the country.
You are by yourself in that channel of snow
and pines and pines,
whether the pines and snow flow backwards smoothly,
whether you drive or you stop or you walk or you sit.

This land waits. It watches. How beautifully desolate
our country is, out of the snug cities,
and how it fits a human. You say you drove.
It doesn't matter to me.
All I can see is the silent cold car gliding,
walled in, your face smooth, your mind empty,
cold foot on the pedal, cold hands on the wheel.

## The Weather

I'd like to live a slower life.
The weather gets in my words
and I want them dry. Line after line
writes itself on my face, not a grace
of age but wrinkled humour. I laugh
more than I should or more
than anyone should. This is good.

But guess again. Everyone leans, each
on each other. This is a life
without an image. But only
because nothing does much more
than just resemble. Do the shamans
do what they say they do, dancing?
This is epistemology.

This is guesswork, this is love,
this is giving up gorgeousness to please you,
you beautiful dead to be. God bless
the weather and the words. Any words. Any weather.
And where or whom. I'd never taken count before.
I wish I had. And then
I did. And here
the weather wrote again.

# Margaret Atwood

*The Animals in That Country*

In that country the animals
have the faces of people:

the ceremonial
cats possessing the streets

the fox run
politely to earth, the huntsmen
standing around him, fixed
in their tapestry of manners

the bull, embroidered
with blood and given
an elegant death, trumpets, his name
stamped on him, heraldic brand
because

(when he rolled
on the sand, sword in his heart, the teeth
in his blue mouth were human)

he is really a man

even the wolves, holding resonant
conversations in their
forests thickened with legend.

    In this country the animals
    have the faces of

animals.

Their eyes
flash once in car headlights
and are gone.

Their deaths are not elegant.

They have the faces of
no-one.


## A Night in the Royal Ontario Museum

Who locked me

into this crazed man-made
stone brain
            where the weathered
totempole jabs a blunt
finger at the byzantine
mosaic dome

Under that ornate
golden cranium I wander
among fragments of gods, tarnished
coins, embalmed gestures
chronologically arranged,
looking for the EXIT sign

but in spite of the diagrams
at every corner, labelled
in red: YOU ARE HERE
the labyrinth holds me,

turning me around
the cafeteria, the washrooms,

a spiral through marble
Greece and Rome, the bronze
horses of China

then past the carved masks, wood and fur
to where 5 plaster Indians
in a glass case
squat near a dusty fire

and further, confronting me
with a skeleton child, preserved
in the desert air, curled
beside a clay pot and a few beads.

I say I am far
enough,   stop here   please
no more

but the perverse museum, corridor
by corridor, an idiot
voice jogged by a pushed
button, repeats its memories

and I am dragged to the mind's
deadend, the roar of the bone-
yard, I am lost
among the mastodons
and beyond: a fossil
shell, then

samples of rocks
and minerals, even the thundering
tusks dwindling to pin-
points in the stellar
fluorescent-lighted
wastes of geology

## Progressive Insanities of a Pioneer

I

He stood, a point
on a sheet of green paper
proclaiming himself the centre,

with no walls, no borders
anywhere; the sky no height
above him, totally un-
enclosed
and shouted:

Let me out!

II

He dug the soil in rows,
imposed himself with shovels.
He asserted
into the furrows, I
am not random.

The ground
replied with aphorisms:

a tree-sprout, a nameless
weed, words
he couldn't understand.

III

The house pitched
the plot staked
in the middle of nowhere.

At night the mind
inside, in the middle

of nowhere.

The idea of an animal
patters across the roof.

In the darkness the fields
defend themselves with fences
in vain:
    everything
    is getting in.

IV

By daylight he resisted.
He said, disgusted
with the swamp's clamourings and the outbursts
of rocks,
    This is not order
    but the absence
    of order.

He was wrong, the unanswering
forest implied:

    It was
    an ordered absence

V

For many years
he fished for a great vision,
dangling the hooks of sown
roots under the surface
of the shallow earth.

It was like
enticing whales with a bent
pin. Besides he thought

in that country
only the worms were biting.

VI

If he had known unstructured
space is a deluge
and stocked his log house-
boat with all the animals
even the wolves,

he might have floated.

But obstinate he
stated, The land is solid
and stamped,

watching his foot sink
down through stone
up to the knee.

VII

Things
refused to name themselves; refused
to let him name them.

The wolves hunted
outside.

On his beaches, his clearings,
by the surf of under-
growth breaking
at his feet, he foresaw
disintegration
                    and in the end
through eyes
made ragged by his
effort, the tension

between subject and object,

the green
vision, the unnamed
whale invaded.

## Death of a Young Son by Drowning

He, who navigated with success
the dangerous river of his own birth
once more set forth

on a voyage of discovery
into the land I floated on
but could not touch to claim.

His feet slid on the bank,
the currents took him;
he swirled with ice and trees in the swollen water

and plunged into distant regions,
his head a bathysphere;
through his eyes' thin glass bubbles

he looked out, reckless adventurer
on a landscape stranger than Uranus
we have all been to and some remember.

There was an accident; the air locked,
he was hung in the river like a heart.
They retrieved the swamped body,

cairn of my plans and future charts,
with poles and hooks
from among the nudging logs.

It was spring, the sun kept shining, the new grass
lept to solidity;
my hands glistened with details.

After the long trip I was tired of waves.
My foot hit rock. The dreamed sails
collapsed, ragged.

       I planted him in this country
       like a flag.


## Game After Supper

This is before electricity,
it is when there were porches.

On the sagging porch an old man
is rocking. The porch is wooden,

the house is wooden and grey;
in the living room which smells of
smoke and mildew, soon
the women will light the kerosene lamp.

There is a barn but I am not in the barn;
there is an orchard too, gone bad,
its apples like soft cork
but I am not there either.

I am hiding in the long grass
with my two dead cousins,
the membrane grown already
across their throats.

We hear crickets and our own hearts
close to our ears;

though we giggle, we are afraid.

From the shadows around
the corner of the house
a tall man is coming to find us:

He will be an uncle,
if we are lucky.


## They Eat Out

In restaurants we argue
over which of us will pay for your funeral

though the real question is
whether or not I will make you immortal.

At the moment only I
can do it and so

I raise the magic fork
over the plate of beef fried rice

and plunge it into your heart.
There is a faint pop, a sizzle

and through your own split head
you rise up glowing;

the ceiling opens
a voice sings Love Is A Many

Splendoured Thing
you hang suspended above the city

in blue tights and a red cape,

your eyes flashing in unison.

The other diners regard you
some with awe, some only with boredom:

they cannot decide if you are a new weapon
or only a new advertisement.

As for me, I continue eating;
I liked you better the way you were,
but you were always ambitious.


## Newsreel: Man and Firing Squad

I

A botched job,
the blindfold slipped, he sees
his own death approaching, says No
or something, his torso jumps as the bullets hit
his nerves  /  he slopes down,
wrecked and not even
cleanly, roped muscles leaping, mouth open
as though snoring, the photography
isn't good either.

II

Destruction shines with such beauty

Light on his wet hair
serpents of blood jerked from the wrists

Sun thrown from the raised and lowered
rifles  /  debris of the still alive

Your left eye, green and lethal

III

We depart, we say goodbye

Yet each of us remains in the same place,
staked out and waiting,
it is the ground between that moves, expands,
pulling us away from each other.

No more of these closeups, this agony
taken just for the record anyway

The scenery is rising behind us
into focus, the walls
and hills are also important,

Our shattered faces retreat, we might be
happy, who can interpret
the semaphore of our bending
bodies, from a distance we could be dancing


## Five Poems for Dolls

I

Behind glass in Mexico
this clay doll draws
its lips back in a snarl;
despite its beautiful dusty shawl,
it wishes to be dangerous.

II

See how the dolls resent us,
with their bulging foreheads
and minimal chins, their flat bodies
never allowed to bulb and swell,

their faces of little thugs.

This is not a smile,
this glossy mouth, two stunted teeth;
the dolls gaze at us
with the filmed eyes of killers.

III

There have always been dolls
as long as there have been people.
In the trash heaps and abandoned temples
the dolls pile up;
the sea is filling with them.

What causes them?
Or are they gods, causeless,
something to talk to
when you have to talk
something to throw against the wall?

A doll is a witness
who cannot die,
with a doll you are never alone.

On the long journey under the earth,
in the boat with two prows,
there were always dolls.

IV

Or did we make them
because we needed to love someone
and could not love each other?

It was love, after all,
that rubbed the skins from their grey cheeks,
crippled their fingers,
snarled their hair, brown or dull gold.

Hate would merely have smashed them.

You change, but the doll
I made of you lives on,
a white body leaning
in a sunlit window, the features
wearing away with time,
frozen in the gaunt pose
of a single day,
holding in its plaster hand
your doll of me.

V

Or:   all dolls come
from the land of the unborn,
the almost-born; each
doll is a future
dead at the roots,
a voice heard only
on breathless nights,
a desolate white memento.

Or:   these are the lost children,
those who have died or thickened
to full growth and gone away.

The dolls are their souls or cast skins
which line the shelves of our bedrooms
and museums, disguised as outmoded toys,
images of our sorrow,
shedding around themselves
five inches of limbo.

## Notes Towards a Poem
## That Can Never Be Written

For Carolyn Forché

i

This is the place
you would rather not know about,
this is the place that will inhabit you,
this is the place you cannot imagine,
this is the place that will finally defeat you

where the word *why* shrivels and empties
itself.  This is famine.

ii

There is no poem you can write
about it, the sandpits
where so many were buried
& unearthed, the unendurable
pain still traced on their skins.

This did not happen last year
or forty years ago but last week.
This has been happening,
this happens.

We make wreaths of adjectives for them,
we count them like beads,
we turn them into statistics & litanies
and into poems like this one.

Nothing works.
They remain what they are.

iii

The woman lies on the wet cement floor

under the unending light,
needle marks on her arms put there
to kill the brain
and wonders why she is dying.

She is dying  because she said.
She is dying for the sake of the word.
It is her body, silent
and fingerless, writing this poem.

iv

It resembles an operation
but it is not one

nor despite the spread legs, grunts
& blood, is it a birth.

Partly it's a job
partly it's a display of skill
like a concerto.

It can be done badly
or well, they tell themselves.

Partly it's an art.

v

The facts of this world seen clearly
are seen through tears;
why tell me then
there is something wrong with my eyes?

To see clearly and without flinching,
without turning away,
this is agony, the eyes taped open
two inches from the sun.

What is it you see then?

Is it a bad dream, a hallucination?
Is it a vision?
What is it you hear?

The razor across the eyeball
is a detail from an old film.
It is also a truth.
Witness is what you must bear.

vi

In this country you can say what you like
because no one will listen to you anyway,
it's safe enough, in this country you can try to write
the poem that can never be written,
the poem that invents
nothing and excuses nothing,
because you invent and excuse yourself each day.

Elsewhere, this poem is not invention.
Elsewhere, this poem takes courage.
Elsewhere, this poem must be written
because the poets are already dead.

Elsewhere, this poem must be written
as if you are already dead,
as if nothing more can be done
or said to save you.

Elsewhere you must write this poem
because there is nothing more to do.

*1981*

## A Women's Issue

The woman in the spiked device
that locks around the waist and between
the legs, with holes in it like a tea strainer
is Exhibit A.

The woman in black with a net window
to see through and a four-inch
wooden peg  jammed up
between her legs so she can't be raped
is Exhibit B.

Exhibit C is the young girl
dragged into the bush by the midwives
and made to sing while they scrape the flesh
from between her legs, then tie her thighs
till she scabs over and is called healed.
Now she can be married.
For each childbirth they'll cut her
open, then sew her up.
Men like tight women.
The ones that die are carefully buried.

The next exhibit lies flat on her back
while eighty men a night
move through her, ten an hour.
She looks at the ceiling, listens
to the door open and close.
A bell keeps ringing.
Nobody knows how she got here.

You'll notice that what they have in common
is between the legs.  Is this
why wars are fought?
Enemy territory, no man's
land, to be entered furtively,

fenced, owned but never surely,
scene of these desperate forays
at midnight, captures
and sticky murders, doctors' rubber gloves
greasy with blood, flesh made inert, the surge
of your own uneasy power.

This is no museum.
Who invented the word *love*?

# Patrick Lane

## White Mountain

Trees in glass robes
cold under the moon's cowl.
Arms hold ice.

Wind carries only the howl
of a dog. Ashes of snow
in grey fire.

There is only a faint glow.
Roads of men advance
and retreat.

Tracks fill with snow.


## Passing into Storm

Know him for a white man.
He walks sideways into wind
allowing the left of him

to forget what the right
knows as cold. His ears
turn into death what

his eyes can't see. All day
he walks away from the sun
passing into storm. Do not

mistake him for the howl you hear

or the track you think you
follow. Finding a white man

in snow is to look for the dead.
He has been burned by the wind.
He has left too much

flesh on winter's white metal
to leave his colour as a sign.
Cold white. Cold flesh. He leans

into wind sideways; kills without
mercy anything to the left of him
coming like madness in the snow.


## The Bird

The bird you captured is dead.
I told you it would die
but you would not learn
from my telling. You wanted
to cage a bird in your hands
and learn to fly.

Listen again.
You must not handle birds.
They cannot fly through your fingers.
You are not a nest
and a feather is
not made of blood and bone.

Only words
can fly for you like birds
on the wall of the sun.
A bird is a poem
that talks of the end of cages.

## Wild Horses

Just to come once alone
to these wild horses
driving out of high Cascades,
raw legs heaving the hip-high snow.
Just once alone. Never to see
the men and their trucks.

Just once alone. Nothing moves
as the stallion with five free mares
rush into the guns. All dead.
Their eyes glaze with frost.
Ice bleeds in their nostrils
as the cable hauls them in.

Later, after the swearing
and the stamping of feet,
we ride down into Golden:

*Quit bitchin.*
*It's a hard bloody life*
*and a long week*
*for three hundred bucks of meat.*

That and the dull dead eyes
and the empty meadows.

## Elephants

The cracked cedar bunkhouse
hangs behind me like a grey pueblo
in the sundown where I sit
to carve an elephant
from a hunk of brown soap
for the Indian boy who lives

in the village a mile back
in the bush.

The alcoholic truck-driver
and the cat-skinner sit beside
me with their eyes closed
all of us waiting out the last hour
until we go back on the grade

and I try to forget the forever
clank  clank  clank
across the grade
pounding stones and earth to powder
for hours in mosquito-darkness
of the endless cold mountain night.

The elephant takes form—
my knife caresses smooth soap
scaling off curls of brown
which the boy saves to take home
to his mother in the village.

Finished, I hand the carving to him
and he looks at the image of the great
beast for a long time
then sets it on dry cedar
and looks up at me:
                    What's an elephant?
he asks me
so I tell him of the elephants
and their jungles. The story
of the elephant graveyard
which no one has ever found
and how the silent
animals of the rain forest
go away to die somewhere
in the limberlost of distances
and he smiles at me
tells me of his father's

graveyard where his people have been
buried for years. So far back
no one remembers when it started
and I ask him where the graveyard is
and he tells me it is gone
now where no one will ever find it
buried under the grade of the new
highway.

## Mountain Oysters

Kneeling in the sheep-shit
he picked up the biggest of the new rams
brushed the tail aside
slit the bag
tucked the knackers in his mouth
and clipped the cords off clean

the ram   stiff
with a single wild scream

as the tar went on
and he spit the balls in a bowl.

That's how we used to do it
when I was a boy.
It's no more gawdam painful
than any other way
and you can't have rams fighting
slamming it up every nanny

and enjoyed them with him
cutting delicately
into the deep-fried testicles.

Mountain oysters make you strong

he said
while out in the field
the rams stood holding their pain
legs fluttering like blue hands
of old tired men.


## Unborn Things

After the dog drowns in the arroyo
and the old people stumble into the jungle
muttering imprecations at the birds
and the child draws circles in the dust
for bits of glass to occupy
like eyes staring out of earth
and the woman lies on her hammock
dreaming of the lover who will save her
from the need to make bread again
I will go into the field
and be buried with the corn.

Folding my hands on my chest
I will see the shadow of myself; the same
who watched a father when he moved
with hands on the dark side of a candle
create the birds and beasts of dreams.

One with unborn things
I will open my body to the earth
and watch worms reach like pink roots
as I turn slowly tongue to stone
and speak of the beginning of seeds
as they struggle in the earth;
pale things moving toward the sun
that feel the feet of men above,
the tread of their marching
thudding into my earth.

*Ecuador*

## From the Hot Hills

For Jaswant Singh Gill

Brought from the hot hills of India
to the cold bleak country of the north
dark men strain bodies into silence
bending and breaking long brown muscles
on the dead weight of timber. Soft
language lost in ignorance
they take the jobs on the green-chain
where no man will work. A job
reserved for drunks who stagger off the train
or the huge bodies of Saskatchewan farm boys
the Sikhs whose names no one knows or cares
to know, respond to *Hey You!* and smile.
Isolate in breathing shacks of snow
they curl their bodies on straw
around the pale flower of a stove
a forty-five gallon drum
fed with salvaged slabs.

The women are alabaster
objects in a town of men.
and any Sikh who dares to speak to one
feels the steel toe of a boot.
The biggest joke of winter was the knowledge
they wiped themselves with their fingers
and one day received cheques
wrapped in toilet paper. Stabbed by cold
they breathe pnuemonia and the numb
distance of their skin.

Together they wait through the winter
knowing it will take three more
before they can bring their women
from the other side of the world.
Locked in the prison of skin

they break on the long weekend
when loggers pelt their shack with stones.
Three are taken to hospital in Kamloops.
with arms and bellies slashed
and when the lone policeman asks
what caused the fight, they tell him
the fight was amongst themselves.
They say they fought over
the memory of their women;
that to keep from going mad
they were driven there with words
believing they could survive
by telling each other stories of love.


## The Carpenter

The gentle fears he tells me of being
afraid to climb back down each day
from the top of the unfinished building.
He says: I'm getting old
and wish each morning when I arrive
I could beat into shape
a scaffold to take me higher
but the wood I'd need
is still growing on the hills
the nails raw red with rust
still changing shape in bluffs
somewhere north of my mind.

I've hung over this city like a bird
and seen it change from shacks to towers.
It's not that I'm afraid
but sometimes when I'm alone up here
and know I can't get higher
I think I'll just walk off the edge
and either fall or fly

and then he laughs
so that his plum-bob goes awry
and single strokes the spikes into the joists
pushing the floor another level higher
like a hawk who every year adds levels to his nest
until he's risen above the tree he builds on
and alone lifts off into the wind
beating his wings like nails into the sky.


## Stigmata

For Irving Layton

What if there wasn't a metaphor
and the bodies were only bodies
bones pushed out in awkward fingers?
Waves come to the seawall, fall away,
children bounce mouths against the stones
man has carved to keep the sea at bay
and women talk with empty wombs
proclaiming freedom to the night.
Through barroom windows rotten with light
eyes of men open and close like fists.

I bend beside a tidal pool and take a crab from the sea.
His small green life twists helpless in my hand
the living bars of bone and flesh
a cage made by the animal I am.
This thing, the beat, the beat of life
now captured in the darkness of my flesh
struggling with claws as if it could tear its way
through my body back to the sea.
What do I know of the inexorable beauty,
the unrelenting turning of the wheel I am inside me?
Stigmata. I hold a web of blood.

I dream of the scrimshawed teeth of endless whales,
the oceans it took to carve them. Drifting ships
echo in fog the wounds of Leviathan
great grey voices giving cadence to their loss.
The men are gone
who scratched upon white bones their destiny.
Who will speak of the albatross in the shroud of the man,
the sailor who sinks forever in the Mindanao Deep?
I open my hand. The life leaps out.


## Albino Pheasants


At the bottom of the field
where thistles throw their seeds
and poplars grow from cotton into trees
in a single season I stand among the weeds.
Fenceposts hold each other up with sagging wire.
Here no man walks except in wasted time.
Men circle me with cattle, cars and wheat.
Machines rot on my margins.
They say the land is wasted when its wild
and offer plows and apple trees to tame
but in the fall when I have driven them away
with their guns and dogs and dreams
I walk alone. While those who'd kill
lie sleeping in soft beds
huddled against the bodies of their wives
I go with speargrass and hooked burrs
and wait upon the ice alone.

Delicate across the mesh of snow
I watch the pale birds come
with beaks the colour of discarded flesh.
White, their feathers are white,
as if they had been born in caves
and only now have risen to the earth

to watch with pink and darting eyes
the slowly moving shadows of the moon.
There is no way to tell men what to do . . .
the dance they make in sleep
withholds its meaning from their dreams.
That which has been nursed in bone
rests easy upon frozen stone
and what is wild is lost behind closed eyes:
albino birds, pale sisters, succubi.

## Of Letters

I sit in the solitude of letters.
Words do not slow the sun.
The sky is clear in the west.

Clouds have passed over me.
Their spun silk hangs
on the bones of the Monashee.

A magpie drifts across the sun.
His long tail writes too swiftly
for me to interpret. On my desk

a wasp I killed last week
after it stung me. Who
will write its poem?

I move toward my fortieth year.
Letters remain unanswered.
The sun slides into the west

and in the east clouds collapse
draping with crystal
the waiting arms of the trees.

## The Great Wall

There is a moment on the wall when a man looks out
over the far horizon and wonders when
they will come.  He does not know who they are.
The wall was built many years ago, long
before he was born and before his father was
born.  All his life has been spent
repairing the wall, replacing the fallen
stones, clearing away the tough grass
that grows like fingers in the masonry.

Inside the wall the land is the same
as outside and once, when he was confused
by the hot wind, he could not remember
which side of the wall he lived on and he
has never forgotten the doubt of that day.
He has seen no one but his family for years.
They were given this work by someone
a long time ago or so his father said
but who it was he did not remember,
it was before his time.

But there comes a moment, there always does,
when a man stops his work, lays down his tools,
looks out over the dry brown distance
and wonders when they will come, the ones
the wall is meant for.  At that moment
he sees between the earth and the sky
a cloud of dust like the drifting spores
of a puffball exploded by a foot.

He knows there is nothing to do but wait,
nothing he can do but stand on the wall.  Everything
is in order, the wall as perfect as a man
can make it.  It does not occur to him
that the cloud might be only a cloud of dust,
something the wind has raised out of nothing

and which will return to nothing. For a moment
he wonders what will happen when they come.
Will they honour him for his work, the hours
and years he has spent? But which side
of the wall do they come from?
No one has ever told him what would happen.

He will have to tell his son, he thinks,
his wife. He wishes his father were alive
to see them coming, but he is not,
and his son, who has already learned
the secrets of stone, is asleep.
It is a day to remember.
In all his life he has never been more
afraid, he has never been happier.

## Against Blue Jade Curtains

For the Companions

Against blue jade curtains
friends talk with first friends,
sadness and the touch of wine.
Our loss is our beginning.
Outside bats dance.
They pay us little attention.
Such knowledge is a blessing.
With wine we too hang upside down,
our laughter the flight of bats,
a small but perfect freedom.

## Small Love Song

Syllable of stone, the lizard lies prone
under the bright dome of the moon.
His patience lasts forever.
I know I am almost old and my bed is made of sand
but even among stones love is possible.
The lizard waits forever in the ruins.
Come to me.
I will wait for you at least one more night.

# Gary Geddes

*Sandra Lee Scheuer*

*(Killed at Kent State University on May 4, 1970 by the
Ohio National Guard)*

You might have met her on a Saturday night
cutting precise circles, clockwise, at the Moon-Glo
Roller Rink, or walking with quick step

between the campus and a green two-storey house,
where the room was always tidy, the bed made,
the books in confraternity on the shelves.

She did not throw stones, major in philosophy
or set fire to buildings, though acquaintances say
she hated war, had heard of Cambodia.

In truth she wore a modicum of make-up, a brassiere,
and could, no doubt, more easily have married a guardsman
than cursed or put a flower in his rifle barrel.

While the armouries burned she studied,
bent low over notes, speech therapy books, pages
open at sections on impairment, physiology.

And while they milled and shouted on the commons
she helped a boy named Billy with his lisp, saying
Hiss, Billy, like a snake. That's it, SSSSSSSS,

tongue well up and back behind your teeth.
Now buzz, Billy, like a bee.  Feel the air
vibrating in my windpipe as I breathe?

As she walked in sunlight through the parking-lot
at noon, feeling the world a passing lovely place,
a young guardsman, who had his sights on her,

was going down on one knee as if he might propose.
His declaration, unmistakable, articulate,
flowered within her, passed through her neck,

served her trachea, taking her breath away.
Now who will burn the midnight oil for Billy,
ensure the perilous freedom of his speech?

And who will see her skating at the Moon-Glo
Roller Rink, the eight small wooden wheels
making their countless revolutions on the floor?


## Letter of the Master of Horse

I was signed
on the King's authority
as master of horse.
Three days
            (I remember
            quite clearly)
three days after we parted.
I did not really believe it,
it seemed so much the unrolling
of an incredible dream.

Bright plumes, scarlet tunics,
glint of sunlight on armour.
Fifty of the King's best horses,
strong, high-spirited, rearing
to the blast of trumpets,
galloping
down the long avenida

to the waiting ships.
And me, your gangling brother,
permitted to ride with cavalry.

Laughter,
children singing
in the market, women
dancing, throwing flowers,
the whole street covered
with flowers.

In the plaza del sol
a blind beggar kissed my eyes.
I hadn't expected the softness
of his fingers
                    moving upon my face.

A bad beginning.
The animals knew, hesitated
at the ramps, backed off,
finally had to be blindfolded
and beaten aboard.

Sailors grumbled for days
as if we had brought on board
a cargo of women.

But the sea smiled.
Smiled as we passed
through the world's gate,
smiled as we lost our escort
of gulls.  I have seen
such smiles on faces of whores
in Barcelona.

For months now
an unwelcome guest
in my own body.

I squat by the fire
in a silence broken only
by the tireless grinding
of insects.

I have taken
to drawing your face
in the brown earth
at my feet.
              (The ears are
              never quite right.)

You are waving,
waving.  Your
tears are a river
that swells, rushes beside me.
I lie for days in a sea drier
than the desert of the Moors
but your tears are lost,
sucked
into the parched throat of the sky.

I am watched daily.
The ship's carpenter is at work
nearby, within the stockade,
fashioning a harness for me
a wooden collar.  He is a fool
who takes no pride in his work,
yet the chips lie about his feet
beautiful as yellow petals.

Days melt
in the hot sun, flow
together.  An order is given
to jettison the horses,
it sweeps like a breeze
over parched black faces.

I am not consulted, though
Ortega comes to me later
when it is over and says:

> God knows, there are men
> I'd have worried less to lose.

The sailors are relieved,
fall to it with abandon.
The first horse is blindfolded,
led to the gunwales, and struck
so hard it leaps skyward
in an arc, its great body
etched against the sun.

I remember thinking
how graceless it looked,
out of its element, legs
braced and stiffened
for the plunge.

They drink long
draughts, muzzles submerged
to the eyes, set out like spokes
in all directions.
The salt does its work.
First scream, proud head
thrown back, nostrils flared,
flesh tight over teeth
and gums
                (yellow teeth,
                bloody gums).
The spasms, heaving bodies,
turning, turning.
I am the centre
of this churning circumference.
The wretch beside me,
fingers

knotted to the gunwales.

They plunge toward
the ship, hooves crashing
on the planked hull.
Soft muzzles ripped
and bleeding on splintered wood
and barnacles.
The ensign's mare
struggles half out of the water
on the backs of two
hapless animals.

When the affair ended
the sea was littered with bodies,
smooth bloated carcasses.
Neither pike pole nor ship's
boats could keep them off.
Sailors that never missed
a meal retched violently
in the hot sun. Only
the silent industry of sharks
could give them rest.

What is the shape of freedom,
after all? Did I come here
to be devoured by insects, or
maddened by screams in the night?

Ortega, when we found him,
pinned and swinging in his bones,
jawbone pinned and singing
in the wind: God's lieutenant,
more eloquent in death.

Sooner or later hope
evaporates, joy itself
is seasonal. The others?

They are Spaniards, no more
and no less, and burn with a lust
that sends them tilting
at the sun itself.

Ortega, listen, the horses,
where are the sun's horses
to pull his chariot from the sea,
end this conspiracy of dark?

The nights are long, the cold
a maggot boarding in my flesh.

I hear them moving,
barely perceptible, faint
as the roar of insects.
Gathering,
gathering to thunder
across the hidden valleys
of the sea, crash of hooves
upon my door, hot quick
breath upon my face.

My eyes, he kissed my eyes,
the softness of his fingers
moving. . . .

Forgive me, I did not
mean this to be my final
offering.  Sometimes the need
to forgive, be forgiven,
makes the heart a pilgrim.
I am no traveller,
my Christopher faceless
with rubbing on the voyage
out, the voyage into exile.
Islanded in our separate
selves, words are

too frail a bridge.

I see you in the morning
running to meet me down
the mountainside, your face
transfigured with happiness.
Wait for me, my sister,
where wind rubs bare
the cliff-face, where we rode
to watch the passing ships
at day-break, and saw them
burn golden, from masthead
down to waterline.

I will come soon.

## The Strap

No other sound was heard throughout the school
as Jimmy Bunn surrendered to the strap.
He stood before me in the counsellor's office
eye to eye, while the desk drawer gaped,
his farmer's hands stretched out in turn
expectant as beggars. My heart was touched.
I gave them more than they had bargained for.
Six on each. The welts, like coins,
inflated as we watched. Nothing he'd done
deserved such largesse, disrupting my sermon
on the Bay of Pigs invasion and how Americans
are hooked on violence, etcetera, etcetera.
They say there's a kinship in aggression
that knits the torturer and his victim;
we came to be the best of friends.
But each excuse and subterfuge exploded
in my brain as he dropped his puffed pink hams
and fought back tears. I put the leather tongue
into the gaping drawer and pushed it shut.

## Jimmy's Place

We found the cow in a grove below the road,
leaning against an alder for support,
her udder swollen, her breath ragged and grating
as a rasp. I could have drowned
in the liquid eye she turned to me.
Her calf, though dead, was perfectly positioned,
forelegs and head protruding from the flaming ring
of vulva. Too large, perhaps, or hind legs
broken through the sac, dispersing fluids.
Much as we tried we couldn't pry it loose
and flesh around the legs began to give
from pressure on the rope. The cow
had no more strength and staggered back
each time we pulled. Tie her to the tree,
I said, being the schoolmaster and thinking
myself obliged to have an answer, even here
on the High Road, five miles south of town
where the island bunched in the jumble
of its origins. It was coming, by God,
I swear it, this scrub roan with her shadow self
extending out behind, going in both directions
like a '52 Studebaker, coming by inches
and our feet slipping in the mud and shit
and wet grass. She raised her head and tried
to see what madness we'd concocted in her wake,
emitted a tearing gunny-sack groan,
and her liquid eye ebbed back to perfect white.

## Saskatchewan: 1949

Father is riding
the ridgepole of the new barn
and dreaming ocean.

He grips the keel

with shipwright's thighs.
Studs and two-by-fours
like bleached, white ribs
take measure of the sky.

He cannot fathom the wash
of tides, war's currents,
love's coups d'état,
that ground him
on this ancient seabed
of prairie.
                    He knows
what his fingers know:
claw hammer, crowbar,
and a clutch of nails.

Close-hauled bedsheets
nudge the house to windward.
Ripe wheat breaks like surf
on beaches of new lumber.

Ahoy!  Ahoy!  cries Noah
from his ark.

Shoals of brown cattle
dot the sweetgrass shallows.
Crows swim up like sturgeon
from the startled corn.

## Philip Larkin

He was a man whose words stopped short
of ecstasy, whose impaired tongue and ear refused
the grand theme, the gesture of extravagance,
and found, instead, out along the side-roads,

pantleg rolled, cycle propped against a tree,
a desperation so quietly profound even toad,
blinking among grass-spears, had overlooked.
He composed no score for happiness, but improvised

a life of common pleasures taken in a minor key:
a few pints with friends who didn't talk of poetry,
an early morning stroll in Pearson Park,
industrialist's gift to dreary, fog-bound Hull,

sausages on campus, a slice of Humber pie.
Hearing-aid turned off, he tunes his inner music,
a private soul station, some such jazz,
communes with Jelly Roll and Beiderbecke,

or watches from his window at the Nuffield,
where Westbourne intersects with Salisbury,
winos rub themselves againt the freshly-painted
thighs of mermaids in the Victorian fountain,

who take their own libations from a conch.
While such doleful enthusiasts drink his health,
all flesh conspires to silence Larkin;
he undergoes a sea-change in the Avenues.

With no more reason to attend, he sings the poem
of his departure, achieves his wish to be alone.
Propped up in bed and talking to himself,
one thing only is denied: the desire of oblivion.

# From *The Terracotta Army*

CHARIOTEER

*I wouldn't call you layabouts a standing army;*
*there's more life in this terracotta nag*

*than in the whole first division.* With that,
Bi leapt on the back of a cavalry pony he had fired

the previous day and dug his heels into the outline
of ribs. I wouldn't have been surprised

to see it leap into action and clear the doorway
with the potter shouting death to the enemy.

Most of the animals were cast from a single mould
and could be distinguished one from the other

only by the application of paint and dyes. I took
exception to this and remarked that, as charioteer,

I found more distinctive characteristics in horses
than in men. Bi swung his legs over the neck

and dropped to the ground. He was no taller
than the ponies he fashioned. Then, with a flourish,

he drew a green moustache on the horse's muzzle
and fell about the pottery amused by his own joke.


PAYMASTER

We stood beside the trenches and looked at the rows
of figures there, bronze horses harnessed in gold

and silver, some of the charioteers in miniature
with robes and hairstyles denoting superior rank;

then the pottery horses with their snaffle bits
and bridles of stone beads. These had been fired

in one piece, except for the tail and forelock.
Most of the men could be seen to wear toques

over their topknots. Kang, of course, had abandoned
such fashions and stood there with an eternal leer

and his pot-belly showing through armour, rivets
forever about to pop. A sensualist. I was astounded

as usual by the loving attention to detail and asked Bi
what thoughts this assembled spectacle called up in him.

*Counterfeit currency,* he said. *A life's work
that will never be seen, poems tossed in bonfires.*

*A poem lives on in the ear, but a single push
will topple all of these.*


BLACKSMITH

Bi remarked on the lethal aspect of the crossbow,
whose bronze trigger mechanism I'd just improved.

Tests had been done that morning on criminal types
who'd failed to comply with laws on standardization.

At short range the crossbow sent a heavy arrow
through the breasts of five men with surprisingly little

loss of speed; it was equally efficient on two others
in full armour, standing back to back outside the gates

of the A-fang palace.  I received a rousing cheer
from the assembled soldiers and nobility;

even the castratos pressed into service in the grounds
and gardens seemed more than slightly impressed.

Bi was sweating profusely and I thought he looked
rather pale in the dim light as he worked on details

of the armoured vest of a kneeling crossbowman.
Where is the dragon, rain-bringer, lord of waters

when we need him, the potter muttered to himself,
wiping the blade of the chisel on his leather apron.


## From *Hong Kong*

### *Sullivan*

There's a strange hush at St. Stephen's
as we wait for them to storm the College.
Nurses drift like butterflies among the injured,
offering a word, a touch, a cigarette.
When the enemy bursts through the door

I'm lying on a cot at the far end of the corridor,
my head bandaged, my leg supported in a sling.
Two soldiers proceed to bayonet the sick and wounded
in their beds, to a chorus of screams and protests.
A nurse throws herself on top of one of our boys

to protect him—it might have been the kid
from Queen's—and they are both killed
by a single thrust of the bayonet.
I suppose they were sweethearts.  Pinned
at last, she does not struggle.  Her hands

open and close once, like tiny wings,
and the dark stain on her white, starched uniform
spreads like a chrysanthemum, a blood-red sun.
I cut the cord supporting my leg, slip on
the nearest smock and stand foolishly at attention,

making the salute. My right index finger
brushes the damp cotton of the bandage.
Later, the butchers are shot by their own officers;
one, apparently, had lost a brother
in the final assault.

## 250-Word Essay Required by the Japanese on the Battle of Hong Kong

On the southeastern shore of Lake Winnipeg, there's a small town called Libau. There wasn't much happening in those days to keep a town going, so we had to settle for a store, a garage and a barber-shop. The Japanese who took over the store in 1935 tried to sell sandwiches and coffee on the side and take in laundry, but nobody had money to pay for groceries, never mind the luxuries. After school, when my chores were done, I sometimes did odd jobs for Mr. Saeto in exchange for food. I piled wood, stocked shelves, or maybe brought him a catch of goldeye from the lake. The first time, I gutted them and cut off the heads and tails, but Saeto shook his head and made clear he wanted his fish intact. Kids used to say the Japanese ate fish-eyes as a delicacy, but I think Saeto used the head and tail for soup. He told me he had a wife in Japan and had been to visit her twice, the first time producing a son, the second time a daughter. I had a lot of respect for him when I heard that. Once, while we were warming our hands in front of the wood-heater, I asked him why he didn't bring his family to Canada. He told me politics was no good; it made people's hearts like stone. In all that time, I never even heard of Hong Kong.

249 words

# Gwendolyn MacEwen

*Poems in Braille*

I

all your hands are verbs,
now you touch worlds and feel their names—
thru the thing to the name
not the other way thru (in winter
I am Midas, I name gold)

the chair and table and book
extend from your fingers;
all your movements
command these things back to their
places; a fight against familiarity
makes me resume my distance

II

they knew what it meant,
those egyptian scribes who drew
eyes right into their hieroglyphs,
you read them dispassionate until
the eye stumbles upon itself
blinking back from the papyrus

outside, the articulate wind
annotates this; I read carefully
lest I go blind in both eyes, reading with
that other eye the final hieroglyph

III

the shortest distance between 2 points
on a revolving circumference
is a curved line; O let me follow you,
Wenceslas

IV

with legs and arms I make alphabets
like in those children's books
where people bend into letters and signs,
yet I do not read the long cabbala of my bones
truthfully; I need only to move
to alter the design

V

I name all things in my room
and they rehearse their names,
gather in groups, form tesseracts,
discussing their names among themselves

I will not say the cast is less than the print
I will not say the curve is longer than the line,
I should read all things like braille in this season
with my fingers I should read them
lest I go blind in both eyes reading with
that other eye the final hieroglyph

## Manzini: Escape Artist

now there are no bonds except the flesh; listen—
there was this boy, Manzini, stubborn with
gut stood with black tights and a turquoise
leaf across his sex

and smirking while the big
brute tied his neck arms legs, Manzini
naked waist up and white with sweat

struggled. Silent, delinquent, he
was suddenly all teeth and knee, straining slack
and excellent with sweat, inwardly

wondering if Houdini would take as long
as he; fighting time and the drenched
muscular ropes, as though his tendons were worn
on the outside—

as though his own guts were the ropes
encircling him; it was beautiful; it was thursday; listen—
there was this boy, Manzini

finally free, slid as snake from
his own sweet agonized skin, to throw his entrails
white upon the floor
with a cry of victory—

*now there are no bonds except the flesh,*
but listen, it was thursday, there was this boy,
Manzini—


## Arcanum One

and in the morning the king loved you most
and wrote your name with a sun and a beetle
and a crooked ankh, and in the morning
you wore gold mainly, and the king adorned you
with many more names

beside fountains, both of you slender
as women, circled and walked together

like bracelets circling water, both of you
slender as women, wrote your names with
beetles and with suns, and spoke together
in the golden mornings

and the king entered your body
into the bracelet of his name
and you became a living syllable
in his golden script, and your body
escaped from me like founting water
all the daylong

but in the evenings you wrote my name
with a beetle and a moon, and lay upon me
like a long broken necklace which had fallen
from my throat, and the king loved you
most in the morning, and his glamorous love
lay lengthwise along us all the evening


## Poem Improvised Around a First Line*

the smoke in my bedroom which is always burning
worsens you, motorcycle Icarus;
you are black and leathery and lean and
you cannot distinguish between sex and nicotine

anytime, it's all one thing for you–
cigarette, phallus, sacrificial fire–
all part of that grimy flight
on wings axlegreased from Toronto to Buffalo
for the secret beer over the border–

now I long to see you fullblown and black
over Niagara, your bike burning and in full flame

* The first line around which it was improvised has disappeared.

and twisting and pivoting over Niagara
and falling finally into Niagara,
and tourists coming to see your black leather wings
hiss and swirl in the steaming current-

now I long to give up cigarettes
and change the sheets on my carboniferous bed;
O baby, what Hell to be Greek in this country-
without wings, but burning anyway


## The Red Bird You Wait For

You are waiting for someone to confirm it,
You are waiting for someone to say it plain,
Now we are here and because we are short of time
I will say it; I might even speak its name.

It is moving above me, it is burning my heart out,
I have felt it crash through my flesh,
I have spoken to it in a foreign tongue,
I have stroked its neck in the night like a wish.

Its name is the name you have buried in your blood,
Its shape is a gorgeous cast-off velvet cape,
Its eyes are the eyes of your most forbidden lover
And its claws, I tell you its claws are gloved in fire.

You are waiting to hear its name spoken,
You have asked me a thousand times to speak it,
You who have hidden it, cast it off, killed it,
Loved it to death and sung your songs over it.

The red bird you wait for falls with giant wings—
A velvet cape whose royal colour calls us kings
Is the form it takes as, uninvited, it descends,
It is the Power and the Glory forever, Amen.

## The Discovery

do not imagine that the exploration
ends, that she has yielded all her mystery
or that the map you hold
cancels further discovery

I tell you her uncovering takes years,
takes centuries, and when you find her naked
look again,
admit there is something else you cannot name,
a veil, a coating just above the flesh
which you cannot remove by your mere wish

when you see the land naked, lock again
(burn your maps, that is not what I mean),
I mean the moment when it seems most plain
is the moment when you must begin again

## Dark Pines Under Water

This land like a mirror turns you inward
And you become a forest in a furtive lake;
The dark pines of your mind reach downward,
You dream in the green of your time,
Your memory is a row of sinking pines.

Explorer, you tell yourself this is not what you came for
Although it is good here, and green;
You had meant to move with a kind of largeness,
You had planned a heavy grace, an anguished dream.

But the dark pines of your mind dip deeper
And you are sinking, sinking, sleeper
In an elementary world;
There is something down there and you want it told.

## Memoirs of a Mad Cook

There's no point kidding myself any longer,
I just can't get the knack of it; I suspect
there's a secret society which meets
in dark cafeterias to pass on the art
from one member to another.
Besides,
it's so *personal* preparing food for someone's
insides, what can I possibly *know*
about someone's insides, how can I presume
to invade your blood?
I'll try, God knows I'll try
but if anyone watches me I'll *scream*
because maybe I'm handling a tomato wrong
how can I *know* if I'm handling a tomato wrong?

*something is eating away at me*
*with splendid teeth*

Wistfully I stand in my difficult kitchen
and imagine the fantastic salads and soufflés
that will never be.
Everyone seems to grow thin with me
and their eyes grow black as hunter's eyes
and search my face for sustenance.
All my friends are dying of hunger,
there is some basic dish I cannot offer,
and you my love are almost as lean
as the splendid wolf I must keep always
at my door.

## The Child Dancing

there's no way I'm going to write about
the child dancing in the Warsaw ghetto
in his body of rags

there were only two corpses
on the pavement that day
and the child I will not write about
had a face as pale and trusting
as the moon

(so did
the boy with a green belly full of dirt
lying by the roadside
in a novel of Kazantzakis
and the small girl T. E. Lawrence wrote about
who they found after the Turkish massacre
with one shoulder chopped off, crying:
'don't *hurt* me, Baba!')

I don't feel like slandering them with poetry.

the child who danced
in the Warsaw ghetto
to some music no one else could hear
had moon-eyes, no
green horror and no fear
but something worse

a simple desire to please
the people who stayed
to watch him shuffle back and forth,
his feet wrapped in the newspapers
of another ordinary day

# From *The T.E. Lawrence Poems*

APOLOGIES

I did not choose Arabia; it chose me.  The shabby money
That the desert offered us bought lies, bought victory.
　　　　What was I, that soiled Outsider, doing
Among them?  I was not becoming one of them, no matter
What you think.  They found it easier to learn my kind
　　　　of Arabic, than to teach me theirs.
And they were all mad; they mounted their horses and camels
　　　　from the right.

But my mind's twin kingdoms waged an everlasting war;
The reckless Bedouin and the civilized Englishman
　　　　fought for control, so that I, whatever I was,
Fell into a dumb void that even a false god could not fill,
　　　　could not inhabit.

The Arabs are children of the idea; dangle an idea
In front of them, and you can swing them wherever.
　　　　I was also a child of the idea; I wanted
　　　　no liberty for myself, but to bestow it
Upon them.  I wanted to present them with a gift so fine
　　　　it would outshine all other gifts in their eyes;
　　　　it would be *worthy*.  Then I at last could be
Empty.

You can't imagine how beautiful it is to be empty.
Out of this grand emptiness wonderful things must surely
　　　　come into being.
When we set out, it was morning.  We hardly knew
That when we moved we would not be an army, but a world.

NITROGLYCERINE TULIPS

We planted things called tulip bombs to knock out
    Turkish trains, or curl up the tracks;
    the Turks were so stupid, it sometimes
    seemed to me too easy. How could they
    expect a *proper* war
If they gave us no chance to honor them?

I called myself Emir Dynamite, and became quite deft
    at the whole business of organized
    destruction. In the back of one train
    which I derailed, was a carriage full of
    dying men; one whispered *Typhus,*
So I wedged the door closed and left them in.

Another time I straightened out the bodies of dead Turks,
    placing them in rows to look better;
    I was trying, I think, to make it
    a neat war. Once there were three hundred
    of them, with their clothes stripped off,
And I wanted nothing more than to lie down with them,

And die, of course—and think of nothing else but
    raspberries cold with rain, instead of
    sending currents into blasting gelatin
    and watching the sad old trains
    blow sky high
With Turks in little bits around everywhere.

DERAA

I started to write something like:
*The citadels of my integrity were lost,* or
    *quo vadis from here, Lawrence?*
                      How pathetic.

I may as well tell you that as a boy my best castle
          was beseiged and overcome by my brothers.

What happened of course was that I was raped at Deraa,
          beaten and whipped and reduced to shreds
          by Turks with lice in their hair, and VD,
          a gift from their officers, crawling all over
          their bodies.
                              I had thought that the Arabs were
Bad enough.  Slicing the soles of a prisoner's feet
          so that when they let him return to his men,
          he went very, very slowly;
                                        but they were merciful.

Imagine, I could never bear to be touched by anybody;
I considered myself a sort of flamboyant monk, awfully
          intact, yet colorful.
                              Inviolable is the word.
But everything is shameful, you know; to have a body
          is a cruel joke.  It is shameful to be under
          an obligation to anything, even an animal;
          life is shameful; I am shameful.  There.

So what part of me lusted after death, as they smashed
          knees into my groin and turned a small knife
          between my ribs?  Did I cry out or not when
          they held my legs apart and one of them rode
          upon me, laughing, and splitting open
          a bloody pathway through my soul?
I don't remember.
                              They beat me until something, some
          primal slime spilled out of me, and fire
          shot to my brain.
                              On a razor edge of reality,
I knew I would come out of this, bleeding and broken,
          and singing.

They lean on the horizon, insolent and wise.

GHAZALA'S FOAL

Ghazala was the second finest camel in all Arabia, and
She did not know it.
                      She had absolutely no mission in life
            and no sense of honor or of shame; she was
            almost perfect.
                      I've seen so many camels die
            that it doesn't matter—the females going on
            until they foundered and died in their tracks,
            the males roaring and flinging themselves down
            and dying unnecessarily out of sheer rage, those
            we scooped out of the snow at Tafileh—but
Mostly I remember Ghazala's foal, getting up and walking
            when it was three hours old, then falling down
            again, in a little heap of slippery limbs.

One of the men skinned it, and Ghazala cried and sniffed
            the little hide.
                      Then we marched again, and often
            she stopped short, and looked around wildly,
            remembering something that was terribly important,
            then lapsing into a blank, dazed stare.
                                        Only
            when the poor, tiny piece of skin was placed
            before her on the ground would she
Murmur something, nudge it, ponder a while, and walk on.


TALL TALES

It has been said that I sometimes lie, or bend the truth
            to suit me.  Did I make that four hundred mile
            trip alone in Turkish territory or not?
            I wonder if it is anybody's business
            to know.  Syria is still there,
            and the long lie that the war was.

Was there a poster of me offering money for my capture,

and did I stand there staring at myself,
daring anyone to know me?  Consider
truth and untruth, consider why they call them
the *theatres* of war.  All of us
played our roles to the hilt.

Poets only play with words, you know; they too
        are masters of the Lie, the Grand Fiction.
        Poets and men like me who fight for something
        contained in words, but not words.

What if the whole show was a lie, and it bloody well was—
        would I still lie to you?  Of course I would.


NOTES FROM THE DEAD LAND

I have died at last, Feisal.  I have been lying
On this hospital bed for five days, and I know
        that I am dead.  I was going back home
        on my big bike, and I wasn't doing more
        than sixty when this black van, death camel,
Slid back from the left side of my head, and ahead,
Two boys on little bikes were biking along, and
        something in my head, some brutal music
        played on and on.  I was going too fast,
        I was always going too fast for the world,
So I swerved and fell on my stupid head, right
In the middle of the road.  I addressed myself
        to the dark hearts of the tall trees
        and nothing answered.

The Arabs say that when you pray, two angels stand
On either side of you, recording good and bad deeds,
        and you should acknowledge them.
        Lying here, I decide that now
        the world can have me any way it pleases.
I will celebrate my perfect death here. *Maktub:*
It is written.  I salute both of the angels.

# Michael Ondaatje

*Early Morning, Kingston to Gananoque*

The twenty miles to Gananoque
with tangled dust blue grass
burned, and smelling burned
along the highway
is land too harsh for picnics.
Deep in the fields
behind stiff dirt fern
nature breeds the unnatural.

Escaping cows canter white
then black and white
along the median, forming out of mist.
Crows pick at animal accidents,
with swoops lift meals—
blistered groundhogs, stripped snakes
to arch behind a shield of sun.

Somewhere in those fields
they are shaping new kinds of women.


*The Diverse Causes*

*'for than all erbys and treys renewyth a man and woman,
and in lyke wyse lovers callyth to their mynde olde
jantylnes and olde servyse, and many kynde dedes that
was forgotyn by neclygence'*

Three clouds and a tree
reflect themselves on a toaster.

The kitchen window hangs scarred,
shattered by winter hunters.

We are in a cell of civilised magic.
Stravinsky roars at breakfast,
our milk is powdered.

Outside, a May god
moves his paws to alter wind
to scatter shadows of tree and cloud.
The minute birds walk confident
jostling the cold grass.
The world not yet of men.

We clean buckets of their sand
to fetch water in the morning,
reach for winter cobwebs,
sweep up moths who have forgotten to waken.
When the children sleep, angled
behind their bottles, you can hear mice prowl.
I turn a page
careful not to break the rhythms
of your sleeping head on my hip,
watch the moving under your eyelid
that turns like fire,
and we have love and the god outside
until ice starts to limp
in brown hidden waterfalls,
or my daughter burns the lake
by reflecting her red shoes in it.

## Elizabeth

Catch, my Uncle Jack said
and oh I caught this huge apple
red as Mrs Kelly's bum.

It's red as Mrs Kelly's bum, I said
and Daddy roared
and swung me on his stomach with a heave.
Then I hid the apple in my room
till it shrunk like a face
growing eyes and teeth ribs.

Then Daddy took me to the zoo
he knew the man there
they put a snake around my neck
and it crawled down the front of my dress.
I felt its flicking tongue
dripping onto me like a shower.
Daddy laughed and said Smart Snake
and Mrs Kelly with us scowled.

In the pond where they kept the goldfish
Philip and I broke the ice with spades
and tried to spear the fishes;
we killed one and Philip ate it,
then he kissed me
with raw saltless fish in his mouth.

My sister Mary's got bad teeth
and said I was lucky, then she said
I had big teeth, but Philip said I was pretty.
He had big hands that smelled.

I would speak of Tom, soft laughing,
who danced in the mornings round the sundial
teaching me the steps from France, turning
with the rhythm of the sun on the warped branches,
who'd hold my breast and watch it move like a snail
leaving his quick urgent love in my palm.
And I kept his love in my palm till it blistered.

When they axed his shoulders and neck
the blood moved like a branch into the crowd.

And he staggered with his hanging shoulder
cursing their thrilled cry, wheeling,
waltzing in the French style to his knees
holding his head with the ground,
blood settling on his clothes like a blush;
this way
when they aimed the thud into his back.

And I find cool entertainment now
with white young Essex, and my nimble rhymes.


## Peter

I

That spring Peter was discovered, freezing
the maze of bones from a dead cow,
skull and hooves glazed
with a skin of ice.
The warmth in his hands
carved hollows of muscle,
his fingers threading veins on its flank.

In the attempt to capture him
he bit, to defend himself,
three throats and a wrist;
that night villagers found the cow
frozen in red, and Peter
eating a meal beside it.

II

They snared him in evening light,
his body a pendulum
between the walls of the yard,
rearing from shrinking flashes of steel
until they, with a new science,

stretched his heels and limbs,
scarred through the back of his knees
leaving his veins unpinned,
and him singing in the evening air.

Till he fainted, and a brown bitch
nosed his pain, stared in interest,
and he froze into consciousness
to drag his feet to the fountain,
to numb wounds.

III

In the first months of his capture
words were growls, meaningless;
disgust in his tone burned everyone.
At meals, in bed, you heard Peter's howl
in the depths of the castle like a bell.
After the first year they cut out his tongue;

difficult
to unpin a fish's mouth
without the eventual jerk
to empty throat of pin and matter.

There followed months of silence,
then the eventual grunting;
he began to speak with the air of his body,
torturing breath into tones; it was despicable,
they had made a dead animal of his throat.

He was little more than a marred stone,
a baited gargoyle, escaped
from the fountain in the courtyard:
his throat swollen like an arm muscle,
his walk stuttered with limp, his knees straight,
his feet arching like a compass.

IV

They made a hive for him in the court,
Jason throwing him bones from the table,
the daughter Tara tousling in detail
the hair that collapsed like a nest
over his weaving eyes.
She, with bored innocence,
would pet him like a flower,
place vast kisses on his wrists,
thrilled at scowls and obscenities,
delighted at sudden grins
that opened his face like a dawn.
He ate, bouldered at their feet,
vast hands shaping rice,
and he walked with them on grit drives—
his legs dragged like a suitcase behind him.

V

All this while Peter formed violent beauty.
He carved death on chalices,
made spoons of yawning golden fishes;
forks stemmed from the tongues of reptiles,
candle holders bent like the ribs of men.

He made fragments of people: breasts
in the midst of a girl's stride,
a head burrowed in love,
an arm swimming—fingers heaved
to nose barricades of water.

His squat form, the rippled arms
of seaweeded hair,
the fingers black, bent from moulding silver,
poured all his strength
into the bare reflection of eyes.

VI

Then Tara grew.

When he first saw her, tall,
ungainly as trees,
her fat knees dangled his shoulders
as her hips rode him,
the court monster, she
swaying from side to side, held
only by the grip of her thighs
on his obtuse neck—
she bending over him,
muttering giggles at his eyes,
covering his creased face with her hair.
And he made golden spiders for her
and silver frogs, with opal glares.

And as she grew, her body
burned its awkwardness.
The full bones roamed
in brown warm skin.
The ridge in her back broadened,
her dress hid seas of thighs,
arms trailed to adjust hair that paused
like a long bird at her shoulder;
and vast brown breasts
restless at each gesture
clung to her body like new sea beasts.

And she smiled cool at Peter now,
a quiet hand received gifts from him,
and her fingers, poised,
touched
to generate expressions.

VII

An arm held her, splayed
its fingers like a cross at her neck
till he could feel fear thrashing at her throat,
while his bent hands tore the sheet of skirt,
lifted her, buttock and neck to the table.
Then laying arm above her breasts
he shaped her body like a mould,
the stub of tongue sharp as a cat, cold,
dry as a cat, rasping neck and breasts
till he poured loathing of fifteen years on her,
a vat of lush oil, staining,
the large soft body like a whale.

Then he lay there breathing at her neck
his face wet from her tears
that glued him to her pain.


## 'The gate in his head'

For Victor Coleman

Victor—the shy mind
revealing faint scars
coloured strata of the brain
not clarity but the sense of shift.
A few lines/the tracks of thought.
The landscape of busted trees
melted tires in the sun
Stan's fishbowl
with a book inside
turning its pages
like some sea animal
camouflaging itself
the typeface clarity
going slow blond in the sun full water

My mind is pouring chaos
in nets onto the page.
A blind lover, dont know
what I love till I write it out.
Then from Gibson's your letter
with a blurred
photograph of a gull.
Caught vision. The stunning white bird
an unclear stir.

And that is all this writing should be then.
The beautiful formed things caught at the wrong moment
so they are shapeless, awkward
moving to the clear.


## Postcard from Piccadilly Street

Dogs are the unheralded voyeurs of this world.
When we make love
the spaniel shudders
walks out of the room,
she's had her fill of children now

but the basset—for whom
we've pretty soon got to find a love object
apart from furniture or visitor's legs—
jumps on the bed and watches.

It is a catching habit having a spectator
and appeals to the actor in both of us,
in spite of irate phone calls from the SPCA
who claim we are corrupting minors
(the dog is one and a half).

We have moved to elaborate audiences now.

At midnight we open the curtains
turn out the light
and imagine the tree outside
full of sparrows
with infra red eyes.


## From *The Collected Works of Billy the Kid*

Christmas at Fort Sumner, 1880. There were five of us together
then. Wilson, Dave Rudabaugh, Charlie Bowdre, Tom
O'Folliard, and me. In November we celebrated my 21st birthday, mixing red dirt and alcohol—a public breathing throughout the night. The next day we were told that Pat Garrett had
been made sheriff and had accepted it. We were bad for progress
in New Mexico and cattle politicians like Chisum wanted the
bad name out. They made Garrett sheriff and he sent me a letter
saying move out or I will get you Billy. The government sent a
Mr. Azariah F. Wild to help him out. Between November and
December I killed Jim Carlyle over some mixup, he being a
friend.

Tom O'Folliard decided to go east then, said he would meet up
with us in Sumner for Christmas. Goodbye goodbye. A few days
before Christmas we were told that Garrett was in Sumner
waiting for us all. Christmas night. Garrett, Mason, Wild, with
four or five others. Tom O'Folliard rides into town, leaning his
rifle between the horse's ears. He would shoot from the waist
now which, with a rifle, was pretty good, and he was always
accurate.

Garrett had been waiting for us, playing poker with the others,
guns on the floor beside them. Told that Tom was riding in
alone, he went straight to the window and shot O'Folliard's
horse dead. Tom collapsed with the horse still holding the gun
and blew out Garrett's window. Garrett already halfway downstairs. Mr. Wild shot at Tom from the other side of the street,

rather unnecessarily shooting the horse again. If Tom had used stirrups and didnt swing his legs so much he would probably have been locked under the animal. O'Folliard moved soon. When Garrett had got to ground level, only the horse was there in the open street, good and dead. He couldnt shout to ask Wild where O'Folliard was or he would've got busted. Wild started to yell to tell Garrett though and Tom killed him at once. Garrett fired at O'Folliard's flash and took his shoulder off. Tom O'Folliard screaming out onto the quiet Fort Sumner street, Christmas night, walking over to Garrett, no shoulder left, his jaws tilting up and down like mad bladders going. Too mad to even aim at Garrett. Son of a bitch son of a bitch, as Garrett took clear aim and blew him out.

Garrett picked him up, the head broken in two, took him back upstairs into the hotel room. Mason stretched out a blanket neat in the corner. Garrett placed Tom O'Folliard down, broke open Tom's rifle, took the remaining shells and placed them by him. They had to wait till morning now. They continued their poker game till six a.m. Then remembered they hadnt done anything about Wild. So the four of them went out, brought Wild into the room. At eight in the morning Garrett buried Tom O'Folliard. He had known him quite well. Then he went to the train station, put Azariah F. Wild on ice and sent him back to Washington.

\*

She leans against the door, holds
her left hand at the elbow
with her right, looks at the bed

on my sheets—oranges
peeled half peeled
bright as hidden coins against the pillow

she walks slow to the window
lifts the sackcloth
and jams it horizontal on a nail
so the bent oblong of sun
hoists itself across the room
framing the bed the white flesh
of my arm

she is crossing the sun
sits on her leg here
sweeping off the peels

traces the thin bones on me
turns toppling slow back to the pillow
Bonney Bonney

I am very still
I take in all the angles of the room

*

I have seen pictures of great stars,
drawings which show them straining to the centre
that would explode their white
if temperature and the speed they moved at
shifted one degree.

Or in the East have seen
the dark grey yards where trains are fitted
and the clean speed of machines
that make machines, their
red golden pouring which when cooled
mists out to rust or grey.

The beautiful machines pivoting on themselves
sealing and fusing to others

and men throwing levers like coins at them.
And there is there the same stress as with stars,
the one altered move that will make them maniac.


## Letters & Other Worlds

*'for there was no more darkness for him and, no doubt
like Adam before the fall, he could see in the dark'*

My father's body was a globe of fear
His body was a town we never knew
He hid that he had been where we were going
His letters were a room he seldom lived in
In them the logic of his love could grow

My father's body was a town of fear
He was the only witness to its fear dance
He hid where he had been that we might lose him
His letters were a room his body scared

He came to death with his mind drowning.
On the last day he enclosed himself
in a room with two bottles of gin, later
fell the length of his body
so that brain blood moved
to new compartments
that never knew the wash of fluid
and he died in minutes of a new equilibrium.

His early life was a terrifying comedy
and my mother divorced him again and again.
He would rush into tunnels magnetized
by the white eye of trains
and once, gaining instant fame,
managed to stop a Perahara in Ceylon
—the whole procession of elephants dancers

local dignitaries—by falling
dead drunk onto the street.
As a semi-official, and semi-white at that,
the act was seen as a crucial
turning point in the Home Rule Movement
and led to Ceylon's independence in 1948.

(My mother had done her share too—
 her driving so bad
 she was stoned by villagers
 whenever her car was recognized)

For 14 years of marriage
each of them claimed he or she
was the injured party.
Once on the Colombo docks
saying goodbye to a recently married couple
my father, jealous
at my mother's articulate emotion,
dove into the waters of the harbour
and swam after the ship waving farewell.
My mother pretending no affiliation
mingled with the crowd back to the hotel.

Once again he made the papers
though this time my mother
with a note to the editor
corrected the report—saying he was drunk
rather than broken hearted at the parting of friends.
The married couple received both editions
of *The Ceylon Times* when their ship reached Aden.

And then in his last years
he was the silent drinker,
the man who once a week
disappeared into his room with bottles
and stayed there until he was drunk
and until he was sober.

There speeches, head dreams, apologies,
the gentle letters, were composed.
With the clarity of architects
he would write of the row of blue flowers
his new wife had planted,
the plans for electricity in the house,
how my half-sister fell near a snake
and it had awakened and not touched her.
Letters in a clear hand of the most complete empathy
his heart widening and widening and widening
to all manner of change in his children and friends
while he himself edged
into the terrible acute hatred
of his own privacy
till he balanced and fell
the length of his body
the blood screaming in
the empty reservoir of bones
the blood searching in his head without metaphor


## The Cinnamon Peeler

If I were a cinnamon peeler
I would ride your bed
and leave the yellow bark dust
on your pillow.

Your breasts and shoulders would reek
you could never walk through markets
without the profession of my fingers
floating over you. The blind would
stumble certain of whom they approached
though you might bathe
under rain gutters, monsoon.

Here on the upper thigh

at this smooth pasture
neighbour to your hair
or the crease
that cuts your back.  This ankle.
You will be known among strangers
as the cinnamon peeler's wife.

I could hardly glance at you
before marriage
never touch you
—your keen nosed mother, your rough brothers.
I buried my hands
in saffron, disguised them
over smoking tar,
helped the honey gatherers . . .

                    *


When we swam once
I touched you in water
and our bodies remained free,
you could hold me and be blind of smell.
You climbed the bank and said

                    this is how you touch other women
the grass cutter's wife, the lime burner's daughter.
And you searched your arms
for the missing perfume
                              and knew

                    what good is it
to be the lime burner's daughter
left with no trace
as if not spoken to in the act of love
as if wounded without the pleasure of a scar.

You touched
your belly to my hands

in the dry air and said
I am the cinnamon
peeler's wife. Smell me.


## Escarpment

He lies in bed, awake, holding her left forearm. It is 4 a.m. He turns, his eyes rough against the night. Through the window he can hear the creek—which has no name. Yesterday at noon he walked along its shallow body overhung with cedar, beside rushes, moss, and watercress. A green and grey body whose intricate bones he is learning among which he stumbles and walks through in an old pair of Converse running shoes. She was further upriver investigating for herself and he exploring on his own now crawling under a tree that has uprooted and spilled. Its huge length across a section of the creek. With his left hand he holds onto the massive stump roots and slides beneath it within the white water heaving against him. Shirt wet, he follows the muscle in the water and travels fast under the tree. His dreaming earlier must have involved all this.

In the river he was looking for a wooden bridge which they had crossed the previous day. He walks confidently now, the white shoes stepping casually off logs into deep water, through gravel, and watercress which they eat later in a cheese sandwich. She chews much of it walking back to the cabin. He turns and she freezes, laughing, with watercress in her mouth. There are not many more ways he can tell her he loves her. He shows mock outrage and yells but she cannot hear him over the sound of the stumbling creek.

He loves too, as she knows, the body of rivers. Provide him with a river or a creek and he will walk along it. Will step off and sink to his waist, the sound of water and rock encasing him in solitude. The noise around them insists on silence if they are more than five feet apart. It is only later when they sit in a pool legs against each other that they can talk, their conversation roaming to include relatives, books, best friends, the history of Lewis and Clark, fragments of the past which they piece together. But otherwise this river's noise encases them and now he walks alone with its spirits, the clack and splash, the twig break, hearing only an individual noise if it occurs less than an arm's length away. He is looking, now, for a name.

It is not a name for a map—he knows the arguments of imperialism. It is a name for them, something temporary for their vocabulary. A code. He slips under the fallen tree holding the cedar root the way he holds her forearm. He hangs a moment, his body being pulled by water going down river. He holds it the same way and for the same reasons. Heart Creek? Arm River? he writes, he mutters to her in the darkness. The body moves from side to side and he hangs with one arm, deliriously out of control, still holding on. Then he plunges down, touches gravel and flakes of wood with his back the water closing over his head like a clap of gloved hands. His eyes are open as the river itself pushes him to his feet and he is already three yards down stream and walking out of the shock and cold stepping into the sun. Sun lays its crossword, litters itself, along the whole turning length of this river so he can step into heat or shadow.

He thinks of where she is, what she is naming. Near her, in the grasses, are Bladder Campion, Devil's Paintbrush, some unknown blue flowers. He stands very still and cold in the shadow of long trees. He has gone far enough to look for a bridge and has not found it. Turns upriver. He holds onto the cedar root the way he holds her forearm.

# Bronwen Wallace

*The Woman In This Poem*

The woman in this poem
lives in the suburbs
with her husband and two children
each day she waits for the mail and
once a week receives
a letter from her lover
who lives in another city
writes of roses   warm patches
of sunlight on his bed
*Come to me* he pleads
*I need you* and the woman
reaches for the phone
to dial the airport
she will leave this afternoon
her suitcase packed
with a few light clothes

But as she is dialing
the woman in this poem
remembers the pot-roast
and the fact that it is Thursday
she thinks of how her husband's face
will look when he reads her note
his body curling sadly toward
the empty side of the bed

She stops dialing and begins
to chop onions for the pot-roast
but behind her back the phone
shapes itself insistently

the number for airline reservations
chants in her head
in an hour her children will be
home from school and after that
her husband will arrive
to kiss the back of her neck
while she thickens the gravy
and she knows that
all through dinner
her mouth will laugh and chatter
while she walks with her lover
on a beach somewhere

She puts the onions in the pot
and turns toward the phone
but even as she reaches
she is thinking of
her daughter's piano lessons
her son's dental appointment

Her arms fall to her side
and as she stands there
in the middle of her spotless kitchen
we can see her growing
old like this
and wish for something  anything
to happen  we could have her go
mad perhaps and lock herself
in the closet  crouch there
for days her dresses withering
around her like cast-off skins
or maybe she could take
to cruising the streets at night
in her husband's car
picking up teenage boys
and fucking them in the back seat
we can even imagine
finding her body

dumped in a ditch somewhere
on the edge of town

The woman in this poem offends us
with her useless phone and the persistent
smell of onions   we regard her as we do
the poorly calculated overdose
who lies in a bed somewhere
not knowing how her life drips
through her drop by measured drop
we want to think of death
as something sudden
stroke or the leap
that carries us over the railing
of the bridge in one determined arc
the pistol aimed precisely
at the right part of the brain
we want to hate this woman

but mostly we hate knowing
that for us too it is
moments like this
our thoughts   stiff fingers
tear at again and again
when we stop in the middle
of an ordinary day and
like the woman in this poem
begin to feel
our own deaths
rising slow within us

## All That Uneasy Spring

All that uneasy spring
we worked in our gardens
as soon as the earth was warm
we planted onions and peas

impatiens in the shade of our hedges
and marigolds in fiery rows along the walks
we set the seedlings out to harden
under sheets of glass
each of us looking up occasionally
to see the other women
in their yards   a series
of mirrored reflections   then
someone would wave from her kitchen
and we'd stop for coffee
leaving our mudcaked shoes
on the steps outside

And all that uneasy spring
our gossip came in whispers
like rumours from another land
divorces and custody disputes
how Anne's husband had kidnapped
her children from school
and Sharon had simply
left one afternoon and not come back
not even called

After the gardens were in
we washed the windows
repainted the lawnchairs
sent the drapes out to be cleaned
and at four
when the children arrived from school
we started the barbecues
scented our wrists
the cool drinks always ready
and the steaks just right
when our husbands pulled in the drive

But all that uneasy spring
when we lay in the dark
under crisp fresh sheets

the things we couldn't say
licked like flames
behind our eyes   our houses
were burning down   our children
screamed and sometimes our own voices
woke us surfacing through layers
of smoke to where our fingers touched
our husbands' bodies cool
and confident beside us
and awake then in that
uneasy dark we would remember
our morning conversations the sounds
of our voices coming back to us
suddenly precious even the smallest details
dirt-stained fingernails
the tiny lines that crinkled
white in sunburned skin
so that turning toward sleep
again we saw each other
standing in those hopeful gardens
while at our feet
the plants burst
dreamlike
from the slow dark ground

## A Simple Poem for Virginia Woolf

This started out as a simple poem
for Virginia Woolf   you know the kind
we women writers write these days
in our own rooms
on our own time
a salute   a gesture of friendship
a psychological debt
paid off
I wanted it simple

and perfectly round
hard as an
egg   I thought
only once I'd said egg
I thought of the smell
of bacon grease and dirty frying-pans
and whether there were enough for breakfast
I couldn't help it
I wanted the poem to be carefree and easy
like children playing in the snow
I didn't mean to mention
the price of snowsuits or
how even on the most expensive ones
the zippers always snag
just when you're late for work
and trying to get the children
off to school on time
a straightforward poem
for Virginia Woolf   that's all
I wanted really
not something tangled in
domestic life the way
Jane Austen's novels tangled
with her knitting her embroidery
whatever it was she hid them under
I didn't mean to go into all that
didn't intend to get confessional
and tell you how
every time I read a good poem
by a woman writer I'm always peeking
behind it trying to see
if she's still married
or has a lover at least
wanted to know what she did
with her kids while she wrote it
or whether she had any
and if she didn't if she'd chosen
not to or if she did did she

choose and why   I didn't mean
to bother with that
and I certainly wasn't going
to tell you about the time
my best friend was sick in intensive care
and I went down to see her
but they wouldn't let me in
because I wasn't her husband
or her father   her mother
I wasn't family
I was just her friend
and the friendship of women
wasn't mentioned
in hospital policy
or how I went out and kicked
a dent in the fender of my car
and sat there crying because
if she died I wouldn't be able
to tell her how much I loved her
(though she didn't and we laugh
about it now) but that's what got me
started I suppose   wanting to write
a gesture of friendship
for a woman for a woman writer
for Virginia Woolf
and thinking I could do it
easily   separating the words
from the lives they come from
that's what a good poem should do
after all and I wasn't going to make excuses
for being a woman   blaming years of silence
for leaving us
so much to say

This started out as a simple poem
for Virginia Woolf
it wasn't going to mention history
or choices or women's lives

the complexities of women's friendships
or the countless gritty details
of an ordinary woman's life
that never appear in poems at all
yet even as I write these words
those ordinary details intervene
between the poem I meant to write
and this one   where the delicate faces
of my children   faces of friends
of women I have never even seen
glow on the blank pages
and deeper than any silence
press around me
waiting their turn


## The Heroes You Had As A Girl

The heroes you had as a girl
were always three grades ahead of you
taller than the boys in your own class
taller even than your brothers
and the layers of muscle ripening
under their thin shirts their jeans
made your palms itch
for something you didn't know how to explain
but wanted to   sitting with your girlfriends
in the hot dry grass
at the edge of the parking-lot
where all day Saturday they worked on their cars
hunched over the greasy mysteries of their engines
occasionally raising their heads
their eyes flicking
to where you were included
as part of the landscape

Sundays they practised more dangerous manoeuvres

till your eyes stung with the smell
of oil and burning rubber
and once they built arches of flaming
orange crates   you remember them spinning
through the air when one car missed
remember the screams that burned your throat
before you realized no-one was hurt
your voices fluttering like foolish birds
on the wild currents of their laughter
and now twenty years later the hero
who drove that car returns as unexpectedly
as the memory and just as out of place
you watch him study a display of bathroom fixtures
in the hardware department of Simpsons-Sears
he's grown fat and balding
and you think how easy it would be
to walk right over tap him
on the shoulder say *hello*
*remember me*   and if he didn't
you could laugh it off
at least you've kept your figure
that's not what stops you now
though something does
and as he walks away
you can feel the dry grass biting
the backs of your legs   the uncomfortable
angle of your knees as you sat just so
practising your own dangerous manoeuvres
not being noticed   not noticing
the other girls   forgetting their names
the shapes of their faces reddening in the sun
(though you remember those burning arches
your throat tightening again around those foolish screams,
you think you could explain it now
and that's what stops you
knowing you want nothing less
than for him to turn
peel off his shirt to show you

burn scars on his chest
and in the sullen landscape of his eyes
you want the faces of those girls
your own among them burning
brighter than any fire


## Common Magic

Your best friend falls in love
and her brain turns to water.
You can watch her lips move,
making the customary sounds,
but you can see they're merely
words, flimsy as bubbles rising
from some golden sea where she
swims sleek and exotic as a mermaid.

It's always like that.
You stop for lunch in a crowded
restaurant and the waitress floats
toward you.  You can tell she doesn't care
whether you have the baked or french-fried
and you wonder if your voice comes
in bubbles too.

It's not just women either.  Or love
for that matter.  The old man
across from you on the bus holds
a young child on his knee; he is singing
to her and his voice is a small boy
turning somersaults in the green
country of his blood.
It's only when the driver calls his stop
that he emerges into this puzzle
of brick and tiny hedges.  Only then
you notice his shaking hands, his need

of the child to guide him home.

All over the city
you move in your own seasons
through the seasons of others: old women, faces
clawed by weather you can't feel
clack dry tongues at passersby
while adolescents seethe
in their glassy atmospheres of anger.

In parks, the children
are alien life-forms, rooted
in the galaxies they've grown through
to get here.  Their games weave
the interface and their laughter
tickles that part of your brain where smells
are hidden and the nuzzling textures of things.

It's a wonder that anything gets done
at all:  a mechanic flails
at the muffler of your car
through whatever storm he's trapped inside
and the mailman stares at numbers
from the haze of a distant summer.

Yet somehow letters arrive and buses
remember their routes.  Banks balance.
Mangoes ripen on the supermarket shelves.
Everyone manages.  You gulp the thin air
of this planet as if it were the only
one you knew.  Even the earth you're
standing on seems solid enough.
It's always the chance word, unthinking
gesture that unlocks the face before you.
Reveals the intricate countries
deep within the eyes.  The hidden
lives, like sudden miracles,
that breathe there.

# Thinking With the Heart

For Mary di Michele

*'I work from awkwardness. By that I mean I don't like to arrange things. If I stand in front of something, instead of arranging it, I arrange myself.'—Diane Arbus.*

*'The problem with you women is, you think with your hearts.'— Policeman.*

How else to say it
except that the body is a limit
I must learn to love,
that thought is no different from flesh
or the blue pulse that rivers my hands.
How else, except to permit myself
this heart and its seasons,
like the cycles of the moon
which never seem to get me anywhere
but back again, not out.

Thought should be linear.
That's what the policeman means
when I bring the woman to him,
what he has to offer for her bruises, the cut
over her eye: *charge him or we can't help you.*
He's seen it all before anyway. He knows
how the law changes, depending on what you think.
It used to be a man could beat his wife
if he had to; now, sometimes he can't
but she has to charge him
and nine times out of ten
these women who come in here
ready to get the bastard
will be back in a week or so
wanting to drop the whole thing
because they're back together,

which just means a lot of paperwork
and running around for nothing.
It drives him crazy, how a woman
can't make up her mind and stick to it,
get the guy out once and for all.
'Charge him,' he says, 'or we won't help.'

Out of her bed then, her house, her life,
but not her head, no, nor her children,
out from under her skin.
Not out of her heart, which goes on
in its slow, dark way, wanting
whatever it is hearts want
when they think like this;
a change in his, probably,
a way to hold what the heart can't
without breaking:  how the man who beats her
is also the man she loves.

I wish I could show you
what a man's anger makes
of a woman's face,
or measure the days it takes
for her to emerge from a map of bruises
the colour of death.  I wish there were words
that went deeper than *pain* or *terror*
for the place that woman's eyes can take you
when all you can hear
is the sound the heart makes
with what it knows of itself
and its web of blood.

But right now, the policeman's waiting
for the woman to decide.
That's how he thinks of it; *choice*
or how you can always get what you want
if you want if badly enough.
Everything else he ignores,

like the grip of his own heart's red
persistent warning that he too is fragile.
He thinks he thinks with his brain
as if it were safe up there
in its helmet of bone
away from all that messy business
of his stomach or his lungs.
And when he thinks like that
he loses himself forever.

But perhaps you think I'm being hard on him,
he's only doing his job after all,
only trying to help.
Or perhaps I'm making too much of the heart,
pear-shaped and muscular, a pump really,
when what you want is an explanation or a reason.
But how else can I say it?
Whatever it is you need
is what you must let go of now
to enter your own body
just as you'd enter the room where the woman sat
after it was all over,
hugging her knees to her chest,
holding herself as she'd hold her husband
or their children, *for dear life*,
feeling the arm's limit, bone and muscle,
like the heart's.
Whatever you hear then
crying through your own four rooms,
what you must name for yourself
before you can love anything at all.

## *Particulars*

To come back, again,
to those Sundays at my grandmother's table,
but by a different way, so that I see
that thin spot in my father's hair
as he bowed his head to ask
*the blessing*—what my grandmother
called it, not thanks—*Bless
this food to our use
and us to Thy service,
in Christ's name,
Amen.* My father stumbling
over the words, perhaps in recognition
of what he was really asking for
(there, in the midst of things,
his whole family listening),
a blessing, on food they'd earned
casting metal, teaching other people's kids
or planted, themselves, in the fields we'd see
as soon as we raised our heads, men and women
embarrassed by prayer, but sticking to it
as they stuck to their stories,
hoarded those private, irreducible histories
that no one else would get a piece of, ever.

To begin to see, a little,
what they taught me
of themselves, their place
among the living and the dead,
thanksgiving and the practical
particulars of grace, and to accept it,
slowly, almost grudgingly,
to come downstairs this morning
as the paper slaps
the front porch, look up, catch
the paper girl with her walkman on
dancing down the street, red tights,

jean jacket, blonde hair, making me
love her, perfectly, for ten seconds,
long enough to call out
all my other loves, locate each one
precisely, as I could this house
on a city map or the day I found
my son, swimming within me.

To try and hear it
in the way we make the most
of what we get, like the man I know
who says he's held Death in his arms.
That's how he puts it, trying
for a way to say *wife* or *Ellen*
and reach far enough to touch her
there, include the whispers
from the hall outside, the hiss
of the oxygen tank, still on,
the sounds his arms made
adjusting to her weight, this
angle of bone, this one
when her head tipped, finally, back.

And to say for myself, just once,
without embarrassment, *bless*,
thrown out as to some lightness
that I actually believe in,
surprised (as I believe
they were) to find it
here, where it seems impossible
that one life even matters, though
like them, I'll argue
the stubborn argument of the particular,
right now, in the midst of things, *this*
and *this*.

# Robert Bringhurst

## The Beauty of the Weapons

*El-Arish, 1967*

A long-armed man can
carry the nine-millimeter
automatic gun slung
backward over the right shoulder.

With the truncated butt
caught in the cocked
elbow, the trigger
falls exactly to hand.

These things I remember,
and a fuel-pump gasket cut
from one of the innumerable
gas masks in the roadside dump.

I bring back manuscript picked
up around incinerated trucks
and notes tacked next
to automatic track controls.

Fruits of the excavation.
This is our archaeology.
A dig in the debris
of a civilization six weeks old.

The paper is crisp and brittle
with the dry rock and the weather.
The Arabic is brittle

with the students' first exposure

to air-war technology and speed.
Ridiculous to say so, but
the thought occurs,
that Descartes would be pleased:

the calculus is the language
of the latest Palestinian
disputations
in the field of theology.

The satisfying feel
of the fast traverse
on the anti-aircraft guns
is not in the notes.

It lies latent and cool
in the steel, like the intricate
mathematics
incarnate in the radar:

the antennae folded and rolled
like a soldier's tent,
sweeping the empty
sky and the barren horizon,

the azimuth and the elevation,
sweeping the empty air
into naked abstraction,
leading the guns.

The signal is swirled until it
flies over the lip like
white, weightless
wine from a canteen cup.

Invisibly, the mechanism sings.

It sings. It sings like a six-ton flute:
east, west, always the same
note stuck in the rivetless throat.

And yet, a song as intricate
as any composition by Varèse,
and seeming, for the moment, still
more beautiful, because,

to us, more deadly.
Therefore purer, more
private, more familiar,
more readily feared, or desired:

a dark beauty with a steel sheen,
caught in the cocked
mind's eye and brought
down with an extension of the hand.


*The Sun and Moon*

In the night's darkness there was once no moon,
and no sun rose into the dawn's light, no sun
sucked the color from the grass.
No moon opened the empty womb,
no moon frosted water, leaf and stone.
No sun burned into the upturned eye at noon
or polished the sparrowhawk's skull
or the coyote's bone.

Each night a girl's lover came to her,
hidden from her sight,
when the light was gone from her night fire.

Each day she searched the eyes
of the young men, certain she would recognize

the daylit shape of eyes whose blind,
dumb gleam in the midnight licked
like a tongue into the corners of her blood.
A month of days, and her lover's secret stood.

Waiting, one night, willing to wait
no longer to know her lover by day, by sight,
she blackened her hands with the soot
from her evening fire.

In the morning she looked for her lover and found
the marks of her hands on the back of her brother.

She ran.  He ran after her,
over the sea's cold meadow, the grass,
the mountains, the trees, to the earth's end
and over.

She became the flaming sun,
and her brother became the husk of the moon,
to chase her, to come to her, brother and lover,
again.

Her virgin blood flows in the dusk
and she wipes it away at dawn.
Her evening fire burns in the dusk
and her morning fire in the dawn,
and he comes out looking, over sea and land,
when her evening fire grows cold and black,

and the marks of her hands
are still on his back.

## Poem About Crystal

Look at it, stare
into the crystal because

it will tell you, not
the future, no, but
the quality of crystal,
clarity's nature,
teach you the stricture
of uncut, utterly
uncluttered light.


## Anecdote of the Squid

The squid is in fact
a carnivorous pocket
containing a pen, which serves
the squid as his skeleton.

The squid is a raised finger or
an opposed thumb.  The squid's quill
is his long, scrupulous nail, which
is invisible.

The squid is a short-beaked
bird who has eaten
his single wing, or impaled
himself on his feather.

The squid, however,
despite his Cadurcian
wineskin and four hundred cups,
does not entertain.

The squid, with his eight
arms and his two
brushes and his sepia,
does not draw.

The squid knows too that the use
of pen and ink is neither recording

impressions nor signing his name
to forms and petitions.
But the squid may be said,
for instance, to transcribe
his silence into the space
between seafloor and wave,

or to invoke an unspoken
word, whose muscular
non-pronunciation the squid
alone is known to have mastered.

The squid carries his ink
in a sack, not a bottle.
With it the squid makes
artifacts.

These are mistakable for
portraiture, or
for self-portraiture, or,
to the eyes of the squid-eating whale,

for the squid, who in the meanwhile grows
transparent and withdraws,
leaving behind him his
coagulating shadows.


## Xenophanes

Earth is the ultimate substance.
What is, is made out of earth.  We
who climb free of it,
milkthistles, mallards and men,
are made out of earth which is driven by water.

I have found chiton shells high

in the mountains, the finprints of fish
in the stonecutter's stone, and seen
boulders and trees dragged to sea
by the river. Water and earth
lurch, wrestle and twist in their purposeless
war, of which we
are a consequence, not an answer.

*

The earth gives birth to the sun
each morning, and washes herself in the water,
and slits the sun's throat every night
with a splintered stone, and washes
herself once again in the water.

Some days the sun, like a fattening
goose, crosses over in ignorant stupor.
Other days, watch: you will see him
shudder and twitch, like a rabbit
caught in the snare—but what
does it matter? One way
or the other, his death is the same.

We must learn to be thought
by the gods, not to think them.
Not to think gods have two eyes and ten fingers,
thirty-two teeth and two
asymmetrical footprints. Not to think
here in the unstopped bowls
of our skulls we hold luminous
godbreath. The mush in our skulls
is compiled, like our toenails,
of rocksalt and silt, which is matted
like felt in the one case, and swollen
like hope in the other:

What is, is earth. What dies
is earth driven by water.

*

The earth has one end. It is under
our feet. You may think
differently; I am convinced
there is no other.

## The Stonecutter's Horses

(*This is in some measure the story of Francesco Petrarca, who
was a gentleman, and a scholar, and a brilliant poet, and a good
Roman Catholic, and the father of an illegitimate daughter
whom he loved very deeply and whose illegitimacy was, for him,
a source of incurable pain. His feelings concerning himself and
his daughter grew so intense that for years he would not speak
her name in public, though he pronounced it often enough and
lovingly enough in private. After her marriage he sought to
simplify his affairs and his explanations by adopting as his foster
son the man he might have called his son-in-law: his daughter's
husband Brossano. With him and few others, Petrarca shared
the story of his precious wound.*

*On the morning of 4 April 1370, in one of the upper rooms
of his house in Padova, in the north of Italy, Francesco Petrarco
summoned his secretary, to whom he dictated in simple Italian
the first draft of his last will and testament. A later version of this
document—the dry and guarded Latin rewrite which Petrarca
considered suitable for public disclosure—still survives. Only
an occasional flash in the Latin suggests the rough glint of its
predecessor. The close, for instance, reads:* Ego Franciscus
Petrarca scripsi qui testamentum aliud fecissem si essem
dives ut vulgus insanem putat. '*I, Francesco Petrarca, have
written this. I would have made a different testament if I were
rich, as the lunatic public believes me to be.' The Italian original
would, I believe, have begun with a meditative wail:* Io,
Francesco, io, io. . . .)

I, Francesco, this April day:
death stirs like a bud in the sunlight, and Urban
has got off his French duff and re-entered Rome
and for three years running has invited me to Rome,
over the bright hills and down the Cassia,
back through Arezzo one more time,
my age sixty-five and my birthday approaching,
the muggers on the streets in broad daylight in Rome,
the hawks and the buzzards. . . .

                       Take this down.

No one has thought too deeply of death.
So few have left anything toward or against it.
Peculiar, since thinking of death can never be
wasted thinking, nor can it be come to
too quickly. A man carries his death with him
everywhere, waiting, but seldom thinking
of waiting. Death is uncommonly like the soul.

What I own other than that ought to fall
of its own weight and settle. But beggars and tycoons
and I are concerned with our possessions,
and a man with a reputation for truth
must have one also for precision.

                    I leave
my soul to my saviour, my corpse to the earth.
And let it be done without any parades.
I don't care very much where I'm buried,
so it please God and whoever is digging.
Still, you will ask. You will badger me.
If I am dead you will badger each other.
But don't lug my bones through the public streets
in a box to be gabbled at and gawked at and followed.
Let it be done without any parades.
If I die here in Padova, bury me here
near the friend who is dead who invited me here.
If I die on my farm, you can use the chapel
I mean to build there, if I ever build it.

If not, try the village down the road.

If in Venezia, near the doorway.
If in Milano, next to the wall.
In Pavia, anywhere.  Or if in Rome . . .
if in Rome, in the center, of course, if there's room.
These are the places I think I might die in
in Italy.
        Or if I happen to be in Parma,
there is a cathedral of which, for some reason,
I am the archdeacon.  But I will avoid
going to Parma.  It would scarcely be possible,
I suppose, in Parma, not to have a parade.

At any rate, put what flesh I have left
in a church.  A Franciscan church if there is one.
I don't want it feeding a tree from which
rich people's children swipe apples.

Two hundred ducats go to the church in which
I am buried, with another hundred to be given
out in that parish to the poor, in small doses.
The money to the church, let it buy a piece of land
and the land be rented and the rental from the land
pay for an annual mass in my name.
I will be fitter company in that sanctuary
then, present in spirit and name only,
than this way, muttering to the blessed virgin
through my hemorrhoids and bad teeth.  I should be glad
to be rid of this sagging carcass.
                Don't write that.

I have cleared no fields of their stones.  I have built
no barns and no castles.  I have built a name
out of other men's voices by banging my own
like a kitchen pan.  My name to the Church
with the money it takes to have it embalmed.
Very few other things.  My Giotto to the Duke.

Most men cannot fathom its beauty. Those
who know painting are stunned by it. The Duke
does not need another Giotto, but the Duke knows painting.

To Dondi, money for a plain ring to remind him
to read me.
                    To Donato—what? I forgive him
the loan of whatever he owes me. And I
myself am in debt to della Seta. Let it
be paid if I haven't paid it. And give him
my silver cup. Della Seta drinks
water. Damned metal ruins the wine.

To Boccaccio, I am unworthy to leave
anything, and have nothing worthy to leave.
Money then, for a coat to keep himself warm
when he works after dark, as he frequently does,
while the river wind stutters and bleats at his window,
and his hand-me-down cordwood fizzles and steams.

My lute to Tommaso. I hope he will play it
for God and himself and not to gain fame
for his playing.
                    These are such trivial legacies.

Money to Pancaldo, but not for the card table.
Money to Zilio—at least his back salary.
Money to the other servants. Money to the cook.
Money to their heirs if they die before I do.

Give my Bible back to the Church.
                                    And my horses . . .
my horses.
                    Let a few of my friends, if they wish to,
draw lots for my horses. Horses
are horses. They cannot be given away.

The rest to my heir and executor, Brossano,

who knows he is to split it, and how he is to split it,
and the names I prefer not to put into this
instrument. Names of no other importance.
Care for them. Care for them here in this house
if you can. And don't sell off the land to get money
in any case. Selling earth without cause
from the soul is simony, Brossano. Real-estate
hucksters are worse than funeral parades.
I have lived long enough in quite enough
cities, notwithstanding the gifts
of free lodging in some of them, long enough, Brossano,
to know the breath moves underfoot in the clay.
The stone quarried and cut and reset
in the earth is a lover's embrace, not an overlay.

The heart splits like a chinquapin pod,
spilling its angular seed on the ground.

Though we ride to Rome and back aboard animals,
nothing ever takes root on the move.
I have seen houses and fields bartered
like cargo on shipboard. But nothing takes root
without light in the eye and earth in the hand.

The land is our solitude and our silence.
A man should hoard what little silence
he is given and what little solitude he can get.

Just the one piece over the mountains
ought, I think, to be given away. Everything
I have ever done that has lasted began there.
And I think my heir will have no need to go there.
If Brossano die before I do,
look to della Seta. And for his part let him
look into that cup. He will know my mind.

A man who can write as I can ought not
to talk of such things at such length. Keep this

back if you can.  Let the gifts speak
for themselves if you can, small though they are.
But I don't like the thought of what little there is
spilling into the hands of lawyers through lawsuits.
The law is no ritual meant to be practised
in private by scavengers.  Law is the celebration
of duty and the ceremony of vengeance.  The Duke's
law has nothing to do with my death
or with horses.
           Done.
               Ask the notaries to come over
precisely at noon.  I will rewrite it
and have it to sign by the time they arrive.

## The Song of Ptahhotep

For George Payerle

Good speech is rarer than jade.  It is rarer
than greenstone, yet may be found among girls
at the grindstones, found among shepherds
alone in the hills.
I know how a man might speak to his grandson;
I cannot teach him to speak to the young women.

Still, I have seen at the well how the words
tune the heart, how they make one who hears them
a master of hearing.  If hearing enters the hearer,
the hearer turns into a listener.  Hearing is better
than anything else.  It cleanses the will.

I have seen in the hills how the heart chooses.
The fists of the heart hold the gates of the ears.
If a grandson can hear his grandfather's words,
the words decades later
may rise like smoke from his heart
as he waits on a mountain and thinks of old age.

In the cave of the ear, the bones, like stars
at the solstice, sit upright and still,
listening in on the air as the muscle and blood
listen in on the skeleton.
Tongues and breasts of the unseen
creatures of the air
slither over the bones in the toothless
mouths of the ears.
To hear is to honor the sleeping snail
in the winter woodbox back of the forge.

You will see the new governor's ears
fill like pockets, his eyes
swell up with the easily seen,
yet his face is a dumped jug.  His bones
wrinkle like bent flutes, his heart
sets and triggers like a beggar's hand.
The new governor's words are orderly, clean,
inexhaustible, and cannot be told
one from another, like funerals, like sand.

I have done what I could in my own time in office.
The river rises, the river goes down.
I have seen sunlight nest on the water.
I have seen darkness
puddle like oil in the palm of my hand.

Speak to your grandson by saying,
good speech is rarer than jade, it is rarer
than greenstone, yet may be found among girls
at the grindstones, found among shepherds
alone in the hills.
The heart is an animal.  Learn where it leads.
Know its gait as it breaks.  Know its range,
how it mates and feeds.
If they shear your heart bald like a goat, the coat
will grow back, though your heart may shudder from cold.
If they skin out your heart,
it will dry in your throat like a fish in the wind.

Speak to your grandson by saying,
my grandson, the caves of the air
glitter with hoofmarks
left by the creatures
you have summoned there.

My grandson, my grandson,
good speech is rarer than jade, it is rarer
than greenstone, yet may be found among girls
at the grindstones, found among shepherds
alone in the hills.  The heart is a boat.
If it will not float, if it have no keel,
if it have no ballast, if it have
neither pole nor paddle nor mast,
there is no means by which you can cross.

Speak to your grandson by saying,
my grandson, the wake of the heart
is as wide as the river,
the drift of the heart is as long as the wind
and as strong as the rudder that glides through your hand.

Speak to your grandson by saying,
good speech is rarer than jade, it is rarer
than greenstone, yet may be found among girls
at the grindstones, found among shepherds
alone in the hills.
The fists of the heart as they open and close
on the rope of the blood in the well of the air
smell of the river.
The heart is two feet and the heart is two hands.
The ears of the blood hear it clapping and walking;
the eyes of the bones see the blooded footprints
it leaves in its path.

Speak to your grandson by saying,
my grandson, set your ear
on the heart's path,
kneeling there in honor
of the sleeping snail.

## For the Bones of Josef Mengele, Disinterred June 1985

Master of Auschwitz, angel of death,
murderer, deep in Brazil they are breaking
your bones—or somebody's bones: my
bones, your bones, his bones, whose
bones does not matter. Deep in Brazil they are breaking
bones like loaves of old bread. The angel
of death is not drowning but eating.

*Speak!* they are saying. *Speak! speak!*
*If you don't speak we will open and read you!*
Something you too might have said in your time.
*Are these bones guilty?* they say. And the bones
are already talking. The bones, with guns
to their heads, are already saying, *Yes!*
*Yes! It is true, we are guilty!*

Butcher, baker, lampshade and candlestick
maker: yes, it is true. But the bones? The bones,
earth, metals, teeth, the body?
These are not guilty. The minds of the dead
are not to be found in the bones of the dead.
The minds of the dead are not anywhere to be found,
outside the minds of the living.

# Robyn Sarah

*Fugue*

Women are on their way
to the new country.  The men watch
from high office windows
while the women go.
They do not get very far
in a day.  You can still see them
from high office windows.

Women are on their way
to the new country.  They are taking
it all with them: rugs,
pianos, children.  Or they are leaving
it all behind them: cats,
plants, children.
They do not get very far in a day.

Some women travel alone
to the new country.  Some
with a child, or children.
Some go in pairs or groups
or in pairs with a child
or children.  Some in a group with
cats, plants, children.

They do not get very far in a day.
They must stop to bake bread on the road
to the new country, and to share
bread with other women.  Children
outgrow their clothes and shed them
for smaller children.  The women too

shed clothes, put on each other's

cats, plants, children, and at full moon
no one remembers the way to the new country
where there will be room for everyone and
it will be summer and children will
shed their clothes and the loaves will
rise without yeast and women will have come
so far that no one can see them, even from

high office windows.

## Maintenance

Sometimes the best I can do
is homemade soup, or a patch on the knee
of the baby's overalls.
Things you couldn't call poems.
Things that spread in the head,
that swallow
whole afternoons, weigh down the week
till the elastic's gone right out of it—
so gone
it doesn't even snap when it breaks.
And one spent week's
just like the shapeless bag
of another.  Monthsful of them,
with new ones rolling in and
filling up with the same junk:  toys
under the bed, eggplant slices sweating
on the breadboard, the washing machine
spewing suds into the toilet, socks
drying on the radiator and falling down
behind it where the dust lies furry and
full of itself. . . The dust!
what I could tell you about

the dust.  How it eats things—
pencils, caps from ballpoint pens,
plastic sheep, alphabet blocks.
How it spins cocoons
around them, clumps up and
smothers whatever strays into
its reaches—buttons,
pennies, marbles—and then
how it lifts, all of a piece,
dust-pelts
thick as the best velvet
on the bottom of the mop.

                    Sometimes
the best that I can do
is maintenance:  the eaten
replaced by the soon-to-be-eaten, the raw
by the cooked, the spilled-on
by the washed and dried, the ripped
by the mended; empty cartons
heaved down the cellar stairs, the
cans stacked on the ledge, debris
sealed up in the monstrous snot-green bags
for the garbage man.

And I'll tell you what
they don't usually tell you:  there's no
poetry in it.  There's no poetry
in scraping concrete off the high chair tray
with a bent kitchen knife, or fishing
with broomhandle behind the fridge
for a lodged ball.  None in the sink
that's always full, concealing its cargo
of crockery under a head
of greasy suds.  Maybe you've heard
that there are compensations?  That, too's
a myth.  It doesn't work that way.
The planes are separate.  Even if there are

moments each day that take you by the heart
and shake the dance back into it, that you lost
the beat of, somewhere years behind—even if
in the clear eye of such a moment you catch
a glimpse of the only thing worth looking for—
to call this compensation, is to demean.
The planes are separate.  And it's the
other one, the one called maintenance,
I mostly am shouting about.
I mean the day-to-day,
that bogs the mind, voice, hands
with things you couldn't call poems.
I mean the thread that breaks.
The dust between
typewriter keys.


## A Meditation Between Claims

You want to close your hand
on something perfect, you want to say
Aha.  Everything moves towards this,
or seems to move, you measure it
in the inches you must let down
on the children's overalls,
tearing the pages off the wall
each month; a friend phones
with news that another friend
has taken Tibetan vows, meanwhile the
kitchen is filling up with the smell
of burnt rice, you remind yourself
to buy postage stamps tomorrow

The mover
and the thing moved, are they two
or one; if two, is the thing moved
within or without, questions

you do not often bother yourself with
though you should; the corner store
is closed for the high holy days,
and though the air has a smell
not far from snow, your reluctance
to strip the garden is understandable

Laundry is piling up
in the back room, Mondays and Thursdays
the trash must be carried out
or it accumulates, each day
things get moved about and
put back in their places
and you accept this, the shape
that it gives a life, though the need
to make room supercedes other needs

If, bidding your guest goodbye,
you stand too long at the open door,
house-heat escapes, and the oil bill
will be higher next month, the toll
continues, wrapping the green tomatoes
in news of the latest assassination.
The mover
and the thing moved, it all
comes down to this: one wants
to sit in the sun like a stone,
one wants to move the stone   which
is better

## Sounding an Old Chord in October

The streetlamp directly opposite
is out, an unaccustomed dark
pools this side of the street.
In the garden the dried bean-pods

rasp on their woody vines,
leave nothing to look forward to
but snow.  Still, expectation
stirs, a dog with ears cocked
for familiar footsteps, lights
in strange windows are taking on
a peculiar intimacy
                         It's the old story,
the thing we'd almost forgotten, last year's
chestnut, bone-smooth to cold fingers
fishing a linty pocket for a fare
(though the rates have gone up again
since the coat was hung away, and any
loose change is purely fortuitous)

A pebble
ricochets off the bus-stop
with the kind of ping metal only makes
when cold, like the twang
of a piano-string that slips
in the dead of night
                         so expecting
the unexpected becomes a way of saying
yes again, this is the thing
we refuse to go on without,
the delicate engineering of a life
to allow for a coincidence of paths,
take it from there

For no other reason
we stare at a little piece of street
between buildings, as if we could will
the arrival of someone unlikely to pass there,
spontaneous, nonchalant
with neither wine nor flowers,
just a dark figure jaunting along
in no sort of hurry
and visible only for seconds
between parked cars.

## C Major Scale, Ascending

Nodding off in the brightness of the morning after. Sun
reflects off a neighbour's window, a warm square on scuffed
floorboards, wavering suddenly as the window is opened (the
glass sheet trembling in its cold frame) with just such a
movement as the heart makes when it comes to itself. . .

For a second one imagines opening one's eyes under water, the
moment of adjustment to a new kind of vision, it's all part of
the same phenomenon, coming out of the womb of early
motherhood with a sudden passion for objectivity and a readiness
to try on new voices, like one's own mother's collection of
small silk scarves in a drawer with tangled jewelry and vestiges
of cologne

Always such moments transcend the time of year or day, but the
sun is a constant, the surprise of it, framing some realization,
highlighting the arbitrary: a scrap of paper on the floor, inked
with the words 'C major Scale, Ascending'—left over from a
college course in harmony but seeming suddenly to embody the
whole of what we can know—

Like the smells of bleach and floorwax, one's grandmother
dusting the piano from bass to treble in a series of minor
seconds, there is this music of chance, for which one learns to
compose oneself, a hand in an upstairs window is glimpsed
pouring coffee from a metal pot, or wind turns an umbrella
inside out and everything is ready to begin again, sun breaks
suddenly on the floor like a dropped egg

## Study in Latex Semi-Gloss

There is nothing new. Does that matter? Somewhere a woman
is painting her rooms. She has tied up her hair and covered it
with a tattered diaper. Alone, in a flat lit by bare bulbs, she

moves from room to room, her sandals sticking to the spread pages of old Gazettes pooled with paint spills. She is looking for something, for a screwdriver with a yellow handle, with which she now pries off the lid of the last can of paint; she is stirring the paint with a wooden stick, stirring it longer than necessary, as if it were batter. Now she pours creamy fold upon fold into the crusted tray. The telephone shrills in another room; it is you, but she won't get there in time to answer. If she did, what could you say that would apply here?

Late into the night bare windows frame her, bending and stretching, wielding the roller on its broomstick. Paint streaks her bare arms and legs; some hairs have escaped the cloth about her head to fall in her eyes, and she pushes them aside with the clean back of her hand. In the alley behind the flat, cats couple with strangled yells. Soon she will shut herself in the tiny bath, blinking at the dazzle which dulls the fixtures to the colour of stained teeth; she will tack a torn towel over the window and drop her clothes—the loose jersey with the sleeves cut off, the frayed corduroy shorts, stiff with spatters of paint, at whose edges bunches of dark thread dangle. The underpants, damp and musky with sweat, will fall limp to her ankles. She will squat in the narrow tub, scrubbing at her skin with washcloth, solvent, fingernails, and after, with the cracked remnant of a bar of green soap which she tries in vain to work into a lather. Rinsing with splashed water, she'll pause and hug her knees, hug in the sag of her tired breasts, then stand, stretch, pat dry with the clean side of a damp towel. On the toilet she'll bend to examine a broken toenail and remain bent, dreaming, staring at the yellowed tiles.

You will have been asleep an hour, by the time she kills the lights and slips naked into a sleeping-bag spread across a bare mattress on the bare floor. The smell of the bag is the smell of woodsmoke and pine, faint, mixed with old sweat. Perhaps it's the smell that makes her smile a little as she feels herself sucked down into the whirlpool of sleep. Somewhere across blocks and blocks of tenements, her children, half-grown, long-limbed, sprawling on foam mats in their father's studio apartment, will stir as a lone car guns its engine in the empty street. She dreams, if she dreams at all, of holes in the plaster, of places where the baseboard is missing, of the bulging and cracking of imperfect surfaces. Dreams the geography of a wall.

There is nothing new. Even what could bloom between you, if you let it, if she let it, goes on as the paint goes on, over old seams, old sutures. Weathers as the paint will weather, flaking along old stress lines. This matters. Think, before you dial again. What have you to do with those children, blinking sleep from their eyes, breakfasting with their father in a booth of the local diner; where will you be when daylight, like cold water, shocks her awake to pull on yesterday's clothes and squat in the kitchen doorway with her mug of instant coffee? Where, when her clear eyes, steady in their purpose, scan the new surface to discover her painter's holidays?

## Excavation from the Bridge

The outlines
fill in slowly:
gouache,

pastel. The
junctures of wet
twigs, to attach

such weight to a few
bare nodes, like
early pickets.

Drops gather and
slip through
fingers, will not

be counted; holes fill

and calcify.  Pressed
into clay, the bones

are hinged and
wingless.  Time
is a muscle, blind,

smooth as a fist.  The
breath, held,
just so.

## The Thread

Diminutions
of autumn.  The light
makes no apology, falling
aslant the bare arms
of the trees.  They have let
slide their holdings; only a
rare branch still flames
toward sundown, caught
at the right angle.  The
afternoon is private, the sun
visits each window, warm
with the last warmth of October, the
screens tick in their metal
frames, mesh hazy with
last summer's dust, they ping
where a late fly, all buzz
and bluster, hurls himself
again and again.  Now he has crawled
down between the screen
and outer pane, the sun
is moving on, touching the last
crescent of screen, a few

dust-motes hover there and gleam,
pearl-like, before they move
out of the light:  and see,
a single thread of spider-silk,
anchored where faintest air
stirs it, gleams
and disappears, and gleams
again.

## To Fill a Life

To fill a life as fitful sky fills windows, or a painter, canvas, to fill
it willfully, to make large movements within a frame, I think is to
be desired—the frame, too, not to contain, but to provoke such
movement. No mirror will show you the lines worry pushes your
face into, for in the looking, curiosity makes other lines. I want to
move far enough away to see you whole, as a child will in a loop
that he makes of finger and thumb. *Look how small I can make you,
Mummy.*

So the unmade beds of children.  So the hats, scarves, mitts,
thrown pell-mell over the radiator, so the smell of damp wool
filling the hall as the heat rises.  On the counter, the jagged shells
of breakfast eggs, a crust of stuck whites like brown lace in the cast
iron skillet still warm on the burner.  So the towels on the
bathroom floor, the steamed mirror, stray hairs in the tub and a
blue worm of dried toothpaste on the edge of the sink.  The tap
dripping, humid air smelling of shampoo.  The face of a life in
motion.  The pegs on the rack by the door, on which are slung
umbrellas, shawls, soft bags of cloth and leather, the straps
wound round each other.

To delight in the weathered, more than in polished planes, to
prefer the visible repair to the thing re-done, I think is to respect
tenancy, its wear and tear, its fixed term.  For each grey hair he
pulls from her head, she gives her youngest son a penny, until

there are so many, he makes a bankrupt of her, no more, she throws up her hands, laughing. Decades later, when she sells the old house, he comes at night and removes from its hinges the door to the back shed, into whose reluctant grain he and his brothers gouged their names and a date, in boyhood. He puts it on his car, he drives it home and stores it under his stairs. Three names on an unhinged door, the first, of a man dead these twenty-two years. All winter, snow blows into the old shed.

To fill a life. To fill one's own shoes, and walk in them till the plies of the soles begin to separate, till the heels are rubbed away, till the toes turn up and the lettering inside has all flaked off. As fitful sky. To go with the drift of things, shifts of the light and weather. Snow blows into the tracks my skis made this morning: erase all that. I am walking on the face of winter. It's like magic, it's like walking on water, it *is* walking on water. Are you listening? I know a man who photographs the bumps on faces, the tiny lines, who celebrates them with his sharpest focus. I know a man who broke his hammer trying to open a window. Each winter new cracks open in the chimney wall, air currents trace fresh strata of soot across the ceiling.

A pulling against the grain. Amoebas of light in the undulation of gauze curtains, the cross and mesh of lines. Water's resistance as the oars reverse direction. Walking upwind. Syncopation, in music, or certain kinds of dissonance. Cloth cut on the bias, hair combed up from the nape. Velvet, rubbed the wrong way with a finger. Or finger and thumb, cleansed to an edge, testing each other's raised grain. Feeling the lines that frame us, whorl and loop, for life, beyond confusion.

I want to move far enough away to see you whole, I want a lens to contain you, even upside down, as a handful of cast type contains its own impression. As winter contains spring, or the residue of snow, the shape of those things it melted around. The broken tricycle, the rusted spade. It is spring, the season for construction; no backward look in the way that old house is gutted for renovation. I watch from across the street, chunks of my life knocked out like bad teeth, the plaster-dust drifting down like a chalky pall over the gardens. Erase all that. Are you listening?

The face of a life in motion. The sound of pianos out of open windows; radios playing to empty kitchens. On the cold side-walk, a ring of footsteps: that sound nearly forgotten. Clothes-lines shrilling on rusty pulleys; the squeak of baby-carriage wheels. Or close your eyes and it's June, pages torn from a child's copy-book are blowing down the street. In the park, by the stone pond, a line of figures in loose clothing practice Tai Chi, their movements sweeping, rhythmical, echoing each other like the arches of the pavillion behind them, reflected in the water. It's early morning. The movements are large, are generous, they flow, and the clothing too as it fills with wind, flapping against the bodies held there in marvelous postures against the light.

## March, Last Quarter

Liveliness only
in tiny things:
the drops of water that hang
at the tips of bare twigs

or the sparrow whose bobbings
at sapling's summit
tremor it
like a bow—

liveliness has made itself small,
has gone into tiny things
and waits there, wise, against
ice and thaw and ice
as we too wait for the air
to be kind again, taking the face

between dumb hands, breathing
love into the ear,
lifting hair.


## Scratch

The tinder words, where are they,
the ones that
jump-start the heart—

> like mirrors at the bends
> of tunnels, that withhold
> your face, but give you
> what is to come;

> like the voice at the end
> of the tunnel, that says
> 'Terminus', almost
> tenderly—

Little twigs that snap
like gunshot as they
consume themselves, little
dry twigs,

little sparks, little pops, little bursts
at the smoky heart of where it
begins again, o,

tender and sunny love! what, are you gone
so far away?

Come home to me now, my
brightness.  Make a small glow.
Make it to move
the heart, that has sat down
in the road

and waits for something
to turn it over. . .

    The roomy heart,
    willing to be surprised.

# Notes on the Poets

## MARGARET ATWOOD (b.1939)

The issues that have been constant in Margaret Atwood's writing all have to do with survival: survival of the individual consciousness in the face of psychic overload; survival of women in a male-dominated society; survival of the community, whether the nation-state or a smaller unit such as the tribe of writers; and survival of the species against increasing violence, technological madness that is destroying culture and environment, and the ever-present threat of nuclear annihilation.

Atwood's poems about psychic overload often include the figure of an immigrant, or pioneer, who is trying to confront a new and possibly hostile environment, where 'unstructured/space is a deluge.' The task of this individual, like that of the artist, is to form gestalts, to shape the chaos, thereby rendering it manageable, perhaps even meaningful. Atwood's response to threats to Canadian sovereignty and cultural survival, posed by the colonial attitude of Canadians and the presence and policies of the United States, has found expression in a variety of works, including *Survival: A Thematic Guide to Canadian Literature* (1972), *The Journals of Susanna Moodie* (1970), and a sequence such as 'Two-Headed Poems'.

Feminist concerns inform her work at every level, not only because most of her personae and narrators are women, but also because she has very consciously addressed such issues as sexual rights, procreative rights, social and vocational rights. The struggle for identity and equality for women finds its fullest dramatic expression in her novels *The Edible Woman* (1970) and *Surfacing* (1972), but the poems of *Procedures for Underground* (1970), *Power Politics* (1973)—from which the surreal and witty 'They Eat Out' was taken—and several recent collections explore the same ideas with mordant humour and a variety of genres, including psychological parables and stinging satires.

Atwood is concerned, in other words, with power politics at every level of existence. Much of her recent work has addressed directly the problems of torture, imprisonment, and other human rights violations, totalitarian regimes, racism, censorship, and hunger. Her task has been to create strategies, literary techniques, with which to bring these issues home to readers. Her poems, and such non-fiction writings as 'Amnesty International: An Address', quoted in the introduction to this anthology, argue for the artist as a witness and provocateur, trying to raise consciousness and initiate change. She said in an interview with Christopher Levenson in *Manna:* 'I would say that I don't think what poetry does is express emotion. What poetry does is evoke emotion from the reader, and that is a very different thing. As someone once said, if you want to express emotion, scream. If you want to evoke emotion it's more complicated.'

Atwood uses anomaly and other dislocating devices to keep the reader alert and involved in the poetic process. She functions as an illusionist, employing perceptual tricks—interjecting apparent non-sequiturs or off-hand comments to distract the reader from the apparent content of the poem, for example, or suddenly shifting the point of view in the middle of a poem. Atwood loves to parody traditional romantic forms and stances; instead of lyrical outbursts, displays of sonority, and heavy emoting, she prefers understatement, the creation of a wry and prosaic voice, and the shock value of surreal and bizarre images. As she explains in *Manna*: 'There are always concealed magical forms in poetry. By "magic" I mean a verbal attempt to accomplish something desirable. You can take a poem and trace it back to a source in either prayer, curse, charm or incantation—an attempt to make something happen. Do you know anything about autistic children? One of the symptoms of that is they mistake the word for the thing. If they see the word "clock" on the paper they pick it up to see if it ticks. If you write "door" they try to open it. That sort of thing is inherent in language in some funny way and poetry is connected with that at some level.'

Atwood was born in Ottawa, but spent much of her childhood in the woods of Northern Quebec, where her father worked as an entomologist. She studied at the University of Toronto and Harvard and has travelled widely. Her work has been acclaimed internationally. She has received a Governor General's Award, been nominated for the Booker Prize, and been published in many languages. In addition to the books mentioned above, her other collections of poetry include *The Circle Game* (1966), *The Animals in That Country* (1968), *You Are Happy* (1974), *Selected Poems* (1976), *Two-Headed Poems* (1978), *True Stories* (1981), and *Interlunar* (1984). Her other novels are *Lady Oracle* (1976), *Life Before Man* (1979), *Bodily Harm* (1981), *Murder in the Dark* (1983), and *The Handmaid's Tale* (1986). *Dancing Girls* (1977) and *Bluebeard's Egg* (1984) are collections of stories. She has written children's books and a second collection of criticism, *Second Words: Selected Critical Prose (1982)*. She lives in Toronto.

## MARGARET AVISON (b.1918)

In 1941 Margaret Avison outlined a modest conception of poetics: 'Literature', she wrote, 'results when: (a) every word is written in the full light of *all* the writer knows; (b) the writer accepts the precise limits of what he knows, i.e. distinguishes unerringly (while writing) between what he knows, and what he merely knows about, by reputation or reflected opinion.' This view, which she endorsed again as recently as 1962, reflects not only the seriousness with which she approaches her craft, but also her view of poetry as a vehicle of discovery. She is a philosophical poet who is moved to search for 'truths' that underlie the world we perceive with our senses. She is not a descriptive poet; she is interested, as she explains in 'Voluptuaries and Others', in 'that other kind of lighting up/That shows the terrain comprehended.' 'Nobody stuffs the word in at your eyes,' she says in 'Snow'. 'The optic heart must venture: a jailbreak/And re-creation.' In order to make this jail-break, the optic heart must see through the pollution of body and mind that produces a society of unconscious grey men and clapboard suburbs, and 'this communal cramp of understanding' ('The World Still Needs'). In a world where salesmanship is valued more than a fine ear, where limited imaginations triumph, the poet can find little that is worth her attention and respect. The landscapes of *Winter Sun* (1960) are bleak and imprisoning, like the landscapes of Eliot's early poetry; like Eliot also, Avison is often forced to search the past for significant moments of illumination. Hence her interest in great men of science whose imaginative leaps have opened up new worlds of knowledge and experience. 'History makes the spontaneous jubilation at such moments less and less likely though,' she laments.

Avison's epistemological concerns have resulted in a number of poems that explore the nature of imaginative perception. Many poems in *Winter Sun* are characterized by rapid shifts of perspective, a kind of poetic equivalent of the use of multiple lenses and camera angles in film-making. To write in the 'full light of *all* the writer knows' involves dispensing with all formal notions of time and space. Like the reader of the stream-of-consciousness novel, the reader of Avison's poetry is often hard-pressed to find a centre of gravity, a fixed point of reference. It is as though, in this world of continuous change, the only certainty is the act of perception itself. Each new poem, for poet and reader alike, is analogous to the swimmer's moment at the whirlpool; if both 'dare knowledge', they will discover perhaps 'the silver reaches of the estuary'.

The austere winter terrain of her first book gives way to gentler landscapes and warmer climates in *The Dumbfounding* (1966), marking a deepening of religious experience. There is also a reconciliation with the physical world that results in poetry at once more concrete and sensuous. These poems are characterized by a careful observation of minutiae, such as the faces of loiterers and the industry of ants; it is the work of a poet fully absorbed in actuality. Here Avison leaves behind most of the rhetorical and esoteric elements that trouble her earlier verse; her sensitivity to the subtleties of language now encompasses the sound of raindrops, 'letting the ear experience this/discrete, delicate/clicking.'

Margaret Avison was born in Galt, Ont., and educated at the University of Toronto. She has been a librarian, a secretary, a research worker, a lecturer in English literature, and a social worker at a mission in down town Toronto. She is one of the finest but least prolific poets in Canada. During the early forties and fifties she contributed to Sid Corman's *Origin*, along with Charles Olson, Denise Levertov, and Robert Creeley. Apart from giving occasional readings and participating in a writers' workshop at the University of British Columbia, she has remained at the edges of the literary arena in Canada. Avison is an enthusiastic supporter of other writers and has translated a number of poems from the Hungarian, which appear in *The Plough and the Pen: Writings from Hungary, 1930-1956* (1963), edited by Ilona Duczynska and Karl Polanyi. *Sunblue* appeared in 1978, followed by a collected edition: *Winter Sun/The Dumbfounding: Poems 1940-1966* (1982).

### EARLE BIRNEY (b.1904)

Birney is a poet who has always believed that moral progress is possible. His observation of the scarred battleground of his own century has troubled him deeply, however, causing him to lash out in anger at human cruelty and indifference and to despair at his own guilt and complicity. These two responses reflect the Marxism of a generation caught in two world wars and a depression as well as the Puritanism of his heritage. The first accounts for his well-known vitriolic satires, such as 'Anglo-Saxon Street', and for his more recent attacks on the economic and political atrocities of the American empire, such as 'Sinaloa' and 'Images in Place of Logging', where he describes 'the men and the metalled/ants that multiply in the browning/pulp of the peeled world.' As early as 1945, Birney had written from Watford Military Hospital lamenting the time-bomb within each man, and pleading: 'O men be swift to be mankind/or let the grizzly take.' Almost twenty years later, he wrote in 'Letter to a Cuzco Priest': 'Pray to yourself above all for men like me/that we do not quench/the man in each of us.'

In 'The Bear on the Delhi Road', Birney suggests the method by which he brings his world under imaginative control. He says: 'It is not easy to free/myth from reality.' He describes the business of trying to make a bear perform, making it dance rather than merely amble among berries. The men of Kashmir try to transform reality, to give it artistic shape for financial gain; however, in so doing, they perform a task not unlike that of the artist, who begins with the real and concrete, whether an object or an experience, and reflects upon it until its 'meaning' (for him) is released. This is the essential structure of the romantic ode, wherein the poet contemplates a height of land (say Tintern Abbey) and is moved to discover some personal and universal significance in his experience. It is certainly the organizing principle at work in 'Vancouver Lights', 'A Walk in Kyoto', and many of Birney's travel poems; and it is a method he shares quite noticeably with Al Purdy.

Birney's energies have always been engaged in coming to terms with his need for a social identity and with his separateness as an artist. Despite his involvement in the war and the universities, he has always been an outsider, beset by internal and external forces that have kept him from feeling fulfilled. He resents society's indifference to the artist and feels intensely that the artist has a cure for society's ills. In 'Cartagena de Indias' he describes what it means to learn that other cultures can honour even their most critical poets. 'I love the whole starved cheating/poetry-reading lot of you,' he says of the Colombians, 'I who am seldom read by my townsmen.' In The Creative Writer, Birney speaks of the situation of the writer in Canada:

*It seems to me that the effective writer is one who is inwardly sure of the entire naturalness of his creative act. For instance, he must be aware that he is writing not merely because he is neurotic. Everybody's a bit queer and slightly mad, but I'm sure that my compulsion to construct more and more unprofitable verses isn't anywhere near as screwball as the compulsion of businessmen to make more and more money. But the writer who does not believe this is hamstrung from the start, haunted by a false diagnosis of his*

*society, and driven either into a permanent state of apology and mock-modesty for his*
*abnormality, or into snarling hatred for the nastiness of the normal.*

This describes accurately many of the tensions Birney has felt during his own lifetime. For him there can be no real resolution of this tension. And there is reason to believe that without it his peculiar *daimon* would cease to function. That is why he is continually on the move, why he is always experimenting in his art.

'Living art,' Birney says, 'like anything else, stays alive only by changing.' His own verse has travelled from the most traditional beginnings—including narrative, meditative lyrics, satires, nature poems, and odes—through years of experiment with typography and orthography, down the long congested road to concrete poetry. Birney is a constant reviser of poems and a contributor to little magazines. 'I don't know exactly where the literary Dew Line is this moment,' he says, 'but I'm sure it lies somewhere in the complicated world of today's little-little magazines and small-press chapbooks.'

Birney's life is as colourful as his art—and as controversial. He was born in Calgary, but spent most of his youth in Banff and in Creston, B.C. He graduated from the University of British Columbia in 1926. His graduate studies in California were interrupted by difficulties, mostly financial, which took him to Utah to teach, and to New York to work for the Trotskyites. With a grant from the Royal Society he completed his doctoral studies in London, Eng., and at the University of Toronto, where he lectured for several years and served as literary editor of *Canadian Forum*. During the Second World War he was a Personnel Selection Officer overseas and then for a short time was Supervisor of Foreign Language Broadcasts to Europe for the CBC. Later he joined the English Department at UBC and was head of the Department of Creative Writing. Birney has been writer-in-residence at the University of Toronto and has travelled widely throughout Asia, Europe, South America, and the United States. He now resides in Toronto.

Birney's reputation as a poet was established with *David and Other Poems* (1942) and *Now Is Time* (1945), for each of which he won a Governor General's Award. Further books have followed, including *The Strait of Anian: Selected Poems* (1948), *Trial of a City and Other Verse* (1952), *Ice Cod Bell or Stone* (1962), *Near False Creek Mouth* (1964), *Selected Poems* (1966), *Rag and Bone Shop* (1970), *The Collected Poems of Earle Birney* (1975), and *Ghost in the Wheels. Selected Poems 1920 - 1976* (1977). Birney has also written two novels,*Turvey* (1949), which won the Stephen Leacock medal for humour, and *Down the Long Table* (1955); two books on the creative process, *The Creative Writer* (1966), and *The Cow Jumped Over the Moon* (1972); and an autobiographical work, *Spreading Time, Book One, 1940-1949* (1980).

GEORGE BOWERING (b.1935)

George Bowering's work has been closely associated with the *Tish* group of poets, who, in reaction to prescribed texts and dominant literary forebears, rejected much of the formalism of modernist poetry in favour of a poetry that was more personal, more clearly rooted in region or place, and committed to a greater degree of open-endedness. Under the influence mainly of American models, such as William

Carlos Williams, Charles Olson, Robert Creeley, and Jack Spicer, these young poets came to regard the poem less as a set-piece, or well-made artefact, and more as a process, a sustained moment of discovery. The poet begins with the physical fact of his own being; thus his preoccupation with breathing, the body, nearby objects and persons. The poem, the created thing, becomes an object in its own right, with laws, a fusion of form and content, a unit of energy passed from writer to reader.

The primitive stance, which involves throwing off the yoke of tradition— including such poetic devices as rhyme, metrics, alliteration, and the simile— has its dangers. R.P. Blackmur sums up the matter well with regard to Thomas Hardy's poetry: 'Hardy was a free man in everything that concerns the poet; which is to say, helpless, without tradition; and he therefore rushed for support into the slavery of ideas whenever his freedom failed him.' The irregular, syncopated rhythms of the speaking-voice can become as dull or flat as the easily anticipated rhythms of the metrical or syllabic line; so, too, the rejection of conventional forms often sends the poet scurrying in search of such structuring devices as the journal entry, the Tarot, the thematically-based sequence of poems about friends, fellow writers, and so on.

In his best work Bowering manages to navigate safely between the Scylla of formlessness and the Charybdis of prescribed forms. His best poems reveal that he is not a primitive at all, but a rather skilled magician and impersonator, absorbing and assimilating the styles of a wide range of poets. His work ranges from the jazz improv poem, such as 'Circus Maximus', through a variation on the traditional poetic elegy in 'Summer Solstice', where he is highly conscious of Auden's 'On the Death of William Butler Yeats' and Yeats's own elegy, 'A Prayer for My Daughter', to rhymed acrostics and a full-scale tribute to Rainer Maria Rilke in *Kerrisdale Elegies*.

Many of Bowering's comments about technique relate to the question of *voice*. 'Not just Wordsworth's vague idea of using common speech,' he says, 'but *how to get your own voice on the page*.' In his book *Al Purdy*, he explains the notion of finding your own voice as 'a writing-school aphorism that inadequately describes the process whereby the poet comes to avail himself of ways to get the individualities of his speech habits into his prosody.' As he says in 'Circus Maximus', a poetic is no more than a single pattern imposed on experience to make it meaningful and tolerable: '(patterns I deny/and that/is part of a pattern).'

Bowering was born in Penticton, B.C. and educated at the University of British Columbia, where he received a B.A. in History and an M.A. in English. In addition to being a co-editor of *Tish*, he served as an aerial photographer in the RCAF, and travelled to Mexico, where, he says, 'I first saw strangers as individuals. I got close to people and that has always been a hard thing for me: to be close to people.' Bowering has been a tremendously prolific writer of poetry, fiction, and criticism. He has also edited various anthologies, as well as the magazine *Imago*, devoted to the publication of the long poem, and is now a contributing editor to *Open Letter*. He taught in Calgary and Montreal before joining the English Department at Simon Fraser University in Burnaby, B.C. He lives in Vancouver.

Bowering has published many books of poetry, including *Sticks & Stones* (1963), *Points on the Grid* (1964), *The Man in Yellow Boots* (1965), *Rocky Mountain*

*Foot* (1969), and *The Gangs of Kosmos* (1969), which together won a Governor General's Award, *Touch: Selected Poems 1960-1970* (1971), *The Catch* (1976), *Selected Poems: Particular Accidents* (1980), *Smoking Mirror* (1982), and *West Window* (1982). His abiding interest in the long poem is evident in his three book-length poems, *George, Vancouver* (1970), *Autobiology* (1972), *Kerrisdale Elegies* (1984), and in *Delayed Mercy and Other Poems* (1986).

Bowering has written several books of criticism, including *Al Purdy* (1970), *A Way With Words* (1982), and *The Mask in Place: Essays on Fiction in North America* (1983). He is also author of various works of fiction, including *The Flycatcher and Other Stories* (1974), *Protective Footwear* (1978), and *Burning Water* (1980), for which he received a Governor General's Award.

## ROBERT BRINGHURST (b.1946)

Robert Bringhurst was born in the United States and raised in the mountains of Montana, Wyoming, Utah, Alberta, and British Columbia. He spent a number of years in the Middle East, Europe, and Latin America, so it is not surprising that he reads and translates from half a dozen ancient and modern languages. In his poem 'The Song of Ptahhotep', the narrator says: 'I have seen at the well how the words tune the heart, how they make one who hears them a master of hearing. If hearing enters the hearer, the hearer turns into a listener. Hearing is better than anything else. It cleanses the will.' Bringhurst has striven to master the art of listening, hearing the voices of the land, hearing the voices of ancient cultures. To be a listener, he has chosen to inhabit the edges of society and to live close to wilderness, although he is also a keen student of typography and printing and has worked as a book designer in Vancouver, where he has lived on and off since 1973, and for McClelland & Stewart in Toronto. He has done a study of postwar Canadian visual art and (with Haida artist Bill Reid) an illustrated collection of Haida stories called *Raven Steals the Light* (1984).

In his poem 'Anecdote of the Squid', Bringhurst draws a clever portrait of the squid as a sort of dissappearing artist who, in the presence of enemies, makes artefacts that are mistaken for the squid itself. Meanwhile, the wily squid 'grows/transparent and withdraws,/ leaving behind him his/coagulating shadows.' Like his squid, Bringhurst belongs to the older tradition of objectivity in art, expressed in Flaubert's statement that the novelist should be 'everywhere felt, but nowhere seen' in his work and in Yeats's comment that, in art, 'all that is personal soon rots'. Bringhurst places himself squarely in this tradition. 'Music that is too human is useless,' he writes in 'Vietnamese New Year in the Polish Friendship Centre'. 'That which is too exclusively human is not human enough. Our deepest passions push us way outside ourselves.' The aim is to discover the artistic means to move beyond the limits of the self to a larger, perhaps deeper, sphere of knowing; this means eschewing confession, domestic reportage, and the other personal fictions that so dominate contemporary poetry in Canada and abroad. Bringhurst's chosen path may be as perilous as it is unpopular: the danger lies in forgetting that art must make its appeal through the senses, not through the intellect alone, and thus drifting too close to abstraction and pretentiousness. And yet Bringhurst's best work has both the concreteness and the luminosity that characterize the classics in this tradition. As he writes in 'Vietnamese New Year', 'art is not a house. Art is an opening made in the air. It is seeing and saying and being what is in the world. . . . Literature is a struggle with *hearing*, *listening*. The writer needs a stethoscopic ear, and he can—I prefer that he should—lay it against the stones and wild grasses as well as against his own chest. And the chests, of course, of other human beings.'

In order to create poetry that is human in the deepest sense, Bringhurst has been drawn to history and narrative. Story, from its origins in parable and myth, is a moral art, instructing as it entertains and engages with its characters and events. Historical events or personages provide a distancing from the present that allows both poet and reader greater imaginative freedom. Asked about his interest in the long poem, he replies: 'I don't live in a world in which the short poem is a welcome or sensible object. What can I do with one if I write it except send it to the editor of some morose or flippant little magazine—or worse, sell it for money to the editor of some hopped-up monthly, where it will function as an ornament between two columns of racy prose and a four-colour ad for Scotch whisky? The short poem is a welcome grace in an ordered life. We do not lead ordered lives. We live in a catastrophic world—a world which the short poem can't convincingly address. A world, therefore, in which, if someone does read a poem, he is likely to read it too earnestly and all wrong, or too quickly, too lightly, and equally wrong. The temptation in such a world is to create an island of answering: to reinvent everything, to write another obese, eccentric monument, in spite of one's best intentions.'

Bringhurst's books include *The Shipwright's Log* (1972), *Cadastre* (1973), *Deuteronomy* (1974), *Bergschrund* (1975), *The Stonecutter's Horses* (1979), *Tzuhalem's Mountain* (1982), *The Beauty of the Weapons: Selected Poems, 1972-82*, and *Pieces of Map, Pieces of Music* (1986).

### LEONARD COHEN (b.1934)

Leonard Cohen's imagination was shaped not only by his Jewish heritage and the Catholic milieu of Montreal, but also by the literary values and antics of the Beat generation, whose bohemianism embodied anew the Blakean notion that the road of excess is the path to wisdom. His earliest poems in *Let Us Compare Mythologies* (1956) and *Spice-Box of Earth* (1961), which are witty, exuberant, and richly embroidered, reveal a fascination with eroticism and violence as means of spiritual transcendence, a theme that finds its fullest expression in his novel *Beautiful Losers* (1966). *Flowers for Hitler* (1964) announces a deepening and maturing of vision; the tone of joyous celebration gives way to darker imaginings. The poet descends morally and imaginatively into the fiery furnaces of Belsen and Auschwitz where, like Conrad's Marlow, he comes face to face with his own emptiness and his own potential for evil. At this point the poems move towards the greater simplicity of form delineated in 'Style', where Cohen hints at the potential for brotherhood and harmony that might be possible beyond the trappings of ego, culture, and nationalism. 'Well, you know, you get wiped out,' he said. 'And the deeper the wipe-out, the deeper the reluctance to use ornament or to use any other faculties that brought you to the wipe-out.'

*Parasites of Heaven* (1966) and *The Energy of Slaves* (1972) give full expression to Cohen's rejection of many of the values and strategies of conventional poetry. The books consist mainly of anti-poems, gestures of refusal, indicating a belief that the act of writing may itself be a betrayal. By the time he had published *Parasites* and *Slaves*, Cohen had already become internationally known for his folksongs. He could afford to announce his demise as a writer; he may also have had serious doubts, given the demands of his musical career and the lessons to be learned in the public arena, about both his poetic talent and the efficacy of poetry as a means of communication. However, there is in Cohen's most serious pronouncements a redeeming degree of humour and self-mockery, so it is not surprising to find, after a six-year silence, that he published a new collection of poems called *Death of a Ladies' Man* (1978), a sort of dialogue of self and soul in which the poet and his alter-ego debate the meaning of art, love, politics, and nation.

Sainthood and renunciation figure prominently in *Death of a Ladies' Man*, as they do in so many of Cohen's song lyrics. The writer of subtle psycho-parables such as 'Story', 'You Have the Lovers', and 'The Stranger Song' turns the interrogation lights on his own motivations and devices, producing a number of astonishing and hilarious prose pieces, such as 'How To Speak Poetry', which embodies as clear a statement as has been made of the dilemma of the modern artist. 'The bombs, the flame-throwers, and all the shit have destroyed more than just the trees and villages. They have destroyed the stage.' In the face of such reality, the poet must become a 'student of discipline', one who offers not advertisements for himself and his sensitivity, but 'data and the quiet organiza-tion of (his) presence'.

This advice recalls a comment Cohen made a decade earlier in an interview with Michael Harris in *Duel:*

> *I think that a decent man who has discovered valuable secrets is under some obligation to share them. But I think that the technique of sharing them is a great study.*
>
> *Now, you can reveal secrets in many ways. One way is to say this is the secret discovered. I think that this way is often less successful because when that certain kind of conscious mind brings itself to bear on this information, it distorts it, it makes it very inaccessible. Sometimes, it's just in the voice, sometimes just in the style, in the length of the paragraph; it's in the tone rather than in the message.*

The sharing of valuable secrets has taken Cohen a considerable distance down the road to asceticism, which is another form of excess. As his career blossomed, his private life was characterized more and more by solitude, simplicity, and meditation. And a recent collection, *Book of Mercy* (1984), is in the form of fifty prayers and incantations that recall the Old Testament Psalms, the Sermon on the Mount, and the tradition of religious verse that moves from Gerard Manley Hopkins through John Donne back to St John of the Cross.

Cohen was born in Westmount, a wealthy English-speaking enclave of Mon-treal, and studied at McGill University. He tried graduate studies for three weeks at Columbia, but returned to Montreal to read in clubs, write his unpublished novel *Ballet of Lepers,* and do a stint in the family clothing business. A Canada Council grant enabled him to travel to England, where he wrote *The Favourite Game* (1963), then to the island of Hydra in Greece, where he wrote much of his poetry and fiction. He returned to Montreal and New York to pursue his musical career, producing a series of highly acclaimed albums. He lives in Montreal, east of The Main.

### GARY GEDDES (b. 1940)

In his poem 'Philip Larkin' Geddes pays tribute to the British poet in terms that define his own poetics: 'He was a man whose words stopped short/of ecstasy, whose impaired tongue and ear refused/the grand theme, the gesture of extravagance'. He concentrates on the often unnoticed desperation of other human beings—a desperation as quiet as that of the Master of Horse, forced to watch the animals in his charge driven overboard; a desperation as profound as that of Paul Joseph Chartier (in the serial poem *War & Other Measures*), whose imagined autobiography, ending with his blowing himself up in a House of Commons washroom, evokes the fundamental political structure of Canada. Such subject matter has prompted the most frequent label applied to Geddes—*political* poet.

Although this summary is appropriate, Geddes does not deal with headline events and transient front-page issues. (It was six years after the Vietnam War that he wrote 'Sandra Lee Scheuer'.) His concerns are discovered 'out along the side-roads', within people and communities not usually thought of as political, and within stories whose refusal of any 'gesture of extravagance' makes a reader blink with disbelief. The political element Geddes so often uncovers is the brutality of the structures human beings use to organize their collective power, or the sudden realization of responsibility for others that comes to individuals in the unpredictable byways of their lives.

Geddes summed up this central and sustained interest of his work in an interview with Louise Schrier in *Anthos* (Nov. 1986): 'I agree with W.H. Auden that all good poetry is political, because it remembers and records what we can't afford to forget about our private and collective pasts.' The primacy of remembering and recording dictates Geddes's preference for narrative, and for the forms of letter/diary and dramatic monologue. The urgent confidences of the epistolary mode, ostensibly addressed to a single privileged reader, shape Geddes's language and line, even when a specific poem does not overtly adopt the conventions of the letter.

*The Terracotta Army* (1984) is a book-length series of dramatic monologues in which various third-century B.C. Chinese military sculptures are imagined addressing their sculptor and questioning both the values of the age and the accuracy of his interpretation. The general strategy of these poems is a technique that Geddes favours even in situations where a strict definition of dramatic monologue would not apply; his interest in the dilemma of the unprivileged is expressed, not in declaiming or in satire, but in trying to imagine his way into the language through which a particular person would express himself.

Narrative is prominent both in Geddes's dramatic monologues and in his letter-poems: what his characters speak has the shape of story. Most of the books, too, are organized as narrative; even a more obviously personal book like *Snakeroot* (1973) conveys the tensions of growing up mainly through anecdotes recounting the rituals of rural Saskatchewan. Geddes's most important and memorable books—from *Letter of the Master of Horse* (1973), *War & Other Measures* (1976) to *Hong Kong* (1987)—are made of discrete poems (sometimes themselves tersely lyrical) assembled into story:

> *I've used in a number of pieces a kind of fragmented narrative form to suggest that the mind works in very unusual ways, does not release its information in a nice straight linear fashion; and that somehow juxtaposing and counterpointing can be much more revealing than telling in a straightforward fashion. The sections in these pieces are like little stopped frames in a film. They're all very short and intense; they have an event going on, and an emotion attached; together they add up to a kind of poetic novel.*

Such arguments, and his own books, made Geddes a primary force in the development of one strain of the long poem in Canada in the 1970s and 1980s: the serial or interrupted narrative, which interweaves elements of different stories (as they are concentrated in the language of various characters) into a larger story.

Geddes seldom attracts attention for unusual vocabulary, or for the extended manipulation of a clever conceit. On the other hand he is not slangily casual or without concern for telling details of image and sound. As he write in *Anthos*:

> *I want the poems to touch people deeply and make them care about themselves, their world, and language itself. This view of poetry does not lend itself to extremes of eclecticism or undue ornamentation. But, I'd say, the techniques and craft are there, for those who want to look carefully. . . . The thrust of narrative allows me certain freedoms that aren't available to the lyric poet, one of which is a degree of monumental distraction (in character, event, terrain) that draws a reader's attention away from the so-called niceties of form.*

(Letter to Ricou, 21.Oct.1987)

So diverted, the reader is less likely to notice the niceties of language than when reading A.M. Klein or Phyllis Webb. But they are there—in exact and mnemonic phrases of echoing sounds, in his attention to the nuances of the language of mass-market consumerism, in the sudden shifts to intense metaphors for love and anger within the casual voice of the storyteller, and in the overtly metalinguistic elements that suddenly appear in *Changes of State* (1986) and *Hong Kong*. Geddes's tone and ear are, to return to the Larkin image, deliberately constrained but not impaired.

Geddes was born and raised in Vancouver, with a four-year interlude on a farm in Saskatchewan. He studied at U.B.C. and the University of Toronto, where he completed his doctorate. He lives in Dunvegan, Ontario, and teaches at Concordia University in Montreal. His other books of poetry include *Rivers Inlet* (1971), *The Acid Test* (1981) and *I Didn't Notice the Mountain Growing Dark* (1986). He also published *Conrad's Later Novels* (1980, criticism), *The Unsettling of the West*

(1986, stories), and the collaborative *Les Maudits Anglais* (1984, a play). He is an editor of several anthologies, including *20th-Century Poetry & Poetics*. His awards include the E.J. Pratt medal, the Americas Best Book Award in the 1985 Commonwealth Poetry Competition, and the 1987 National Magazine Award.

LAURIE RICOU

### RALPH GUSTAFSON (b. 1909)

Ralph Gustafson was born of Anglo-Swedish stock in Lime Ridge, Quebec, and raised in Sherbrooke. He graduated from Bishop's University in Lennoxville, then studied at Oxford. After a brief stint of teaching at St Alban's School in Brockville, he returned to England in 1933 and remained there until 1939, publishing his first two books of poetry. Gustafson lived in New York from 1939 until 1963, working during the war for British Information Services, summarizing attitudes to Britain in the American press. He returned to Canada in 1963, living in North Hatley and serving as poet-in-residence at Bishop's from 1966 until his retirement in 1977. Gustafson won a Governor General's Award in 1974 for *Fire on Stone* and was the recipient of the A.J.M. Smith Prize. He has travelled widely, been a music critic for radio, and an anthologist—he edited three anthologies for Penguin, including the early *Anthology of Canadian Verse (English)* (1942) and *The Penguin Book of Canadian Verse* (1958; rev. 1967). Besides many collections of poetry, he has published two collections of short stories: *The Brazen Tower* (1974) and *The Vivid Air* (1980).

Leon Edel has suggested that Gustafson's poetry falls into three distinct periods, corresponding roughly to his British, American, and Canadian years. From the English, Gustafson certainly seems to have learned a good deal about measure and compression in the closed lyric; and from the Americans, especially Wallace Stevens, he learned that poetry can accommodate ideas, or wise talk, that it can be richly meditative. The poems produced during these two periods are dense, angular, syncopated, labyrinthine, and given to large-scale pronouncements and generalizations about historical events and human motivations. Inside his tortured syntax, the journalist is often at odds with the man who feels; the singer, with the thinking man. But in the late 1950s something unusual happened to change Gustafson's style. Whether the result of his marriage or of his travels in Canada—perhaps both—new energies were released into his poetry. The new landscapes and experiences could not be contained in short lyrics and meditations, but demanded an opening out toward longer discursive and narrative modes that would permit the cataloguing of names, the recording of minutiae, and the creation of a sense of movement through vast distances in a world far removed from the claustrophobic bed-sitters and flats of London and the garrets of Manhattan. The poems became longer, the lines shorter, reflecting modes developed by Lawrence Ferlinghetti and Gary Snyder in the U.S., and Earle Birney and Al Purdy in Canada. This new sense of emotional and physical space—which was doubtless a factor in his decision to return home—pushed Gustafson towards extended forms, particularly the poem-sequence, to which he brought outrageous wit, lyric skills, and an eye for significant detail.

In his selected essays on poetry and music, *Plummets and Other Partialities* (1987), Gustafson claims that 'Of all the constructions which a poem may take, the sequence, the poem by sections, is the one, I think, most peculiarly contemporary. The architecture accommodates the modern temper. Its structure and complex of meditation, irony and extension, convey the contemporary world of incompletion and, at the same time (in accordance with Poe's injunction) maintain tension.' Yet, against the abuses of the long poem—'Sprawling, self-licensed, half prose, half thought'—Gustafson also makes the case for the short lyric or Impromptu poem, as an 'inspired accident', 'the devil in a halo': 'The structuring, invisible, cogent, is from learning; the vitality of its cadence is from metrical control; the verbal music is from the tuned ear.' Although he continues to shift gears regularly from his complex, angular and epigrammatic occasional poems to the longer meditative pieces, Gustafson's greatest achievement may well lie in those delicate, lucid, almost oriental evocations of place in the Eastern Townships, where meaning is found to reside in the concrete particulars of daily life.

Gustafson's poetry collections include *The Golden Chalice* (1935), *Alfred the Great* (1937), *Flight into Darkness* (1944), *Rivers among Rocks* (1960), *Rocky Mountain Poems* (1960), *Sift in an Hourglass* (1966), *Ixion's Wheel* (1969), *Selected Poems* (1972), *Fire on Stone* (1974), *Corners in the Glass* (1977), *Sequences* (1979), *Landscape with Rain* (1980), *Conflicts of Spring* (1981), *Gradations of Grandeur* (1982), *The Moment Is All: Selected Poems* (1983), *Directives of Autumn* (1984), *Impromptus* (1984), and *The Collected Poems of Ralph Gustafson* (1987).

### D. G. JONES (b.1929)

Doug Jones was born in Bancroft, Ont., and educated at McGill and Queen's Universities. He began writing as an undergraduate at McGill, where he won several prizes in creative writing. His early work was encouraged and ultimately published by Louis Dudek and Raymond Souster in magazines and in book form by Contact Press. Jones has taught at several universities in Canada and is a member of the English Department at the University of Sherbrooke, where he served as an editor of *Ellipse*, a quarterly review designed to present the work of French and English writers in translation. He has published four books of poetry—*Frost on the Sun* (1957), *The Sun Is Axeman* (1961), *Phrases from Orpheus* (1967), and *Under the Thunder the Flowers Light Up the Earth* (1977), for which he received a Governor General's Award—and a major analysis of image and theme in Canadian literature, *Butterfly on Rock* (1970). He lives in North Hatley, Que.

There is a passage in *Butterfly on Rock* that is both an acute comment on the state of poetry in Canada and a useful summary of Jones's own poetic development: 'Having reached the Pacific, Canadians have begun to turn back on themselves, to create that added dimension Teilhard de Chardin calls the noosphere. . . . more than ever before, we have arrived at a point where we recognize, not only that the land is ours, but that we are the land's.' His first three volumes of poetry represent the stages in his own journey towards a 'true' landscape. In *Frost on the Sun* Jones was preoccupied with violence and disintegration, but only as poetic *subjects*, not as pressing realities that must find poetic resolution. In *The Sun Is Axeman*, however, a hostile nature is presented, one that is stunted and barren, mute and unsympathetic, unlike anything in the pastoral world of his early poems. Many of the poems present the unpredictable landscapes of dreams, landscapes that may splinter into betrayal and degeneration. In *Phrases from Orpheus* Jones experiences some sort of dark night of the soul, in which he asks: 'how shall I love/this earth,/which is my certain death?' Jones feels in all things a potential for violence, for disintegration, but he understands this at a psychological level to be a fundamental aspect of reality. In the later poems, myth functions not as ornament but as a controlling structural element; these poems are successful, not because they rewrite old myths, but because they reveal something of the poet's own world. In a letter to the present writer, Jones wrote: 'It is always a case of seeing through a conventional pattern or faded myth to something more immediate, vital or violent, and the renewal of the old or the creation of a new myth more adequate to that immediate experience.' *Orpheus* also includes a number of poems that grow out of very personal emotional experience, but experience that is controlled and manipulated. These poems are extremely well turned and yet they retain a psychological depth that is quite remarkable.

As important as Jones's discovery of his own noosphere is his discovery of the means of giving it imaginative expression. In 'Clotheslines' he argued that 'the most common things/clothes hung out to dry/serve as well as kings/for your imagery.' The truth is that common things serve better than kings, as Jones discovers in *The Sun Is Axeman*. His early poetry had been too general, too abstract. The sense of logic, or intellect, was oppressive; too often sound and image were under severe strain from having to flesh-out the skeleton of thought that held a poem together. However, in poems such as 'Portrait of Anne Hébert' and 'For Françoise Adnet', the images grow with the poem; they are not grafted on. The metaphors are organic, drawing the reader towards, rather than away from, the subject. Jones begins to use common objects quite naturally and his poetry makes its appeal through the senses, not merely through the intellect. He forsakes his idealized landscapes for the colour and texture of the actual world around him.

The search for a more precise and more immediate form of expression took Jones briefly to Pound and the Imagists and then to moderns such as Auden. In 'Portrait of Anne Hébert' the language is natural, the syntax simple and insistent, suggesting that the poet is too caught up in the making to be fanciful or verbose. Here, and in the more complicated poems of *Phrases from Orpheus*, Jones is concerned with 'articulating a highly intense and obscure complex of feelings with extreme economy ... with a certain simplicity and yet dramatic power.' One poem that seems to realize this difficult goal is 'These Trees Are No Forest of Mourners'; its sureness and simplicity are striking. The best of Jones's later poems have this sculptural quality; their success lies not in exhaustive detail, but rather in precision and economy of phrasing. We are left, as in the Chinese paintings that Jones admires, with only an image—and a space in which that image can grow.

In *Under the Thunder the Flowers Light Up the Earth*, he explores metaphors of growth and decay, love and violence, in poems that attain a lyrical intensity not present in his earlier work. In the persona of Archibald Lampman he also writes a remarkable poem sequence to 'Kate' (Katherine Waddell, with whom Lampman was in love) that touches upon the violence and prudery of the Canadian psyche.

## A.M. KLEIN (1909-1972)

Abraham Moses Klein was born in Ratno, in the Ukraine, and the following year his family moved to Montreal. He began writing seriously as a student at McGill University (1926-30), where he first met A.J.M. Smith, F.R. Scott, Leon Edel, and Leo Kennedy. In 1930 he entered law school at the University of Montreal and received his LL.B. in 1933. He married Bessie Kozlov in 1933 and became editor of the *Canadian Jewish Chronicle* in 1938; the following year he began a long association with Sam Bronfman, as a speech writer and public-relations adviser. While his literary reputation grew over the years—with the winning of a Governor General's Award in 1949 for *The Rocking Chair and Other Poems* (1948) and the great critical success of his novel *The Second Scroll* (1951)— Klein was never quite satisfied and was easily distracted into causes and kinds of writing for which he was neither gifted nor temperamentally disposed. He was a lawyer with the spirit and instincts of a poet and scholar; an employee of big business with a socialist's conscience and vision; and a deeply religious, if unorthodox, Jew with an intense need to reach, and be appreciated by, a much wider audience. While these pressures and contradictions contributed to his eventual breakdown and long silence, it must be said that his unusual burdens fired a remarkable talent and inspired a body of work unique in vision and seldom surpassed in craft.

In his 'Portrait of the Poet as Landscape' Klein speaks of the poet as someone compulsively engaged in naming, cataloguing, deciphering. Klein's tools included French, English, Latin, Yiddish, and Hebrew and a love of language that expressed itself in infectious wit, outrageous pedantry, free-wheeling word-play, and a propensity for exotic vocabularies and frequent allusions to religious and literary classics. His biographer, Usher Caplan, calls attention in *Like One That Dreamed* to Klein's earthy humour and Joycean playfulness, qualities also noticed by his friend and fellow-poet P.K. Page: 'His puns were unbelievable— he just couldn't resist them. Language was marvelously flexible on his tongue, he could bend it any way at all, make it do anything. Klein had that sense of the child in him, to delight in language and play with it. His joyfulness, his delight in things—he was so alive to the world.'

Klein took pleasure in deciphering Joyce's *Ulysses*, and his writings on Joyce that have survived can be found in *Accent* X, 3 (1950) and *New Directions* 13 (1951). He identified with Joyce's breadth of imagination, verbal genius, and bawdy humour, not to mention his lovingly portrayed Jewish hero, Harold Bloom. But Klein was also drawn to the religious and linguistic intensities of Jesuit poet Gerard Manley Hopkins, from whom he learned much about poetic syntax and sound-patterning. Klein's devotion to craft and his love of language helped him rise above the causes and the occasions that triggered much of his poetry, so that he could make co-exist, in a single literary context, the humour and horror of

Nazism, the sacredness and profanity of elements of French-Canadian culture, and the sublimity and ridiculousness of artistic ambition and endeavour.

Klein's publications also include *Hath Not a Jew* (1940), *The Hitleriad* (1944), *Poems* (1944), and *Collected Poems* (1974), edited with an introduction by Miriam Waddington. Klein's influence and example have been felt by many Canadian poets—notably Layton, Mandel, Cohen, and Solway—in terms of linguistic play and tactics for using and exploring the poet's Jewishness. However, as Waddington points out, Klein's influence among these and other poets has even more to do with the later work, where 'he put into poetry his double and sometimes triple tradition, extending ancient biblical metaphors to include modern grain elevators in a northern landscape, and finding a new metaphysic in such folk objects as rocking chairs and spinning wheels.'

Aside from his splendid 'Portrait of the Poet as Landscape', Klein refused to delineate his poetics: 'I do not intend to give you "a brief statement of my attitude towards my art, etc." I am surprised that you ask it. You know such questions elicit only the sheerest of arrogant balderdash. What shall I say in reply: "I sing because I must!"—How phoney! Or that I wish to improve the world with my rhyme!—How ridiculous! Or that I seek to express the standards of my age, etc. Me, I will have none of that cant. Simply expressed, I write poetry only to reveal my civilization, my sensitivities, my craftsmanship. This, however, is not to be quoted.' (*Like One That Dreamed: A Portrait of A.M. Klein*, 1982, edited by Usher Caplan).

## ROBERT KROETSCH (b.1927)

Robert Kroetsch was born in the small farming community of Heisler, Alberta, which has remained a dominant element in his imaginative life. In 1948 he graduated from the University of Alberta and went to work as a civilian education and information specialist for the U.S. Army, spending time in Labrador and the North. He began graduate studies at McGill University, but received his M.A. from Middlebury College in 1957 and his Ph.D. from the University of Iowa in 1961. After several years of teaching in the English Department at the State University of New York in Binghamton—where he co-edited *Boundary 2*, a journal of post-modern literature—Kroetsch began teaching intermittently in Canada, accepting a permanent position at the University of Manitoba in 1978. He has become an important figure regionally and nationally, not only for his poetry and fiction, but also for the vigour and contagion of his critical essays.

In contrast to what he, and many other critics, perceive to be a puritanical and conservative streak in the Canadian consciousness, Kroetsch espouses a Dionysian aesthetic. As the narrator of his novel *Badlands*, Anna Dawe, says: 'God help us we are a people raised not on love letters or lyric poems or even cries of rebellion or ecstasy or pain or regret, but rather old hoards of field notes. Those cryptic notations made by men who held the words themselves in contempt but who needed them nevertheless in order to carry home, or back if not home, the only memories they would ever cherish: the recollections of their male courage and their male solitude.'

One of the chief preoccupations of Kroetsch's poetics has been to find alternatives to the lyric, with its expectations of closure and coherence. Kroetsch's pursuit of the long poem—not the narrative that so interested Pratt, but the fragmented epic and poem-sequence—has involved a struggle against the presumed systems and grids of inherited story, employing (instead of character and a linear unfolding of plot) such structuring devices as stone hammers, ledgers, seed catalogues, and grammar itself. Under scrutiny these ordinary things become objects of meditation, assuming, or acquiring, a larger symbolic value: the stone hammer undergoes transformations from natural object to weapon, artefact, functional object, and imaginative touchstone; the ledger serves as a clever device—with its columns of inventory, credit, and debit—for tallying up private and collective guilt in the accounting that is fundamental to all thinking lives; seeds and catalogues of seeds provide a wonderful metaphor for exploring the images of growth so germane to our survival as individuals and as a nation; and the conjunctive structures 'and/but' in *The Sad Phoenician* function as a maddening, if humorous, expression of the alternating currents of motivation and sexual desire, entry and withdrawal, braggadocio and bathos.

Ron Smith, in an Afterword to *The Stone Hammer Poems*, insists that Kroetsch's 'preoccupation with the need to "uninvent" the old mythologies and invent or create a new mythology that is central to his prairie locale, is a revolutionary act that is key to the revelatory process found in all his writings. It is this process that allows Kroetsch to cross geographical and aesthetic boundaries in his art.' As a poet and theorist, however, Kroetsch is, above all, playful. He sees the poet as trickster or lover rather than priest. Kroetsch endorses the idea of the poem as something more than literary document; he praises 'hubbub' and 'commotion', conditions in which the poem is 'Freed from picture, into the pattern and tumble of sound.'

Kroetsch's poetics may be gleaned from *The Crow Journals* (1980) and two issues of *Open Letter* devoted to his work. 'What has come to interest me now,' he writes in the latter, 'is what I suppose you can call the dream of origins. Obviously, on the prairies, the small town and farm are not merely places, they are remembered places, even dreamed places. When they were the actuality of our lives, we had realistic fiction, and we had almost no poetry at all. Now, in this dream condition, as dream-time fuses into the kind of narrative we call myth, we change the nature of the novel. And we start, with a new and terrible energy, to write the poems of the imagined real place.'

Kroetsch's poetry books include *The Ledger* (1975), *The Stone Hammer Poems* (1975), *Seed Catalogue* (1977), *The Sad Phoenician* (1979), and *Field Notes* (1981). His novels include *But We Are Exiles* (1965), *The Words of My Roaring* (1966), *The Studhorse Man* (1969), for which he received a Governor General's Award, *Gone Indian* (1973), *Badlands* (1975), *What the Crow Said* (1978), and *Alibi* (1983).

## PATRICK LANE (b. 1939)

In an essay entitled 'To the Outlaw', first published in John Gill's *New: American & Canadian Poetry* (1971), Patrick Lane writes passionately of the poet as an outlaw, a half-mad fugitive who inhabits the margins of society, the darkest corners: 'A poet is neither trained nor taught. He is the outlaw surging beyond the only freedom he knows, beauty in bondage. . . . The poem is a place of beauty that goes beyond knowledge and understanding.' For Lane, then, the poem would appear to be a sort of prison or cage in which experience is captured, its terrors rendered beautiful in words. Appropriately, images of confinement—jails, cages, rooms, attitudes, roles, social classes, political systems—abound in his poems. Animals—creatures that ought to exist outside the mental and physical prisons man makes, but are constantly being trapped, victimized, or rendered extinct—stalk through the pages of Lane's books, especially birds, those exotic and romantic reminders of our earthbound nature and our deepest yearnings for escape.

Another facet of Lane's romantic stance is his conviction that he writes about lower-class working experience from the INSIDE IN, rather than from the OUTSIDE IN. He insists that 'the personal is the only universal truth, the "everyman"', and argues that his 'search for enlightenment . . . is always balanced with my social commitment to the lower class, of which I am a member, with all its rage and pathos.' Thus he identifies strongly with Chilean poet Pablo Neruda and with the plight of peoples in the Third World countries he has visited; so, too, he advocates a poetry along lines suggested in Neruda's essay 'Towards an Impure Art': 'A poetry impure as the clothing we wear, soup-stained, soiled with our shameful behaviour, our wrinkles and vigils and dreams. . . .'

The form and content of most of Lane's early work falls within such 'impure' bounds. His messages are not pretty; they are full of guilt and suffering, separation and loss. Gradually, however, the image of the tight-lipped loser who inhabits these poems gives way to a wiser, more reflective persona, capable of greater understanding and a broader historical reference. After the early work, which had been excessively anecdotal, Lane began to discover in the basic materials of his poetry *significant* form, which has more to do with the resources of language than with events themselves. Similarly, his considerable metaphorical gifts, which previously seemed unsuited to an age committed to understatement and economy, became more and more capable of profound and startling effects: the metaphor in 'Stigmata', for example, 'the scrimshawed teeth of endless whales,/the oceans it took to carve them', derives its power not from mere cleverness, but rather from the poet thinking his way into the image. For the reader this results in the shock of recognition, and delight at being confronted with a proposition (the creature shaped by the element it inhabits) so profoundly simple that it has escaped attention.

Whether he is writing about love, nature, the destruction of the Incas, or the castration of a ram, Lane is capable of a delicate but biting lyricism. In 'Mountain Oysters', for example, the speaker describes the quick and efficient slitting of the ram's scrotum and subsequent eating of the fried testicles with an excruciating matter-of-factness and verbal understatement ('brushed the tail aside/slit the bag/tucked the knackers in his mouth/and clipped the cords off clean'); these techniques, and the colloquial indifference of the farmer's off-hand remarks, serve to heighten the sense of pain and horror Lane wishes to communicate. The idea of 'cutting delicately' and then eating the testicles invokes a sense of incongruity, and calls up old-wives' tales about strength and sexual prowess being derived from eating the organs of certain animals; then Lane beautifully juxtaposes the dining scene with an image of rams in the field, 'holding their pain/legs fluttering like blue hands/of tired old men.'

Ultimately there is a degree of poetic learning and a real commitment to literature in Lane's work that is of greater significance than his 'outlaw' stance. As he works with the longer line and explores certain metrical and syllabic possibilities that he had eschewed in his earlier work, Lane becomes more and more capable of appropriating other voices, other times.

He was born in Nelson, B.C. and has lived intermittently in the interior of British Columbia, mostly in Vernon, until recently, when he settled in Saskatoon. His travels have taken him to Europe, China, and South America. As his poems indicate, he has tried his hand at a wide variety of jobs, mostly manual. He was co-founder of Very Stone House, a small publishing venture Lane often operated in transit out of a series of doomed Volkswagen vans, and has been writer-in residence at Concordia University and the Universities of Manitoba and Alberta. He teaches part-time at the University of Saskatchewan. His books include *Letters from a Savage Mind* (1966), *The Sun Has Begun to Eat the Mountains* (1972), *Passing Into Storm* (1973), *Beware the Months of Fire* (1973), *Unborn Things* (1975), *Poems New and Selected* (1979) which won a Governor General's Award, *Old Mother* (1982), and *Selected Poems* (1987).

## IRVING LAYTON (b.1912)

Because he is so outspoken and graphic in his denuncia-tions, Layton is the best-known and most controversial figure in Canadian poetry. Like Auden, he believes that the writing of poetry is a political act; as he explains in the Preface to *The Laughing Rooster*:

*In this country the poet has always had to fight for his survival. He lives in a middle-class milieu whose values of money-getting, respectability, and success are hostile to the kind of integrity and authenticity that is at the core of his endeavour. His need to probe himself makes him an easy victim for those who have more practical things to do—to hold down a job, amass a fortune, or to get married and raise children. His concern is to change the world; at any rate, to bear witness that another besides the heartless, stupid, and soul destroying one men have created is possible.*

Layton's barbs are not limited to the middle-class. He is equally critical of educational institutions. He rejects Culture as 'that underarm perspiration odour of impotent old men'; and he describes good taste as 'something to wipe our unstodgy behinds with'.

Layton is a man of contradictions. He would have us believe that he is a brawling, irreverent, wild-eyed poet with no use for conservative values. Despite his swagger and cultivated disdain, however, Layton is neither a primitive nor a sensualist. His satire, bombast, and erotica are the masks for his fine, beleaguered sensibility. His need to project an image of controversy has often made him espouse issues and causes that seem inconsistent with his expressed poetic vision, with the vision of poetry as freedom. Perhaps it is a comment on our country, rather than on Layton, that his second-rate poems of social gesture should attract more attention than his most delicate, refined verse.

If Layton himself remains an enigma, his literary significance is more certain. Like Whitman in the United States, he has done much to stimulate interest in poetry and to loosen its choking collar. He has reminded us that there are no inherently unpoetic subjects—there are only unpoetic minds. Poetry, he says, is 'a self authenticated speaking, a reaching down into the roots of one's being'. The poet is someone who knows 'the terror and ecstasy of living daily beyond one's psychic means'. Layton is a conscious craftsman, but he insists that 'without the material given the poet when his Unconscious (soul) is stirred into activity by a powerful emotion, his intelligence and craftsmanship are of no use to him whatever.' His own best poems are a perfect blend of passion and restraint, of a conscious and an unconscious ordering of materials.

Layton's poetry is concerned with three main subjects: sexual love, power, and imagination. Like most men he is attracted to the subject of large-scale expenditures of energy, especially violence. He believes that men are basically aggressive and that battles and wars are a means of psychic cleansing. Sexual love is, for Layton, another form of encounter that has its creative and destructive aspects. Man can dominate reality, Layton tells us in 'The Fertile Muck', not only by love, but also by imagination. Art is the supreme synthesizer; it can contain paradox and contradiction because it deals with the truth that lies between opposites, as we have learned from poets like Blake and Yeats. As Layton explains in 'The Birth of Tragedy': 'Love, power the huzza of battle/are something, are much;/yet a poem includes them like a pool/water and reflection.'

Of his long meditation, 'A Tall Man Executes A Jig', Layton has this to say: 'More than any other poem of mine, this one fuses feeling and thought in an intense moment of perception. Of truth. Truth for me, of course. That's the way I feel about gnats, and hills, and Christian renunciation, the pride of life and crushed grass-snakes writhing on the King's Highway. I like poems that are subtle and circular—the perfect form of a serpent swallowing its own tail and rolling towards Eternity. A meditative music, the feelings open as the sky. Formless poems give me the pips. If ideas, I want to see them dance' (Poet's Choice, 1966, edited by Paul Engle and Joseph Langland).

Layton was born in Roumania. While a child he went with his parents to Montreal, where he has spent most of his life. He studied agricultural science at Macdonald College and economics at McGill University, and taught in a boys' private school before taking up his teaching position at Sir George Williams University. In the forties Layton was associated with Louis Dudek and John Sutherland in the editing of First Statement, a controversial magazine that later merged with Preview to become Northern Review. In the fifties he joined with Dudek and Raymond Souster in the founding of the influential Contact Press. Since then Layton has taught, travelled, edited books, read his poetry on campuses across the country, and been an active commentator on current affairs. He was a professor of English at York University, but is now retired and lives in Montreal.

Since the publication of *Here and Now* (1945), Layton has published many books of poetry, including *The Improved Binoculars* (1956), *A Red Carpet for the Sun* (1959), for which he received a Governor General's Award, *Balls for a One-Armed Juggler* (1963), *The Laughing Rooster* (1964), *Collected Poems* (1965), *Periods of the Moon* (1967), *The Shattered Plinths* (1968), *The Whole Bloody Bird* (1969), *The Collected Poems of Irving Layton* (1971), *Lovers and Lesser Men* (1973), *The Darkening Fire* (1975), *The Unwavering Eye* (1975), *For My Brother Jesus* (1976), *The Covenant* (1977), *The Poems of Irving Layton* (1977), *The Gucci Bag* (1984), *Final Reckoning* (1987), and *Fortunate Exile* (1987).

## DOROTHY LIVESAY (b.1909)

In an essay entitled 'Song and Dance' (*Canadian Literature*, No. 41, Summer 1969), Dorothy Livesay says: 'I suppose that all my life I have fought against obscurantism! For me the true intellectual is a simple person who knows how to be close to nature and to ordinary people. I therefore tend to shy away from academic poets and academic critics. They miss the essence.' Livesay's search for the 'essence' has led her through a series of transformations, from her earliest imagist and symbolist lyrics about love and isolation; through her activist 'agitprop' writings of the forties and fifties; and, finally, to her confessional and feminist writings of the sixties and seventies.

The constant fact in her art, as in her life, has been the struggle to reconcile her need for privacy and her need for community. At times Livesay has likened this struggle to the search for the 'perfect dancing partner' or the perfect muse. As she says in 'Song and Dance', writing was a form of dance that 'could extend to an identification with a community, a nation, a world.' Poetry is for Livesay a manifestation of that ideal union between two people, poet and reader: 'Not a dance of touch, but one where the rhythm itself created an unseen wire holding two people together in the leap of movement.'

At various points in her life, Livesay has espoused a 'realist' credo, such as that expressed in 'Without Benefit of Tape', where she insists that poetry must originate in everyday experience and 'living speech'. Her documentary poems clearly grow out of this 'realist' impulse. She describes 'Call My People Home' as her 'most thoroughly documented "public" poem', one that is able to 'combine a sense of personal poignancy and alienation with a sense of social purpose.' What interests her about this form, as she says in 'The Documentary Poem: A Canadian Genre' (*Contexts of Canadian Criticism*, edited by Eli Mandel), is its capacity to create a 'dialectic between the objective facts and the subjective feelings of the poet.' Livesay's best work certainly lies at the extremes of private and public statement—in the lyric and the narrative; and the documentary is the form in which, for her, both of these elements come together. The passion of the poet finds its engagement and release, not in didacticism or righteous indignation, but rather in a total absorption in character and event. And yet, regardless of the documentary impulse that gives rise to it, 'Call My People Home' derives its illusion of reality less from accurate reference to historical fact than from the linguistic inventiveness and imaginative sympathy of the poet. The subjective needs of the poet drive her to penetrate the surfaces of history in order to create myth, to plumb the depths of what we call archetypal experience.

Although her recent work has been more stridently feminist in its utterances, Livesay has always been concerned about the role of women in society. There is no shortage of women in her poetry, from ruined maids and overburdened housewives to political activists. The world of these women is often circumscribed by roles, attitudes, domestic conditions. They move awkwardly and uncomfortably within rooms, framed windows, magic circles of children, drowning in, but miraculously saved by, the profusion of detail in their lives; and rejoicing in the evidence of growing things—a bird, a grandchild, a geranium.

Livesay rejects the elegiac preoccupations of much modern writing. 'We are optimists,' she says, 'Blakean believers in the New Jerusalem. We cannot see man's role as tragic but rather as divine comedy. We are alone—so what? We are not always lonely. Laughter heals, the dance captures, the song echoes forth from the tree-top. I won't stop believing this until every tree in Canada's chopped down; I thumb my nose at those who say that nature, and with it human nature, is becoming "obsolete".'

No doubt she inherited both her interest in poetry and her concern for social issues from her parents, who were literary people active in the field of journalism. Livesay was born in Winnipeg and lived there for ten years before her family moved to Ontario. She graduated from the University of Toronto in 1931 and then studied at the Sorbonne, exploring the influence of the French Symbolists on modern English poetry. During the Depression she was a social worker in Toronto, Montreal, and New Jersey. After 1936 she lived in Vancouver, where she worked at the YWCA, taught, and contributed to political and literary magazines, including Alan Crawley's *Contemporary Verse*. When her husband died, Livesay returned to Paris, where she worked for UNESCO before being posted to Zambia for three years. She has taught widely and been a writer-in-residence at various Canadian universities, including the University of Manitoba, where she founded *CV/II*, a periodical of poetry and reviews. She has been honoured for her literary contributions with four honorary doctorates and the Order of Canada. She now lives in Victoria, B.C.

Livesay's works include *Green Pitcher* (1928), *Signpost* (1932), *Day and Night* (1944), *Selected Poems* (1957), *The Unquiet Bed* (1967), *Collected Poems. The Two Seasons* (1972), *Ice Age* (1975), *The Raw Edges* (1981), The *Phases of Love* (1983), and *The Self-Completing Tree: Selected Poems* (1986). Her two prose books are *A Winnipeg Childhood* (1975) and *Right Hand Left Hand* (1977). Livesay has edited *The Collected Poems of Raymond Knister* (1949) and two anthologies of poetry by women: *Forty Women Poets of Canada* (1972) and *Woman's Eye* (1974). She was twice the recipient of Governor General's Awards for poetry and received the Lorne Pierce Medal for Literature in 1947.

## PAT LOWTHER (1935-1975)

Pat Lowther was born and grew up in North Vancouver, at that time a rugged sparsely populated landscape such as the one she describes in 'Coast Range': 'Just north of town/the mountains start to talk/back-of-the-head buzz/of high-stubbled meadows/minute flowers/moss gravel and clouds.' This close proximity to, and awareness of, nature in its raw and primitive state was to be a constant in her life and poetry. She reveals an almost visceral awareness of the terrain she inhabited, participating in its energy and transformational character whether her subject is mountains, craneflies, or the waters of Furry Creek.

Images of earth, and stone in particular, are everywhere present in her poetry. She identifies strongly with Chilean poet Pablo Neruda and his involvement with his people at the baserock level of their work upon the earth. Neruda, she says, is 'the man who moves/under the hills,/the man who kisses stone'; he is someone who, transported suddenly to the west coast of Canada, 'would know where/the clamshell middens are'. Like Neruda, Lowther knows that it 'isn't easy/to keep moving thru the perpetual motion of surfaces' in a world where the bodies are 'laid/stone upon stone'; but the process is necessary: 'You are changing, Pablo,/becoming an element/a closed throat of quartz/a calyx/imperishable in earth'.

At the psychological level, Lowther's preoccupation with stone, the most resistant of the things in the physical world, represents a desire to eliminate the surfaces, edges, boundaries that separate peoples from each other and from objects in nature. The sense of *relation*, of the position objects bear in relation to one another, fascinates her: thus she concerns herself with the silence between words, or the spaces between notes of music; she regards love as a kind of intersection; she sees certain gadgets and phenomena, such as phone booths and hot-line shows, as symbols of our struggle to reach beyond the limits of our own skin into other spheres of knowing. 'The world falls through my forehead', she says, 'resistlessly as rain.'

Lowther was intensely conscious of the major intellectual issues of her time: the role of women in society and the nature of political involvement. Yet her feminist concerns were only a part of her larger concern with extending consciousness, as she suggests in a note to her poems in *Mountain Moving Day* (1973, edited by Elaine Gill for The Crossing Press):

*I see the woman's revolution as part of a new outreach of consciousness. The liberation of women from imposed self-images is happening. Even the most hostile and fearful women are absorbing it subliminally right along with the cream depilatory commercials. New assumptions are being accepted below the level of consciousness. . . .*

*At one time I believed we humans were coming to the end of our evolutionary cycle—devolving like dandelions Now I see the half breeds of the future passing like migrating birds, and I begin to have a kind of tentative hope.*

For Lowther poetry is a means of effecting change in individuals *and* in society. In 'Regard to Neruda', she states: 'Often now I forget/how to make love/but I think I am ready/to learn politics.' For the poet, learning politics involves exercising full control over the language and its precious resources. The poem itself becomes a magical tool or vehicle for transporting the reader from one level of consciousness to another, and from a position of estrangement from the things, events, and people of this world to one of full participation and involvement.

Although many of her poems are political at this deeper level, Lowther has also written about specific political events in recent history. 'Chacabuco, The Pit', which deals with the aftermath of the U.S.-assisted overthrow of the government of Salvador Allende in Chile, is a powerful hymn to survival, to the earth and its people. What interests Lowther is not so much the betrayal of human values evident in the overthrow, but rather the miraculous persistence of the human spirit which, like the sexual energy that keeps the species from extinction, is a 'holy mystery/beyond refusal'.

Lowther's poetry is remarkable less for its 'fashionable' content than for its maturity and control. Whether she is writing brief imagistic pieces, confessional lyrics, or passionate meditations, she is extremely conscious of prosody—not with rhythm as an aspect of poetry, but with what Pound called the 'articulation of the total sound of the poem'.

Before she was murdered in 1975, Pat Lowther had published three books of poetry: *This Difficult Flowering* (1968), *The Age of the Bird* (1972), and *Milk Stone* (1974). Her reputation was growing rapidly. She had been elected national chairman of The League of Canadian Poets and was teaching Creative Writing at the University of British Columbia. *A Stone Diary*, which had been accepted before her death, was published posthumously in 1976; *Final Instructions* appeared in 1980.

## GWENDOLYN MacEWEN (1941-1987)

Gwendolyn MacEwen rejected self-indulgent, therapeutic poetry and the 'terribly cynical and "cool" poetry written today'. She believed that the poet can and must say things; and she wrote with the conviction that she had discovered things sayable, and worth saying. 'I write basically to communicate joy, mystery, passion,' she said '. . . not the joy that naïvely exists without knowledge of pain, but that joy which arises out of and conquers pain. I want to construct a myth.'

MacEwen's poetry might well be discussed in terms of the peculiar ground it inhabits between the 'realists' and the 'myth-makers' in Canadian poetry. From the beginning she had repudiated the actual world for one that is ancient and mythic, believing that imagination can reconcile the antinomies in life. 'I believe there is more room inside than outside,' she says in the introduction to *A Breakfast for Barbarians*. 'And all the diversities which get absorbed can later work their way out into fantastic things, like hawk-training, IBM programming, mountain-climbing, or poetry.' Like Blake and Yeats, she drew her inspiration from things occult, mystical, rather than from traditional mythology. She was most alive to the myth and ritual contained in ordinary experience; her motorcycle Icarus bears little resemblance to the original. Her landscapes and figures are mostly dream-like, not bound by normal conventions of space and time; her characters are symbolic, their movements ritualistic.

'I am involved with writing as a total profession, not as an aesthetic pursuit,' she said. 'My prime concern has always been with the raw materials from which literature is derived, not with literature as an end in itself.' Of course one of the primary sources of raw material for the writer is literature itself. MacEwen had long been preoccupied with the figure of the artist, whether the Egyptian scribes 'who drew/eyes right into their hieroglyphs' or the solitary figure of the dancer. As she says in 'Finally Left in the Landscape',

> Yet still I journey to this naked country
> to seek a form which dances in the sand.
> This is my chosen landscape.

She chose this landscape, but not without certain misgivings, as she suggests in 'Poems in Braille'. Here she expresses the conflict she feels between art and life, between the world of names and the world of things, between dance and action. For her, as for the Platonist, things are but the shadows of a real world. Words, the names we give to things, are more real because they are our attempt to describe the other-worldliness of things; they are the windows through which we view reality. However attractive this landscape, the poet cannot help but doubt its sufficiency at times. MacEwen is aware that the whole of the message may not be contained in the medium, that it may be found in the very *things* she eschews. 'I do not read the long cabbala of my bones/truthfully', she admits. She asks to follow Wenceslas, who could behold a peasant gathering fuel and be moved and involved in that experience—that is, see it in terms of itself. 'I should read all things like braille in this season', she concludes:

> with my fingers I should read them
> lest I go blind in both eyes reading with
> that other eye the final hieroglyph

Although her usual method was to begin with names, to decode language for what it may reveal about the human condition, MacEwen appears, in the *The Shadow-Maker*, to be moving more in the direction of realism. One poem is a comic exaggeration of an encounter with a fool who abuses language profoundly on a train between Fredericton and Halifax; another is a reflective account of actual experiences and impressions during travel. In terms of poetic technique, MacEwen resembles the incantatory and prophetic Yeats. Yeats claimed to have 'tried to make the language of poetry coincide with that of passionate, normal speech', to have searched for 'a powerful and passionate syntax'. Although she emphasizes the passionate more than the normal aspect of speech, she often combines, like Yeats, the oracular and the vernacular in a single poem. 'O baby, get out of Egypt', she writes in 'Cartaphilus'. 'An ancient slang speaks through me like that.' She employs the dramatic gesture and direct speech ('listen—there was this boy, Manzini') of the actor or storyteller who is intent upon delivering his message. It is a spoken poetry, a poetry of chant or incantation. MacEwen had the habit of reciting her own poetry from memory; and the ritual was quite spellbinding. Hers is a passionate plea for life, for beauty. 'To live consciously is holy', she said. The conscious man will not be one-sided; he will find a balance between his passion and his reason, between 'the complex dance of fire and blood' and 'the accurate self'.

Gwendolyn MacEwen was born in Toronto. She first published poetry when she was fifteen, in *The Canadian Forum*. At eighteen she left school to take up a full-time career as a writer. After her Canada Council grant in 1965 to research a historical novel in Egypt, she received the CBC New Canadian Writing Contest Award (1965), the Borestone Mountain Poetry Award, and a Governor General's Award for *The Shadow-Maker* (1969). She translated, prepared plays and talks for radio, read poetry in universities and schools, and was writer-in-residence at the University of Toronto. She died in November 1987.

Her poetry publications include *Selah* (1961) and *The Drunken Clock* (1961) (both privately printed), *The Rising Fire* (1963), *A Breakfast for Barbarians* (1966), *The Shadow-Maker* (1969), *The Armies of the Moon* (1972), *Magic Animals: Selected Poems Old and New* (1974), *The Fire-eaters* (1976), *The T.E. Lawrence Poems* (1982), *Earth Light: Selected Poetry* (1982), and *Afterworlds* (1987). Her works of fiction include *Julian the Magician* (1963), *King of Egypt, King of Dreams* (1971), *Noman* (1972), and *Noman's Land* (1985).

### ELI MANDEL (b.1922)

Eli Mandel was born in Estevan, Sask., and lived in that province until he joined the Army Medical Corps in 1943 and went overseas. When he returned from the war, he completed an MA from the University of Saskatchewan and taught at the Collège Militaire Royale de St Jean. He has since completed a PH.D. in English at the University of Toronto, taught at the University of Alberta, and become a Professor in the Fine Arts and Humanities Departments at York University. His first poems were published in *Trio* (1954) with those of Gael Turnbull and Phyllis Webb. His numerous published books of poetry include: *Fuseli Poems* (1960); *Black and Secret Man* (1964); *An Idiot Joy* (1967), for which he received a Governor General's Award; *Crusoe: Poems Selected and New* (1973); *Stony Plain* (1973); *Out of Place* (1977); *Life Sentence* (1981); and *Dreaming Backwards: The Selected Poetry of Eli Mandel, 1954-1981* (1981). Mandel is also an important critic and anthologist; he shows an unusual talent for critical synthesis. Apart from his numerous essays he has published *Criticism: The Silent Speaking Word*, a series of broadcasts for the CBC, and *Another Time* (1977), a collection of essays on Canadian poetry. He edited *Poetry '62* (with Jean-Guy Pilon), *Five Modern Canadian Poets* (1970), *Contexts of Canadian Criticism* (1971), and *Poets of Contemporary Canada: 1960 - 1970* (1972).

Mandel's early poetry was admired for its use of classical mythology as a means of exploring experience obliquely. His 'Minotaur Poems' and many of the Fuseli poems were written under the critical inspiration of Northrop Frye and the poetic example of James Reaney and Jay Macpherson. The early poems, though they are well-turned, polished pieces, often lack conviction, as if the weight of the traditional masks weakens, or stifles, the poet's own voice. In all of these poems there is a lyrical poet caged and threatening to break out. In *Black and Secret Man* Mandel becomes more personal, more inward. He is, to use his own definition of the modern poet, a man in search of himself; and his voyage of discovery takes him into difficult, troubled waters. He wanders through the ranks of his own ghosts, rifles his personal files of guilt and suffering, discovering in the process new and exciting materials.

The form of Mandel's verse has changed radically. It has moved from a rational ordering of materials in the direction of fragmentation and logical discontinuity, from language that is heavily rhetorical to a more colloquial idiom. Gradually he leaves behind 'the poise and thrust of speech' that 'gleams like polished steel' for a rougher, more halting, though possibly incoherent, form of expression. Some of his latest poems echo the last speeches of Samuel Beckett's characters in combining grunts, non-sequiturs, and erratic description with philosophical profundities and lyrical outpourings. Mandel has read and absorbed the critical theories of George Steiner in *Language and Silence*. As a Jew, a writer, and an academic, he is in a natural position to understand the limitations of rational discourse and also the dangers inherent in the indiscriminate use of language. Although his poetic explorations of these themes are sometimes too self-conscious and academic, his new directions are undeniably promising. The Auschwitz poem, for example, is a beautiful rendering of the intellectual and verbal disintegration that accompanies extreme psychic shock, as well as being a profound comment on the labyrinthine nature of moral perception.

Like Atwood, Mandel is fond of perceptual tricks, of unexpected shifts in tone or diction or point of view that startle the reader into consciousness, although his verse always seems more personal and affective. Atwood, like Flaubert's ideal artist, is everywhere felt but nowhere seen in much of her verse; Mandel, on the other hand, is a poet who is both seen *and* felt. He does not use alienating devices to refine himself out of existence but to give another dimension to his poetry. But this is not to say that Mandel's materials are more genuinely personal than Atwood's. In a poem such as 'Pictures in an Institution' he claims to reject his Greek and anthropology, his second-hand textbook knowledge, for the raw materials of memory. 'I take,/brutal to my thoughts, these lives, defy/your taste in metaphor', he says. The three self-consciously comic and anti-poetic 'notices' in the poem seem at first designed to conceal the poet's embarrassment at the deeply personal nature of the materials. Nevertheless it is well to remember that poets are good liars, creatures with a 'forked tongue', to use Mandel's phrase; thus the 'notices' in the poem may also be regarded as devices calculated to heighten the personal emphasis by trying to call attention away from it to the banal or the merely comic. That such questions should be raised at all is a fair indication that Mandel is successful in his efforts to create the illusion of fact. Mandel would no doubt agree with Frederick Philip Grove's view that the artist's concern is not with fact but with truth.

For Mandel, the poet is a paradoxical creature, one who partakes of the divine but who also needs to be carefully watched like the wizards, thieves, hunchbacks, and idiots that inhabit his poetic world. The poet, like Houdini, is an escape artist, continually seeking newer and more difficult emotional and verbal nets or mazes to escape from, because he is most alive during those moments of struggle, of challenge. 'I am crazed by poetry,' Mandel admits; but he means the kind of madness that is truly sane, that demands the experience of bondage in order to understand the meaning of liberty. He describes himself as a man 'reeling with messages' and there is in his verse a kind of apocalyptic frenzy, or passionate intensity, that reminds one at times of Layton, at times of Yeats.

## JOHN NEWLOVE (b.1938)

There are many dimensions to John Newlove's poetry. To readers familiar with his verse the tone of 'wearied intellectuality' that he refers to in 'In This Reed' seems predominant. He wrote from a mood of despair and disenchantment that reminds one of post-war English poets such as Philip Larkin. Newlove's is a poetry of alienation, peopled with derelicts, hitch-hikers, whores, outsiders of all sorts.

The poet appears as an outsider wandering in some no-man's-land between a vanishing past and a never-to-be realized future. Memory is another country he inhabits frequently, but memory, like everything else in Newlove's cosmos, breaks down. The vision of *Black Night Window* is dark indeed; but in *The Cave* Newlove's landscape is even more desolate. He moves from the bleakness of the Prairies and the unending highway to a more primal landscape of swamps and sea. It is a book of terse confessions, tortured examinations of failed relationships and breakdowns in communication, cynical meditations on history and 'progress'. The poet experiences not only the disintegration of personality, of identity, but also the collapse of the objective world; he is a man caught between the engine and the sea; in 'the cave/of time/with trees/and war/falling/down . . . —and/Jesus,/goodbye,/goodbye.'

In these poems Newlove often writes in a halting, disjunctive, matter-of-fact manner, giving the impression of resistance to the poetic process itself. As his vision darkens there is a corresponding paring down of language. The poems become like etchings, painstakingly made, or distillations of complex thoughts and feelings. In *The Cave* Newlove's spareness reaches such a point that he says in 'The Flower': 'I am too tense/decline to dance/verbally.'

Alongside the poetry of exhaustion and despair, however, are poems of historical interest and poems of great lyric intensity. He has an exceptional concern for rhythm and cadence and has written short lyrics that rival the best of Cohen and Layton. 'Ride Off Any Horizon' best illustrates Newlove's lyricism and his range of poetic materials. It is interesting first of all because it demonstrates one of the primary ways in which Newlove's imagination works. To ride off any horizon is to let the mind follow any idea or feeling for which there is an appropriate sound pattern, to let the mind be carried along by the verbal associations. The various sections of 'Ride Off Any Horizon' contain almost all of the areas of experience that concern Newlove in his poetry: the vast, untamed Prairies barely touched by the forces of industrialization; the Prairies of the Depression; the destruction of the Indians that finds its most powerful expression in 'The Pride'; the place of boyhood and family memories and emotional relationships; and, finally, the lonely crowds and concrete wilderness of the city. These images are held together by the refrain both aurally and grammatically, so that the poem has the kind of unity that is usually associated with narrative or ballad.

Newlove writes with directness and candour about personal relationships. His is not simply a poetry of self-exposure; he seldom stops short of a precise, rhythmical expression of feeling. Where he cannot find the measure to control a feeling, he will occasionally turn on a gentle but perfectly pitched irony. In 'The Pride' he also pioneers the documentary mode, where a delicate balance must be struck between historical fact and imaginative recreation. This short narrative asserts the power of, and the pride that must be taken in, aboriginal history and culture; their stories from the collective past will enable us to acquire 'the knowledge of/our origins, and where/we are in truth,/whose land this is/and is to be?'

Newlove was born in Regina and lived for a number of years in Russian farming communities on the eastern edges of Saskatchewan, where his mother was a school teacher. He has lived and worked in various parts of Canada—in Vancouver, Terrace, Toronto, and Ottawa; but the major geographical influence on his life and verse is the Prairies, with its oppressed Indians, ethnic minorities, and the vastness and austerity of its terrain. As he says in *Black Night Window*: 'Everyone is so/lonely in this/country that/it's necessary/to be fantastic.' Newlove's poetry has been widely published in magazines in Canada and abroad and has appeared in numerous anthologies. He has worked as a publisher's editor and been writer-in-residence at several Canadian universities. His publications include *Grave Sirs* (1962), *Elephants, Mothers & Others* (1963), *Moving in Alone* (1965), *Notebook Pages* (1966), *What They Say* (1967), *Black Night Window* (1968), *The Cave* (1970), *The Fat Man* (1977), and *The Night the Dog Smiled* (1986).

### ALDEN NOWLAN (1933-1983)

Alden Nowlan has chronicled movingly and convincingly the harshness and hypocrisy of life in the Maritimes. His poems tell of the repressions that are a part of that heritage. 'I am a product,' he says 'of a culture that fears any display of emotion and attempts to repress any true communication.' Like Souster, he is moved by his immediate environment, especially by economic conditions that grind down the human spirit. He is a poet of the underprivileged. 'In my childhood and early youth I experienced the kind of poverty that scarifies and warps the soul.' His is a dark world indeed, a world brutalized by poverty, ignorance, fear, greed, and lust. Anyone familiar with the fictional world of Hugh MacLennan's *Each Man's Son* will recognize Nowlan's landscapes at once.

Poetry for Nowlan was a means of establishing communication; like the atheist's prayer, it was a 'reaching out in fear and gentleness'. He can write of violence, loneliness, and despair with great compassion. In 'Britain Street' he tells of the unhappy conditions between parents and children in the depressed areas, 'where the very names/of their young were curses'. In this climate of brutality and hatred, the poet reclaims the abused, debased names and restores to them some dignity; he gives them a newer, more humane context, invests them with beauty and feeling. Though not a moralist, he is capable of fine moral discriminations, as in 'In Those Old Wars', where he reflects on the debasing effects of power and the (sometimes) ennobling effects of defeat. His attitude towards his own serious illness was typical:

*When I was in hospital, every time that I was operated on I thought I was going to die.*
*The thing I was worried about after worrying about what would become of my wife and*

*son was how much I wanted to write—how much time I'd wasted when I could have been*
*writing. Every time I went down in the elevator to get operated on, I thought . . . how many*
*more things I wanted to say. For that reason, my illness was good for my writing. As*
*Nietzsche says, 'What does not kill me, strengthens me.'*

Nowlan claimed that his work as a journalist gave him a sense of writing for
an audience. 'You learn a great respect for the audience when you do newspaper
work,' he said. 'And, another thing, it made me very aware of people.' Not
content to be a mere recorder of experience (from the outside), he tried to fathom
the psychology that underlies experience, the relation between the feeling and
the act. He brought to poetry the novelist's gift of characterization, the capacity
to embody a feeling or idea in an image of action. 'I don't like hypocrisy and I
don't like fakes,' he said in typical fashion. 'I think the most important division
in the world is between the people who are real and the people who are fakes.'
Journalism also left its mark on his style. He wrote with a disarming directness
and simplicity, as if he had time for neither fakes nor literary games. The pressure
to 'get things said' seemed to preclude rhetoric, ornament. As he explained in
'And He Wept Aloud':

> *oh, admit this, man, there is no point in poetry*
> *if you withhold the truth*
> *once you've come by it*

The naturalness of Nowlan's diction, his ear for the nuances of the speaking
voice, the rightness of his enjambment—these things speak for the sincerity of his
desire to offer his truth in the simplest, most unadorned manner possible. As
Robert Bly suggests in the prefatory note to *Playing the Jesus Game*, Nowlan is a
poet entangled not in words, but in the universe. 'Human feeling is all that
counts,' he said. 'To hell with literature . . . it's a kind of reassurance that there are
people out there, listening. Makes me sort of visualize my poems wandering all
over the place tapping people on the shoulder and saying: "Hi there, I'm Alden
Nowlan, who are you?"' To the charge that he was a regionalist, Nowlan replied:
'I don't write about Maritime people in capital letters, as if they were some special
species. I have certain feelings and responses—I could well have these same
feelings and responses if I lived in Montreal, but I'd write about them in a
different way, simply because I'd have a different experience and see different
things if I lived in Montreal.' Nowlan's portrayal of human emotions moved from
the objective early poetry, which was often saved from lapsing into sentimental-
ity by his sense of irony and wry humour, to a more personal, confessional poetry.
Whatever his subject or manner, however, his unusual moral sympathy gave the
poetry warmth and great appeal.

Nowlan was born in the Nova Scotia backwoods. He left school at twelve and
worked as a farm labourer, a sawmill helper, the manager of a hillbilly orchestra,
and the editor of the *Hartland Observer*, finally joining the *Telegraph-Journal* of
Saint John, N.B. Nowlan received a number of awards, including Canada Council
grants, a Guggenheim fellowship, and a Governor General's Award (for *Bread,
Wine and Salt*). He engaged in various freelance writing projects and was writer-
in-residence at the University of New Brunswick from 1969 until his death.

Nowlan worked closely with theatre people in the Maritimes, writing a play called *Frankenstein* (1976) with Walter Learning, one called *One Dollar Woman*, and another about Sherlock Holmes. His published collections of poetry are *The Rose and the Puritan* (1958), *A Darkness in the Earth* (1959), *Wind in a Rocky Country* (1960), *Under the Ice* (1961), *The Things Which Are* (1962), *Bread, Wine and Salt* (1967), *the mysterious naked man* (1969), *Playing the Jesus Game* (1970), *Between Tears and Laughter* (1971), *I'm a Stranger Here Myself* (1974), *Smoked Glass* (1977), and *I Might Not Tell Everybody This* (1982). Some of his short stories are collected in *Miracle at Indian River* (1968); his autobiographical novel, *Various Persons Named Kevin O'Brien*, appeared in 1973.

## MICHAEL ONDAATJE (b.1943)

Michael Ondaatje was born in Ceylon where he lived for eleven years. Educated at Dulwich College in England before coming to Canada in 1962, he studied at Bishop's University, the University of Toronto, and Queen's University, where he completed an M.A. on Edwin Muir. Ondaatje has published numerous books of poetry: *The Dainty Monsters* (1967); *The Man with Seven Toes* (1969), a macabre narrative set in the primitive wilds of Australia; *The Collected Works of Billy the Kid* (1970, winner of a Governor General's Award), a novelistic sequence of poems and prose that explores, often in a stream-of-consciousness manner, the physical and psychic life of the famous American folkhero; *Rat Jelly* (1973); *There's a Trick wth a Knife I'm Learning to Do* (1979); and *Secular Love* (1986). His works of prose include *Coming Through Slaughter* (1976), the autobiographical *Running in the Family* (1982), and *In the Skin of a Lion* (1987). Ondaatje has published one critical study, *Leonard Cohen* (1970); made several short films, including one on concrete poet bp Nichol called *Sons of Captain Poetry*, and *The Clinton Special*, about Theatre Passe Muraille's 'The Farm Show'; and edited *Personal Fictions* (1977), and *The Long Poem Anthology* (1979). He lives in Toronto and teaches at Glendon College.

Ondaatje has an acute eye for the bizarre, the 'abnormal', the out-of-the-way. His landscapes are peopled with strange beasts, cripples, lost, violent souls, animals—all moving in and out of focus, emerging from and receding into some uncharted region of racial memory. He is fascinated with energy, especially as it is manifested in the form of violence. His poetry is a catalogue of scars, whether the psychic scar that defines an emotional relationship or the disastrous historical event that shapes the destiny of a nation or civilization. Even in the domestic world, which he calls 'a cell of civilized magic', the poet perceives division, the struggle for space and survival.

Thomas Mann remarked that the 'abnormal', the bizarre, is the best, if not the only, route to the 'normal'. Ondaatje's figures, like the parade of freaks and grotesques in a Fellini film, are important for what they reveal of the obsessions, perversions, and fears of so-called normal men. This is not to suggest that his poetry is unrelentingly black or morbid. It is not. He does not revel in the depiction of violence, but brings to bear on his materials considerable integrity and restraint. This is especially obvious in 'Elizabeth' and 'Peter', where the use of understatement heightens the dramatic impact of events. Ondaatje also has a sense of humour, an engaging capacity for the comic and the ironic. If his characters often have blood on their hands and violence on their minds, they are just as likely to have shaving-cream on their chins and dragons in their tennis nets. His poems never seem to be reworkings of a single feeling or mood, because his ability to assume a variety of points of view enables him to describe events and sensations from the inside, as it were. Furthermore, the strong narrative element keeps him from overloading or overworking a single image and gives the poetry a sense of movement and space.

If Ondaatje has a poetics, it is expressed in his poem '"The gate in his head": for Victor Coleman'. 'My mind is pouring chaos/in nets onto the page', he writes. Words are the unique threads that, properly woven, can snare strange, unexpected things. Ondaatje recognizes the importance of form in poetry; even his most casual, personal poetry is held together by some linguistic device. But he rejects an undue emphasis on formal structure. In a letter to the present writer he states his 'distrust of all critics and nearly all dogmatic aesthetics and all rules and all clubs/cliques/schools of poetry'; instead, he expresses a 'wish to come to each poem and let it breed in its own vacuum and have its own laws and order.' He prefers the 'caught vision' of a blurred photograph to the standard reproduction of a recognizable reality:

> *The beautiful formed things caught at the wrong moment*
> *so they are shapeless, awkward*
> *moving to the clear.*

The wrong moment is the right moment: that is the secret of Ondaatje's peculiar form of myth-making. He catches his subject when it is moving *towards* clarity, when it is neither completely vague and unrecognizable nor completely clear and obvious. He can only use the traditional nets of classical mythology by altering our perception of them, by coming at them from unexpected angles. Otherwise they are too static and destroy the subject they are called upon to illuminate.

Ondaatje is a kind of dramatist of disaster, with a cinematic concern for detail, for the appropriate image, for angles of vision. Like Bergman and Fellini, he has a special talent for finding the striking image, the image that remains hooked in the mind long after other details or events have faded. The fantastical aspects of his work should not draw attention from the fact that he has a powerful shaping instinct. He says, in an interview with Christoper Levenson in *Manna*, that he aimed in *Billy the Kid* to create a 'mental shorthand', where you have a 'person thinking very naturally and yet have the lines withdrawing and changing meaning depending on whether line B referred to line A or to line C. So a formal punctuation had to be removed and so it had to be suggested in the phrase or in the way the line fell on the page.' Similarly, in an interview with Sam Solecki in *Spider Blues*, he insists on the importance of 'architecture', which is a matter of 'repeating and building images and so making them more potent'; 'what I want is something more physical, something having to do with the placing of a scene in one place and not in another—that kind of thing. How one *composes* a book. How one turns the real everyday object into something more by placing it in exactly the right place, with the right tone. There is an architecture of tone as well as of rhythm. What academics are obsessed with is who won the horse race or what it really means. But if you watch a replay you start discovering form. You don't watch the horse in front anymore—the leading horse representing "content"—but the horse in fourth place saving himself. I think that writers think about and are interested in that kind of thing, the undercurrents of shape and tone as opposed to just the meaning.'

## P.K. PAGE (b.1917)

'I am a traveller,' P. K. Page has written. 'I have a destination but no maps. Others will have reached that destination already, still others are on their way. But none has had to go from here before—nor will again. One's route is one's own. One's journey unique. What I will find at the end I can barely guess. What lies on the way is unknown. How to go? Land, sea or air? What techniques to use? What vehicle?' ('Traveller, Conjuror, Journeyman', *Canadian Literature*, No. 46, Autumn 1970.)

Patricia Kathleen Page has been a traveller in both her life and art. She was born in England but raised in Calgary and Winnipeg, where her father was stationed with the Strathcona Horse. From her family, which she describes as closely knit and not at all typical, she seems to have gained an appreciation for the arts, as her parents engaged in writing and drawing and were excellent carvers. She says she 'first came to writing by being an adolescent, which is enough to make anyone write.' After living briefly in the Maritimes, she moved to Montreal, where she worked as a scriptwriter for the National Film Board and became associated with Patrick Anderson and F. R. Scott in the editing of *Preview* magazine. Her first major publication was in *Unit of Five* (1944), an anthology of five poets edited by Ronald Hambleton. Page lived abroad for many years, in Mexico, Australia, and Brazil, where she began to draw under her married name, P. K. Irwin. She now lives in Victoria, B.C.

Page's search for the techniques with which to make her spiritual and aesthetic journey is a fascinating study. Her early poetry, which she now describes as 'clotted with images', explores the contradictions that underlie everyday experience: the terrible and explosive beauty of childhood; the haunting presence of boredom and madness associated with the deadly routine of jobs; the vanity and self-delusion that infects the most charitable and earnest of actions and statements. Such subjects lent themselves readily to a richly textured and highly allusive style, in which the interplay of elements of prosody and figurative language served to heighten the sense of irony and paradox. A poem such as 'The Stenographers', for example, strikes one as a kind of tapestry of metaphor, on which the routines and nitty-gritty of office life are described in terms that draw attention to their tedium, mechanization, and mind-deadening qualities: 'the brief bivouac of Sunday', 'the inch of noon', 'the winter of paper'. Such detail and stylization give imaginative expression to the problem of workers alienated from the product of their labours as no Marxist treatise could do. Page does not glorify or romanticize the secretaries; but her metaphors leave no doubt that such conditions are, ultimately, dehumanizing: 'In their eyes I have seen/the pin men of madness in marathon trim/race round the track of the stadium pupil.'

Time and travel have altered Page's conception of life and art, shifting her attention from social and political surfaces to internal psychological states. Actually, her account of her development as an artist serves as a useful analogy for her poetic progress as well. The shock of learning another language, as she says in 'Questions and Images' (*Canadian Literature*, No. 41, Summer 1969), was like being born a second time, growing from silence through a linguistic childhood and adolescence towards a radically altered adulthood, in which all her perceptions underwent a sea-change. Since she could not write poetry, she began to draw, going first through a realist phase in which she had to 'see with the eye of an ant' in order to appropriate the new and exotic environment; then, she says, 'the pen began dreaming. It began a life of its own', to the point where the painter could look into the macaw's eye and be 'drawn through its vortex into a minute cosmos which contained all the staggering dimensions of outer space.'

Here the poet and painter speak the same language, both being concerned, as she says in 'Stories of Snow', with that 'area behind the eyes/where silent, unrefractive whiteness lies.' No other poet in Canada, with the possible exception of Atwood, has been so intensely concerned to explore the nature of visual perception. Eyes abound in her poems, as do lenses, cameras, field glasses. Perspectives are almost always unusual; compositional elements play an important part; images may be blurred, superimposed, surprisingly juxtaposed, viewed through strangely distorting lenses. These perceptual elements, including a concern for colour and light and shade, combine with an imagistic precision that recalls her experience in film. As Munro Beattie has observed, 'Several of her poems might serve as scripts for little experimental films for "art" theatres. Action flows into action, image melts, "by a slow dissolve", into image.'

After Canada, which she has described as a 'whim-oriented culture', Page found the order and interconnectedness of the cultural symbols in Mexico liberating. She came to realize that, for her, art was not an end in itself so much as a means to an end, a path to wisdom. 'Poetry', she says 'was more than ever in the perceiving.' Art, whether poetry or painting, becomes a technique of transformation or metamorphosis, a vehicle for conducting us on that route that leads through the looking-glass, beyond the senses to 'some unseen centre'. 'Without magic the world is not to be borne,' she insists. 'A good writer or painter understands these laws and practices conjuration.'

Page's skills as a conjuror are everywhere present in her poetry, from the metaphysical wit that draws strange and wonderful analogies to the deftness and precision with which she uses words: she is a master of her craft. However, the formal or manipulative aspect of her work seldom submerges the realistic, or referential, side; her best poems remain immediately accessible and thoroughly mysterious.

Page's publications include a novel, *The Sun and the Moon*, which was published in 1944 under the pseudonym Judith Cape and reprinted with eight short stories in 1973 under the title *The Sun and the Moon and Other Fictions*. Her books of poetry are *As Ten As Twenty* (1946); *The Metal and the Flower* (1954), which won a Governor General's Award; *Cry Ararat!* (1967); *Poems Selected and New* (1974); *Leviathan in a Pool* (1974); *Evening Dance of the Grey Flies* (1981); and *The Glass Air: Selected Poems* (1985). She has also published an autobiographical work, *Brazilian Journal* (1987).

### E.J. PRATT (1882-1964)

Edwin John Pratt was born in Western Bay, Newfoundland, the son of a Methodist minister. After graduating from St John's Methodist College, he spent four years as a teacher and minister in coastal villages before entering the University of Toronto. A succession of degrees followed—B.A. in Philosophy (1911), M.A. (1912), B.D. (1913), and Ph.D. in Theology (1917)—after which he joined the English Department of Victoria College, where he remained until his retirement in 1953. Pratt was an enthusiastic and respected teacher, as well as an active force in the social and intellectual community of the University. He was also editor of *Canadian Poetry Magazine* from 1936 to 1942.

Pratt's critical reputation has been uneven, depending on the whims and fluctuations of the literary stock market in Canada. He began writing long poems in an age that valued brevity and economy; he espoused humanistic values—such as courage, endurance, and solidarity—when the dominant mode was irony and understatement, and the chief expression was a tight-lipped dismissal of society and its destructive ways. Yet Pratt's work was never naïvely optimistic; in fact, human weakness and vanity come up for regular drubbings in his work. Although Poe has called the long poem 'a contradiction in terms' and the English critic B.S. Johnson describes the narrative poet as a 'literary flat-earther', the long poem still remains the dominant form in Canada and Pratt is its chief architect. His verse narratives restored drama, psychological depth, structural complexity, intelligence, and verbal texture to a form that had lost its energy and direction.

Pratt almost single-handedly upheld the expansive tradition in Canadian poetry, arguing for a poetry that is 'a grand binge' rather than a snack at a funeral; his use of rhyme, metrics, and blank verse has often blinded readers to the spare brilliance of his early poems, such as 'Newfoundland' and 'The Shark', and the rich contribution he has made to poetic diction, ushering in—with the scholar's resourcefulness and the child's delight—whole new vocabularies from science, technology, and anthropology in narratives such as 'The Titanic'. Earle Birney, in 'E.J. Pratt and his Critics', calls him 'a man whose capacity for feeling is so great he is like a smelter furnace demanding stacks of raw material for fuel' and draws attention to Pratt's insistence on the need for sufficient passion to turn these rough facts into tempered steel.

As Pratt wrote in the *Canadian Poetry Magazine* in 1936:

*A poem can be written only by some one who knows how to write: there is no exception to that rule. Poetry is an exacting, difficult craft, and it takes years of hard work, and education and a sense of the language. Rhyme and metre do not make a poem; they produce by themselves nothing but doggerel. The real flesh and blood of poetry lies in turns of phrases, vivid images, new and unusual thoughts and manners of expressing them. A good poem is good because it is an unusual, imaginative, arresting way of writing English. We do not speak in poetry, except at rare moments; and if a poet writes so simply as to give the effect of spoken language, that effect is all the more startling and novel.*

*To be able to use this language one must learn it, and that takes, among other things, reading. Practically all the great poets of our language were very highly educated, and the majority were scholars of enormous learning, commanding a large number of languages living and dead. Shakespeare, Burns and Keats are usually regarded as proving the contrary, but their capacity to respond to the books they did read was tremendous, and of no great poet is it untrue to say that his genius would have starved to death without books, for all his observations and experience of life. The reason is very simple: the poet is a literary man, and he has to know something about his trade. . . . Of course, reading the classics is not everything. . . . People will always try to resist reading modern poets, but very few ever succeeded in becoming good poets who took that attitude to the poetry of their own time. Contemporary poetry should be studied by everyone who wishes to add something further to it.*

Although he pioneered the narrative or contemporary epic, Pratt also prepared the way for Atwood, Kroetsch, and Ondaatje by parodying in *Towards the Last Spike* both the epic form and the values it traditionally espoused—nationhood, heroism, and reason—thus laying the groundwork for *Power Politics, The Collected Works of Billy the Kid*, and *Seed Catalogue*. Milton Wilson fully understood the importance of Pratt's poem when he said, 'I have the notion that the problems involved in *Towards the Last Spike* are going to be the central problems in the poetry of our future. . . . [Pratt writes] narratives, no doubt, but discontinuous narratives which are always turning, on the one side, into documents, letters, and jokes, and on the other, into pure lyrics.'

Pratt's publications include *Newfoundland Verse* (1923), *The Witches' Brew* (1925), *Titans* (1926), *The Iron Door* (1927), *The Roosevelt and the Antinoë* (1930), *The Titanic* (1935), *Still Life and Other Verse* (1943), *Dunkirk* (1941), *Behind the Log* (1947), *Brébeuf and His Brethren* (1940), and *Towards the Last Spike* (1952). Pratt's *Collected Poems* appeared in 1944 and again in 1958, this time with a long introduction by Northrop Frye. His poetry received three Governor General's Awards.

### AL PURDY (b.1918)

Purdy was born in Wooler, Ontario and educated at Albert College in Belleville. At sixteen he dropped out of school and began his wanderings, working at odd jobs, putting in time with the RCAF in British Columbia, and trying his hand at writing. Although his first book of poems was published in 1944, he did not seriously consider supporting himself by writing until he sold a script to the CBC in 1955. He moved to Montreal and then to Roblin Lake at Ameliasburg, Ontario, where he has lived for many years. From Ameliasburg he has travelled to the Cariboo, Newfoundland, Baffin Island, Cuba, Greece, and England, and has been writer-in-residence at various universities. Of this incessant wandering he says: 'I write poems like spiders spin webs, and perhaps for much the same reason, to support my existence . . . unless one is a stone one doesn't sit still. And perhaps new areas of landscape awaken old areas of one's self. One has seen the familiar landscape (perhaps) so often that one ceases to really see it.'

Purdy's development has been haphazard and independent, a product of his continued experiment and chance discovery of interesting talents rather than of absorbing any major influences. He objects as much to the 'sweetness and iambic smoothness' of academic poets like Richard Wilbur as to the 'togetherness ... of the Duncan-Creeley-Olson bunch.' 'I have no one style,' he said in a letter to Charles Bukowski, 'I have a dozen: have got to be virtuoso enough so I can shift gears like a hot-rod kid—I doubt that my exact combo ever came along before. Unlike some, I have no ideas about being a specific kind of poet. I mean, I don't make rules and say THIS is what a poet HAS to be. I don't know what the hell a poet is or care much. I do know what he isn't sometimes.'

Despite his objections to the contrary, Purdy has developed a speaking voice that is unmistakable. His poetry is most recognizable in terms of its language and structure. One of its main characteristics is a peculiar mixing of chattiness and profundity, of homely observation and mythical or historical allusion. Purdy is an extremely well-read poet. He has a firm grasp of what he calls 'the gear and tackle of living'; the imagery in a single poem can be drawn from a number of different sources, sometimes with considerable success. He peoples his rural Ontario with ghosts from the near and distant past, with echoes of ancient Greece and United Empire Loyalist salons; in his particular Baffin Island may be seen the shades of Diefenbaker, Odysseus, Laurence Olivier, King John, and Gary Cooper.

Structurally, Purdy's verse is equally recognizable. He has a tendency to leave his poems open-ended, to leave a subject deliberately unresolved. In poems of this sort there is no subject outside the poem other than the perceiving consciousness of the poet; in other words, the subject of the poem is the *process itself*, the process of trying to come to terms with a feeling or experience. Philosophically, a preoccupation with process is understandable; it implies an awareness that at best 'truth' is difficult to discover, at worst it is completely relative. From an aesthetic point of view, however, a desire for honesty and verisimilitude in this area does not always work to the poem's advantage. Carried too far it can become a cliché, a short-cut. If this happens the reader is likely to feel that at times a poet should lie, that he should be prepared to offer up small truths directly rather than try successfully for the larger truth.

Whatever objections one may have to Purdy's open-endedness and his habit of undercutting something that is obviously important to both himself and the reader, there can be no doubt about his very considerable talent. His 'exact combo' is unlike anything else in Canadian poetry. He has an inexhaustible capacity to surprise and delight, to upset whatever critical expectations his own poems might encourage. His answer to his critics, and perhaps the reason for his popularity, is suggested in the following comment he makes on the nature of the poetic process:

*There ought to be a quality in a good poet beyond any analysis, the part of his mind that leaps from one point to another, sideways, backwards, ass-over-electric-kettle. This quality is not logic, and the result may not be consistent with the rest of the poem when it happens, though it may be. I believe it is said by medicos that much of the human mind has no known function. Perhaps the leap sideways and backwards comes from there. At any rate, it seems to me the demands made on it cause the mind to stretch, to do more than it is capable of under ordinary and different circumstances. And when this happens, or when you think it does, that time is joyous, and you experience something beyond experience. Like discovering you can fly, or that relative truth may blossom into an absolute. And the absolute must be attacked again and again, until you find something that will stand up, may not be denied, which becomes a compass point by which to move somewhere else. . . . And sometimes—if you're lucky—a coloured fragment may slip through into the light when you're writing a poem.*

There are many coloured fragments in Purdy's poetry. The way his mind stretches to assimilate new areas of experience, the way it leaps in unexpected directions, often at considerable psychic cost to the poet, is truly remarkable.

Purdy's best verse is predominantly elegiac. Like Roberts and Carman, he is sensitive to manifestations of change, to the passing of time. He loves to reflect upon things historical. There is something about events and people out of the past that releases his imagination in new and exciting ways. Thus his identification with the decaying world of Prince Edward County in Ontario, his attraction to the outbacks of British Columbia, and his passionate response to the Inuit's encounter with the white man's technology on Baffin Island. Perhaps the values and the certainty that the shifting present never affords him are found in abundance in the past. In poems such as 'The Runners' and 'Lament for the Dorsets' there is little uncertainty or self-consciousness; instead, the poet achieves a rare beauty and precision.

Since the publication of his first book in 1944, Purdy has published numerous major collections, including *Poems for All the Annettes* (1962, 1968, 1973); *The Cariboo Horses* (1965), for which he received a Governor General's Award; *North of Summer* (1967); *Wild Grape Wine* (1968); *Love in a Burning Building* (1970); *Selected Poems* (1972); *Sex and Death* (1973); *The Poems of Al Purdy* (1976); *Sundance at Dusk* (1976); *No Other Country* (1977); *Being Alive* (1978); *The Stone Bird* (1981); *Piling Blood* (1984); and *The Collected Poems of Al Purdy* (1986), which won a Governor General's Award. He has also published a limited deluxe edition of poems from his trip to Greece called *The Quest for Ouzo* (1970). In addition, Purdy has edited two anthologies—*Storm Warning* (1971) and *Storm Warning II* (1976)—and a collection of Canadian views of the United States, *The New Romans* (1968).

## ROBYN SARAH (b.1949)

 Robyn Sarah was born in New York to Canadian parents and studied at McGill University and the Quebec Conservatory of Music. Her poems have appeared widely in magazines and anthologies, including *Aurora* (1980) and *The Inner Ear* (1983), and have been enthusiastically received by reviewers. According to *University of Toronto Quarterly*, her work is notable for its 'tone, its flawless cadences, an imagination rooted in natural things. . . . Each word and image seems set miraculously simple and right.' Her books of poetry include *Shadowplay* (1978), *The Space Between Sleep and Waking* (1981), *Anyone Skating on that Middle Ground* (1984), and *Becoming Light* (1987). She lives with her family in Montreal, teaches at Champlain College, and is co-founder, with Fred Louder, of Villeneuve Editions.

'People sometimes ask me what poets have influenced me,' Sarah says in an unpublished interview with Louise Schrier, 'and when I think about that, I say that my writing has been more influenced by two prose writers—Katherine

Mansfield and James Agee—who are very, very conscious of sound in their work. You feel, reading them, that every syllable, every punctuation mark, is exactly right. I'm jarred by bad sound, by the sound of a bad sentence. I think that has to do with my exposure to music.' In addition to sound, her work, like Agee's fiction, pays loving attention to objects in our daily lives, not so much objects in nature as man-made objects and our palpable relations with those objects. Poems such as 'Maintenance' and 'A Meditation Between Claims' reveal a quiet, engaging intelligence that is alert to the intersection of differing realities, the point at the window 'where hot meets cold', and to the celebration of ordinary, perhaps worn, surfaces, where 'things may be taken at face value', where the attentive observer may discover 'always a/small surprise.'

Sarah's poems express a 'delight in the weathered . . . planes' and a 'respect for tenancy, its wear and tear, its fixed terms.' In the same interview, she discusses this dimension of her work: 'I don't find the distances between people depressing; I find it a fact of life like other facts of life. It's there, it's a thing that can be talked about. I don't find cracks in plaster or worn floor boards depressing or dismal. I'm moved by the signs of life in these things, the signs that this floor has been walked on, this house has been lived in, people have been here, people have tried to repair things and they've fallen apart again . . . it just strikes me as part of the process of the passage of time . . . I write about them because they're part of the fabric of life.' To some readers Sarah's absorption in the nitty-gritty of domestic life will seem characteristic of contemporary writing by women; to others it will recall the almost mystical relationship with the physical world, natural or man-made, to be found in the work of Emily Dickinson and Elizabeth Bishop. 'We need to make room in our lives,' Sarah says, 'for something other than dailiness, for something other than taking care of our physical needs. And a poem, then, does much more than that—it makes room for the dance, if you like, for moments of grace.'

Sarah draws many of her titles and structural metaphors from music and painting, but it is the concreteness and specificity of her language, not the artistic allusions, that invest her poetic world with such vividness and luminosity. In commenting on this dimension of her work, however, she shifts the emphasis away from observation, or vision, and towards craft. 'I don't have a good visual memory. I create the illusion of having it by focusing on certain details very intensely and allowing this to suggest what else there may be in that room. . . . I don't like speaking in an abstract way. I find that often an emotion or a mood can be conveyed better by evoking the physical objects that are present at the time, rather than talking about the mood itself.'

### F.R. SCOTT (1899-1985)

Frank Scott was born and raised in Quebec City, where his father was an Anglican minister and a poet. He graduated from Bishop's College in Lennoxville, was a Rhodes scholar at Oxford, and then studied Law at McGill University, where he graduated and joined the Faculty in 1928. He was Dean of Law from 1961 to 1964 and retired from McGill in 1968. Scott found no difficulty reconciling his artistic and political impulses. He was active in founding the League for Social

Reconstruction in 1932 and the Canadian Commonwealth Federation (the CCF, which eventually became the NDP), drafting its Regina Manifesto and acting as the CCF's National Chairman from 1942 to 1950. He contributed to *Social Planning for Canada* (1935), edited *Canada Today: A Study of Her National Interests and National Policy* (1943), wrote *Canada and the United States* (1941), and co-edited with Michael Oliver *Quebec States Her Case* (1964). Scott not only became an expert on international law and constitutional affairs, but also defended D.H. Lawrence's *Lady Chatterly's Lover* in the courts and won a case against the notorious Padlock Law of the Duplessis government.

'What is my personal conception of poetry?' Scott wrote. 'If I could define it, it would not be too different from my conception of life itself. The making of something new and true. An exploring of the frontiers of the world inside and the world outside man. And a kind of umbilical contemplation from within the poem itself of its own dynamic and central structure.' His examination of the world outside man began with a number of imagistic poems about nature, particularly related to the northness of Canada, its remote lakes and vast rock formations such as the Canadian Shield; this early work, in terms of its subject matter and visual intensity, has much in common with the work of the Group of Seven. Against the serene and austere aspects of nature in Canada, Scott pits the human work of building and 'civilizing', though he does this in terms that are not entirely Romantic; he admires the work of human hands where it constructs, by way of its 'cabin syllables', art and language, and such humanizing enterprises as education, medicine, and government. However, his keen intellect and training in law gave him sufficient insight to identify and the wit to parody all that is bogus and destructive in human affairs, so that even a largely affirmative poem such as 'Laurentian Shield' ends with the ambivalent phrase, 'the long sentence of their exploitation.'

Scott's lively satires and diatribes against hypocrisy and waste in government, or prudery and racism in society, are seldom without redeemingly infectious humour and word-play, making generous use of puns and *double entendre*. In 'Lakeshore', for example, man's primitive ancestors emerging from sea-slime are described as 'landed gentry'. Scott employed the minimalist techniques of the Imagists in composing his pithy epigrams; he adopted the argumentative modes of eighteenth-century poetry to construct his essays in verse; and he used ballad measures, in the manner of Robert Service, to evoke the full comedy of Canadian attitudes towards sex. Perhaps his most characteristic and successful mode is the extended metaphor, which he employs in 'Lakeshore', 'Laurentian Shield', and 'For Bryan Priestman' where, in a poem that recalls the tone and measure of Auden's 'Musée des Beaux Arts', Scott uses the language of the laboratory to evoke the death by drowning of a professor of chemistry.

In an essay entitled 'The Poet in Quebec Today' (*English Poetry in Quebec*, edited by John Glassco, 1965), Scott describes the process of his own poetic development: 'My early poetry was influenced by the geography in Quebec. Coming back from Oxford, where for the first time in my life I was brought into direct contact with the European tradition, in which one soaked up the human achievements of great individuals and great nations past and present, and where always one was drawn back toward antiquity, I found Quebec presented a totally different kind of challenge. Here nothing great seemed to have been achieved in human terms. I was shocked by the ugliness of the cities and buildings by comparison with those that I had recently lived in, and there seemed so little that one wished to praise or draw inspiration from in our social environment or past history. But the Laurentian country was wonderful, open, empty, vast, and speaking a kind of eternal language in its mountains, rivers, and lakes. I knew that these were the oldest mountains in the world, and that their rounded valleys and peaks were the result of long submersion under continents of ice. Geologic time made ancient civilizations seem but yesterday's picnic. This caught my imagination and I tried to express some of this feeling in what I call my Laurentian poems. It was a form of "internalization", and it sufficed me at first for poetic inspiration.

'As I became more involved in the human society about me, particularly after the great financial crash of 1929, the ensuing depression, and the emergence of revolutionary and reform political movements in which I participated, I found that I reacted negatively in my writing and turned easily to satire. The satire was the holding up of the existing society against standards one was formulating in one's mind for a more perfect society. It was not revolutionary poetry; it was satiric poetry, which is quite a different thing, though somewhat allied.'

Scott's poems appeared in the *McGill Fortnightly Review*, of which he was an editor in 1925, but his writing was not widely noticed until it appeared in *New Provinces: Poems of Several Authors* (1936), which he co-edited with his friend and fellow-poet A.J.M. Smith. Scott was co-founder of *Preview* in 1942, which merged three years later with *First Statement;* 1945 also saw the publication of *Events & Signals*. Then came Scott's *Overture* (1954), *The Eye of the Needle* (1957), *The Blasted Pine: An Anthology of Satire, Invective, and Disrespectful Verse, Chiefly By Canadian Writers,* co-edited with A.J.M. Smith (1957), *Signature* (1964), *Selected Poems* (1966), and *The Collected Poems of F.R. Scott* (1981), for which he received a Governor General's Award. Scott had received this award previously for *Essays on the Constitution: Aspects of Canadian Law and Politics* (1977).

### RAYMOND SOUSTER (b.1921)

Souster's chief concern has been to keep singing in the face of despair. As he says in 'Good Fortune', 'life isn't a matter of luck/of good fortune, it's whether/the heart can keep singing/when there's really no reason/why it should.' His imagination is peopled with the victims of wars and industrial 'progress', whores, cripples, beggars, down-and-outs of every sort. He takes upon himself their guilt and shame and tries to communicate the terrible sense of human waste that weighs upon him. Souster is equally troubled by the impermanence of things. At times he displays a gentle nostalgia for the innocence and good times of the past, lamenting the passing of friends and shared interests and the disappearance of familiar landscapes under a jungle of concrete and cereal-box architecture. Although he is incapable of sustained irony or satire, Souster often strikes out at the instruments of change and destruction like an animal that has been hurt or cornered. His most convincing response is to celebrate signs of man's capacity for joy or, at least, survival; he searches out pockets of beauty and spontaneity in the rubbish heap of the century, as in 'Top Hat' or 'Victory', where he celebrates the determination of a 'bum' who beats the street-cleaning machine to a castaway cigarette butt.

Souster is predominantly a poet of content. Robert Creeley applies this name to the poets of the thirties. 'There are also those men', he says, ' . . . who extend to their writing of verse concerns which haunt them, again reasonably enough, in other areas of living. They are in this way poets of "content", and their poems argue images of living to which the content of their poem points. They argue the poem as a means to recognition, a signboard as it were, not in itself a structure of "recognition" or—better—cognition itself.' Creeley is thinking here of Kenneth Fearing, but his description applies well to Souster, for whom the sociological impulse seems more pressing than the aesthetic. This view is not inconsistent with Souster's idea of the poet's function. In 'The Lilac Poem' he speaks of the impermanence of all things, even poetry. If art itself is subject to the eroding effects of time, the artist is best employed as a recorder or photographer of the human condition at a particular moment in history; or rather—and perhaps this is his main function—as an entertainer who can divert man's attention away from the sources of his despair. The short poem is itself a function of the poet's view of the impermanence of all things; and it is especially characteristic of modern poetry. As Frost suggests, the good poem provides 'a momentary stay against confusion'.

This does not mean that Souster has no interest in form, in prosody. He is sufficiently steeped in American poetry, especially in the work of Ezra Pound and William Carlos Williams, to have absorbed not only a distaste for the baggage of poetic tradition, but also a preoccupation with certain formal elements in verse. His own poetry is not metrical; he prefers the shifting rhythms of speech to the monotony of the metronome. Like Bowering, he avoids the use of mythical allusion and archaism, preferring instead poetry with a base in actual experience. Souster understands Pound's dictum that 'It is better to present one Image in a lifetime than to produce voluminous works.' He has written a number of excellent imagist poems, such as 'Study: The Bath' and 'The Six-Quart Basket', that have the clarity and economy of the *haiku*. Occasionally Souster is tempted to comment on the image, to tag on a moral that leaves attention outside the poem, as in 'The Hunter'; but his best poems are either pure image or pure voice. The poems of lyrical reflection are less likely to misfire, because the poet begins with a mood that is strong enough to arrange the materials it gathers to express itself, rather than with an image that is often too weak to support itself without assistance from the voice of the poet. These reflective verses speak for Souster's integrity as a man and as a poet; they are beautifully turned and reveal a quiet concern, or empathy, that is always surprising, sometimes moving.

Souster was born in Toronto and has spent all of his life there except for the war years, 1941-5, when he was in the RCAF in the Maritimes and in England. Of his beloved Toronto, he says:

*I suppose I am truly an unrepentant regionalist. As Emile Zola put it to Paul Bourget: 'Why should we be everlastingly wanting to escape to lands of romance? Our streets are full of tragedy and full of beauty; they should be enough for any poet.' All the experiences one is likely to encounter in Paris can be found in this city. Toronto has a flavour all its own. . . . My roots are here, this is the place that tugs at my heart when I leave it and fills me with quiet relief when I return to it.*

Like Wallace Stevens, Souster has been wedded simultaneously to the muses of both poetry and commerce: until his retirement he was employed some four decades by the Canadian Imperial Bank of Commerce in downtown Toronto. His involvements in the poetic community are many. He edited a mimeographed magazine called *Combustion* (1957-60) and was a founder-editor of Contact Press. He edited *New Wave Canada: The New Explosion in Canadian Poetry* (1966), and *Generation Now* (1970), an anthology of poetry for schools. He was also a founding member of the League of Canadian Poets.

Souster has published many books of poetry, including *When We Are Young* (1946); *Go to Sleep, World* (1947); *Shake Hands with the Hangman* (1953); *Selected Poems* (1956), edited by Louis Dudek; *A Local Pride* (1962); *Place of Meeting* (1962); *The Colour of the Times* (1964), his collected poems, which received a Governor General's Award; *Ten Elephants on Yonge Street* (1965); *As Is* (1967); *Lost & Found* (1968); *So Far So Good* (1969); *Selected Poems* (1972); *On Target* (1973); *Doubleheader* (containing *As Is* and *Lost & Found*, 1975); *Rain-check* (1975); *Extra Innings* (1977); *Collected Poems* in four volumes (1980 ff.); and *The Eyes of Love* (1987).

## ANNE SZUMIGALSKI (b. 1922)

Anne Szumigalski (née Davis) was born in London, England, and raised in Hampshire. During the war she worked with refugees and as an interpreter with the British Red Cross, speaking French, German, and Dutch fluently, as well as some Polish and Russian. She was with the first Civilian Relief Unit to enter Europe after D-Day. She met her husband, an ex-P.O.W., in Germany and immigrated to Canada in 1951. She has lived in Saskatoon since 1956 and been an active participant in the development of the Saskatchewan Writers' Guild. Szumigalski raised four children and has been a tireless editor and supporter of young poets; she has also taught imaginative writing in schools and at the Saskatchewan Summer School for the Arts in Fort San. She has served as writer-in-residence at the Winnipeg Public Library; and two of her books have been nominated for a Governor General's Award.

Szumigalski's poetry is unusual in Canada for its obliviousness to the attractions of place. When asked the reasons for this feature of her work, she said: 'If landscape is important to my work, it's the inner landscape. The world of imagination is so much larger. That's where I prefer to reside.' The inner world of her poems is one of transformations, talking corpses, bizarre contracts binding people together, real and psychic surgery; it is a fantastical landscape stretching between birth and death, with the wonderful concreteness and illogic of dreams.

Szumigalski's later work explores the formal possibilities of the prose poem, a form that appears on the printed page without line-breaks, but that still retains the density of image, sound, and rhythm associated with lyric poetry. The prose poem is a highly charged form, whose impact and compression require that it not extend beyond two or three pages. Because its appearance on the page serves to free the prose poem from some of the conventions and expectations of the lyric poem, this form lends itself well to both the psychological intensity and the dream-like juxtapositions that are central to Szumigalski's poetry. Although she sometimes uses the prose poem for narrative purposes, she never strays far from either the length or the compression required to sustain lyric intensity. Whether structured around a feeling, an anecdote, or an idea, these compact, richly textured pieces seem always to strive beyond quotidian reality, to a region where image becomes symbol and where symbol achieves the status of archetype.

Szumigalski's poetry collections include *Woman Reading in Bath* (1974), *A Game of Angels* (1980), *Doctrine of Signatures* (1983), *Risks* (1983), and *Dogstones: Selected and New Poems* (1986). She is also co-editor (with Don Kerr) of *Heading Out: The New Saskatchewan Poets* (1986).

### MIRIAM WADDINGTON (b. 1917)

Miriam Waddington (née Dworkin) was born to Russian-Jewish parents in Winnipeg, though she spent her adolescent years in Ottawa. She completed a B.A. in English at the University of Toronto in 1939 and married Patrick Wadding-ton, a journalist, the same year. After writing briefly for newspapers and magazines, she studied social work, receiv-ing her M.A. from the University of Pennsylvania. Until her divorce in 1960, Waddington lived in Montreal, raising a family, doing social work, and writing poems that would appear in *First State-ment*, *Preview*, and her first three books: *Green World* (1945), *The Second Silence* (1955), and *The Season's Lovers* (1958). She returned to Toronto to work for the North York Family Services and to teach English at York University from 1964 until her retirement in 1983. She was the recipient of the J. J. Segal Award in 1972 and an honourary D.Litt. from Lakehead University in 1975. Her other collec-tions of poetry are *The Glass Trumpet* (1966), *Call Them Canadians* (1968), *Say Yes* (1969), *Driving Home* (1972), *The Price of Gold* (1976), *The Visitants* (1981), and *Collected Poems* (1986). She is also author of *Summer at Lonely Beach and Other Stories* and a critical study, *A.M. Klein* (1970), and is the editor of *The Collected Poems of A.M. Klein* (1974).

Waddington's career as a social worker has played an important role in her poetry, shaping both the content and the form of her work. Much of the early work examines the world of poverty, unemployment, deviance, and crime; these poems, for the most part, make use of traditional poetic devices such as rhyme, metre, and stanzaic form: the chaos of the material itself seemed to demand a rigorously ordered poetic form. Alongside these documentary pieces are tender poems about nature, love, and the loss of innocence, in which Waddington presents herself as poet-healer, 'a splint against your sorrows.' Gradually her poetic interests shifted from public to private concerns, with a corresponding loosening of form, particularly the use of the short line. Of this shift, she writes: 'This change was unconscious and had something to do with *zeitgeist*. New hope, new ways of understanding the world, and—along with the atom bomb—new anxieties were everything. There no longer seemed to be time for the spinning out of long literary lines. The tempo of short lines suited the times and suited me.

The short line serves Waddington's purposes well in the personal poems, as well as in the Jewish and folkloric pieces, where there is a Chagall-like playfulness and where the momentum allows her to assume the role of ecstatic celebrant, 'the tender and brooding outsider' concerned with 'subtle melodies' and 'obscure lives', listening for the 'old lost songs'. In *Call Them Canadians* Waddington was invited to write poems to accompany a stunning collection of photographs of Canadians at work and at play, in love and in mourning. This commission produced some of her finest work and rescued Waddington from the solipsism and lack of density that are a possible legacy of the short line. The visual images lift the poet beyond the interfering ego, providing the sensory detail to charge her imagination; and the public function of the volume encourages her in the direction of greater substance and universality, resulting in poems that are lively, textured, and fully accessible.

### BRONWEN WALLACE (1945-1989)

Bronwen Wallace was born in Kingston, Ontario, where she now lives and works in a centre for battered women and children and teaches intermittently in the English Department at Queen's University. Her poems were first published jointly with work by Mary di Michele in *Marrying in the Family* (1980). Subsequent books of poetry are *Signs of the Former Tenant* (1983), *Common Magic* (1985), and *The Stubborn Particulars of Grace* (1987). She has edited books for Quarry Press and collaborated with Chris Whynot on two films: *All You Have To Do* (1982) and *That's Why I'm Talking* (1987).

Wallace is an archeologist of the emotions. The reader of her poems moves, layer by layer, deeper into the substratum of feelings, back to primal moments of fear, pain, and humiliation. Wallace searches out the 'hidden lives' within us, the small invasions of change and memory that crack open the shells of our ordinary lives. She speaks of the 'unexpected rituals' and objects that 'may tell the stories of our lives/more accurately than we ourselves could.' Thus the poems are full of maps, dreams, mirrors, the reflections of which produce a sense of infinite regression into the past, where we brush our earliest beginnings and, perhaps, feel 'our own deaths rising within us'.

'My fascination with narrative poetry grows out of my fascination with how we tell the story of our own lives', she said in a conversation with the present writer. . . . 'The story of my poems is simply "what happens"; beyond that—or rather through that—is the voice of the narrator moving closer and closer to the discovery of the mystery which lies at the centre of her life and every life. I try to keep the language simple and commonplace, the rhythm that of everyday speech. In doing so, I hope to have the poem reflect what I believe: that there is no such thing as ordinary, and that in these commonplace details the mystery of each life is revealed.'

Wallace's work falls squarely into the oral tradition of story-telling, with its asides, digressions, and associative leaps. The process, as she has indicated, is one of 'detours and double-backs, leaps', a constant 'Re-mapping' and reconstruction of the past by each subsequent retelling. She speaks of 'our terrible need to know everything', which explains not only the force that drives her poems, but also the power these poems have for the reader, whose own life and motives are often opaque and inexplicable. As keeper of the stories, Wallace has mastered the so-called digression, or lateral shift, so common to the tradition of oral story-telling, wherein the narrator appears to have forgotten or abandoned the main story momentarily, but has, in effect, deepened the narrative by bringing new material to bear. These objects, places, sounds, names, and persons—surfacing dream-like in her narratives—serve as signposts and exempla for the reader-pilgrim journeying through her poetic landscapes.

Wallace acknowledges the influence on her work of the poetry of Al Purdy and Galway Kinnell, but says her biggest influence has been the 'kitchen-table conversation', with all its revelations, its codes and formulas, and its meander-ings. Her parables, whether direct or self-consciously narrated, draw the reader in by deliberately delaying information at crucial moments and by projecting the image of a narrator who is struggling, humbly and somewhat erratically, to get to the bottom of things in her own life and the lives around her. 'The poem', she says, 'never goes from A to B to C as I thought it would. I discover it as I go. I agree with Flannery O'Connor, too, that if I don't discover something during the writing, my reader won't either.'

## PHYLLIS WEBB (b.1927)

Phyllis Webb's poetry, because it presents a world that often seems devoid of meaning and consolation—a world of suf-fering, betrayal, gratuitous violence, and death—raises ques-tions about the aim of art. What, we find ourselves asking, can be the point of writing about such things? Is the aim of art—if indeed it can be said to have an aim—to confirm our suspicions that life has no meaning, or that its purpose is by no means certain or benign? Can so unrelentingly bleak a picture be anything but depressing?

However bleak it may appear to be at the level of content, Webb's poetry is an affirmation of the human spirit, of the power of the imagination to confront and reshape reality. As Albert Camus argues in his famous treatise, *The Rebel*, there is no such thing as a nihilistic work of art; even if literature 'describes nostalgia, despair, frustration, it still creates a form of salvation. To talk of despair is to conquer it. Despairing literature is a contradiction in terms.' What is important in Webb's poetry is the style, the way in which she imposes *form* on whatever elements from reality she uses.

One has only to look closely at 'Love Story' to understand the terrifyingly delicate balance Webb can achieve between the realist and formalist elements, by virtue of an unremitting attention to the visual, auditory, and intellectual nuances of words. Rather than describe the death of the infant in graphic detail, Webb chooses rather to stylize the killing, speaking of the ape's biting of the neck in metaphorical terms as 'tasting time' and of the attack as something general rather than specific: 'and his nails rooted sudden fire in the ribs of Adam.' Reference to the infant's belly as 'plush' on which the ape 'bobbed nervously' serves, finally, to heighten rather than diminish the horror of the imaged scene by drawing attention to elements of texture and cushioning effect that the reader would otherwise gladly forgo.

On the rare occasions when she has spoken about her art, Webb's concern has been, primarily, with craft. In an article called 'Polishing Up the View', which appeared in *CV/II*, Vol. 2, No. 4, December 1976 (transcribed from a tape in the Aural History Department of the Provincial Archives, Victoria), Webb speaks briefly of the influence of American poets Charles Olson, Robert Creeley, and Robert Duncan, all of whom she met in the summer of 1963 at the University of British Columbia. She singled out Duncan on the grounds that he had 'the most to offer me because he is a great explorer in the realm of form.' Of her own explorations in form she is very specific, talking about the difficulty of ordinary sentence structure, which is 'based on an opposition of ideas, so that you get "buts" and "thoughs" and "althoughs" and "ifs" and so on. . . . it seemed to me that this had some philosophical significance and that I had to break through the oppositions that are presented to us in everyday thought and get a more refined synthesis'.

Of her poem 'Making', Webb has written: (*Poet's Choice*, 1966, edited by Paul Engle and Joseph Langland):

*I was surprised when this poem arrived with its 'Quilted', but this, the patchwork quilt, was the given of the poem and became the central image controlling the range of ideas, keeping the concepts always in touch with the homely making.*

*I like the sound of this poem; I like the way 'Making' travels its keyboard and shakes up the far end of the alphabet. After the first draft I immediately thought to cast it into a syllabic pattern based on the first stanza. But then I decided that the poem was already made: the rhythm was there, the oddness that seemed to me right, though I had not sought it, was there, and there was easiness too. For the poem simply happened on the May morning as I sat in the sun with my back against the wall.*

*It seems to me to be the answer to its companion piece, 'Breaking', which had concluded with such awful tolerance, 'What are we whole or beautiful or good for/but to be absolutely broken?' 'Making''s unhysterical, determined, open relativism is here both ethic and aesthetic. That's why I like the poem—because it says my centre.*

As is evident in her poems and in the emphases of her critical writings on the poetic line, the creative process, and the genesis of poems, Webb is extremely conscious of even the smallest nuance of rhythm or sound. Her dissatisfaction with the verbosity and heavy-handedness of conventional rhetoric led her, in the mid-1960s, towards the minimalism of *Naked Poems* (1965), with their short lines and abbreviated manner; the same questing and curiosity led her, in the 1980s, to explore the 8th-century Persian form called the ghazal, whose discrete but tonally-linked couplets accommodated themselves particularly well, in *Water and Light* (1984), to the verbal dexterity and imaginative leaping that are Webb's hallmarks. Webb is also a continuing explorer of life and its meaning, personally and collectively. Her work touches not only upon the philosophical anguish of modern life, but also upon some of the issues, events, and personalities that have shaped our age.

Phyllis Webb was born in Victoria and raised there and in Vancouver. She studied English and Philosophy at UBC from 1945 to 1949, ran unsuccessfully as a CCF candidate in the provincial elections, and worked as a secretary in Montreal, where she also attended Macdonald College and McGill and came into contact with F. R. Scott and Ronald Sutherland. Her poems were first published in *Trio*, along with those of Eli Mandel and Gael Turnbull. For the next fourteen years she lived intermittently in England, Montreal, Paris, Vancouver (where she taught English at UBC), and Toronto, where she produced the CBC 'Ideas' program. She now lives on the Gulf Islands. Her publications include *Even Your Right Eye* (1956), *The Sea Is Also a Garden* (1962), *Naked Poems* (1965), *Wilson's Bowl* (1980), and *The Vision Tree: Selected Poems* (1982), which won a Governor General's Award. Her critical writings and thoughts on the creative process appear in *Talking* (1982).

# Index of Poets